World Cities beyond the West

This study is the first systematically to cover those cities beyond the core that most clearly can be considered world cities: Bangkok, Cairo, Hong Kong, Jakarta, Johannesburg, Mexico City, Moscow, Mumbai, São Paulo, Seoul, Shanghai, and Singapore. Fourteen leading authorities from diverse backgrounds bring their expertise to bear on these cities across four continents and consider the major regional and global roles they play in economic, political, and cultural life. Conveying how these cities have followed various pathways to their present position, they offer multiple perspectives on the interplay of internal and external forces and demonstrate that any comprehensive discussion of world cities has to engage a multiplicity of perspectives. With an introduction from Josef Gugler and an afterword from Saskia Sassen, this substantial volume makes a major contribution to the world cities literature and provides an important new impetus for further analysis.

Josef Gugler is Professor in Residence in Sociology at the University of Connecticut where he directed the Center for Contemporary African Studies until recently. Previously he served as Director of Sociological Research at the Makerere Institute of Social Research, Uganda. Research and teaching have taken him to a number of African countries as well as India and Cuba, and he has held visiting appointments in several universities in Europe and the U.S. He has co-authored and edited five volumes on urbanization in developing countries, most recently *Cities in the Developing World* (1997) and *The Urban Transformation of the Developing World* (1996).

World Cities beyond the West

Globalization, Development, and Inequality

Edited by

Josef Gugler

CAMBRIDGE UNIVERSITY PRESS
Cambridge, New York, Melbourne, Madrid, Cape Town, Singapore, São Paulo, Delhi

Cambridge University Press
The Edinburgh Building, Cambridge CB2 8RU, UK

Published in the United States of America by Cambridge University Press, New York

www.cambridge.org
Information on this title: www.cambridge.org/9780521830034

First published 2004
Reprinted 2006

A catalogue record for this publication is available from the British Library

Library of Congress Cataloguing in Publication data
World cities beyond the West: globalization, development, and inequality / edited by
Josef Gugler
p. cm.
Includes bibliographical references and index.
ISBN 0 521 83003 6 – ISBN 0 521 53685 5 (pb)
1. Cities and towns. 2. Cities and towns – Developing countries. 3. Globalization.
I. Gugler, Josef.
HT119.W67 2004
307.76′09172′4 – dc22 2003060605

ISBN 978-0-521-83003-4 hardback
ISBN 978-0-521-53685-1 paperback

Transferred to digital printing 2008

Contents

Figures

Maps

Tables

Contributors

JANET ABU-LUGHOD recently retired from the Graduate Faculty of the New School for Social Research where she taught both sociology and historical studies. She is also Professor Emerita at Northwestern University where she taught sociology and directed several urban studies programs. In 1999 she received the award for lifetime contributions to Urban Sociology of the American Sociological Association's Community and Urban Sociology Section and a similar recognition of her distinguished scholarly career from the Section on the Political Economy of the World System.

MARIA HELENA MOREIRA ALVES is Director of Institutional Relations at Movimento Viva Rio in Rio de Janeiro. She was the principal investigator in a participatory research project that involved workers of the Ford and Saab-Scania plants in São Paulo as well as the leadership of automobile workers unions in the United States, Canada, and Sweden in the 1980s. She has taught at various universities in Brazil, Chile, and the United States, and has been involved in popular education programs in Brazil for almost three decades.

JAMES H. BATER is Professor of Geography at the University of Waterloo. He has held visiting appointments at the University of Chicago, Sheffield University, and the University of Toronto. His current research involves examination of the impact of privatization and urban management in Moscow, Nizhniy, Novgorod, Samara, and St. Petersburg.

OWEN CRANKSHAW is an Associate Professor in the Department of Sociology at the University of Cape Town. He has held research positions at the Centre for Policy Studies and the Human Sciences Research Council in South Africa. He has also lectured at the University of Natal, University of the Witwatersrand, and the London School of Economics. His research focuses on changing patterns of racial and occupational inequality in South Africa, urbanization, squatting, and residential segregation.

DEAN FORBES is Pro Vice Chancellor (International) and Professor in the School of Geography, Population and Environmental Management at Flinders University of South Australia. He has previously held appointments at the Australian National University, Monash University, and the University of Papua New Guinea. He has worked as a consultant for several United Nations agencies and the Australian government, and has undertaken a secondment with AusAID, Australia's international development agency.

JOSEF GUGLER is Professor in Residence in Sociology at the University of Connecticut where he directed the Center for Contemporary African Studies until recently. Previously he served as Director of Sociological Research at the Makerere Institute of Social Research, Uganda. Much of his work has been devoted to urbanization in poor regions, especially Africa. Research and teaching have taken him to a number of African countries as well as India and Cuba, and he has held visiting appointments in several universities in Europe and the US.

YEONG-HYUN KIM teaches in the Department of Geography at Ohio University. Her research focuses on globalization, world cities, urban politics, and development. She maintains a special interest in South Korea, her country of origin, and India where she is currently doing research on global auto firms' operations in large cities.

SUSAN PARNELL is an Associate Professor in the Department of Environmental and Geographical Science at the University of Cape Town. She has held appointments at SOAS, University of London, and the University of the Witwatersrand. Most recently she has been involved in aspects of the reconstruction of the apartheid city, advising local and national government as well as international donors. She serves on the board of several local NGOs concerned with poverty alleviation and gender equity in post-apartheid South Africa.

SUJATA PATEL was born in Bombay and has spent most of her life there. Currently she is Professor in the Department of Sociology at the University of Pune. Her research has been concerned with class conflict and industrial relations; the relationship between caste, communalism, and reservation; Gandhi; and gender and urban problem in mega-cities in India.

JANET SALAFF is Professor of Sociology at the University of Toronto. She studies the intersection of families and the urban community, mainly Chinese families. She has written about the family and industrialization (Hong Kong), the family and state policy (Singapore), and family and work (Canada, Taiwan, Inner Mongolia). She is currently doing research on transnational migration of Chinese families between Toronto and China and Hong Kong.

SASKIA SASSEN is the Ralph Lewis Professor of Sociology at the University of Chicago, and Centennial Visiting Professor at the London School of Economics. At the center of her research are global dynamics, translocal processes, and the production of space. This has led her to focus on capital and labor flows, the articulation of cities with global processes, and the participation of national states in shaping and enabling global and translocal processes and institutional arrangements. She chairs the Information Technology and International Cooperation Committee of the Social Science Research Council (USA).

ALVIN Y. SO is a Professor of the Division of Social Science at the Hong Kong University of Science. He previously taught at the University of Hawai'i where he received the Regents' Medal for Excellence in Teaching. He co-edited the *Bulletin of Concerned Asian Scholars* and served as Chair of the Asian-American Section of the American Sociological Association. His researches include social class, development, and democratization in East Asia.

PETER M. WARD holds the C. B. Smith Sr. Centennial Chair in US–Mexico Relations at the University of Texas at Austin, where he is Professor in the Department of Sociology and in the Lyndon B. Johnson School of Public Affairs. He is also Director of the Mexican Center, and in 2002 became Editor-in-Chief of the *Latin American Research Review.* He previously taught urban geography at the University of Cambridge and University College London, and has served as advisor to various Mexican government ministries and agencies.

DOUGLAS WEBSTER divides his time between an appointment as Consulting Professor at the Asia Pacific Research Center of Stanford University and his position as Senior Urban Advisor to the National Planning Board of Thailand. He is also an active advisor to the World Bank's East Asia Urban Unit. In association with the World Bank and the Ford Foundation, his current research at Stanford focuses on peri-urbanization in Bangkok and Manila in Southeast Asia, and in Hangzhou and Chengdu in China.

WEIPING WU is an Associate Professor of Urban Studies and Planning at Virginia Commonwealth University. She has been a consultant for the World Bank and was a Research Fellow at the Brookings Institution in Washington, DC. Her research interests include comparative urban development and policy, rural–urban migration, and economic development and planning. A native of China, she particularly keeps abreast with urban development issues in China and East Asia.

SHAHID YUSUF has served the World Bank in numerous capacities for over two decades, most recently as Director of the *World Development Report 1999/2000*. He is co-editor of the *World Bank Research Observer*, and a member of the World Bank Editorial Committee as well as its Research Committee. Much of his work has focused on Asia.

Acknowledgments

In my endeavor to pursue a global approach to world cities in poor countries across four continents I was fortunate in that many people readily shared their knowledge and their insights with me. I would like to thank in particular Janet Abu-Lughod, Mike Douglass, Myra Marx Ferree, William G. Flanagan, Saskia Sassen, Richard E. Stren, and Weiping Wu.

We are indebted to the National Academy of Sciences' Committee on Population for sponsoring a two-day workshop that brought nearly all contributors together; to Charles M. Becker, Saskia Sassen, Richard E. Stren, and Yue-man Yeung who acted as our discussants on that occasion; and to Barney Cohen who was most supportive in this endeavor. Prior to the workshop, the overseas participants had the opportunity to meet for a one-day conference at the University of Connecticut thanks to the efforts of Wayne Villemez.

All royalties from this volume have been vested in Oxfam.

JOSEF GUGLER

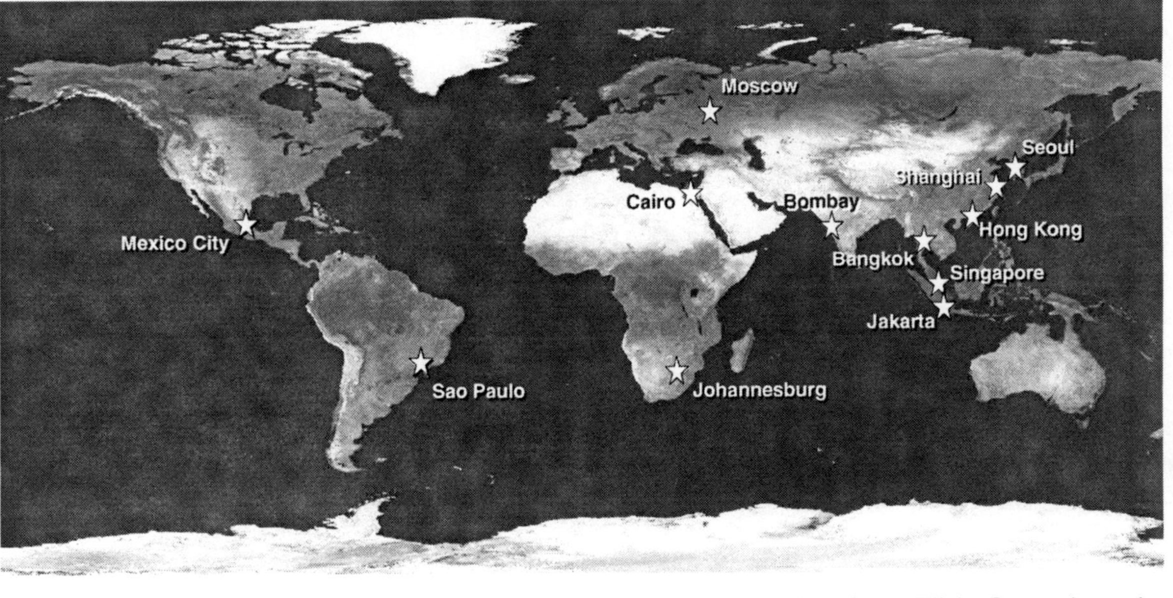

Graphic design by Daniel L. Civco, based on The Blue Marble, NASA Goddard Space Flight Center, image by Reto Stockli, enhancements by Robert Simmon

Introduction

Josef Gugler

> There is a first-world elitist bias to the globalization literature. Globalization is written from the metropolitan centre. Many of these writings are guilty of doing "bad geography" by only examining one or two representations of globalization.
>
> (Short *et al.* 2000, p. 317)

The notion of "world cities" has become prominent in the social sciences in recent years, and the literature has expanded at a rapid pace. Most of this literature, however, is focused on cities at the core of the world system. Much of it is devoted to the triumvirate of New York, London, and Tokyo, and where it moves beyond this "first tier" it usually explores North American and Western European cities.[1] This volume seeks to broaden the inquiry beyond these cities, to adopt, as Robinson (2002) put it recently, a more cosmopolitan approach. We focus beyond the West in terms of political economy rather than geography.

A number of cities beyond the core play major regional and global roles.[2] They make up a substantial proportion of "second-tier" world cities and must be part of any analysis. This is all the more important as these cities differ from their core counterparts in a number of ways.[3] They are more subject to the economic, political, and cultural impact of core actors – governments, corporations, international organizations, universities, the media, even if there is considerable variation in their dependent status. Most are located in poor countries, and the resources

[1] The academic debate on world cities was launched by Friedmann (1986) and reprised in *World Cities in a World System* (Knox and Taylor 1995). Sassen's *The Global City* (2001, first published in 1991) stands as the landmark study. Sassen (1997) and Yeoh (1999) offer overviews of the burgeoning field – and demonstrate how lopsided its development has been in terms of research and analysis remaining by and large limited to core countries.

[2] The core is here understood to comprise Western Europe, the US, Canada, Japan, Australia, and New Zealand.

[3] Dick and Rimmer (1998), however, argue the convergence of spatial patterns between Southeast Asian and US cities. And Cohen (1996) suggests that cities in the "North" and the "South" are becoming more alike in the problems they share: growing unemployment, declining infrastructure, deteriorating environment, collapsing social compact, and institutional weakness.

they can draw on are much more limited even as they too have to make heavy investments in infrastructure to meet the standards expected by foreign investors and professionals. On the other hand nearly all have younger populations and are not yet faced with the issues of a greying population confronting core countries.

This study is the first systematically to cover those cities beyond the core that most clearly can be considered world cities, whereas previous work has focused rather haphazardly on one or a few cities, a region at best. Several of the cities presented are here considered for the first time in terms of the major regional and global roles they play. Our joint endeavor distinguishes itself from most previous work in two other major respects. For one, we move beyond the economic realm to consider the political and cultural dimensions. For another, instead of remaining within narrow disciplinary boundaries, this volume brings together leading authorities on these cities who came from several disciplines and pursue a range of different approaches. Most identify themselves as geographers or sociologists, one is based in an interdisciplinary urban studies program, and three bridge the academic/practice divide: an economist works at the World Bank, an urban planner has been Senior Urban Advisor to a national government for a number of years, a political scientist has been an activist in a workers' movement since it played a leading role in forcing a military regime out of power. Our ideological inclinations vary as well.

In all, fourteen authors from diverse backgrounds bring their particular expertise to bear on twelve world cities across four continents. They present the full array of perspectives on world cities beyond the core. Having critically engaged each other and four discussants at a conference – some of us had a workshop as well – their contributions combine to provide a complex picture of world cities beyond the core. They convey how these cities have followed various historical pathways to their present position; they explore the interplay between internal and external forces; and they demonstrate that any comprehensive discussion of world cities has to engage a multiplicity of perspectives. We thus establish the basis for a more general understanding of world cities and provide new impetus to their analysis.[4]

As we look back on our undertaking systematically to cover world cities beyond the core three conclusions stand out. First, these cities are extraordinarily diverse. They have had very different histories, their

[4] Ward (1995) has pointed out how research in poor countries on major topics such as urban social movements, informal–formal sector interactions and interdependence, and the dynamics of household and female insertion in the labor market, has stimulated work elsewhere.

present economic and political circumstances vary, they are variously articulated with their respective regions and across the globe, and their demographic dynamics differ. The foremost conclusion of our systematic approach is how problematic most generalizations about world cities are.

Secondly, the transformation of the city center into an elite enclave is one pattern that is common to virtually all our cities. It reflects the fact that the standard of living of a significant proportion of the population in these cities has dramatically improved. It also conveys strikingly that the severe inequalities characteristic of most non-core countries, and of their cities in particular, have been further exacerbated in their world cities. At the same time, increased integration in the global economy has exposed the populations of these cities to sudden reversals of fortune that are not cushioned by public systems of support such as may be found in rich countries.

The third conclusion that these accounts of twelve cities across four continents impose is that any general analysis of world cities has to recognize, along with the forces of globalization, the strength of the state and the power of popular movements. Of course – our first conclusion applies – states may be weak, popular movements may be dormant, but for more than half the cities considered here either the state or a popular movement has constituted a major driving force. The state and civil society have to be brought into the analysis of world cities.

Regional and global articulations

Cities beyond the core are important. In demographic terms, most of the world's largest cities are found outside the core. According to the most recent estimates, twelve out of the world's sixteen largest cities, each with more than 10 million inhabitants, were outside the core in the year 2000. Three of the cities we consider here, Mexico City, Mumbai/Bombay, and São Paulo, with between 16 and 18 million people, were among the world's five largest cities (United Nations 2002). But the selection of cities for this volume has not been guided by sheer population size – half the cities considered here have populations of less than 10 million (Table I.1). Rather, we are presenting a selection of strategic places.

Some of the cities presented here play major roles in the global economy, all hold dominant positions at the regional level or within very large countries such as China and India. In terms of the "new global dimensions" emphasized by discussions of world cities, most of these cities concentrate command functions and are key locations for finance and specialized services for firms. They "function as regional or global nodes in the world economy," they are "global cities" as defined by Sassen

Table I.1 *Economic and demographic indicators for cities and countries*

	City						Country			
	Global network connecticity (score)	Headquarters and subsidiaries (number)	Stock market capitalization (US$ million)	Regional, interregional, and total international destinations of direct flights[a]	Population (million)	Annual population growth rate (%)	Population (million)	Annual population growth rate (%)	GNI at PPP per capita (US$)	
	2000	1996	2002	2001	2000	1995–2000	2001	1980–2001	2001	
Hong Kong	0.71	40	506,131	12 + 63 = 75	6.9	1.99	7	1.4	25,560	Hong Kong SAR[b]
Singapore	0.65	35	117,338	34 + 74 = 108	4.0	2.90	4	2.6	22,850	Singapore
São Paulo	0.54	25	123,807[c]	17[d] + 8[e] + 22 = 47	18.0	1.74[f]	172	1.7	7,070	Brazil
Mexico City	0.49	28	103,137	16[g] + 32[e] + 9 = 57	18.1	1.46	99	1.8	8,240	Mexico
Mumbai/ Bombay	0.48	8	131,011	3 + 47 = 50	16.1	2.62[f]	1,032	1.9	2,820	India
Jakarta	0.48	15	29,921[c]	4 + 25 = 29	11.0	3.69	209	1.6	2,830	Indonesia
Bangkok	0.44	22	46,084	14 + 77 = 91	7.4	2.23[f]	61	1.3	6,230	Thailand
Shanghai	0.43	1 + 16	463,080[c]	16 + 24 = 40	12.9	−0.35[f]	1,272	1.2	3,950	China
Moscow	0.42	6	124,198	48 + 86 = 134	8.4	−0.55[f]	145	0.2	6,860	Russia
Seoul	0.41	3 + 23	248,533	42 + 51 = 93	9.9	−0.73	47	1.0	15,060	South Korea

Johannesburg	0.41	8	184,622	40 + 26 = 66	3.0	3.61	43	2.1	10,910	South Africa
Cairo	0.35	9	26,094[c]	18[h] + 20[i] + 39 = 77	9.5	1.32[f]	65	2.2	3,560	Egypt
London	1.00	5 + 45	2,217,324[c]	113 + 169 = 282	7.6	n.a.	59	0.2	24,340	United Kingdom
New York	0.98	24 + 45	13,810,429[c]	8[d] + 5[j] + 75 = 134	16.7	0.47	285	1.1	34,280	United States
Tokyo	0.69	30 + 36	2,251,814[c]	10 + 71 = 81	26.4	0.51	127	0.4	25,550	Japan

[a] International flights within a city's region (East Asia, Southeast Asia, South Asia, Eastern Europe and Central Asia, Western Europe, Middle East, Africa, the Americas) and between regions scheduled for September 2001.

[b] Special Administrative Region of China.

[c] The stock market capitalization includes other stock market(s) in the same country.

[d] International flights to destinations in South America, the Caribbean, Central America, and Mexico.

[e] Flights to destinations in the US and Canada.

[f] The annual population growth rate is for a period extending before and/or after 1995–2000.

[g] International flights to destinations in South America, the Caribbean, and Central America.

[h] International flights to destinations in Africa.

[i] International flights to destinations in the Middle East.

[j] Flights to destinations in Canada.

Sources: Global network connectivity from Taylor (2002); headquarters and subsidiaries from Godfrey and Zhou (2000); flight departures from OAG (2001); city population and annual growth from United Nations (2002); country data, including stock market capitalization, from World Bank (2003).

(2000, pp. 4, 59). The only two globally comprehensive data sets available at this time serve to make the point.[5]

Beaverstock *et al.* (1999) scored cities as global service centers in terms of the significant presence of major firms providing producer services in accountancy, advertising, banking/finance, and law.[6] More recently Peter Taylor *et al.* (2002) have moved beyond the mere presence of such offices to their importance and to their significance in terms of the global firms they represent to offer a measure of global network connectivity. They again drew on global service firms, this time covering accountancy, advertising, banking/finance, insurance, law, and management consultancy. But they now focused on the office networks of the 100 firms they studied. They assessed the service value of the offices in a given city in terms of their size and their extra-locational functions, e.g. as regional headquarters. And they measured the global network connectivity of a city by multiplying the service value of each firm present in the city by the firm's service value in every other city and summing the product for the firms (Table I.1). Four of the cities presented in this volume ranked among the eighteen cities scoring highest in 2000, and they included all the non-core cities in that top tier. Another seven of our cities were among the twenty-five cities ranked next.[7] Cairo, however, stood only in fifty-ninth position (Taylor 2002). Still, the Middle Eastern metropolis merits inclusion for the major economic, political, and cultural role it plays in the region. Cairo also illustrates how a region's fortunes, or in this case ill fortunes, affect a city's regional and global role.

A measure of the command functions located in world cities is provided by Godfrey and Zhou (1999, 2000) who surveyed the headquarters of the world's 100 largest corporations, as measured by gross annual revenue, and their first-level subsidiaries. Only four had their headquarters in cities covered here in 1996: three in Seoul and one in Shanghai. But when we consider the first-level subsidiaries of those top corporations, a quite different picture emerges that attests to the role these cities play within their regions: five of our cities rank among the ten cities that had more

[5] Short *et al.* (1996) present such other data as were available on cities as major financial centers, seats of corporation headquarters, telecommunication nodes, transportation nodes, and sites of global spectacles by the mid-1990s. These data were extremely limited, and their significance was quite problematic. There has not been much progress since except for the work of P. J. Taylor and his associates and of Brian Godfrey and Yu Zhou that I draw on here.

[6] Taylor (2000) offers a spirited argument for the significance of these indicators in assessing world city status.

[7] Another five non-core cities ranked among the forty-three cities with the highest global network connecticity: Beijing, Buenos Aires, Istanbul, Kuala Lumpur, and Warsaw. Except for Istanbul, they are situated in regions where cities included in this volume score higher and are more important in other respects as well.

than twenty-two first-level subsidiaries, and they included all the non-core cities among those ten. Another three of our cities were among the next twenty-two cities, home to more than fourteen first-level subsidiaries (Table I.1).[8] The strong showing of Seoul and Shanghai on this measure stands in striking contrast to their low global network connectivity. While these cities are the seats of considerable corporate power, they remain relatively self-centered in the provision of producer services.

The stock market capitalizations of nine of our cities exceeded US$100 billion in 2002, putting them amongst the world's twenty-four largest stock markets (World Bank 2003).[9] Most of our cities are home to their country's only stock market. The exceptions, Cairo, Jakarta, São Paulo, and Shanghai, boast the country's predominant stock market. The capitalization of stock markets bears little relationship to global network connectivity or command functions. Rather it is a function of the size of the national economy the stock market represents, i.e. the product of income level and population size (Table I.1). Singapore, however, is enlarged beyond its national base by the role it plays in regional finance, and to a lesser extent such is the case of Johannesburg.

International flights offer a measure of the connectedness of cities. I have used data on the number of foreign cities that can be reached with scheduled direct flights (Table I.1). They show no relationship to any of the three indicators considered so far but rather present a distinct dimension of world city status. Specific factors appear to account for the major differences across our cities. Moscow, until recently the capital of an empire, stands out as offering as many direct flights, disproportionately provided by Aeroflot, to foreign destinations as New York, even if the frequency of flights and the passenger volume is considerably lower. Singapore, in spite of its tiny population, ranks second, testimony to the success of its government in making it an attractive point of transit and the national airline a carrier of choice. Jakarta, on the other hand, appears to have been dramatically affected by its political/economic crisis.

I have further distinguished between destinations within a country's region and those beyond. In East Asia, Hong Kong overshadows Shanghai in connections beyond the region. Both have few direct flights to destinations within East Asia, whereas Seoul connects with many cities in China. In Southeast Asia, Bangkok rivals Singapore in interregional connectedness, due in part to its attractions as a tourist destination, while

[8] Another six non-core cities are among the thirty-two cities that had more than fourteen first-level subsidiaries of the world's 100 largest corporations: Beijing, Bogotá, Buenos Aires, Caracas, Istanbul, and Manila.

[9] Only two other non-core cities, Kuala Lumpur and Rio de Janeiro, had stock market capitalizations exceeding US$100 billion.

being little connected within the region. In South Asia, Mumbai/Bombay suffers from India's political isolation vis-à-vis its immediate neighbors. Cairo is equally well connected with Africa and the Middle East. Johannesburg has more direct flights to African destinations than any of our other cities, or London for that matter. São Paulo and Mexico City are evenly matched in terms of direct flights to destinations in the Americas south of the Rio Grande, but tourist traffic to the Caribbean and Mexico puts New York far ahead of them. Mexico City is well connected with US cities – and appears to lose many of its passengers headed beyond the Americas to US airlines.

World cities outside the core do not have the reach of the major global players in terms of the "new global dimensions." However, they do not simply stand in an hierarchical relationship as intermediaries for New York, London, or Tokyo. Sometimes they are collaborators: foreign interests draw on Hong Kong expertise in approaching China. But in China as elsewhere these cities are also competitors at the regional level: Johannesburg capital has been competing with British, French, and US interests in Africa south of the Sahara since the end of the international sanctions against the apartheid regime that had constrained it.

A focus on the "new global dimensions" plays to the strengths of a few world cities in the core and overlooks their vulnerability. The United States, for one, has a large trade surplus in services, but that has been dwarfed for many years by even larger trade deficits in goods that make the world's biggest economy utterly dependent on foreign credit. And a more encompassing approach to the world economy brings to the fore the importance of a number of cities outside the core. If they are second-level players in the "new global dimensions," they have proved themselves formidable competitors in manufacturing. Here their role is not regionally circumscribed. In manufactures such as automobiles, they supply their region but also export to what used to be known as "industrial countries." In other manufactures, ranging from textiles to consumer electrical goods to electronics, they have by and large displaced manufacturing in the now "deindustrializing" countries that constitute their principal markets. Already by 1996, nearly one out of five transnational corporations was based beyond the core (Sassen 2000, p. 23).

A full appreciation of the strategic roles non-core cities play requires that we broaden our purview to embrace the realm of culture. Two dimensions stand out. Several of the cities presented here are important media producers and/or play a global role in propagating an ideology. The most prominent example of a city as ideological proponent is historic rather than contemporary. Moscow emerged as Russia's center of Christian Orthodoxy in the mid-fifteenth century and came to celebrate its role as the "third Rome," a place where liturgy would never be compromised by the politics of religion as it had been in Rome and Constantinople. Then, with the victory of the Bolshevik revolution, Moscow became the leader of the socialist revolution. Today the New Labor Movement in São Paulo prides itself on exporting its ideas across the globe. An altogether different ideological role is played by Singapore. Its proclamation of "Asian values" is all too readily dismissed by Western commentators who fail to acknowledge the relationship between these values and the remarkable economic achievements of this and other Asian countries.[10]

In the leisure media, in film, television, and music, a number of our cities dominate their regions, and some reach well beyond. In the early years after the Bolshevik revolution, Moscow became the global leader in cinematographic innovation. More recently Bollywood, i.e. the film industry of Mumbai/Bombay, established itself as the world's foremost film producer. Together with other Indian studios it now produces more than twice as many films as the US (UNESCO 2001). They supply 95% of the Indian market, three times the share national film production holds in any other country, except for the US (Barbaroux 2001). Bollywood exports to the large Indian diaspora as well to regional markets, e.g. in Africa. Cairo is the predominant producer for the Arab world and has come to be known as "Hollywood on the Nile." Johannesburg is set to play a similar role in Africa south of the Sahara. Hong Kong rivals the US in numbers of films produced. It has moved beyond its regional audience to make inroads in Hollywood's heartland. And so has Shanghai.[11]

The cities considered here are major players in the regional and global economy, and some play a major cultural role in their region and beyond. Their scope for political action, however, is usually quite limited. Political action in the international arena remains by and large the prerogative of states; the era when city-states exercised political control over large regions is long gone. Several of the cities we consider here are not even the capitals of their countries.[12] World cities are, however, key sites for protest movements. The impact of popular movements in Mumbai and

[10] Teheran may be similarly seen as a global ideological center, in this case a resurgent Islam that rejects Western ways.

[11] Larkin's (1998, pp. 140–192) analysis of the success of Indian films in northern Nigeria, where they have all but displaced films from Hollywood and Hong Kong, serves to emphasize that conceptions of global cultural flows that privilege the centrality of the West fail to recognize the common historical process of peripheries that are engaged alongside centers in contemporary cultural production.

[12] I included Shanghai rather than Beijing in this volume because of its growing importance in the global economy, but the capital of the world's largest, and increasingly powerful, nation clearly plays a major regional and global role.

São Paulo has been particularly far-reaching, but several more of our cities spawned protest movements that led to regime change.

The diversity of world cities

The cities we consider here are remarkably diverse. We have just had some indications how their regional and global articulations vary. They are also differentiated by history, economy, polity, and demography.

Spread across four continents, our cities are heirs to a large array of cultures. The vagaries of history intersected with locational advantages to establish their strategic position. Most have a long history – Cairo became the capital of Egypt more than a thousand years ago, others are more recent colonial creations. And their historical legacies vary greatly. The roles these cities have played at the national, regional, and global level have changed over time. For example, it may be argued that Moscow has been a world city for centuries, but its role changed dramatically under three different political regimes. At the same time there is a striking continuity in that it is these cities' service functions rather than manufacture that continue to distinguish them.

Eventually our cities came to be profoundly affected by the West, the more so as nearly all took on major significance in the era of European expansion. Most came into prominence in the nineteenth century as the principal trading and transshipment center for a rich hinterland. Usually they were developed by European interests as part of a commercial network based on colonial control. In São Paulo much of this development took place after Portugal had relinquished control and was the work of European settlers. In the case of Shanghai, European powers were not prepared to colonize China, but established firm control in this along with a few other coastal cities. When the Japanese entered the fray at the beginning of the twentieth century, they occupied Korea and developed Seoul. They failed in their subsequent attempt to control China. The Kingdom of Siam maintained its control over Bangkok, but the city's rise was also due to its strategic maritime location.

Only two of our cities were developed inland by European interests. Both were situated in settler colonies. Mexico City, while built on a precolonial capital, emerged as a major administrative and commercial center in the Spanish Empire. British and Dutch settlers established Johannesburg on the wealth of the world's richest gold deposits. Moscow distinguishes itself by both its inland location and the indigenous roots of its emergence as a world city.

Spatial patterns and architecture bear witness to history. Given the cost of investments in infrastructure, housing, manufacturing plants, and office space, changes usually come slowly, but they tend to accelerate in times of boom or bust. The form the physical expansion of cities takes may vary, but each city connects increasingly with other expanding urban areas, making boundary definitions ever more problematic: the most recent United Nations (2002) estimate puts the population of Johannesburg at 3.0 million, but about 7.3 million people live in the metropolitan area.[13]

The cities considered here are significantly involved in the global economy, but they remain affected by the national economies in which they are embedded (Table I.1). We may distinguish three categories of countries where our cities are situated: two rich cities/city-states, i.e. Singapore and Hong Kong with per capita gross national incomes (GNI), at purchasing power parity (PPP), around US$24,000 in 2001;[14] six middle-income countries, i.e. Brazil, Mexico, Russia, South Africa, and Thailand, with incomes ranging from US$6,230 to US$10,910, and South Korea at about US$15,000; and four low-income countries, i.e. China, Egypt, India, and Indonesia, at between US$2,820 and US$3,950. As countries' income levels vary, so do their definitions of "the poor" and "the middle class," and the size of the categories so defined.

Past history and present opportunities of cities are shaped by the region in which they are situated, and by the competition of other cities in the region. Once China embarked on free-market reforms, Hong Kong faced increasing competition from Shanghai even as the opportunities in the world's largest market expanded dramatically. Seoul stands in the shadow of Tokyo. Bangkok's position was strengthened as some of its neighbors faltered. Cairo's opportunities have been severely limited by political conflicts in the Middle East that culminated in a series of wars – but the opportunities of its regional competitors, Beirut, Damascus, Baghdad, were even more diminished. Johannesburg began to take on a leading role in Africa south of the Sahara once the South African apartheid regime was removed, but this is the world's poorest region, and major countries are rent by political conflict and war.[15]

Some cities have secured a specific niche in their regional economy. Bangkok has established itself as a regional center for tourism, health services, and administrative services for corporations and international

[13] Excellent satellite images of all our cities, except Singapore, are presented in Beckel 2001.

[14] Purchasing power parity converts currencies to US dollars according to their purchasing power, i.e. one dollar has the same purchasing power over domestic GNI that the US dollar has over US GNI.

[15] When Nigeria and the Belgian Congo/Zaïre became independent in 1960, Lagos and Léopoldville/Kinshasa appeared set to become the major regional centers in Africa south of the Sahara, while Johannesburg was handicapped by the increasing isolation of the apartheid regime. But four decades of disastrous political developments in the two countries thwarted the potential of their leading cities.

organizations in Asia. The film industry of Mumbai dominates South Asia. São Paulo boasts the largest concentration of industry in Latin America. Mexico City seeks to become the region's financial center.

Many of the cities we consider here have operated within a quite stable political environment for a generation or more. Elsewhere, changes in political regime led to profound transformations. The collapse of the Soviet Union and the abrupt transition to a market economy have brought wrenching changes to Moscow. The repercussions of the collapse of the apartheid state in South Africa have transformed Johannesburg. And the political crisis that continues to unfold in Indonesia holds the prospect of altogether altering the course on which Jakarta has been proceeding.

The political context in which cities evolve toward world city status varies greatly. Hong Kong flourished under the laissez-faire capitalism established by Britain in its crown colony. The corporatist state in Singapore was remarkably successful in pursuing programs of social engineering that transformed social relations. Shanghai is booming under continuing state-party control that has slowed down the dismantling of inefficient state industries and provided a shield during the Liquidity Crisis that burst on emerging economies in the 1990s. If the state is powerful in Hong Kong, Shanghai, and Singapore, it was successfully challenged by the labor movement in São Paulo which played a key role in the demise of the military regime in Brazil and continues to push for further democratization.[16] In Brazil and elsewhere, more or less forceful trends towards democratization entail pressures for decentralization and devolution that take resources away from cities that were heretofore privileged, especially so if they held capital city status. The conflict is likely to be exacerbated where city, state, and/or national government are controlled by different parties, as is often the case in Mexico City, Mumbai, and São Paulo.[17]

Their cosmopolitan history has bequeathed racial, ethnic, and/or religious diversity on most of our cities. Such diversities are usually reflected in spatial segregation and often come to the fore in political conflicts as group identities are manipulated. Religious difference has become a central element in the politics of Mumbai, and its citizenry has suffered repeated outbursts of sectarian violence. As the intersections of class and race shift in Johannesburg, it remains to be seen how race relations evolve,

[16] Roberts's (1997) quite recent discussion of "citizenship," i.e. political, civil, and social rights, in Latin America, which had Brazil lagging the countries of the Southern Cone, may already be in need of revision.

[17] Even in the absence of major party divisions, nearly all the cities considered here suffer from divided jurisdictions that impede the effective administration of their metropolitan areas.

and whether ethnic divisions among Africans that were fostered under white minority rule have been effectively buried.

The distinctive demographic characteristic of our cities is that their populations are younger than those of their counterparts in the core. Three factors all affect the age distribution in that same direction. Their populations tend to have higher fertility; their life expectancy is shorter; and many cities experience substantial in-migration from rural areas. At the same time there is considerable variation in the demographic dynamics of the cities considered here in terms of both natural population growth and migration.[18]

The demographic transition is more or less advanced in the countries where these cities are situated (Table I.1). We may distinguish two stages. Brazil, Egypt, India, Indonesia, Mexico, and South Africa are well into the transition, with annual rates of population growth ranging from 1.6 to 2.2% in the last two decades.[19] China, South Korea, and Thailand are even further along with growth rates little over 1%, but it remains to be seen whether population growth in China will rebound as the severe restrictions on fertility are relaxed. Russia had joined industrial countries with very low growth rates earlier. In recent years population growth rates declined further in all these countries.

Declines in mortality and fertility are likely to occur earlier in urban areas, and especially so in cosmopolitan cities such as those presented here. They translate into increasing dependency ratios and fewer new entrants into the labor force. The last effect comes with a considerable time lag, but it is reenforced by the expansion of educational systems. The demographic transition affects urban population growth indirectly as well: slower natural population growth in rural areas reduces the pressures for out-migration to urban areas.

High rates of rural–urban migration used to cause much alarm, but in recent years population growth in most of our cities has been little different from national growth (Table I.1).[20] Taking into account that urban natural population growth tends to be lower in urban than in rural areas, total city growth rates approaching national rates still imply a certain amount of net rural–urban migration. But by now rural–urban migration

[18] In some cities many residents maintain close ties with what they consider their "home," i.e. the community from which they, or their parents, migrated. Such involvement has major social and political implications. For a discussion of the urban–rural connection in Africa, see Gugler (2002).

[19] Hong Kong and Singapore have rather high growth rates, but a large part of their population growth is due to immigration.

[20] Our data sources cover different time periods for city and population growth. Still, data on national population growth 1990–2001 (World Bank 2002) lend support to the generalizations made here.

makes a substantial impact only in a few cities: Bangkok, Jakarta, Johannesburg, and Mumbai. In the case of Johannesburg, the disappearance of the apartheid-era restrictions on the movement of Africans precipitated a large influx of Africans formerly restricted to rural areas and the relocation of Africans and whites within the metropolitan area.

A number of countries, most prominently China, the Soviet Union, and South Africa, have controlled migration towards their cities, more or less successfully. It would appear that wherever it is politically acceptable thus to create second-class citizens, and where migration controls can be enforced with some degree of effectiveness, governments attempt to limit rural–urban migration and/or migration to the most privileged cities. States of course remain sovereign to control immigration even as they promote free trade and have lost all control over communication. The city-state Singapore can regulate migration across its borders according to the requirements of its labor market. Hong Kong was in a similar situation while it was a British crown colony. Now, as a Special Administrative Region of China, it continues effectively to control migration. When a Court of Final Appeal ruling opened the doors to the immigration of an estimated 1.5 million Chinese, the Hong Kong government had the decision overturned by the Chinese legislature. Moscow continues to control in-migration in spite of federal legislation abolishing the Soviet-era restrictions on the free movement of Russian citizens.

Twelve world cities

The specificity of the cities presented here intersects with the disciplinary and ideological bent of the authors to provide accounts that vary greatly in focus. In particular, they vary in the emphasis put on three driving forces: the global political economy, the state, and popular movements. The extent to which the contributions privilege one over the other serves to organize the book.

Globalizing cities

Their skylines distinguish world cities from other cities in poor countries. Office towers, five-star hotels, and luxury apartments stand out. Meeting the standards expected by foreign investors and professionals requires heavy investment in infrastructure. These cities, unlike their counterparts in rich countries, tend furthermore to attract a disproportionate share of investment in manufacturing. They crowd out other cities competing for foreign investment and what limited investment capital can be mobilized within the national economy.

Weiping Wu and Shahid Yusuf detail how the dramatic policy changes of the recent past in China have translated into huge investments in industry and infrastructure in Shanghai. In one of the poorest countries amongst those we are considering here, investment in the urban infrastructure of the premier industrial city ballooned from 6 billion yuan in 1991 to 53 billion in 1998. To take just one example, the paved road surface per capita doubled over those seven years. Wu and Yusuf argue that for Shanghai to succeed in the global competition, China has to continue the process of opening up to the outside world. Presumably this will entail further exacerbating inequalities across the huge country.

Yeong-Hyun Kim demonstrates that while strategies to attain world city status, or to consolidate such status, invariably give high priority to attracting foreign investment and expertise, international standing can be pursued through other avenues as well. She relates how Seoul followed its success in dramatically expanding manufacturing and exports by attracting world-class sports events. The city modernized its infrastructure for the 1988 Summer Olympics, and the high-profile media event gained Seoul international recognition. International tourism rose, and the city emerged from its cultural isolation. The trend was reenforced as Seoul hosted the 2002 World Cup Finals. Beijing's efforts to follow the example of Seoul succeeded in making it the third Asian city to host the Summer Olympics, in 2008.

The Asian Miracle, the Debt Crisis of the 1980s, the Russian Implosion, the Liquidity Crisis of the 1990s, and the current global recession have demonstrated time and again that the economic fortunes of countries can change quite abruptly. The impact of the global economy, in boom and in crash, is felt most dramatically in world cities heavily dependent on foreign investments, exports, and tourism. Huge inflows of capital are followed by abrupt reversals. Markets for exports shrink overnight. Tourists suddenly stay away. The consequences are particularly severe in poor countries where the people exposed to such sudden reversals of fortune are not cushioned by public systems of support such as exist in rich countries. Instead these shocks are mediated, to a greater extent than in rich countries, through political systems, social structures, and cultural patterns. Moscow has remained shielded from the worst consequences of Russia's precipitous decline by its powerful political position. In Bangkok, family support, the solidarity of workplace communities, and the employment practices of Japanese firms, cushioned severe economic shocks and allowed the city to strengthen its position relative to most of its foreign competitors.

Douglas Webster points out that globalization, and its crises, differentially affect different parts of the city and different sectors of its population. Globalization policies have often been pursued at the expense of the elderly, children, and women, and they are usually more vulnerable than others in times of crisis. Webster relates how the consequences of hyper growth and economic crises varied across Bangkok, its suburbs, and its periphery.

Janet Abu-Lughod emphasizes how Egypt's open door policy has burdened the lower and lower middle classes, how investments in Cairo's infrastructure have taken resources from social services for the poor. She suggests that the rising support for the Islamic movement may be related in part to the relative decline in the living standard of these classes. The success of the chauvinistic Shiv Sena movement in Mumbai can be similarly traced to ever-increasing inequalities.

As the global involvement of cities in poor countries increased, a significant proportion of their population came to pursue a dramatically improved standard of living. It contrasts sharply with the living conditions of those around them: if a two-class structure is becoming more pronounced in rich countries, the chasm is exacerbated in most poor countries. Three or four of our cities, however, boast remarkably low levels of poverty relative to both, the inequalities thought to be characteristic of world cities, and the general inequality that prevails in nearly all poor countries. While they were situated in poor regions, they could control the in-migration of the poor, either at international borders, i.e. Hong Kong and Singapore, or through restrictions on migration, e.g. Moscow and, until recently, Shanghai. These cities admitted only those poor they could productively employ, and their welfare policies were not swamped by those kept outside the gates.

The most visible manifestation of the sizeable new consumer elite is the striking transformation of the city center to be found in virtually all our cities. Offices, hotels, luxury housing, and up-scale shops and restaurants have displaced low-income residents. If Moscow's center was both privileged and heterogenous in social composition in Soviet times, low-income earners now give way to those successful under the new dispensation, their foreign partners, and office buildings. In Jakarta, the government embarked on the wholesale "modernization" of the city center, eradicating the *kampung*. The Seoul Olympics lent legitimacy to massive urban restructuring that involved the displacement of poor neighborhoods over public opposition. Elsewhere long-established residents have at times offered resistance. It was fairly ineffectual in Cairo's formerly walled city, where housing stock was left to decay, or cleared to widen thoroughfares and give tourists unobstructed views of major mosques: in recent decades the population in the medieval quarters declined from close to half a million to 300,000. In Mexico City, on the other hand, the working class has shown considerable capacity for political organization in defense of its residential interests and remained predominant in the inner city; still, even there population in the city center has declined dramatically.

High-standard infrastructure and distinctive enclaves of those incredibly rich by local standards set world cities apart from other cities in poor countries. Their industrial, commercial, and financial opportunities draw a disproportionate share of local and foreign capital. And the exceptional opportunities their labor markets promise encourage in-migration not only from rural areas but also from other cities. They drain human capital – the best educated, most skilled, strongly motivated from within the country and beyond. And their expanding middle class offers employment to a large number of low-income service workers, especially in domestic work, retail sales, and security services.[21] The sex ratio of these cities are likely to be affected by their regional and global status in three ways: urban–urban migration entails less family separation than rural–urban migration; to the extent that male migrants from rural areas find better opportunities in these cities than in other cities, they are more likely to have their families join them; and women migrating independently find these cities more attractive in terms of both job opportunities and the rapidly changing position of women in such cosmopolitan centers. All three effects entail higher proportions of women in these strategic cities than in other cities.

Peter Ward reminds us that while we speak of global cities, such cities are much more involved with some regions than with others. This is the case of New York, London, and Tokyo, but it applies even more so to the cities we consider here. Mexico City is a particularly striking case because, unlike any other of the countries in which our cities are situated, Mexico has a common border with a rich country, indeed the world's largest economy. More than half of foreign investment comes from the US. The shift from import-substituting industrialization to exported-oriented growth marginalized Mexico City in some measure as it encouraged manufacture closer to the US market. The integration of the two quite dissimilar economies has been given further impetus by the North American Free Trade Agreement. At the same time, Mexico City enjoys

[21] Brockerhoff (1999) has shown, for developing countries, that the largest cities of countries and their capitals tended to grow substantially faster than other cities between the 1970s and the 1990s. Regional and global status might be expected likewise to stimulate in-migration and boost population growth. However, recent growth of our cities is not particularly high compared to other cities in the same countries.

the opportunity to take advantage of its key position in two overlapping regions: North America and Latin America. In particular, Mexico City aspires to become the principal Latin American center for financial services.

The importance of the state

The state plays an important role in the affairs of world cities, but its impact varies across our twelve locales. Many of our cities have been profoundly transformed by state power – either in the guise of state socialism or as corporatist capitalism. As Russia and China abandoned the state socialist model, they engaged in transitions which have turned out to be extremely difficult. In the process they integrated themselves more closely into the global economy, but the outcomes remain hard to predict.

James Bater shows how political transformations through three regimes profoundly affected the fortunes of Moscow. Moscow was the most important commercial and industrial region of the Russian Empire for virtually all of the Tsarist period, but it lost its position as the Empire's capital to St. Petersburg in 1712. The global–local connection was strong in Soviet days when Moscow's role as the center of world communism translated into a privileged position for its citizenry and shaped the very ecology of the city. At this time Moscow is as yet in the early stages of establishing its role as a major player in the global economy. But its dominant position in a large economy, rich in natural resources and human capital, and its reach over neighboring countries in Eastern Europe and Asia hold out great promise.

Beijing played a role similar to that of Moscow in the ideological confrontations, support of allies, and proxy wars of the second half of the twentieth century. If this was the epoch of the Cold War in Western eyes, it was also the time of a fierce contest between Beijing and Moscow, over the leadership of developing countries in particular. Today China is further along than Russia in establishing itself as a major force in the global economy. Shanghai boasts a stock market far larger than any other outside the core, except for Hong Kong, now also part of China (Table I.1). Taken together these two stock markets have overtaken, by a large margin, all their rivals except New York, Tokyo, London, Paris, and Frankfurt. At the same time China, because of the size of its economy, enjoys greater freedom of action vis-à-vis foreign political powers and world markets than is the lot of any other poor country. Still, with China's entry in the World Trade Organization the policy of shielding inefficient state industries from competition is coming to an end.

The rapid integration of parts of the Chinese economy with the global economy has entailed the emergence of severe inequalities within cities and among regions across the huge country. Urban inequalities will be further exacerbated as state industries are abandoned to their fate in the market economy. These inequalities stand in stark contrast to the rather egalitarian patterns of earlier days, even if those days saw severe urban/rural inequities that in effect relegated rural dwellers to second-class citizenship.[22] It remains to be seen whether the state-party apparatus can continue effectively to contain urban protest and regional dissension.

Alvin So recounts how Hong Kong pursued a trajectory separate from China since it became a British colony in 1842. He provides an analysis of the interplay between the colonial power, the powerful state next door overshadowing the tiny enclave, and regional dynamics that forged the fortunes of Hong Kong. The rulers changed in 1997, and the Hong Kong "Special Administrative Region" is no longer all that separate from China. At this time it would appear that the future of Hong Kong will be even more closely directed by government in Hong Kong and in Beijing. As a British colony Hong Kong could by and large restrict immigration to those that could be productively employed, and the authorities have continued effectively to control migration. We may surmise, however, that the Chinese government, given a choice, will direct resources away from Hong Kong which stands as an island of privilege in a poor country.

Janet Salaff examines how the state's social engineering transformed the lives of Singapore's citizenry. An expanding system of quality education and training established a highly skilled labor force. A pension scheme ensured a high savings rate. Central-city slums and village settlements were replaced by high-rise buildings, and the apartments were increasingly owner-occupied. The population thus was drawn ever more tightly into the market economy, and a growing proportion of women joined the labor force. Singaporeans became less dependent on the support of kin and neighbors. Residential and occupational mobility further weakened community ties. The assurance of economic security in old age, the employment of women, and ante-natal policies led to a precipitous drop in fertility. Within less than a generation, the state had "modernized" the family. This transformation greatly reduced differences in family styles, even while it reproduced class differences. These policies were explicitly designed as part and parcel of a corporatist approach to economic

[22] Whyte and Parish (1984) produced the classic account of what was the largest program of urban social engineering ever, perhaps the most far-reaching as well: the efforts to transform the city that were carried out in China – and abandoned. Chen and Parish (1996) and Davis (1997) provide updates.

development that made Singapore into an affluent world city within just a generation. The success of these policies in turn provided the resources for the ambitious social programs. Unlike cities with rural hinterlands, these programs were shielded from the poor that could not be productively employed: they were kept outside the city-state's gates.

Dean Forbes details how the Suharto regime's "New Order" politics shaped Jakarta. The Indonesian economy and polity were centralized in the national capital which is the hub of domestic and international transport networks. Almost half of all employment created by foreign and domestic investment in Indonesia has been located in Jabotabek, the metropolitan area. Wages were higher, and standards of living superior, than elsewhere in Indonesia, but the regime's attempts to control migration to Jakarta failed. The city thus became characterized by stark social and economic disparities. When the Liquidity Crisis hit in 1997, an autocratic regime that had lasted more than three decades soon disintegrated. The economic shock, more strongly felt in Jakarta than elsewhere in Indonesia, thus was exacerbated by political developments. Pressures mounted for political power and economic resources to be decentralized across the far-flung country. The resolution of the continuing political crisis will profoundly affect Jakarta's future. In the meantime political uncertainty constrains its global aspirations.

The strength of popular movements

Political changes tend to be initiated in world cities. They are home to powerful financial and commercial interests, a sizeable professional class, a substantial working class, and a large student body. Such environments are more receptive to global social trends, even as they develop their own variants. And they provide an attractive arena for protest movements – which is likely to be well covered by national and international media. Popular movements in these cities constitute an important third level of political actors beyond the global and the state.

Jakarta has been the primary setting for the political and economic crises that shook Indonesia over the last few years. Student and worker demonstrations were an important catalyst in the events leading to the resignation of Suharto. Student groups maintained demonstrations of opposition to the successor regime of Habibie. Students and other demonstrators provided an important source of support for the election of Wahid and, to a lesser extent, his successor Megawati Sukarnoputri.

Maria Helena Moreira Alves shows how urban workers successfully changed the politics of São Paulo and beyond. If the state transformed the lives of Singapore's citizenry, São Paulo's workers transformed the local and national polities. The concentration of foreign and national investment had made São Paulo into Latin America's foremost industrial city – and it spawned the New Labor Movement in the late 1970s. The movement came to play a major role in undermining the military regime and bringing civilian rule to Brazil eventually. From the labor movement the powerful *Partido dos Trabalhadores* (PT) emerged. The PT came to control São Paulo, other major cities, and some states. Its leader Luis Ignácio da Silva was elected President of Brazil in 2002. São Paulo had become an "exporter of ideas," ideas that transformed the politics of Brazil, that shaped the negotiations over the protections for labor in MERCOSUR, the common market of the Southern Cone, and that reverberate across the globe in organizations such as the World Social Forum. São Paulo is a remarkable case of globalization profoundly impacting a city through foreign direct investment, of an effective labor movement arising in the multinational production sites, and of this movement in turn having a profound impact on the city, on the nation, on the region, and across the globe.

Sujata Patel joins Alves in emphasizing the importance of local popular movements. However, the movements in São Paulo and Mumbai/Bombay are quite distinct in terms of recruitment and ideology. In São Paulo the movement was launched and continues to be spearheaded by an industrial worker elite, whereas the Shiv Sena in Mumbai effectively displaced an earlier trade union movement that in its heyday had wielded considerable power. The Shiv Sena set out as an ethnic movement recruiting from the Marathi-speaking underclass to fight for the rights of the "sons-of-the-soil." Subsequently it shifted to projecting itself as a Hindu party. Shiv Sena's populist religious mobilization reenforced similar trends in the state of Maharashtra and at the national level. Throughout the movement defined itself in opposition to communists and secularists and promoted vigilante politics. Traditions of democracy, multiculturalism, and civility have declined in a city that used to pride itself on being India's most cosmopolitan city.

Owen Crankshaw and Susan Parnell, in the last contribution, relate the transformation Johannesburg experiences at this time. Soweto, the large city where the majority of Johannesburg's African workers had been ghettoized, was the scene of the fiercest and most effective internal opposition to the apartheid regime. In this case, unlike São Paulo and Mumbai, a global popular movement played a major role in supporting the opposition and boycotting South Africa – a process of globalization quite different from the common understanding of globalization. Now we witness the unraveling of the urban configuration the white minority regime created and see Johannesburg taking on a leading role in Africa south of the Sahara. Alongside the demise of apartheid policies, a dramatic decline in manufacturing employment and an increase in service sector employment have contributed to growing intra-racial inequality between urbanized Africans and immigrants from rural areas.

Conclusions

This volume is the first systematically to cover those cities beyond the core that most clearly can be considered world cities. It presents twelve cities in four continents in their economic, political, and cultural dimensions. Leading authorities on these cities, representing several disciplines, offer a range of different approaches.

Three conclusions stand out. For one, these cities are extraordinarily diverse. They have had very different histories, their present economic and political circumstances vary, they are variously articulated with their respective regions and across the globe, and their demographic dynamics differ. The foremost conclusion of our systematic approach is how problematic most generalizations about world cities are. This diversity has policy implications. Any policy intended to improve a city's global standing needs to focus on specific circumstances rather than simply trying to emulate some presumed model.

Second, globalization has brought dramatic improvements in the standard of living of a significant proportion of the population in these cities. The most visible manifestation of this consumer elite is the striking transformation of the city center to be found in virtually all our cities. The consequent displacement of inner-city residents is only the most striking aspect of the more general issue: the severe inequalities characteristic of most poor countries, and of their cities in particular, have been further exacerbated in most of these world cities. At the same time, as the economic fortunes of these cities have become ever more closely entwined with the global economy, their populations have been exposed to sudden reversals of fortune that are not cushioned by public systems of support such as exist, in varying degrees, in rich countries.

The final conclusion that these accounts impose is that any general analysis of world cities has to recognize, along with the forces of globalization, the strength of the state and the power of popular movements. States demarcated the path to world city status taken by several of our cities. While the policies pursued were usually intended to further global integration, they were also very much shaped by political and cultural context and differed from one state to another. The popular movements that imposed their imprint on a number of our cities in turn pursued a range of altogether different agendas. The state and civil society have to be brought into the analysis of world cities. These cities evolve in the interplay among three powerful agents: globalization, the state, and popular movements.

REFERENCES

Barbaroux, Evangéline 2001. "Mondialisation: l'état du cinéma vu par 50 cinéastes de la planète," *Cahiers du Cinéma*, 557: 46–75.

Beaverstock, J. V., Taylor, P. J., and Smith, R. G. 1999. "A Roster of World Cities," *Cities*, 16: 445–458.

Beckel, Lothar (ed.) 2001. *Megacities: The European Space Agency's Contribution to a Better Understanding of a Global Challenge*. Salzburg: Geospace Verlag.

Brockerhoff, Martin 1999. "Urban Growth in Developing Countries: A Review of Projections and Predictions," *Population and Development Review*, 25: 757–778.

Chen, Xiangming and Parish, William 1996. "Urbanization in China: Assessing an Evolving Model," in Josef Gugler (ed.), *The Urban Transformation of the Developing World*. Oxford: Oxford University Press, pp. 60–90.

Cohen, Michael A. 1996. "The Hypothesis of Urban Convergence: Are Cities in the North and the South Becoming More Alike in an Age of Globalization?," in Michael A. Cohen, Blair A. Ruble, Joseph S. Tulchin, and Allison M. Garland (eds.), *Preparing for the Urban Future: Global Pressures and Local Forces*. Woodrow Wilson Center Special Studies. Washington, DC: Woodrow Wilson Center Press, pp. 25–38.

Davis, Deborah 1997. "Social Transformation of Metropolitan China since 1949," in Josef Gugler (ed.), *Cities in the Developing World: Issues, Theory, and Policy*. Oxford: Oxford University Press, pp. 248–258.

Dick, H. W. and Rimmer, P. J. 1998. "Beyond the Third World City: The New Urban Geography of South-east Asia," *Urban Studies*, 35: 2303–2321.

Friedmann, John 1986. "The World City Hypothesis," *Development and Change*, 17: 69–84.

Godfrey, Brian J. and Zhou, Yu 1999. "Ranking World Cities: Multinational Corporations and the Global Urban Hierarchy," *Urban Geography*, 20: 268–281.

(2000) Unpublished data.

Gugler, Josef 2002. "The Son of the Hawk Does Not Remain Abroad: The Urban–Rural Connection in Africa," *African Studies Review*, 45 (1): 21–41.

Knox, Paul L. and Taylor, Peter J. (eds.) 1995. *World Cities in a World System*. Cambridge: Cambridge University Press.

Larkin, Brian 1998. "Uncertain Consequences: The Social and Religious Life of Media in Northern Nigeria," Ph.D. dissertation, New York University.

OAG 2001. *OAG Flight Guide Worldwide: September 2001*. Oak Brook, IL: OAG.

Roberts, Bryan 1997. "The Social Context of Citizenship in Latin America," in Josef Gugler (ed.), *Cities in the Developing World: Issues, Theory, and Policy*. Oxford: Oxford University Press, pp. 350–365.

Robinson, Jennifer 2002. "Global and World Cities: A View from off the Map," *International Journal of Urban and Regional Research*, 26: 531–534.

Sassen, Saskia 1997. "Cities in the Global Economy," *International Journal of Urban Sciences*, 1 (1): 11–31.
(2000 [1993]). *Cities in a World Economy*. Sociology for a New Century. 2nd edition. Thousand Oaks, CA, London, and New Delhi: Pine Forge Press.
(2001 [1991]). *The Global City: New York, London, Tokyo*. 2nd edition. Princeton: Princeton University Press.
Short, John Rennie, Breitbach, Carrie, Buckman, Steven, and Essex, Jamey 2000. "From World Cities to Gateway Cities: Extending the Boundaries of Globalization Theory," *City*, 4: 317–340.
Short, J. R., Kim, Y., Kuus, M., and Wells, H. 1996. "The Dirty Little Secret of World Cities Research: Data Problems in Comparative Analysis," *International Journal of Urban and Regional Research*, 20: 697–717.
Taylor, Peter J. 2000. "World Cities and Territorial States under Conditions of Contemporary Globalization," *Political Geography*, 19: 5–32.
(2002) Unpublished data.
Taylor, Peter J., Walker, David R. F., Catalano, Gilda, and Hoyer, Michael 2002. "Diversity and Power in the World City Network," *Cities*, 19: 231–241.
UNESCO 2001. www.unesco.org/culture/industries/cinema/html_eng/product.shtml.
United Nations 2002. *World Urbanization Prospects: The 2001 Revision*. New York: United Nations.
Ward, Peter M. 1995. "The Successful Management and Administration of World Cities: Mission Impossible?," in Paul L. Knox and Peter J. Taylor (eds.), *World Cities in a World System*. Cambridge: Cambridge University Press, pp. 298–314.
Whyte, Martin King and Parish, William L. 1984. *Urban Life in Contemporary China*. Chicago: University of Chicago Press.
World Bank 2002. *2002 World Development Indicators*. Online data base.
2003. *2003 World Development Indicators*. Online data base.
Yeoh, Brenda S. A. 1999. "Global/Globalizing Cities," *Progress in Human Geography*, 23: 607–616.

Part 1

The impact of the global political economy

1 Shanghai: remaking China's future global city*

Weiping Wu and Shahid Yusuf

Among the leading Chinese cities, Shanghai is arguably the one best positioned to emerge over the next two decades as a major regional hub or even a world city comparable to Hong Kong and Singapore. Since the early 1990s, the Shanghai municipal authorities, with the support of the central government, have embarked upon a multipronged strategy to achieve this goal. The strategy seeks to capitalize on Shanghai's industrial capabilities to build a high-technology manufacturing sector, to greatly expand the logistics infrastructure already in place, and to create a complex of finance and business services that rival those of Hong Kong.

We believe that actions enabling Shanghai to acquire the status initially of a regional center would need to encompass at least two strands: the first involves greater openness, comparable to that enjoyed by Hong Kong. This is primarily in the hands of the central government. The second calls for municipal policies to enhance Shanghai's competitiveness as a metropolitan area.

This chapter starts with an overview of Shanghai's historical and recent development. With special emphasis on key areas of industry, services, transport, infrastructure, and real estate, we then indicate the kinds of policies, devised by both the national and municipal governments, that would enable Shanghai to graduate from being a national to a regional – and possibly, in the distant future, a global hub of the front rank. And last we show how such policies are being implemented in Shanghai.

History and geography

First established as a fishing village in the tenth century, Shanghai became a county seat in 1074. Merchant families from nearby Ningbo (in Zhejiang Province) were instrumental in making it an integral part of the

* This chapter draws substantial materials from Yusuf and Wu (2002). We wish to thank Josef Gugler, Yue-man Yeung, Xiangming Chen, Deepak Bhattasali, and participants in a National Academy of Sciences' Committee on Population workshop for their insightful comments.

coastal trading system, and Shanghai grew steadily to become a regional commercial center. The succession of "unequal treaties" imposed by external powers on China starting with the Treaty of Nanking of 1849 led to the opening of treaty ports. Shanghai was among the earliest treaty ports. By 1853, it had surpassed Guangzhou (Canton) as China's premier trading city (Yusuf and Wu 1997).

Often called the "crucible of modern China," Shanghai entered the stage of modern commercial and industrial development in the second half of the nineteenth century (Wei 1987).[1] Banking and other producer services began taking root soon afterwards. At the same time, Shanghai also was the city where China's first modern institutions of higher learning were established, starting a tradition that has endured and flourished since. During its golden age in the 1920s, with a population over 2 million, Shanghai was "a meeting ground for people from all countries, a great and a unique city, one of the most remarkable in the world" (Pott 1928, p. 1). Ranked as the seventh largest city in the world in 1936, no modern Asian city from that period could "match Shanghai's cosmopolitan and sophisticated reputation" (Yeung 1996, p. 2).

After 1949, however, the city experienced more than thirty years of neglect and disinvestment. Shanghai was one among a handful of Chinese cities in the early 1950s that had a functioning modern industrial sector, the supporting infrastructure, and the necessary skills. Tightly controlled by the central government, Shanghai was the single largest contributor of the country's revenue and served as a major pillar of the planned economy (Wu 1999a). Despite its growing population, Shanghai was not able to upgrade its infrastructure and the city remained largely the same as in the 1940s. It was only after the success of reforms in south China that Shanghai finally embarked on a rapid path of modernization in the late 1980s.

Today, with a population of over 16 million and land area of 6,377 square kilometers within the metropolitan area, Shanghai is the biggest of three cities – the two others are Hangzhou and Wuxi – that together comprise the principal urban region in China (see Map 1.1).[2] The metropolitan area, governed by the Shanghai municipal government – equivalent to a provincial government because of Shanghai's special administrative status – consists of sixteen urban districts (nine of them are located in the central city) and three suburban counties (see Maps 1.2 and 1.3).

[1] Many academic volumes have been devoted to Shanghai's past, chief among which are Goodman 1995; Howe 1981; Johnson 1995; Lu 1999; Murphy 1953; and Wei 1987.

[2] The other major urban regions are Beijing–Tianjin–Tangshan and Hong Kong–Guangzhou–Shenzhen (Wang 1998, p. 265).

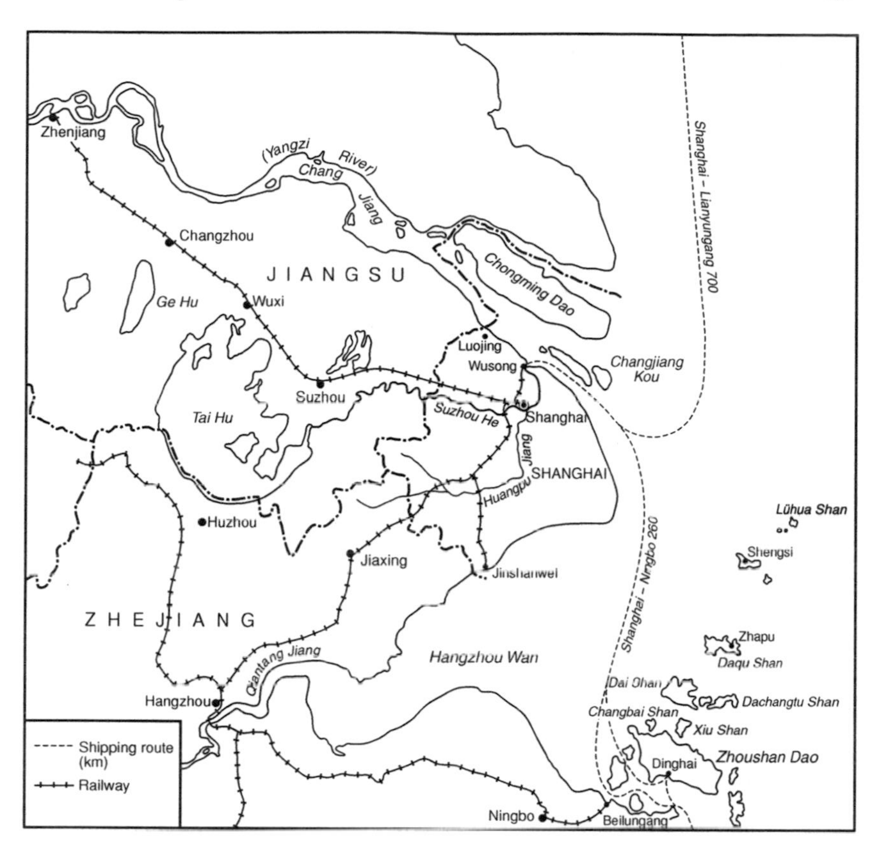

Map 1.1 Shanghai–Hangzhou–Wuxi urban region
Source: Shi *et al.* 1996.

Continuing efforts of decentralization have offered district governments substantial autonomy in tax collection, budget allocation, infrastructure provision, and planning.

Shanghai has a gross domestic product (GDP) of $60 billion (2001), a highly diversified industrial base responsible for 5.5% of national industrial output, and an expanding services sector that now accounts for over half of the municipal GDP (see Table 1.1, McDaniels and Zhao 2001, and *Business China*, Economist Intelligence Unit, 11 September 2000). The interaction between these two diversified sectors offers substantial agglomeration economies. But only a fraction of such economies have been fully exploited because of the persisting compartmentalization of industrial subsectors and research facilities, a resilient

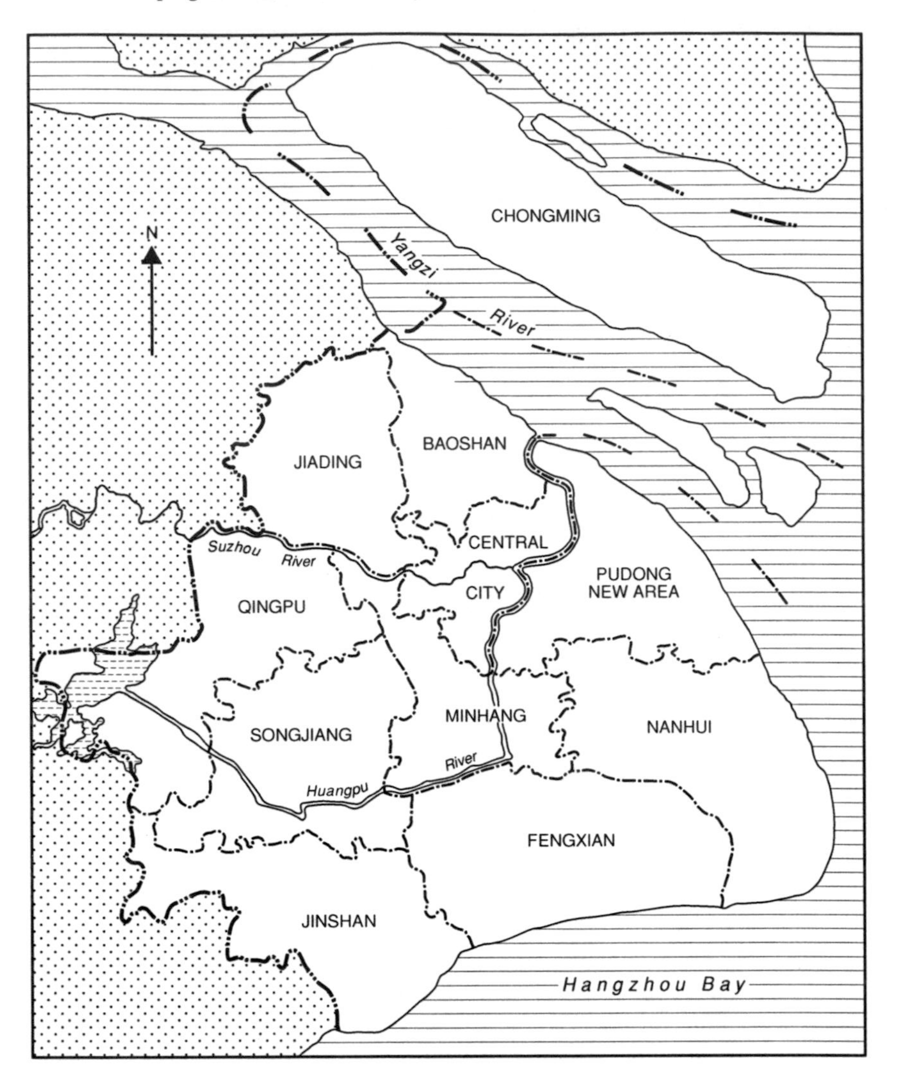

Map 1.2 Administrative division of Shanghai municipality
Source: Yeung 1996.

legacy of a socialist planning system now being displaced piecemeal by the market system. After a decade of industrial restructuring, municipal authorities are paying closer attention to the development of high-tech products and six manufacturing subsectors – automobiles, electronics and telecommunications equipment, power station equipment,

Map 1.3 Urban districts in central Shanghai
Source: Yeung 1996.
Note: Two districts, Huangpu and Nanshi, have been consolidated into one (Huangpu).

Table 1.1 *Indices of gross domestic product in Shanghai (1952 = 100)*

	GDP	Primary sector	Secondary sector	Tertiary sector	Transport and communications	Wholesale retail and food services	Banking and insurance	Real estate
1985	1,596.6	244.2	2,602.9	715.0	1,833.1	391.3	3,076.7	1,154.0
1986	1,666.9	243.8	2,707.0	757.9	1,906.4	394.0	3,544.4	1,065.1
1987	1,791.9	237.2	2,907.3	825.4	1,973.1	397.9	4,274.5	1,175.9
1988	1,972.9	248.2	3,180.6	929.4	2,085.6	461.2	5,185.0	1,198.2
1989	2,032.1	248.9	3,231.5	995.4	2,164.9	465.8	6,548.7	1,286.9
1990	2,103.2	259.6	3,322.0	1,048.2	2,437.7	476.2	6,961.3	1,020.5
1991	2,252.5	260.6	3,547.9	1,137.3	2,627.8	547.0	7,135.3	1,575.7
1992	2,585.9	261.6	4,158.1	1,273.8	2,869.6	643.9	7,784.6	1,905.0
1993	2,971.2	254.5	4,852.5	1,441.9	3,079.1	727.0	9,193.6	2,133.6
1994	3,396.1	261.9	5,541.6	1,669.7	3,300.8	803.3	11,924.1	2,656.3
1995	3,875.0	278.7	6,361.8	1,888.4	3,565.4	921.4	12,568.0	7,190.6
1996	4,378.8	292.6	7,067.9	2,224.5	4,007.5	1,029.2	16,313.3	8,923.5
1997	4,934.9	304.9	7,817.1	2,618.2	4,344.1	1,227.8	20,587.4	10,288.8
1998	5,433.3	311.6	8,458.1	2,992.6	4,717.7	1,355.5	23,016.7	12,696.4
1999	5,987.5	318.5	9,219.3	3,381.6	5,250.8	1,506.0	26,216.0	14,600.9
2000	6,634.2	329.3	10,122.8	3,817.8	6,022.7	1,673.2	30,489.2	16,849.6
2001	7,310.9	339.2	11,337.5	4,149.9	6,552.7	1,934.2	28,141.5	20,371.2

Source: Shanghai Statistical Bureau 2002.

steel, petrochemicals, and home appliances (*Shanghai Star*, 28 May 1999).[3]

Entering the twenty-first century, Shanghai is a city competing aggressively for the mantle of China's premier metropolis in the face of competition from an established center – Hong Kong, and other aspirants such as Beijing. Its share of the nation's GDP is almost twice that of Beijing, and its growth is among the highest of any city in China. In Shanghai's favor are the lower overall living and business expenses relative to Hong Kong[4] and the support and incentives it has received from the central government. The appointment first of Jiang Zemin (1985) and then of Zhu Rongji (1987) as mayors of Shanghai put in place leaders with close links to Beijing. In 1990, Deng Xiaoping lent his support to the city by calling for rapid development of the Pudong New Area project on farmland to the east of the city, proposed in the early 1980s by the then mayor of Shanghai Wang Daohan. The project was formally launched by premier Li Peng in April 1990. This was followed by a number of preferential measures, which, among others, allowed Shanghai to establish a stock market, a free trade zone and a number of service industries. Jiang Zemin's appointment as Party Secretary and Zhu Rongji's entry into the ranks of the ruling circle first as Vice Premier and then Premier further strengthened Shanghai's links with the capital and support for its development ambitions. Thus in 1995, eighteen super-special policies gave preferential status to projects in Pudong, 700 million yuan (approximately $84.5 million) in annual loans from the center plus a number of other benefits that have enabled Shanghai to sustain the tempo of activity and of change (Yatsko 2001). Between 1990 and 2000, the central and municipal governments invested a total of $22 billion in Pudong and by 1999, it accounted for a fifth of metropolitan GDP of Shanghai.

The attention given to Shanghai represented in part the attempt by the center to promote development in the northern part of the country to balance the rapid advances taking place in the southeastern region (Ochi 1997). More broadly, it reflects the increasing attention being given to urban areas where China's wealth is concentrated. Moreover, Shanghai has invested heavily in transport facilities and the latest fiber optics based

[3] Shanghai is the leading producer of many items in each of these categories, accounting for nearly half of all sewing machines produced and close to a third of power-generating equipment (Yeung and Li 1999).

[4] A comparison of Hong Kong and Shanghai compiled by *Business Week* in mid-2001 indicates that living and business operating expenses in Shanghai are far lower than in Hong Kong, e.g., rental for prime office space is US$6.30 per square foot versus $1.90; a two-bedroom apartment is $3,500 versus $1,000; a personal assistant, $3,500 per month versus $500; a business lunch for two is $51 versus $24; a taxi to the airport from downtown is $48 versus $24. See *Business Week*, "A City under Siege," 23 July 2001.

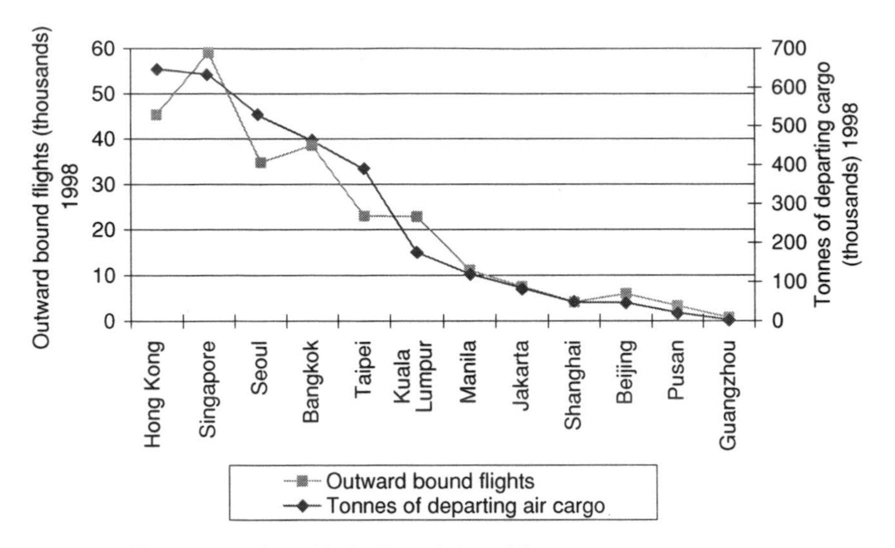

Figure 1.1 Air traffic in East Asian cities
Source: International Civil Aviation Organization 1998.

and mobile communications technology so essential for the growth of local producer services and for integrating with the international business community (Wu and Wong 1997).[5]

Around Shanghai and extending westward along the Yangtze River Valley is one of the two most prosperous economic hinterlands in China with an urban population of 200 million and a GDP of nearly $300 billion (1995 dollars at market prices).[6] The southeastern region, comprised of Hong Kong and the Pearl River Delta, has registered equivalent growth rates and has a superior transport and communication facilities. But the size of the Yangtze Basin economy, its momentum during the 1990s, and its contiguity to the Qingdao–Yantai–Jinan region are certainly impressive. When we look into the future, the pattern of development in the Yangtze Basin, the productivity of the diversified agricultural economy, the vast scale of rural industrial activities, and the speed with which transport and communications infrastructure are being built up, all suggest that this region competes strongly with other parts of the country.[7]

[5] By the end of the 1990s, the number of phone lines per 1,000 people had reached 286 and of mobile phones 155 per 1,000 in Shanghai as against 299 and 45 per 1,000 respectively in Beijing (*Asiaweek*, "Best Cities," 15 December 2000).

[6] Yeung and Li (1999) notes that the Yangtzi Basin accounts for a third of China's population and 40% of GDP.

[7] Shanghai is China's largest seaport, accounting for 18% of total cargo. The total volume of traffic handled by the Shanghai Port Authority in 1998 was 90.5 million tons, of which

Preeminence in a national context, however, is only one of several attributes of a regional or global hub. Several types of function are commonly associated with world city status. These include finance, transnational corporate headquarter functions, global services, transport, information, a site for international conferences, exhibitions and cultural activities (Douglass 2000).[8] Governments across the world have begun to promote the advancement of their key metropolises into regional or global hubs by acquiring some or all of these functions. As Figure 1.1 shows, in the East Asia region, Hong Kong and Singapore lead the way with respect to international flights and international airfreight movements. However, both Beijing and Shanghai have achieved respectable levels in a short space of time and are registering high growth rates as China's economic importance continues to rise.

Becoming a world city – greater openness

Economic liberalization

Relative to many other countries, China remains a closed society where central and subnational governments manage with foreigners, control movement into and out of the country, regulate Internet traffic, and take a minimalist view of individual rights vis-à-vis the state.[9] The political system is firmly in the grip of the Communist Party. And although the Shanghai municipality, with the status of a province, enjoys substantial fiscal and administrative autonomy, it is subject to the same strictures as the rest of the country regarding relations with the outside world.

By containing links with the rest of the world, the Chinese authorities make it harder for Shanghai to capitalize fully on foreign direct investment (FDI) in infrastructure building, international production networking, and the growth of producer services. Although Shanghai's rapid development over the past decade has contributed to its continued national dominance, key elements of national policy have kept Shanghai from moving closer to the ranks of cities that can claim to be the leading regional hubs. China's limited attractiveness for the international business community,

21 million tons was coal and 27.6 million tons was containers. Bulk traffic-coal and fertilizers declined through the 1990s (Shanghai Statistical Bureau 1999).

[8] In recent years Shanghai has created the facilities to hold international exhibitions and made considerable efforts to become a part of the global conference and exhibition circuit.

[9] Notwithstanding the fact that total trade was $851 billion (2003), making China the ninth largest trading nation with one of the highest B2B transactions in the world (Pearson 2000).

which affects the prospects of its cities, was underlined by an *Economist* survey (7 March 1998, p. 114). Hong Kong had a score of 8.5 out of 10 during the period 1992–1996, ahead of Britain, the Netherlands, Singapore, Canada, and the United States. China was not among the top thirty countries.

Openness has many dimensions, including trade, the circulation of labor, the legal framework finance, and culture. China's accession to the World Trade Organization (WTO) will result in a significant liberalization of trade through the adoption of rules and incentive mechanisms shared by other members.[10] It will involve China directly in international governance associated with trade and related issues. It is also likely to result in a far-reaching dismantling of barriers to trade in manufacturing, agricultural products, and many kinds of services and greater penetration of foreign entities in the financial sector, telecommunications, and other areas.[11] These would accelerate the reform of the state enterprise sector currently being downsized through closure, merger, or privatization. The movement of workers is linked to the provision of residence permits. In this regard, Shanghai took the first small step in 2002, when it granted sixty professionals from elsewhere in China and abroad the right to live in the city and engage in business (*Business China*, Economist Intelligence Unit, 24 June 2002, p. 11).

Improved communications with other countries is another dimension of the move towards openness. This already is being pursued with great vigor through heavy investments in telecommunications, amounting to $400 billion between 1994 and 2000, which has provided fixed and mobile telephone services to more than 155 million users.[12] The number of people with Internet access rose from 8.9 million users in 1999 to almost 34 million by the end of 2000.[13] For this investment and the inter-linkages it provides to yield their full returns, domestic rules and

[10] See Martin *et al.* 1999. Recent work by Frankel and Roemer (1999) provides added support for the relationship between trade and increase in incomes. They find that a 1% increase in the ratio of trade to GDP raises per capita incomes by 0.5% by stimulating factor accumulation and productivity. The relationship between trade and growth has been noted in cross-country studies by Sachs and Warner (1995 and 1997). On China see Li and Zhai 2000; Yu 1998 and 2000 and *Financial Times*, "The Big Lie of Global Inequality," 9 February 2000.

[11] *Wall Street Journal*, "China Weighs Lifting Curbs on Foreign Firms," 10 January 2000; *Financial Times*, "China to Speed up Financial Reform before Joining WTO," 21 January 2000.

[12] *Far Eastern Economic Review*, "Surf's up," 4 March 1999. China surpassed Japan in the first quarter of 2000 as the country with the largest number of cell phone users 51.7 million (*China Business*, 11 September 2000). The number of landlines exceeded 100 million in June 2000 (Hartford 2000).

[13] *Financial Times*, "China's Risky Leap Forward," 12 August 1999; *Financial Times*, "China Survey," 1 October 1999; Hartford 2000; *Oxford Analytica*, "China: Internet

laws will have to evolve to recognize individual freedoms to use the burgeoning channels of communication.[14]

This leads to a third and related aspect of openness, which is the framework of commercial laws and regulations governing business dealings and financial transactions. Starting in the mid-1980s, China has been gradually building a legal infrastructure, training lawyers, assimilating laws, and instituting legal procedures that are increasingly a common currency worldwide. But the nature of Chinese legal and regulatory practices, as well as the approach to enforcing regulations, still differs markedly from that of more open industrialized countries. For example, there is legislation providing redress where administrative power is misused, but only under certain conditions when the government is involved, and no redress is available when the Party is involved. The courts cannot challenge the right of the police to impose administrative punishments and send people to jail without a trial.[15] This can result in uncertainty, inhibits business dealings, and raises transaction costs, especially for foreigners.

China's vast potential market tempts foreign companies and financial houses and is responsible for cumulative foreign investment in China projected to reach $388 billion (committed amount) by the end of 2001.[16] But the lack of transparency and the problems of coping with complex local regulations are a disincentive. The persistence of high transaction costs resulted in a reappraisal of business opportunities in China by many foreign corporations and a slowdown of FDI in 1999 (*Financial Times*, "China Survey," 1 October 1999).[17] Although FDI rebounded to an average of $53 billion in 2002–2003, narrowing the institutional gulf in legal and regulatory matters between China and other countries will be a key aspect of greater openness.

China's plans to liberalize transactions on the capital account were interrupted by the East Asian crisis of 1997–1998 that battered five

Impact," 10 May 2001; *China Quarterly*, Chronicle and Documentation, No. 170, June 2002. The number of Internet users in Shanghai rose from 3.3 thousand in 1996 to 102 thousand in 1998. And the number of long-distance telephone lines (not all local phone lines can dial long distance directly) increased from 59,000 to 84,000 over the same period (Shanghai Statistical Bureau 1999, p. 244).

[14] Attempts by the Chinese government to control the use of the Internet through closer regulation and the fostering of state-owned websites would only slow the process of opening (*Financial Times*, "Beijing set to step-up curbs on Internet," 22 March 2000; and Kennedy 2000).

[15] *Oxford Analytica*, "China: The Legal Environment," 29 July 1998; *Oxford Analytica*, "China: Rule by Law," 25 October 1999.

[16] *Business China*, "And the Winner Is . . . ," Economist Intelligence Unit, 26 March 2001.

[17] During the first eight months of 1999, contracted foreign direct investment fell by 20% over the previous year to $25.3 billion (*Oxford Analytica*, "China: Global Engagement," 21 December 1999). However, inflows rose in 2000 and are expected to reach $45 billion (*China Business*, 17 July 2000).

countries in the region but left China largely unscathed. In the immediate aftermath of the crisis it was thought that China avoided succumbing to the crisis because it deferred the deregulation of the capital account until it had built up adequate supervisory capability and thereby contained the inflow of short-term and portfolio capital. Malaysia's experience with controls on capital outflow also lent credence to this line of thinking. However, closer analysis of the entire crisis episode and of the use of capital account controls not just in East Asia but also in Latin America suggests that the story is much more complex and capital controls are relatively ineffective in insulating domestic and financial markets from international markets and may have had less bearing on vulnerability than the state of the financial systems in the crisis-hit East Asian economies and their neighbors.[18]

A major challenge for China during the medium term is to strengthen the financial system (Newfarmer and Liu 1998). As markets become more sophisticated, new derivative instruments appear, and trade contacts continue to expand, restraining capital outflow is likely to prove extremely difficult and even containing inflows would pose problems. Thus capital controls are likely to inflict transactions costs, and raise borrowing costs for small- and medium-scale enterprises, and so long as the yuan is not fully convertible, China's integration with the international markets will be only partial (Edwards 1999). Moreover, if they reduce the pace of banking reform they could involve a substantial waste of resources.[19]

Strengthening market institutions

Shanghai is embarked on the road to becoming a financial center, but it lags behind Hong Kong (Enright *et al.* 1997; Meyer 2000). So far the central government and the municipal authorities have taken only the

[18] Poorly managed and lightly supervised banks in some of the East Asian countries invested their resources without due analysis of risk often in sectors favored by the government, in affiliated businesses, or in real estate. This gradually increased the proportion of non-performing assets and implicitly enlarged the contingent liabilities of the government. As awareness of this banking fragility became more widespread and doubts grew as to the ability of governments to rescue the banking sector, a silent flight of capital commenced. A succession of events then precipitated a full-fledged crisis. Even China was not immune to this silent flight, reflected in the country's large errors and omissions in the balance-of-payment accounts and the huge flow of FDI into Hong Kong, which exceeded $52 billion in 2000. See Kaminsky and Schmuckler (2000) on capital controls on the financial market institution.

[19] Nonetheless, with capital flowing back into the East Asia region and financial reform still in its early stages, the risks from bubbles and a resurgence of problems remain.

first few steps by creating some of the physical infrastructure and inviting international financial entities of all kinds to establish offices. Commercial banks, investment and brokerage houses, insurance firms, other market makers, and telecommunications companies have responded by establishing footholds in the city.[20] By the end of 2001, twenty-one foreign banks had established their main offices in Shanghai. But thus far, the authorities have restricted retail banking activities, securities trading, and insurance and only recently permitted foreign banks operating in Shanghai to make loans in local currency. Many other elements must be put in place, for example, permitting foreign intermediaries to compete for local deposits and services such as credit cards and home mortgages before Shanghai becomes even a regional crossroads for the international financial community (Chowdhury 2000).[21]

One of these is the lowering, as is proposed under the WTO rules, of barriers to trade – a step that would promote trade, sustain growth, and lead to a continuing decline in poverty. Second is the opening of China's capital account, which, along with full convertibility, would permit the freer flow of capital in and out of the country. A third is a framework of rules and laws governing financial and other entities that delineate and enforce rights in a transparent and predictable manner, especially those pertaining to contracts, intellectual property, bankruptcy procedures, and foreclosure. Fourth is a regulatory framework to monitor activities, build the institutions that will ensure stable market functioning, and induce innovations conducive to growth as well as efficiency. Fifth is the reform of financial entities to enhance their autonomy and efficiency and enable them to compete against foreign organizations, a development that would permit a gradual dismantling of the many curbs on the activities of foreign firms, including investment in Chinese banks. In 2001, the nonperforming loans (NPLs) at the Bank of China were estimated to be close to 29% of assets and those of the other major state banks are likely to be comparable if not larger (*Financial Times*, "Loans Move Turns up the Heat on Big Four," 16 May 2001). Furthermore, as state-controlled banks channel over two-thirds of bank credit to state enterprises, half of which have been making losses during 1998–1999, the percentage of NPLs is likely to increase. Return on assets in the banking system was less than 0.2% in 1999.[22]

[20] *Wall Street Journal*, "Alcatel office to be launched in Shanghai," 18 January 2000.

[21] With accession to the WTO, competition in financial services could increase if China reforms its banking sector and levels the playing field (Harner 2000).

[22] *Financial Times*, "China Survey," 1 October 1999; *Far Eastern Economic Review*, "Mission Critical," 9 September 1999; and World Bank 1999b.

The final element relates to the continuing development and deepening of the financial and insurance markets, a process that has been ongoing since the early 1990s.[23] Markets for stocks, other financial instruments, and foreign exchange are now functioning in China, along with adequate mechanisms for clearing transactions and settling payments. Over 1,160 enterprises were listed on the Shanghai or the Shenzhen stock exchanges by the end of 2001 and market capitalization was close to 4.4 trillion yuan ($530 billion).[24] But the insurance industry is still woefully underdeveloped. The institutional base created must evolve much further before China can attain parity with other industrializing countries, not to mention the advanced economies. Shanghai has a head start in the sphere of financial market development in China, which is meaningful in a national context but not yet in regional terms.[25]

Pathways to the world city – competitiveness and livability

While the critical policies determining economic openness will be largely decided by the central government, and the prosperity of Shanghai's hinterland will be a function of policies pursued by a host of entities, Shanghai's municipal authorities also have a large role to play in enhancing the city's competitiveness and quality of life. They have had a firm hand in determining the timing, pace, and configuration of the city's development (Han 2000). Since the mid-1990s, a set of strategic development objectives has been defined and to a degree implemented. A key element is to advance into a world city level of high-tech manufacturing, business services, transport and communications facilities, commercial facilities, and availability of skills (cited in Chan 2000). This calls for action in a number of areas, building on a variety of ongoing initiatives. Shanghai is active in each of these areas, but it faces difficult choices and

[23] Development of the domestic financial market will be aided by a series of government moves, among which is the raising of the ceilings on stock market investments by insurance companies from 5 to 10%. This will increase the volume of liquidity available to finance new share issues (*Financial Times*, "China to boost liquidity in share market," 21 March 2000).

[24] Between 2000 and 2001, market capitalization fell by 9.5%. *China Quarterly*, Chronicle and Documentation, No. 170, June 2002.

[25] It is debatable whether with two major financial centers already in the region – Tokyo and Hong Kong, there will be a role for a third center of equivalent scale, especially given the advances in communications favoring a few large nodes linked to many smaller ones in a hierarchical system (Coyle 1997). However, it was estimated that the capitalization of China's stock markets could grow to $2 trillion by 2007 putting China in second place in Asia after Japan (*Economist*, "Credit Where it's Due," 9 September 2000, and *Business China*, "Open for Business," Economist Intelligence Unit, 12 March 2001).

many steps may involve complex negotiations with the central government as well as neighboring provinces.

Similar to cities in south China, Shanghai has acquired greater local autonomy since the late 1980s when the city negotiated a more favorable fiscal agreement with the central government. Its leadership also has undergone marked change. The current municipal leaders are generally better educated, technically trained industrial managers and professionals. More of them are now native to the city instead of outsiders directly appointed by the central government, tilting the balance of power between center and Shanghai more towards the city. They share in the vision of a market economy, of the creation of formal institutions, and the promotion of science and technology (Chen 1998). This section outlines some of the progress Shanghai has made and likely hurdles it will face, including:

- Continuing efforts to build links with the world economy by improving the physical and business infrastructure and attracting FDI.
- Industrial consolidation accompanied by land use policies inducing a shift of industry away from the core areas and permitting mixed commercial and residential use of prime urban land.
- A coordinated development of transport, housing, and infrastructure to minimize congestion and improve urban livability, through organizational streamlining and the use of new financial instruments.
- Taking measures to ensure an adequate supply of entrepreneurship, skills, and labor from within the municipality and through migration.

Building regional linkages

Enhancing its external linkages has been a key objective of Shanghai. The new international airport in Pudong that opened in September 1999 marks a significant step in the city's long-term goal to become an aviation hub in the Asia and Pacific region.[26] A second runway in planning will further augment its capacity. A magnetic levitation high-speed train connects the airport to the city center and the planned Beijing–Shanghai expressway. This is supplemented by high-speed ferries running from a terminal adjacent to the airport to nearby ports in Zhejiang Province. Foreign airlines have responded to the city's rising significance as a business center and the growth in airport capacity by increasing the volume of

[26] The airport opened with a 4,000-meter runway and one terminal building, with an annual capacity of handling 20 million passengers and 0.75 million tons of freight. When completed eventually with the planned four runways, the airport will be able to handle 70–80 million passengers and 5 million tons of cargo every year (*Shanghai Star*, 19 March 1999).

service (see above). Since 1999, several new, non-stop flights have been added, including KLM Royal Dutch Airlines to Amsterdam, Austrian Airlines to Vienna, and China Eastern Airlines to Japan's Fukushima. Shanghai now has non-stop flights reaching most of the world's important urban centers. By 2001, Shanghai was the fifth busiest container port ahead of Rotterdam, with annual traffic of 6.3 million twenty-foot equivalent (TEU) containers. When Yangshan port is completed in a few years, Shanghai will have the capacity to absorb traffic from Southeast Asia that is currently channeled through Hong Kong. At that point, Shanghai could emerge as the third most important port worldwide (*Financial Times*, "Shanghai Sets Date for Deep Water Port Project," 1 March 2002).

Becoming a major cyber hub is yet another ambitious undertaking in Shanghai's building of external linkages. A five-year key project has been launched to integrate all the circuits and pipelines for telecom services into an underground broadband pipeline (*China Daily*, 21 December 2000). Upon completion in 2005, this project will not only offer a strong backbone for the city's development as an Internet-smart metropolis, it will also improve the aesthetic quality of the environment while reducing the number of accidents caused by open-air circuit poles and lines. Rapidly increasing Internet usage also relates to the export orientation of Shanghai-based enterprises and the steadily improving quality of the telecom facilities is helping integrate Shanghai with the world economy. Greater broadband access and the use of mobile technology, as in Singapore and Japan, will enhance the utility of the Internet although this will require resolving some thorny issues regarding standards, technology, and links with households and freedom of access.[27]

Helping Shanghai to plant industrial roots a century ago, foreign investment is now a major force pushing the city ahead with systematic change. By 2001, the stock of utilized foreign investment reached US$57.5 billion, of which about US$11.5 billion involved technology imports (Shanghai Statistical Bureau 2002). Because of its industrial depth, modernizing infrastructure, and skilled workforce, Shanghai has outpaced other Chinese cities in the race to attract FDI.[28] By attempting to cut the time needed to receive approval for a new business from over three months to less than half that time, the city is hoping to draw abreast of its neighbors such as Kunshan City (*Far Eastern Economic Review*, "Holding the Purse Strings," 5 July 2001). A return on capital investment, 2% higher

[27] Kennedy 2000; *Oxford Analytica*, "China: Equity Market Development," 17 August 2000.

[28] For instance, FDI inflows to Shanghai in 1998 were $3.64 billion as against $2.06 billion in Beijing and $2.52 billion in Tianjin (Shanghai Statistical Bureau 1999).

than the national average (8%) is an additional inducement. The city is also courting more investors from the United States and Japan, while experiencing a decline of FDI originated in Hong Kong. Funding from overseas sources has been instrumental in the building of the city's new subway system, new industrial districts, and the hotel and other facilities needed to attract large numbers of businesses and tourists (Wu 1999b; Wu 2000). Shanghai's strategic location and external linkages, on the other hand, also lure domestic firms to invest in the city and use it as a springboard to the world market.

Reflecting the city's drive to rejuvenate its mature industrial base, manufacturing sectors are attracting more foreign investors. As of July 2000, 254 of the Fortune 500 companies have invested or established offices here (*China Daily*, 18 July 2000), and the chief examples are Alcatel, Volkswagen, General Motors, NEC, DuPont, and IBM. This could be a prelude to the shift of some regional headquarters functions to the city. The largest gains in output value are registered in such rising industries as telecommunications equipment, integrated circuits and computers, biomedical technologies, and new materials (Shanghai Statistical Bureau 1999). Shanghai is likely to regain its industrial edge and competitiveness through these industries as products from its traditional light industries (e.g., electronics, textiles, and garment) have been losing ground in domestic markets. Efforts also are taken to revamp the textile and garments industries through attracting more brand name fashions from overseas, and a series of international fashion exhibitions has been organized for this purpose.

The development of high-tech industry in Shanghai is being spearheaded by the creation of Zhangjiang Science Park in Pudong, some 25 kilometers from the Pudong International Airport. This park, which will eventually cover 25 square kilometers had attracted $4.47 billion worth of investment by the end of 2000, much of it in biopharmaceutical and information technology (IT) industries. The turnover during the year was close to $1 billion and has been rising rapidly as increasing numbers of foreign and private firms have been drawn to the park. The success of the park to date is traceable to a number of factors, among which the planning by the park and authorities and management of park services have played a significant part. Firms that have located at Zhangjiang have been favorably impressed by the access to venture capital and to financial, auditing, consulting, legal, and executive search services. Other cities in China, most notably Beijing and Tianjin, have also been quick to set up technology parks, but none of the other cities have been as effective in providing firms with the environment and services conducive to the emergence of a networked cluster of high-technology firms.

Since the early 1990s, Shanghai has been actively promoting investment in services, with the backing of the central government. Foreign insurers have been allowed to operate only in Shanghai, and all foreign banks currently licensed to deal in the domestic currency are in Shanghai's Pudong New Area (*Far Eastern Economic Review*, "Pudong Rises to the Task," 2 November 2000). An intensive effort is underway to transform the face of the main shopping thoroughfare – Nanjing Road – and make it a world class shopping area comparable to Oxford Street and the Champs-Elysees. This will take some doing; however, the city is attempting to attract international retailers and provide the green spaces and varied attractions that could push turnover from the current $1 billion per annum closer to $3 billion, the level of Oxford Street (Desvaux *et al.* 2002). Deals jointly financed by funds from Hong Kong and Taiwan also are helping Shanghai to rejuvenate its motion picture industry, which gave the city the title of Hollywood of China in the 1930s.[29]

Creating new space of production for industrial consolidation and investment promotion

To appeal to foreign investment and international businesses, several new industrial districts (often called Economic and Technology Development Zones, ETDZ) have been created since 1984. Special regulations comparable to those offered by other coastal provinces have been extended to these districts: tax exemptions for enterprises doing business with foreign companies for a limited duration, tax holidays for new factories set up with foreign investment, and exemption from import duty for production materials used by these facilities (Wu 1999a). To ensure broad-based future development, the city is also strengthening the industrial, science, and technology capabilities of the new districts. The existing stock of FDI and the quality of services is gradually improving Shanghai's bargaining position vis-à-vis foreign companies, enabling it to press for joint ventures, local contracting, and technology transfer (Yeung and Li 1999).

The Pudong New Area is the focus of the effort to produce for the international market. The designated space is a triangular area adjacent to and east of the central city, stretching from the east bank of the Huangpu River to the southwest of the Yangtze estuary and covering over 522 square kilometers. Planned for a three-phase development, Pudong is designed

[29] Recently a powerful animation company has been set up, with dreams of becoming China's Disney and subsequent creation of the nation's first higher-learning animation program (*Variety*, "China Sets Sights on Animation," 3 January 2000).

to relieve the spatial pressure on old Shanghai. It already contains China's largest free trade zone, a fully operational export processing zone, a high-technology development zone,[30] and a large number of new residential communities. The modern facilities – and the concessions – in Pudong have already attracted many businesses. Baoshan Steel Corporation, China's largest steel conglomerate, has put up a facility. One of the largest department stores in Asia has been built here, with investment from the Japanese retail giant Yaohan. And a US$2 billion General Motors facility has been turning out Buick cars, the second major joint auto production line in Shanghai. Over seventy foreign and joint-venture companies have set up research and development facilities in its industrial parks (*Far Eastern Economic Review*, "Pudong Rises to the Task," 2 November 2000).

Pudong also provides Shanghai with a new central business district (CBD) that can house a variety of business activities and, most importantly, financial and business services that are the backbone of other major world cities. The traditional commercial centers of the city are formed by two avenues, Nanjing Road and Huaihai Road, which are already approaching saturation as redevelopment proceeds downtown. The building of Pudong's Lujiazui CBD – an area of 1.7 square kilometers on the east bank of the Huangpu River – has been guided by the long-term ambitions of the city and facilitated by an international consultative planning process in which experts from France, Britain, Italy, and Japan participated (Olds 1997). A host of financial institutions, corporate headquarters, as well as commercial and cultural activities are being housed there, including the Shanghai Stock Market and over forty foreign banks – the only area in the country where foreign banks are allowed to have regular business operations in local currency by the central government.

Competing with the parks such as Zhangjiang in Pudong are the Minhang ETDZ, Hongqiao ETDZ, and Caohejing High-Tech Park, all located to the west of the central city. With more specialized functions, these zones have sought niches in such modern industries as electronics, medical equipment, computers, telecommunications, bioengineering, aerospace and precision instruments, and new construction materials. Although these zones have been more successful than past efforts of creating satellite towns, a large proportion of Shanghai's industrial base still remains in the central-city districts (Gaubatz 1999). This is in contrast with Beijing where industrial activities are being concentrated in the outer suburbs.

[30] A Software Park is being developed jointly by the Ministry of Information Industry and the city government.

Additional measures need to be put in place to consolidate and relocate industry out of downtown locations so that their place can be taken by higher-value-added service activities. Apart from being a source of congestion and environmental pollution, many of these factories are highly inefficient operations that deserve to be shut down. To solve problems associated with fragmented industrial land use, Shanghai has largely relied on relocating factories from the central city to the new industrial districts available for expansion. Between 1991 and 1998, about 12,000 work units as well as 400,000 households were moved from downtown to the city's outskirts (*Shanghai Daily*, 1 September 2000).

The rationalization of land use and the utilization of the new industrial estates, however, will not proceed smoothly unless the prevailing system of land allocation and charges is changed. Land lease awards need to be made through auctions with standard lease terms and payments rather than being assigned through negotiation. Land values, therefore, are determined through competitive and transparent auctions and not by public authorities. Evidence from a few cities, including Shanghai, suggests that central-city factories could fully finance redevelopment if they were permitted to sell their land to real estate development corporations through competitive bidding procedures (Dowall 1993). Shanghai has begun to experiment with the concept of location rent to speed up industrial relocation. This is based on the significant difference in land value for parcels at a central location and a remote site, which can be a critical financial gain for the industries (Han 2000). The city also plans to set up a more transparent auction system for land use rights.

Caution needs to be exercised as the new districts will inevitably compete with the central city for resources. It may be wise to prioritize their development as competition among them is not necessarily conducive to growth. The challenge also lies in pursuing specialization without foregoing the benefit of agglomeration. Shanghai's development funds will be insufficient if they are spread too widely and may be wasted in premature overbuilding. This is evident in some parts of Pudong where many of the lower-grade residential and commercial buildings remain vacant (approximately half at the end of 2001), largely the result of significant mismatches between supply and demand.

Shanghai's property development is yet to be regulated by either a functioning land market or sound planning.[31] The use of real estate business as the key to the rebuilding of the increasingly depressed domestic market

[31] It is not clear whether, in a capitalist system, a functioning land market should be the sole mechanism through which urban land is allocated (see Haila 1999).

Table 1.2 *Improvements in Shanghai's infrastructure services, 1991 and 1998*

	1991	1998
Per capita paved road (square meters)	2.3	5.0
Per capita open space (square meters)	1.1	3.0
Per capita living space (square meters)	6.7	9.7
Capacity for treating wastewater (million tons/day)	0.4	1.9
Access to gas (%)	62.0	91.5[a]
Per capita annual domestic water consumption (tons)	71.2	104.6[a]
Wastewater treated (%)	7.6	30.2[a]

[a] 1996 figures.

Source: Shanghai Statistical Bureau 1997 and 1999; Shanghai Construction Commission 1997.

(seen in the late 1990s), as promoted by China's Premier Zhu Rongji, also led to overbuilding of commercial real estate and luxury residences. The accumulation of excess capacity resulted in a sharp drop in rents during 1996–1999. However, in mid-2000 the city enacted a new regulation depriving all district and county governments of the approval right of land leasing. Instead the Shanghai Municipal Housing and Land Administration has the sole authority, and can stop the leasing approval of land for such projects as shopping malls, entertainment centers, golf courses, and grade A villas and office buildings (*Shanghai Star*, 4 August 2000). These steps have had some effect as by early 2001 occupancy rates for grade A office buildings were up to 94% in the central business area and 78% elsewhere (*Far Eastern Economic Review*, "Filling Up Fast in Shanghai," 19 April 2001). By mid-2002, the average vacancy rate for "Grade A" buildings throughout the city was just 12% (*Far Eastern Economic Review*, "Hong Kong's Mr. Shanghai," 15 August 2002). In addition, commercial space rents in Shanghai were firmer than elsewhere in East Asia.

Renewing urban infrastructure

Shanghai's determination to renew itself can best be seen in its effort to overhaul the city's aging infrastructure since the early 1990s.[32] Unmet demand is shrinking as Shanghai makes progress in virtually every infrastructure service (see Table 1.2). Improvements are particularly rapid in

[32] China devotes 10% of GDP to infrastructure and housing development, with housing alone accounting for 6% of GDP. This has resulted in an oversupply of housing in the medium and higher price range.

road construction, park expansion, and wastewater treatment. Shanghai now treats 30% of its wastewater, compared to an average level of about 7% in all Chinese cities. A number of large infrastructure projects have been completed, such as three bridges and two tunnels across the Huangpu River, an inner ring road, elevated north–south and east–west throughways, and two new subway lines.[33] Furthermore, the first phase of a new light rail system is operational. The city recently unveiled a twenty-year blueprint for the construction of eleven subway lines, seven light rail lines, and three suburban railways. So by 2020, the city will have a total of 325 kilometers of subway and 136 kilometers of light rail (*Shanghai Daily*, 19 June 2000).

The city also has moved gradually to address infrastructure deficiencies that have significant impact on the quality of environment. An essential characteristic of a livable city is an environment with access to clean drinking water, clean waterways, effective solid waste disposal, and clean air (Douglass 2000). To remove itself from the list of heavily polluted cities by the World Health Organization, Shanghai has invested in a new combined wastewater collection system, solid waste and nightsoil management, environment-friendly diesel engines for buses (as well as imposing tighter restrictions on exhausts), and by moving the collection point further upstream increased the supply of potable water from the Huangpu River. One of the most ambitious undertakings has been the Shanghai Environment Project initiated in the mid-1990s, with the backing of World Bank loans (World Bank 1994).

Investment in infrastructure services has increased steadily, with a greater emphasis on city streets, sewerage systems, and other municipal works (see Table 1.3). The infrastructure sector now receives the level of attention from the municipal government it deserves and accounts for about one tenth of Shanghai's total fixed asset investment.[34] About 2% of the city's gross national product went into environment-related capital works in 1995 and this share would likely increase to about 4%. Much of Shanghai's success in renewing infrastructure can be attributed to a comprehensive program of resource mobilization and expenditure management beginning in 1990 (Yusuf and Wu 1997).

[33] Shanghai's Narada Group, a private company, is one of a number of new firms involved in building and operating toll roads in the metropolitan area (*Far Eastern Economic Review*, "Roads to Riches," 23 September 1999).

[34] Total fixed asset investment includes investment in capital construction, technical upgrading and transformation, investment by urban and rural collective units, real estate investment, investment by urban and rural residents in private housing construction, and other investment of ownership units (Shanghai Statistical Bureau 1999).

Table 1.3 *Investment in Shanghai's urban infrastructure (billions of yuan), 1981–2001*

	1981	1986	1991	1992	1993	1994	1995	1996	1997	1998	1999	2000	2001
Electric power	0.35	0.57	1.98	1.97	2.58	4.16	5.73	7.76	8.02	8.96	8.31	6.46	7.22
Transportation	0.24	0.66	1.45	1.50	3.18	3.68	2.59	6.97	8.51	10.88	10.22	4.88	6.07
Postal and telecomunications	0.04	0.18	0.46	0.64	1.47	3.59	5.34	7.76	6.10	7.27	6.39	6.87	10.77
Public utilities	0.06	0.57	0.92	1.26	3.79	2.68	3.50	4.83	5.22	5.84	6.42	10.44	9.23
Municipal works	0.09	0.50	1.34	3.06	5.78	9.71	10.21	10.57	13.43	20.20	18.80	16.33	17.79
Total	0.78	2.48	6.14	8.43	16.79	23.82	27.38	37.88	41.29	53.14	50.14	45.00	51.08
As percentage of TIFA	14.4	16.9	23.8	23.6	25.7	21.2	17.1	19.4	20.9	27.0	27.0	24.1	25.6

Notes: TIFA, total investment in fixed assets. Public utilities include water supply and drainage, residential gas and heating supply, and public transportation. Municipal works include city streets, bridges, tunnels, sewerage, parks, sanitation and waste management, and flood control.
Source: Shanghai Statistical Bureau 2002.

First, municipal authorities have increased user charges for some infrastructure services including bus fares, gas supplies, water, wastewater discharge, and municipal sanitation services. Second, Shanghai has begun to raise funds by leasing land, in the process attracting a large volume of FDI into real estate development including commercial and apartment complexes catering to foreign companies (Wu 2000). Shanghai's population density, its relative prosperity, and the nature of commercial development now underway mean that real estate in the municipality is extremely valuable. This has induced many state enterprises to move their factories out of the downtown areas and lease the land for commercial purposes (*Far Eastern Economic Review*, "China's Land Grab," 13 April 2000). Third, the city has set up separate transport and energy funds in municipal revenue collection, guaranteeing much of the funding for the two sectors. Last, since 1986 Shanghai has tapped into the international market to lure direct investment and build-operate-transfer schemes.[35] The issuing of domestic construction bonds also has been growing steadily, capturing the high level of household savings.

In addition, progress in infrastructure building would not have been possible without large-scale organizational reforms. As a part of Shanghai's reform to unify financial and administrative responsibilities for municipal bureaus, the Shanghai Urban Construction Investment and Development Company was formed in 1992 to mobilize, allocate, and manage funds for urban construction. This state-owned company has employed a wide range of financing mechanisms, particularly through such non-state channels as construction bonds, the stock market, and service concessions. It has entered into concessions with non-state enterprises to operate the bridges and tunnels across the Huangpu River. It also has established a number of subordinate entities, mainly in charge of water supply, which are listed on the Shanghai Stock Market (Wu 1999b). Available official information shows that in 1995 and 1996, funds mobilized by the company accounted for about 76% and 90%, respectively, of Shanghai's total urban infrastructure revenue.

Another important element of Shanghai's institutional reform is greater managerial autonomy for public utility agencies. To the extent feasible, municipal service departments have been given full responsibility for planning, investment, operations, and maintenance. These departments also are adopting an independent cost-accounting system to facilitate sector management and financing. For instance, a sewerage company has been created to maintain the newly constructed sewerage system. A major

[35] See *Wall Street Journal*, "Water Business Is Hot as More Cities Decide to Tap Private Sector," 9 November 1998.

reform materialized in 2000 when the city consolidated water and urban transportation functions scattered across up to nine different municipal agencies in the past into two bureaux that would have full authority over decision making, operations, and maintenance (*China Daily*, 15 May 2000). Other avenues, which would allow enterprises serving as contractors to provide selected services, are under consideration and some bus services are already under concession. The city is also commercializing some of its waste disposal business and a company from neighboring Jiangsu Province has won the contract to collect garbage, a job shunned by many locals (*Shanghai Star*, 24 July 1998).

Substantial progress has been made in raising the supply of better-quality housing since the early 1990s through heavy investment (increasing from 4.3 billion yuan in 1990 to 46.7 billion in 2001, Shanghai Statistical Bureau 2002). The objective is to raise the per capita living space from 11 square meters currently to 23 square meters (*Business China*, "A Room of One's Own," Economist Intelligence Unit, 7 May 2001). The city is replacing 3.6 million square meters of endangered structures and shanty apartments, mostly in the old central city. The accessibility of housing to the average family is on the rise as a result of reforms, among the most comprehensive in the nation (Wu 1999a). But the quality of apartment dwellings, their location, and associated facilities remains a source of dissatisfaction with half of all buyers. The city, employers, and employees all contribute through a newly established public reserve fund to finance housing purchases over time. Since 1998, all banks have been able to supply mortgages to qualified homebuyers on behalf of the public reserve fund. In addition to new home purchases, many people have bought property or use rights to the homes they were assigned under the old welfare housing system and some also trade such rights on the secondary housing market to acquire better housing.[36] By early 2001, officials estimated that about 60% of all families had bought their own homes, either from their employers or from private developers (*Far Eastern Economic Review*, "Windows of Opportunity," 3 May 2001).

The creation of a mortgage finance market, the assignment of leasehold rights, and the permission to trade in the secondary market are important steps in housing reform. But the coverage still remains fairly restricted, the residential property market is insufficiently differentiated and collateral requirements enforced by banks are strict, while the credit provided is relatively short term (*Financial Times*, "China Survey," 1 October 1999). Further reforms will be required to ensure that the large volume

[36] In the first half of 1999, more than 20,000 families engaged in such trading (*Shanghai Star*, 30 July 1999).

of public sector housing is properly commercialized by granting property/lease rights to current residents and the remaining public-owned welfare housing is adequately maintained.[37] Although an active resale market for homes has emerged (and in 2002 it exceeded the market value for new homes), a further rationalization of fees, taxes, and rules interfering with the sale of apartments will help raise the value of resale closer to the 80–90% of the total transactions observed in Western countries (*Financial Times*, "Secondhand Home Sales in Shanghai Good News for Banks," 8 April 2002; *Economist*, "Sticky as Treacle," 16 June 2001).

Further institutional reform also will be needed to minimize political pressures on infrastructure providers, giving them sufficient autonomy to collect fees, make price adjustments, undertake service planning, and have incentives to assume full financial responsibility. Public agencies still have a long way to go in devising appropriate commercial rules and encouraging private participation and competition. Permitting majority private shareholders in infrastructure construction or wholly private infrastructure facilities is unlikely in the foreseeable future unless underwritten by build-operate-transfer schemes. And the private sector may be hesitant to incur greater responsibility and risk as investment in infrastructure provision is usually for a significant duration and the period of implementation can affect investment return. Private interests, therefore, may be better utilized in the areas of infrastructure operation and maintenance, with public transportation, waste disposal, and sanitation services as prime candidates.

Labor market prospects

While policy, infrastructure, and investment are certainly important, successful cities draw their energy from entrepreneurial dynamism and the quality of the workforce. In an economy with accelerating technological innovations and rising specialized service functions, the labor force needs good basic education and skills, and market institutions should permit a high degree of flexibility. Measures to ensure an adequate supply of entrepreneurship, skills, and labor will be one of Shanghai's biggest challenges as its state enterprises move away from the practice of providing the workforce with tenured employment and guaranteed pensions along with health, housing, and other benefits.

[37] In 1999, Shanghai terminated the welfare housing system that had been allocating housing to all urban residents at nominal rent levels, in either work units housing or municipal public housing. However, qualified low-income residents can still rent public housing in the future, and many existing residents are not forced to purchase property/lease rights to their housing.

The foremost challenge is relocating workers displaced by the large-scale closure and divestiture of state enterprises, which is particularly difficult for middle-aged workers close to retirement in the city's core industries like textiles. Labor use in these enterprises is highly compartmentalized with workers trained in a narrow specialization. Therefore, the retraining of workers, either for reassignment within their enterprises in response to production shifts or to facilitate employment after closure, greatly influences internal and external labor mobility. For the moment, the city has opted for the absorption of surplus workers in low-skill service operations where job prospects have multiplied and retraining is minimal. Specifically, these workers find employment in retail, repair and maintenance works, grounds maintenance, household services, and cleaning services.

Shanghai's workers command a wider range of skills compared to other industrial cities in China, but the share of professional and technical personnel lags far behind key global centers. Shanghai has begun to address this educational gap and two measures have been taken to attract new, young talent into the city. Enrollment for local students in universities and colleges, as well as in vocational schools, has been increased substantially.[38] Shanghai also has relaxed restrictions on enterprises in hiring personnel with college or graduate education from other parts of China by allowing them more quotas for urban household registration. In particular, the city welcomes students who are returning from overseas, either temporarily or permanently, to open new businesses.

The rapidly aging population presents Shanghai with another difficult challenge. Those over age sixty-five accounted for 12.5% of the total population in 1996 and 13.3% in 1998, and on current trends are expected to account for 26% in the year 2020 (*Shanghai Star*, 5 June 1998). Shanghai now ranks uppermost among Chinese cities in population aging, about twenty years ahead of the national trend. It is perhaps the only city in China that is witnessing a phenomenon similar to that occurring in countries with substantially higher income levels. A growing number of retirees demand better pensions, housing, and medical benefits.

The significant growth in the share of old age cohorts in the population is partly the result of a low birth rate. As the one-child family planning policy has been fairly effective in large cities, natural growth of the population was only about 0.35% in 1990 and −0.23% in 1996 (Shanghai Academy of Social Sciences 1997). At the same time, life expectancy

[38] The city has seen an increase in annual enrollment for universities from 19,000 in 1991–1995 to 30,000 in 1996–2000, for adult continuing education from 10,000 to 18,000, and for vocational schools from 22,000 to 35,000. See Shanghai Academy of Social Sciences 1997.

for men has risen from seventy-one years to seventy-five years, and for women from seventy-four years to seventy-nine years between 1969 and 1998 in Shanghai (*Liberation Daily*, 29 July 1999). Much of the growth of the resident population between 1985 and 1995 can be traced to the return of Shanghai-born youth, displaced during the Cultural Revolution (1966–1976).

The projected decline in the city's workforce can be offset by an increasing volume of migrant workers, as is the case elsewhere in the world.[39] Shanghai is already relying on temporary migration (without change of household registration) as an alternative to permanent migration (with household registration change) in meeting its labor force needs. About 3 million temporary migrants, largely permitted by relaxed migration policies, are now working and living in metropolitan Shanghai, most of whom do not have urban status and are therefore not counted as part of the resident population. Nevertheless, many temporary migrants stay in the city for a prolonged period of time and often with their families.[40] Without urban household registration, these temporary migrants do not have access to free education, subsidized housing, and pensions. The impact can be severe for migrant families with children. When families of large size migrate together, income disparities between urban residents and migrants also increase (World Bank 1997).

Accommodating migrants and attracting those with the required skills are likely to be a long-term issue facing municipal authorities. This will require a change in the provision of adequate housing as well as services. A new type of housing is becoming available in some areas of Shanghai – migrant housing complexes managed by subdistrict and township agencies. Some involve reuse of old temporary housing while others are new residential compounds built by large enterprises. Yet enterprise-provided dormitories and private housing rentals are still the most common housing choices available to migrants, in which they live in conditions considerably worse than local residents.

To sustain, let alone improve, the quality of its workforce while preventing social stratification and urban poverty, Shanghai will have to tackle

[39] Projections by several local research institutions show that, because of the aging population, the numbers of the resident workforce (age 15–59) will begin to decline after 2005 and by about 2 million in 2030. See Shixun Gui, "Shanghai's Population Trends and Social Security Pensions" (Shanghai: East China Normal University, mimeo, 1999).

[40] For instance, the city's 1997 Floating Population Survey reports that close to a half million migrants have lived in the city for over five years (Zhang *et al.* 1998). So far the city allows migrants to stay for a prolonged period as long as they properly maintain and renew temporary residence permits. Periodically, the Public Security Bureau conducts random checkups and deports those without work and residence permits back to their origin.

the laws governing migration. Migrant workers and entrepreneurs will provide much of the human impetus for the city's future development. Housing reform, for instance, can help improve migrants' quality of life and prevent slum formation. Specifically, migrants can be allowed to participate in the secondary housing market, where apartments are more affordable. Migrants also need greater access to jobs and educational facilities previously open to local residents only. Of course, these measures do not fully address the costs and hardship migrants bear as a result of the household registration system, whose reform will have to be initiated by the central government. It is clear that the current practice of linking household registration and the provision of urban services is likely to widen the rural–urban divide and social differentiation within cities. To respond properly to the need for migration requires that this linkage be reformed.

Conclusion

In a globalizing world, cities at or near the apex of the international urban hierarchy are among the favored few that have acquired large economic, cultural, and symbolic roles. As urbanization continues and service activities – especially IT and finance related – take on an even greater prominence, the number of regional and global centers could increase, but only if they satisfy some exacting requirements. Shanghai, located in one of the most rapidly developing parts of the world, may well be one of them. If the Chinese economy can sustain its growth rate, it will rival the US in a few decades. And if Shanghai is able to retain its preeminence in the Chinese context, then it is likely to be the East Asian city with the best prospect of becoming a global center.

However, Shanghai's chances depend on the extent to which China "opens up."[41] It also rests on a host of municipal policies that focus the municipality's industrial strength on high-tech manufacturing, substantially enlarge its base of IT and producer services, ensure an adequate supply of skills, expand the availability of housing and infrastructure services in line with demand, and improve the quality of life. Shanghai is in the vanguard of change in a number of areas, but, as we have indicated, the tempo of reforms needs to be sustained. In particular, it needs to nurture an internationally competitive services sector by dint of reform and by attracting FDI. The emphasis on industry, housing, and infrastructure will certainly have payoffs, but so long as the volume and quality

[41] An important influence will be the significant degree of foreign ownership of assets resulting from FDI.

of services lag, Shanghai will have difficulty making it into the ranks of regional hubs. Openness, combined with policy measures that induce competitiveness, is most likely to lead to outcomes that are in Shanghai's long-term interests.

REFERENCES

Chan, Roger C. K. 2000. "Shanghai: Development Strategy and Planning Implications," in *Proceedings of International Conference on Re-Inventing Global Cities.* Center of Urban Planning and Environmental Management, University of Hong Kong, pp. 168–183.

Chen, Shi 1998. "Leadership Change in Shanghai: Toward the Dominance of Party Technocrats," *Asian Survey*, 38 (7): 671–688.

Chowdhury, Neel 2000. "Can Citibank Crack the China Market?," *Fortune*, 142 (6), (18 September).

Coyle, Diane 1997. *The Weightless World.* Cambridge, MA: MIT Press.

Desvaux, Georges, Li, Guangyu, and Penhirin, Jacques 2002. "Shanghai Shopping," *McKinsey Quarterly*, 17 (5) (March): 17–27.

Douglass, Mike 2000. "Mega-Urban Regions and World City Formation: Globalization, the Economic Crisis and Urban Policy Issues in Pacific Asia," *Urban Studies*, 37 (12): 2315–2335.

Dowall, David E. 1993. "Establishing Urban Land Markets in the People's Republic of China," *Journal of the American Planning Association*, 59 (2) (Spring): 182–192.

Edwards, Sebastian 1999. "How Effective are Capital Controls?," *Journal of Economic Perspectives*, 13 (4): 65–84.

Enright, Michael J., Scott, Edith E., and Dodwell, David 1997. *The Hong Kong Advantage.* Oxford and New York: Oxford University Press.

Frankel, Jeffrey and Roemer, David 1999. "Does Trade Cause Growth?," *American Economic Review*, 89 (3): 379–398.

Gaubatz, Piper 1999. "China's Urban Transformation: Patterns and Processes of Morphological Change in Beijing, Shanghai and Guangzhou," *Urban Studies*, 36 (9) (August): 1495–1521.

Goodman, Bryna 1995. *Native Place, City and Nation: Regional Networks and Identities in Shanghai, 1853–1937.* Berkeley: University of California Press.

Haila, Anne 1999. "Why is Shanghai Building a Giant Speculative Property Bubble?," *International Journal of Urban and Regional Research*, 23 (3) (September): 583–588.

Han, Sun Sheng 2000. "Shanghai between State and Market in Urban Transformation," *Urban Studies*, 37 (11): 2091–2112.

Harner, Stephen M. 2000. "Financial Services and WTO: Opportunities Knock," *China Business Review* (March–April): 10–15.

Hartford, Kathleen 2000. "Cyberspace with Chinese Characteristics," *Current History* (September): 255–262.

Howe, Christopher (ed.) 1981. *Shanghai: Revolution and Development in an Asian Metropolis.* Cambridge: Cambridge University Press.

International Civil Aviation Organization 1998. *Traffic: Commercial Air Carriers*, Montreal.

Johnson, Linda Cooke 1995. *Shanghai: From Market Town to Treaty Port, 1074–1858*. Stanford, CA: Stanford University Press.

Kaminsky, Graciela, and Schmuckler, Sergio 2000. "Short and Long-run Integration: Do Capital Controls Matter?," in Brookings Institution (ed.), *Brookings Trade Forum 2000*. Washington, DC: Brookings Institution.

Kennedy, Gabriela 2000. "E-commerce: The Taming of the Internet in China," *China Business Review* (July–August): 34–39.

Li, Shantong and Zhai, Fan. 2000. "Prospects of China's Economic Development in the Next 20 Years." Mimeo. Development Research Center, Beijing.

Lu, Hanchao 1999. *Beyond the Neon Lights: Everyday Shanghai in the Early Twentieth Century*. Berkeley: University of California Press.

McDaniels, Iain and Zhao, Sophie 2001. "Shanghai Snapshot," *China Business Review*, 28 (5): 42–45.

Martin, Will, Dimaranan, B., and Hertel, T. W. 1999. "Trade Policy, Structural Change and China's Trade Growth." Mimeo. World Bank, Washington, DC.

Meyer, David R. 2000. *Hong Kong as a Global Metropolis*. Cambridge: Cambridge University Press.

Murphy, Rhodes 1953. *Shanghai: Key to Modern China*. Cambridge, MA: Harvard University Press.

Newfarmer, Richard and Liu, Dana M. 1998. "China's Race with Globalization," *China Business Review* (July–August): 8–13.

Ochi, Hiroo 1997. "The Environment for Locating Business Operatives in Major East Asian Cities." Japan Development Bank Research Report, No. 65, Tokyo.

Olds, Kris 1997. "Globalizing Shanghai: The 'Global Intelligence Corps' and the Building of Pudong," *Cities: The International Journal for Urban Policy and Planning*, 14 (2) (April): 109–123.

Pearson, Margaret M. 2000. "China's Track Record in the Global Economy," *China Business Review* (January–February): 48–51.

Pott, Francis Lister Hawks 1928. *A Short History of Shanghai*. Shanghai: Kelly and Walsh, Ltd.

Sachs, Jeffrey D. and Warner, Andrew 1995. "Economic Reform and the Process of Global Integration," *Brookings Papers on Economic Activity*. Washington, DC.

1997. "Fundamental Sources of Long-Run Growth," *American Economic Review*, 87 (2): 184–188.

Shanghai Academy of Social Sciences 1997. *Shanghai Entering the New Century: Issues in Social Development*. Shanghai: Shanghai Academy of Social Sciences Press.

Shanghai Construction Commission 1997. *Shanghai Urban Construction: Achievements in the Eighth Five-Year Plan Period and Long-Term Plans*. Beijing: China Statistical Publishing House.

Shanghai Statistical Bureau 1996–2002. *Statistical Yearbook of Shanghai*. Beijing: China Statistical Publishing House.

1997. *Shanghai Investment and Construction Statistical Yearbook, 1997*. Shanghai: Shanghai News Press (*Shanghai Xinwen Chubanju*).
Wang, Yukun 1998. "Urban Development Towards the Year 2000," in Yue-man Yeung (ed.), *Urban Development in Asia: Retrospect and Prospect*. Hong Kong: Chinese University of Hong Kong Press.
Wei, Betty Peh-T'i 1987. *Shanghai: Crucible of Modern China*. Oxford and New York: Oxford University Press.
World Bank 1994. *China: Shanghai Environment Project*. Washington, DC: World Bank, processed.
1997. *Sharing Rising Incomes: Disparities in China*. Washington, DC: World Bank.
1999. "China." Mimeo, World Bank, Washington, DC.
Wu, Friedrich and Wong, Jill. 1997. "China's Financial Powerhouse," *China Business Review* (March–April): 14–20.
Wu, Fulong 2000. "The Global and Local Dimensions of Place-Making: Remaking Shanghai as a World City," *Urban Studies*, 37 (8): 1359–1377.
Wu, Weiping 1999a. "City Profile: Shanghai," *Cities: The International Journal for Urban Policy and Planning*, 16 (3) (May): 207–216.
1999b. "Reforming China's Institutional Environment for Urban Infrastructure Provision," *Urban Studies*, 36 (13) (December): 2263–2282.
Yatsko, Pamela 2001. *New Shanghai*. New York: John Wiley and Sons.
Yeung, Yue-man. 1996. "Introduction," in Y. M. Yeung and Sung Yun-Wing (eds.), *Shanghai: Transformation and Modernization under China's Open Policy*. Hong Kong: Chinese University Press.
Yeung, Yue-man and Li, Xiaojian 1999. "Bargaining with Transnational Corporations: The Case of Shanghai," *International Journal of Urban and Regional Research*, 23 (3): 513–533.
Yu, Qiao 1998. "Capital Investment, International Trade and Economic Growth in China: Evidence in the 1980s–1990s," *China Economic Review*, 9 (1): 73–84.
Yu, Yongding 2000. "Globalization from China's Perspectives." Mimeo. Chinese Academy of Social Sciences, Institute of World Economics and Politics, Beijing.
Yusuf, Shahid and Wu, Weiping 1997. *The Dynamics of Urban Growth in Three Chinese Cities*. New York: Oxford University Press for the World Bank.
2002. "Pathways to a World City: Shanghai Rising in an Era of Globalization," *Urban Studies*, 39 (7): 1213–1240.
Zhang, Shenghua *et al.* (eds.). 1998. *The Current Status and Future of Shanghai's Floating Population*. Shanghai: Shanghai: East China Normal University Press.

2 Seoul: complementing economic success with Games

Yeong-Hyun Kim

The notion of "world city" has fascinated many national and urban politicians in the way that "global competitiveness" has enthralled corporate executives around the world. The pursuit of world city status has become part of election rhetoric and viewed as a challenging but worthwhile political project for most large cities both in the developed and developing worlds (W. Kim 1998; Machimura 1998; Olds 1995; Öncü and Weyland 1997; Todd 1995). There has, however, been more confusion than agreement on how the term should be defined and how a city could achieve the status of a world city (Hill and Kim 2000). Many have tried to identify the social, economic, and cultural characteristics that distinguish the leading world cities, London, New York, and Tokyo, from the rest (Beaverstock *et al.* 2000; Budd 1999; Sassen 1991), although it is arguable whether the common ground among these top three can be translated into what it takes to be a world city. Few cities around the world can even dream of housing the globally known stock markets, corporate headquarters, bankers, lawyers, and real estate developers that have made the three world cities so special. There has been a growing body of literature examining what the second-, third- or lower-tier world cities have and dream of having (Dick and Rimmer 1998; Lo and Yeung 1996; Short and Kim 1999; Short *et al.* 2000; Yeoh 1999). Although there has not been a general consensus on the global ranking of cities, it certainly enriches the world cities research to investigate how "other" world cities have achieved their present positions at the international level. In the case of Seoul we will see how a developing country's capital city has used international sports events to boost its global standing.

Emergent world city status has hardly been the outcome of any brilliant political projects. It might be one of many politically calculated exaggerations that national or city government officials emphasize their efforts to bring world city status to their cities, but the chief characteristics of world cities have grown out of economic, social, and cultural factors rather than political projects (Budd 1999; Thrift 1994). This does not mean, however, that the attainment of world city status by governments'

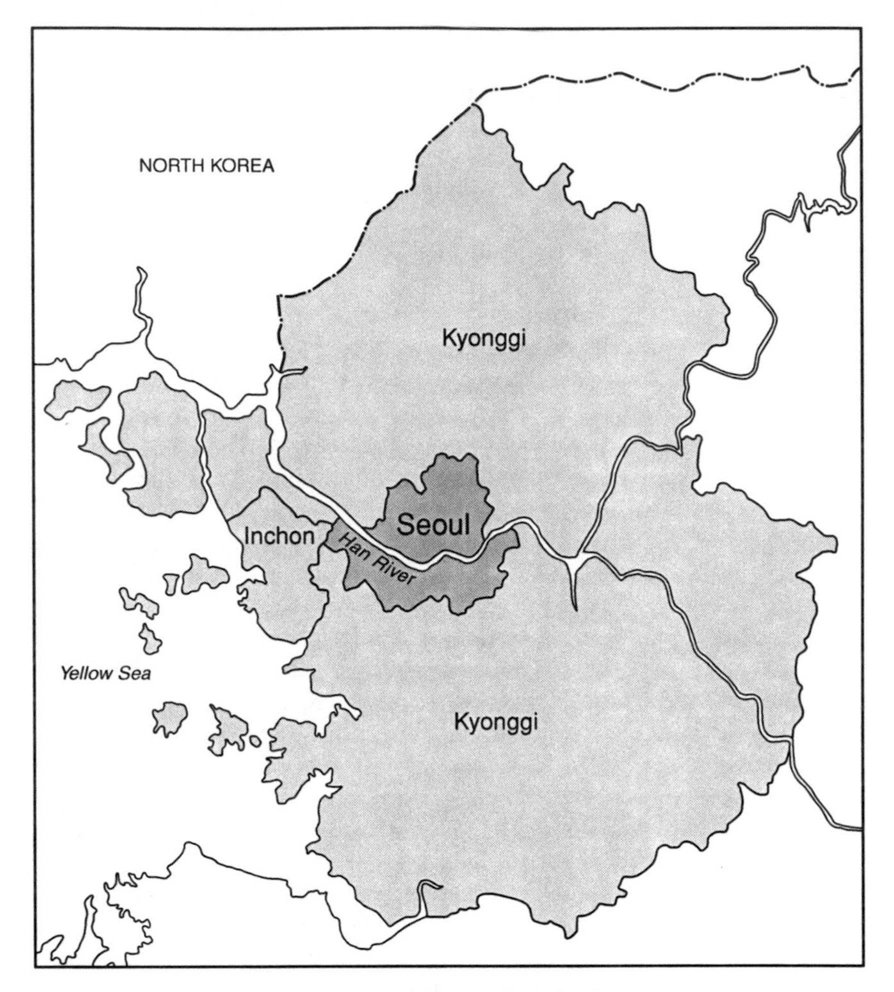

Map 2.1 Seoul and Seoul Metropolitan Region

well-coordinated efforts is impossible. Governments at the national or city levels may not be particularly effective in relocating Fortune 500 companies' headquarters to their cities, but they can promote the hosting of international sports competitions, which can provide an avenue towards becoming a world city. Some cities have been very successful in putting their names on the map of world cities by staging mega events that brought international media attention and other benefits. Like Sydney, which hosted the 2000 Summer Olympics, Seoul is clearly one of the few success stories. It hosted the 1988 Olympic Games and recently co-hosted the 2002 World Cup Finals with Tokyo. With Mexico City, which hosted the Games in 1968, Seoul is one of only two Olympic cities in the developing world.

Seoul has been better known as the capital city of South Korea (hereafter Korea), a newly industrializing economy in Asia, than as an international center. With Tokyo, Hong Kong, and Singapore at the top of the Asian urban hierarchy, Seoul has not been able to assume a commanding position in the region. Seoul has long aspired to escape from the shadow of Tokyo, a neighbor that has been in a dominant position vis-à-vis Seoul in literally every sense throughout modern history. The city has often been considered a subsidiary to Tokyo in terms of international airline services, multinational corporations' regional operations, and global news coverage. As the Korean economy has radically expanded its global role in the past few decades, Seoul's dependence on Tokyo has certainly been reduced, yet the latter remains an overbearing neighbor. After Tokyo, Hong Kong and Singapore constitute a second tier of Asian cities ranked ahead of Seoul in most world cities studies. Compared to these two city-states with hefty histories of international engagement, Seoul lacks an international orientation in its economy and culture. However, Seoul has been able to attach its name to world-class events by hosting international sports competitions.

The 1988 Olympics were viewed as the unprecedented opportunity for Seoul to expand and intensify its global engagement economically, culturally, and politically while showing off the phenomenal economic progress made after the Korean War (Seoul Olympic Organizing Committee 1989). Having staged the Olympics successfully, Seoul was in a good position to prepare for the World Cup Finals, which it hosted jointly with Tokyo in summer 2002. The hosting of these two most prestigious international sports competitions may not have been sufficient to make Seoul a leading world city in Asia, but it has certainly served to enhance Seoul's international visibility.

In this chapter, I first briefly review the history of Seoul's growth and spatial restructuring over the past few decades. The second section reviews Seoul's position in the Asian urban hierarchy and compares the city with its regional rivals, in particular Hong Kong and Singapore. Third, I outline the relationship between world city status and international mega events by looking at cities that have recently applied to host the Summer Olympics. I proceed to examine the effects of the 1988 Olympics in globalizing the city and heightening its international reputation. The fifth section explores how Koreans viewed their hosting of the 2002 World Cup jointly with Japan. Their dream of Seoul becoming an outright world city by upstaging Tokyo before the entire world is critically

Table 2.1 *Population in Seoul, Outer Seoul, and Seoul Metropolitan Region, 1949–2000*

	Seoul	Outer Seoul[a]	Seoul Metropolitan Region[b]	
				Share of national population (%)
1949	1,446,019	2,740,594	4,186,613	20.8
1955	1,574,868	2,363,660	3,938,528	18.3
1960	2,445,402	2,748,765	5,194,167	20.8
1965	3,793,280	3,102,325	6,895,605	23.6
1970	5,535,725	3,358,022	8,893,747	28.3
1975	6,889,502	4,039,132	10,928,634	31.5
1980	8,364,379	4,933,862	13,298,241	35.5
1985	9,639,110	6,181,046	15,820,156	39.1
1990	10,612,577	7,973,551	18,586,128	42.8
1995	10,231,217	9,957,929	20,189,146	45.3
2000	9,981,649	11,924,347	21,905,996	46.3

[a] Inchon and Kyonggi Province.
[b] Seoul and Outer Seoul combined.
Source: National Statistical Office, South Korea (2001).

examined. I conclude by summarizing my assessment of Seoul's efforts to gain world city status and the implications for world cities research.

A six-century old city transformed

Hanyang, as it was then called, became the capital of Korea when the Yi dynasty relocated its palace there in 1394. The Japanese colonial government, which had established control over Korea in 1910, changed its name to Kyongsong. Liberation in 1945 was followed by the division of Korea into North and South Korea. Seoul was given its current name in 1949 when it became the capital city for only the southern half of Korea. If in the past it had been located at the very center of the Korean peninsula, it was now close to the border between two hostile countries.

The first Korean census reported slightly less than 1.5 million people living in Seoul in 1949 (Table 2.1). Key to Korea's economic success was the dramatic growth of export-oriented manufacturing, and a major proportion of the new industry was established around Seoul. The city thus became a primary magnet for migrants from the rest of the country (Hong 1996). Despite efforts, which often involved the use of force, by both the national and the city government to curtail the flow of migrants (Park

1995), Seoul grew rapidly until the 1980s and reached the 10 million mark in 1988. The city has accounted for well over 20% of the national population since the mid-1970s, while the second-largest city, Pusan, remained home to less than half that population. Seoul has come to be a typical primate city, not just in terms of population, but with an overwhelming presence in the country's politics, finance, business, higher education, culture, and identity.

While Seoul's once-uncontrollable population growth has slowed down in recent years – indeed, Seoul has recently lost a small fraction of its population for the first time in its modern history according to the 2000 census – Outer Seoul has come to accommodate even more residents. Outer Seoul consists of the City of Inchon and Kyonggi Province, and the combined area of Seoul and Outer Seoul is commonly referred to as the Seoul Metropolitan Region or Capital Region (Map 2.1). The recent growth of Outer Seoul has been attributed to, among others, mounting mega-city problems in Seoul, including traffic jams and rising rents, the government's restrictions on the (re)location of industries inside Seoul, and massive construction of apartment complexes in cities in Kyonggi Province (Kwon 1995). These apartments have by and large housed middle- and lower-middle-class populations who could no longer afford skyrocketing housing prices in Seoul. Seoul's sprawl into Outer Seoul has been notably different from the pattern of suburbanization characteristic of American metropolises. While American suburbs are mainly filled with middle- and upper-middle-class populations fleeing the city, and commercial centers servicing them, Outer Seoul has accommodated households and industries crowded out of Seoul. In recent years Outer Seoul has become the primary destination for migration flows in Korea (Kim 1995). The Seoul Metropolitan Region, accounting for 46.3% of the national population in 2000, became a mammoth metropolis with around 22 million people, one of the largest around the world.

Seoul has undergone relentless urban restructuring to accommodate the establishment of manufacturing industries and the population expansion. Given the rapid pace of these developments, there was a continuous need to upgrade the city's infrastructure. The 1980s, in particular, saw a marked improvement in Seoul's urban transit system and amenities as well as numerous large-scale real estate developments. The Seoul Olympics provided the government with a legitimate reason to conduct massive urban restructuring throughout the city in spite of public opposition against the displacement of poor neighborhoods (Kim and Choe 1997). Like many other Olympic cities, Seoul disregarded the voices of the powerless in its preparation for the mega event. A Spanish visitor (Zincone 1989, p. 218) summed up the effects of the Olympics on Seoul's urban redevelopment: "On first coming to Seoul, the European visitor feels a mixture of admiration and melancholy. Admiration, because everything seems so new, so big, so well ordered, and so rational. Melancholy, because everything also seems too new, too big, too well ordered, and too rational."

The urban restructuring in preparation for the Olympics contributed to the rapid development of Kang Nam, the part of Seoul that lies south of the Han River which runs through the city. The northern part, Kang Buk, had been home to more than 80% of the city's residents up until the 1960s, but its southern counterpart attracted residential and office developments from the mid-1970s onwards. Most Olympic facilities were located in Kang Nam and triggered massive office developments in neighboring areas in the 1980s and 1990s. Seoul's population is now almost evenly distributed on the two sides of the Han River. While Kang Buk remains the primary urban center that serves as the major site of government administration and corporate headquarters, Kang Nam has become known for the disproportionate concentration of financial firms, business services, and upper-middle-class residential areas. As the Kang Nam area continues to attract international events and the affiliates of multinational corporations, it has emerged to represent a new, internationally connected Seoul.

Seoul in the Asian urban hierarchy

Seoul has long been the capital, primate city, and international gateway of Korea. It has, however, not been able to command much respect in the region. Tokyo stands at the apex of the Asian urban hierarchy. Although some argue for Hong Kong and Singapore as more internationally connected regional centers (Beaverstock *et al.* 1999, p. 25), Tokyo is a world city competing with London and New York (Short and Kim 1999; Yeung 1996). Tokyo's preeminent status among Asian cities is clearly due to Japan's economic success over the past half century. There has been a great deal of confusion on which cities make up the second tier in Asia. Seoul would like to be seen as part of that second tier in Asia, or at least the Pacific Asian region, but some recent studies on world cities suggest otherwise (Table 2.2). While Friedmann (1995) and Short and Kim (1999) rank Seoul in the second tier with Osaka and Singapore respectively, Seoul is clearly behind Hong Kong and Singapore in other studies.

Studies with different research focuses and data sets feature different urban hierarchies, and this is a primary reason for inconsistencies and contradictions in world cities research (Beaverstock *et al.* 2000; Short and Kim 1999). Friedman (1995) lists a number of indicators that he took

Table 2.2 *Asian urban hierarchy in selected world cities studies*

	World cities Friedmann (1995)		Command centers Short and Kim (1999)
1	Tokyo	1	Tokyo
2	Singapore	2	Osaka
3	Seoul	3	Seoul
4	Osaka	4	Beijing
5	Hong Kong		

	Headquarters and first-level subsidiaries Godfrey and Zhou (1999)		Corporate services Beaverstock *et al.* (1999) Taylor (2000)		Transport and telecommunications Rimmer (1999)
1	Tokyo	1	Tokyo	1	Tokyo
2	Hong Kong	2	Hong Kong	2	Hong Kong
3	Singapore	2	Singapore	3	Singapore
4	Seoul	4	Seoul	4	Taipei
5	Oaska	5	Jakarta	5	Seoul
6	Beijing	5	Osaka	6	Beijing
7	Bangkok	5	Taipei	7	Bangkok
8	Taipei	8	Bangkok	8	Kuala Lumpur
9	Shanghai	8	Beijing	9	Osaka
10	Jakarta	8	Shanghai	10	Kaohsiung
10	Manila	11	Istanbul	11	Manila
12	Guangzhou	11	Kuala Lumpur	12	Kobe
13	Kuala Lumpur	11	Manila	13	Osaka
				14	Pusan
				15	Shanghai

into account in his global urban hierarchy, but he does not provide the data sets used for his research. Short and Kim (1999) use the locations of the world's largest corporations' headquarters, banks' head offices, stock markets, and advertising agencies' main offices to rank cities around the world. The success of Seoul-based multinational corporations, *chaebols*, has evidently played the key role in raising Seoul's ranking when locations of corporate headquarters are considered.

Pointing out the shortcomings of an exclusive focus on the location of multinationals' headquarters, Godfrey and Zhou (1999) include multinationals' first-level subsidiaries in identifying the global urban hierarchy. They argue that studies of multinationals' headquarters overrate cities like Seoul where a few conglomerates account for a significant proportion of the national economy. Their global urban hierarchy, which is measured by locations of headquarters and first-level subsidiaries of the world's

100 largest corporations, includes, in order, New York, Tokyo, London, Hong Kong, Singapore, Milan, Paris, Mexico City, Madrid, and Seoul. The position of Hong Kong and Singapore as the second-tier cities in Asia is also confirmed by the Globalization and World Cities (GaWC) Research Group and Network's studies on corporate services around the world (Beaverstock *et al.* 1999; Taylor, 2000). Using the location data of global prime accountant firms, advertising agencies, banks, and law firms, they rank the two Asian city-states in the second tier of their world cities roster, while Seoul is placed in the fifth with eighteen cities ahead of it. Seoul, compared to Hong Kong and Singapore, particularly lacks international banking and legal services. The buoyancy of the Hong Kong and Singapore stock exchanges has overshadowed Seoul's presence in global corporate service markets. Seoul is also placed behind Hong Kong, Singapore, and even Taipei in the Asian transport and telecommunications network (Rimmer 1999). While Hong Kong and Singapore serve as hubs and international gateways of Asia, Seoul is in the main just the connecting point between South Korea and the rest of the world.

Alongside housing multinational corporations, major international law firms, and large airports, a city's openness (or connectedness) to the rest of the world is an important factor in determining its world city status. Seoul has a less than grand history of interactions with foreign cultures and economies. It took many years for Seoul to have significant contact with the outside world after the Korean War. Given that Seoul has been the outright international gateway for the Korean economy, an economy that has aggressively participated in international trade over the past few decades, it is ironic, but true, that it developed little "globalness" in either cultural or economic contexts until recently. Unlike Hong Kong and Singapore, Seoul did not serve as a focal point of international trade. Without an appreciable history of immigration, Seoul's ethnic composition remains overwhelmingly Korean. Foreigners account for only 0.6% of Seoul's population in 1999 (Seoul Metropolitan Government 2000b), an extremely low figure compared to Singapore's 18.8% (Singapore Department of Statistics 2000) and Hong Kong's 7.1% (Hong Kong Special Administrative Region of the People's Republic of China 2000). This nearly homogeneous structure of Seoul entails the absence of ethnic subcultures. The city has also lacked the transnational connections that immigrants would develop by retaining economic and cultural links with their home countries.

While Hong Kong and Singapore have established their economies around multinationals' foreign direct investment (FDI) over many years, Seoul's economic development has depended almost exclusively on local capital. Border-crossing capital movements were heavily controlled until the early 1990s when the Korean government, following the worldwide trend towards financial liberalization, began to show a commitment to the opening of its capital markets. But even then Korea, concerned about the loss of economic sovereignty, did not welcome foreign companies' direct investment. Only in 1995 did Korea attract more than $0.5 billion of FDI, while Hong Kong and Singapore drew $3.3 and $7.2 billion respectively (UNCTAD 1999). The International Monetary Fund restructuring measures following the 1997 Korean financial crisis, however, played a key role in lifting the remaining barriers to free capital flows. The recent explosion of mergers and acquisitions of crisis-hit local companies by foreign investors has resulted in a dramatic increase in FDI flows to Korea. In 1998, FDI in Korea amounted to $5.1 billion, and it grew to $15.5 billion the following year, and Seoul alone attracted $3.0 billion in 1998 and $6.3 billion in 1999. The recent rush of buy-outs by foreign investors has significantly increased the openness of the Korean economy, but it has also reinforced anti-globalization sentiments among Koreans. Multinationals' mergers and acquisitions have ranged from insolvent banks to automobile manufacturers and neighborhood grocery stores. This sudden foreign intrusion has spurred strong reactions from various consumer groups and trade unions hit by the financial crisis and subsequent restructuring. Whether Seoul can cultivate globalness in its culture and economy to the level of Hong Kong's and Singapore's will depend on how this resistance plays out in the future.

A considerable gap has separated Seoul from its two regional rivals on most measures. Some of this gap has, however, been reduced through Seoul's success in attracting international mega events, particularly the Summer Olympic Games and the World Cup Finals.

World-class events and world city status

Cities use international events to boost their economies and reputation and to legitimize their claim to world city status. World fairs and Expos were once praised as vehicles for economic growth and urban redevelopment by politicians and urban planners. More recently the Olympics have come to be viewed as promising events to spur host cities' international visibility and economic development (Rutheiser 1996; Cashman and Hughes 1999). A *New York Times* article sums up what difference the Olympics can make to the host city: "When we last visited Sydney in 1993, just a few days after it was awarded the Games, it was a pleasant and pretty place, but it felt parochial. Today, befitting a metropolis of four million, it feels like a major international city. The streets are thick with new skyscrapers" (Weisenhaus and Mustain 2000, p. 11).

Among the numerous alleged benefits that world-class sports events would bring to the host city, four stand out (Dunn and McGuirk 1999; French and Disher 1997; Larson and Park 1993; Rowe and McGuirk 1999; Syme *et al.* 1989). The first and most important benefit is the massive media exposure before, during, and after the event that enhances the city's reputation at the national level and in the world at large. The second benefit is the economic boom created by the construction and tourism associated with the event. The third is the legacy of sporting venues and urban infrastructure built for staging global spectacles. The fourth is urban redevelopment accompanied with the construction of stadium and leisure facilities. In addition to these benefits, hosting a globally watched sports competition can play a significant role in boosting civic pride among residents. The successful hosting of such events helps heighten confidence in national/urban governments and associated institutions, and this is particularly important in developing countries.

Casting doubt on these benefits, however, a growing body of literature has investigated whether mega events, such as the Olympics, have indeed generated what the national or city Olympic committees have projected (Cashman and Hughes 1999; Wilson 1996). Expenditures on infrastructure, facilities, and event operations have been weighed against revenues from tourism, broadcasting rights, and sponsorships. The effects of mega events in urban redevelopment, particularly the massive displacement of poor neighborhoods, have also been critically scrutinized (Rutheiser 1996). Alongside these studies, mounting attention has recently been paid to the urban or national politics of the bidding for such events and their hosting (Cochrane *et al.* 1996; Hiller 2000; Loftman and Nevin 1996; Whitson and MacIntosh 1993). Some pointed questions have been raised: who took the initiative to bid for the event? What policies and rhetoric have been employed to solicit public support? How has the private sector's involvement in the bidding/hosting process been justified? And finally, which groups have been the prime beneficiaries of the event? The core argument of this "new urban politics" literature is that high-profile prestige events are promoted as an opportunity to boost the economy, reputation, and social unity of hosting places, that they are nothing more than hegemonic devices by which a handful of politicians and entrepreneurs fulfill their ambitions (Harvey 1989).

Despite such critiques of mega event projects by academics, liberal media, and vocal activist groups, many cities around the world bid for the Olympic Games, World Cup Finals, exhibitions, fairs, and conventions. And the majority of citizens show their support for the bidding process and excitement when their cities or countries are awarded the right to stage international events. The enthusiastic popular responses when Athens and Sydney were chosen as venues for the Olympics are still fresh in mind. It does not seem particularly convincing that all of those cheering people are manipulated by exaggerated projections of economic benefits, landmark sports facilities, and world-class urban infrastructure, as many have argued (Harvey 1989; Hiller 2000; Hubbard 1996). Not everyone who thinks the Olympics are a good idea is engaged in hegemonic behavior, either by wishing to exert hegemony or by virtue of having been duped (Schuster 1999). In their case study of Vancouver's World Fair, Ley and Olds (1988, p. 209) conclude, "The cultural dupes posed by mass culture theorists are less visible on the ground than they are in nonempirical speculation." Alongside politicians' political motives and entrepreneurs' businesses interests, public support might be what makes cities keep seeking high-profile mega events.

Cities that applied to host the Olympic Games between 1988 and 2008 and received serious consideration by the selection committees are listed in Table 2.3. Countless other cities that made significant efforts at the local, national, and international level to host the Olympics, but were not adequately supported or noticed, are not listed. Since 1988 none of the cities that have been finalists for the Summer Olympics has been in the top tier of world cities, except for Paris. The finalists may be separated into three categories, allowing for some exceptions. The first group consists of "second-tier cities" in developed countries that have tried to move up to the first tier by hosting the Olympics. They include Amsterdam, Berlin, Osaka, Rome, Stockholm, and Toronto, none of which has been recognized as outright world cities. Indeed, these are the most aggressive chasers of rotating spectacles and conventions around the world (Short and Kim 1998). In the second group we find declining industrial cities in Europe. Having been devastated by the global restructuring of manufacturing industries in the 1970s and 1980s, traditional industrial cities such as Birmingham, Manchester, and Lille have used an Olympic bid as a means to revive their failing economies, to embellish their images, and to project themselves as high-tech or cultural centers (Cochrane *et al.* 1996; John and Cole 1998; Loftman and Nevin 1996 and 1998). The third group includes national centers in developing countries which expected the Olympics to boost their global reputation, improve urban infrastructure, and provide their citizens with international exposure. Thus the majority of candidates in the 2004 and 2008 Olympics bids are "Third World cities": Bangkok, Beijing, Buenos Aires, Cairo, Cape Town, Havana, Istanbul, Kuala Lumpur, Rio de Janeiro, St. Juan, and St. Petersburg.

It is very much debatable whether hosting world-class events like the Summer Olympics can bring world city status. Without a significant

Table 2.3 *Cities bidding for the Summer Olympics, 1988–2008*

	2008	2004	2000	1996	1992	1988
Host city	Beijing	Athens	Sydney	Atlanta	Barcelona	Seoul
Finalists	Istanbul	Buenos Aires	Beijing	Athens	Amsterdam	Nagoya
	Osaka	Cape Town	Berlin	Belgrade	Belgrade	
	Paris	Rome	Istanbul	Manchester	Birmingham	
	Toronto	Stockholm	Manchester	Melbourne	Brisbane	
				Toronto	Paris	
Runners-up[a]	Bangkok	Istanbul				
	Cairo	Lille				
	Havana	Rio de Janeiro				
	Kuala Lumpur	St. Juan, Puerto Rico				
	Sevilla	St. Petersburg				
		Sevilla				

[a] The International Olympic Committee did not make the lists of runners-up public until its 2004 Olympic city selection.
Source: Adapted from Monaco (2000).

concentration of multinational corporations, financial institutions, corporate services, and telecommunications and transportations networks, the successful bidding and staging of the Olympics would be a hollow claim to world city status. The failure of Mexico City after the 1968 Olympics speaks volumes about the fact that the Olympics alone are not sufficient. Why would so many cities bid for the Olympics then – particularly cities in the developing world that fall far short of the requirements of becoming a world city? One possible answer is that, since it is not clear where to start in the path to world city status, many cities in developing countries consider hosting the Olympics a first step to take.

Most large cities in developing countries suffer from the fact that their international image is vague or altogether negative. They receive little international media attention but for natural and social disasters. Third World cities tend to be seen as a combination of shantytowns, traffic chaos, environmental pollution, and inefficient government. The media exposure that the Olympics bring can change such biased perceptions by showing the host city's modern cityscapes and well-organized traffic system – as Tokyo and Seoul did in the 1964 and 1988 Olympics, respectively. Hosting the Olympics and other world-class events is an effective way of showing what a city or a nation has achieved over the years. Once a city has established a positive image, policies designed to attract investment and tourists have better prospects of success, and world city status may come within reach.

The Seoul Olympics: a breakthrough for the South Korean capital

The 1988 Seoul Olympics have been the proudest event for Koreans yet. The Games, with 160 countries participating, were the largest global spectacle ever staged up to that time, and Seoul was the second Asian city after Tokyo to host the Summer Olympics. In addition, although North Korea sabotaged the Olympics, Seoul was able to attract athletes from most of the then socialist countries. Given the fact that the two previous Olympics, Moscow in 1980 and Los Angeles in 1984, were not truly global spectacles, it was a great accomplishment for the International and Seoul Olympic committees to have international goodwill back at the center of this sporting event. Seoul was fortunate to avoid another politically crippled Olympics, which was not an unlikely prospect at the time (Pound 1994).

The bid for the Olympics was considered by the Korean and Seoul governments as early as the late 1970s, but the decision to "go for it" was made in 1980 when the country was recovering from a military coup led by then President Chun (Seoul Olympic Organizing Committee 1989). Indeed, the new administration was heavily criticized for even bidding for the Olympics, since the odds seemed to be very much against it. The use of the Olympics to legitimize the military dictatorship was repeatedly denounced by those opposed to Seoul hosting the expensive international sports competition (Kim 1997). A survey following the Olympics, however, found that about 90% of Koreans felt positive about the event (Kim *et al.* 1989). It is clear that despite lingering worries about extreme actions from North Korea, the heavy economic burden, and manipulative Olympic politics, the Seoul Olympics were a great success for Koreans.

It is difficult to quantify the economic gains and costs of the Olympics, since most sporting facilities have been used for other purposes after the event and, on the other hand, much of the human and indirect investment was not counted. Still, the Seoul Olympics generated a substantial profit of $497 million, which laid to rest the issue of the Olympic debt widely raised while the event was prepared (Hill 1996; Kim *et al.* 1989). Perhaps the most tangible result of hosting the Olympics has been the sharp increase in the number of international tourists coming to Korea, and Seoul in particular, since the mid-1980s even though Seoul lacks the natural or historical assets that attract tourists from distant lands to cities such as Barcelona or Sydney (Figure 2.1). The economic boom that Korea enjoyed in the mid-1980s was generally considered another positive effect of the 1988 Olympics, even if a causal relationship between the event and the national economic performance cannot be established. The country achieved double-digit annual economic growth rates during the entire second half of the 1980s. The Olympic period was the best for the export-oriented Korean economy, which in 1988 accounted for 8.2% of total exports from developing countries (Y. Kim 1998).

Alongside these gains, the Olympics benefited Seoul in four major ways. First, the Olympics and the associated media events increased Seoul's international visibility as soon as the city was awarded the right to stage the Games in 1981 (Larson and Park 1993). Besides the obscurity that is the fate of even major cities in the developing world, the image of a war-torn country had continued to overshadow the dramatic progress that Seoul had made since the Korean War. And as one of two capital cities of a divided nation, Seoul had long been portrayed as a symbol of Cold War tensions. The Korean government effectively used the Olympics to reinvent its capital city as an emerging center in Asia and enhance the country's global standing (*Economist* 2000a).

The Seoul Olympics also served the South Korean government to belittle its northern opponent (Hill 1996; Pound 1994). The economic

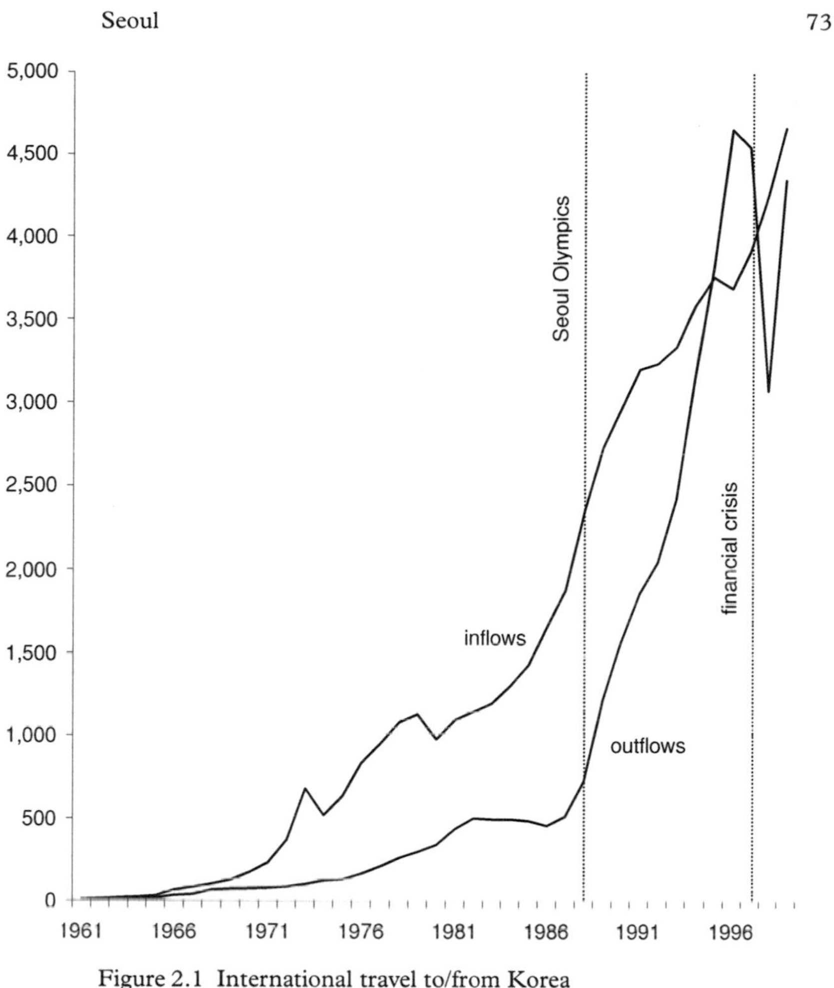

Figure 2.1 International travel to/from Korea
Source: Korea National Tourism Organization 2000.

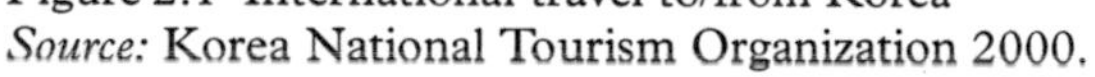

success broadcast to the world stood in sharp contrast to the economic difficulties that North Korea suffered, and was viewed as a demonstration of the superiority of the capitalist system over its socialist competitor. And while a potential boycott by the then socialist countries was a serious concern, given the strained relationships between the two Koreas, most officially recognized South Korea by sending their athletes to Seoul (Pound 1994). The Olympics served the government in domestic politics as well. Many Koreans who were ambivalent about the military government became enthusiastic supporters, even if voices of dissent remained (Kim *et al.* 1989).

Third, the Seoul Olympics played a very important role in the city's urban redevelopment (Seoul Olympic Organizing Committee 1989). The Han River waterfront redevelopment was completed as part of the Olympic preparation. The subway system was extended in the mid-1980s. A number of landmarks carrying Olympic names were built during this time, among them the Olympic Bridge, the 88 Freeway, and the Olympic Park. The staging of the Olympic Games provided a compelling rationale for the massive displacement of poor neighborhoods, many of which were transformed into business and financial districts.

Finally, the Seoul Olympics played a significant role in opening the eyes of the people of Seoul to the wider world. They tasted other cultures as they hosted 160 national teams and hundreds of thousands of tourists from many parts of the world. Seoul had not been a cosmopolitan city by any means, and this exposure to the Other led to an increasing interest in the outside world in the years following the Olympics. The explosive growth of overseas travel since the late 1980s is a good indication of how the Olympics fostered growing openness and globalness in Seoul (Figure 2.1). In 1989 the Korean government lifted restrictions on international travel. The outflow of Korean tourists grew apace after the Olympics and by 1995 outnumbered the inflow of foreign tourists. The financial crisis led to a sharp decline in overseas travel in the late 1990s, but this proved to be temporary.

A sharp increase in the number of resident foreigners is viewed as another indication of the Seoul Olympics' effects in diversifying the city's culture (Y. Kim 1998). Prior to the Olympics, the presence of foreigners, mostly Chinese Koreans and US military personnel, carried little significance: Chinese descendants had been assimilated into the mainstream long ago, and American soldiers lived in restricted military bases. Except for a very limited number of visitors, such as business personnel, tourists, and language instructors, foreigners were a rare sight in the streets of Seoul. Some change in Seoul's ethnic homogeneity could, however, be detected by the late 1980s when migrant workers from Southeast Asia and China flocked to Seoul. Small local manufacturing firms, who had suffered from both an emerging trend of deindustrialization and a surge in wages, welcomed these workers. Most of these foreign workers became aware of Seoul's economic growth and job opportunities through the broadcasting of the Olympics (Y. Kim 1998). By the late 1990s, about 230,000 foreigners were estimated to work legally or illegally in the city (*Economist* 2000b). The remittances sent by foreign workers to their own countries increased from $26.3 million in 1990 to $179.7 million in 1996 (Ministry of Labor 1997).

The 2002 World Cup Finals and the shadow of Tokyo

Having made a success of the Olympics, Korea applied for the 2002 World Cup Finals and was awarded the right to co-host the event with Japan. It would have thrilled Koreans if Seoul had beaten Tokyo in the bidding process, but the Fédération Internationale de Football Association (FIFA) named Seoul as the venue for the opening ceremony and Tokyo, or rather Yokohama, for the closing. The rivalry and hatred between Korea and Japan dates back to the first half of the twentieth century when Japan colonized Korea. Tokyo has held the upper hand in most aspects of the rivalry against Seoul throughout modern history. Koreans viewed the World Cup Finals as an unprecedented opportunity for Seoul to gain "legitimate" world city status by being equal to, if not outperforming, Tokyo. They wanted their city to compare favorably with Tokyo in terms of, among others, stadium, event organization, telecommunications technology, and traffic management. The Seoul World Cup Stadium, with a capacity of 63,930 seats, was newly built for the world's most celebrated soccer festival. Koreans took pride in having a brand-new soccer-only stadium named after the event, while Yokohama International Sports Stadium was built in 1997 and used for field games as well as soccer (Seoul Metropolitan Government 2000a).

The World Cup Finals have not been viewed as significant an event as the Olympics for cities in their efforts to increase their status. The primary reason for this is the fact that the Finals have usually been staged in countries with strong soccer traditions. While the Olympic sites have been limited to large cities in developed countries, Mexico City and Seoul the only exceptions over the past century, six of a total of sixteen World Cup Finals prior to 2002 were held in Latin America: Uruguay (1930), Brazil (1950), Chile (1962), Mexico (1970 and 1986), and Argentina (1978). The other final matches were played in Western European countries, except for the 1994 Finals in the US. Thus the 2002 FIFA World Cup Korea/Japan has been the first Finals staged outside of Europe and the Americas. Second, since the Finals are a soccer-only competition that requires a number of soccer stadiums, they tend to be awarded to a country rather than a specific city. In the 1994 World Cup, for example, nine American cities hosted a total of fifty-two games. Although cities hosting the opening or closing ceremonies have been watched by as many as Olympic sites have, if not more, bidding for the right to stage the World Cup depends very much on the decision of the national football association and government. And indeed, while academics have paid a good deal of attention to the role of football games in politics, nationalism, and class identities (Dauncey and Hare 1999; Duke and Crolley 1996), cities bidding for the World Cup, and those hosting it, have attracted little interest.

Although no one can dispute the Olympics' claim to be the premier global sporting event with a colossal number of athletes from all over the world participating, the World Cup Finals boast a larger global media audience. The 1998 World Cup Finals in France attracted a cumulative television audience of 37.1 billion; the final match between the Brazilian and French alone was watched by 4 billion viewers (Cashman 1999, p. 5). The 2002 Finals were expected to draw at least 41 billion viewers around the world (KOWOC 2000), and the FIFA's unofficial numbers show that this expectation was exceeded. In contrast, the global television audience for the 1996 Atlanta Olympic Games was estimated at 19.6 billion people. This triumph of the World Cup Finals over the Olympics in attracting television audience owes much to the wide appeal of soccer and the one-month stretch of the event compared to the two-week long Olympics. Among the major factors in soccer's worldwide popularity are the recent successes of African teams at international competitions, the soccer boom in the US after the 1994 World Cup, and the commitment of Asian countries to improve the competitiveness of their national teams (Sugden and Tomlinson 1998).

The Korean Football Association decided in 1989 to bid for the 2002 World Cup Finals and lobbied for the Finals to be staged outside of Europe and the Americas (KOWOC 2000). Japan, however, having successfully hosted the World Under-17 Championships in 1993, emerged as the leading contender in the bid. The bidding competition between Japan and Korea became so fierce, and even corrupt, that the hosting of the soccer tournament in 2002 had to be split between the two countries (*Economist* 1996; Sugden and Tomlinson 1998, pp. 111–121). While Japan advertised in the bid its well-developed infrastructure and promised financial support for the development of African football, Korea capitalized on a football tradition that has been rich by Asian standards and the Finals' potential contribution to the reunification of the two Koreas. Both countries promoted very polished images as potential World Cup venues, but neither was strong enough to eliminate the other.

Many Koreans were ambivalent about co-hosting the Finals with Japan during the years leading up to the event, given the historical relationship between the two countries. They feared that Japan would claim credit for the success of the 2002 World Cup, and that Tokyo would be attracting all the media attention. These nationalistic sentiments and worries forced the Korean Football Association to lobby fiercely to secure the opening ceremony for Seoul. The labeling of the event was another source of tension in the early negotiations among FIFA, Korea, and Japan (Sugden and Tomlinson 1998, p. 120). Calling on French and Spanish spellings, Korean representatives insisted the Finals' official name be the 2002 FIFA World Cup Korea/Japan. Koreans were given virtually everything they asked for, yet they remained extremely concerned that Tokyo would upstage Seoul in infrastructure, broadcasting, event operation, security, and international tourism (Seoul Metropolitan Government 2000a). These concerns appeared to grow as the event approached.

In the event, things turned out much better for Korea than expected. The World Cup Finals started with the opening game in Seoul, and the two host countries divided evenly a total of sixty-four matches during the following weeks. Korea received more than its share of international media attention due to its national team's strong showing. The Korean Red Devils stunned the world by reaching the semifinals, and their fans wearing red shirts became one of the most memorable images in the entire event. Although it is still early to assess how the 2002 World Cup Finals have boosted Seoul's world city status, the event certainly left Koreans in an upbeat mood. It may be too much of a dream for Seoul to move to the top of the Asian urban hierarchy in the near future, yet it is the case that Seoul has markedly improved its international standing by faring well in hosting the most watched international sports competition.

Conclusion

Seoul is one of very few cities in developing countries to improve its international reputation by hosting world-class events such as the Olympics and the World Cup Finals. These high-profile media events have served to complement Seoul's economic success in the pursuit of world city status. Seoul used to receive little attention at the international level, and such attention as it received tended to be negative. If this is the fate of most large cities in the developing world, Seoul's image was further tarnished by the Korean War and the Cold War. The city's international image gradually brightened as the success of the Korean economy affected perceptions around the globe, yet a dramatic change came in the 1980s when the city became known as the site of the 1988 Summer Olympics. With the successful staging of the Olympics, Seoul began to appear on the maps of world cities. Alongside this increased international visibility, the Olympics played a significant role in heightening Seoul's globalness through increases in international tourism, the arrival of foreign companies, and an influx of migrant workers from foreign countries.

As a co-host city of the 2002 World Cup Finals, Seoul underwent another round of "ingenious make overs," as foreign observers phrased it, to be world class in every aspect. The term "international standards" was applied to, among others, stadium, entertainments, city traffic, and street signs while Koreans were preparing for the event. The fact that Tokyo was a joint venue of the Finals added to the strong motivation for Seoul to present itself as a world-class city. The Finals reenforced a perception of Seoul as a world city rather than just the capital of Korea. The achievement is due to a strategy followed by neither Hong Kong nor Singapore, a strategy which remained beyond the reach of all but one of the developing countries that attempted to pursue it.

REFERENCES

Beaverstock, Jonathan V., Smith, Richard G., and Taylor, Peter J. 2000. "World-City Network: A New Metageography?," *Annals of the Association of American Geographers*, 90 (1): 123–134.

Beaverstock, J. V., Taylor, P. J., and Smith, R. G. 1999. "A Roster of World Cities," *Cities*, 16 (6): 445–458.

Budd, Leslie 1999. "Globalization and the Crisis of Territorial Embeddedness of International Financial Markets," in Ron Martin (ed.), *Money and the Space Economy*. Chichester: John Wiley and Sons, pp. 115–137.

Cashman, Richard 1999. "The Greatest Peacetime Event," in Richard Cashman and Anthony Hughes (eds.), *Staging the Olympics: The Event and its Impact*. Sydney: University of New South Wales Press, pp. 3–17.

Cashman, Richard and Hughes, Anthony (eds.), 1999. *Staging the Olympics: The Event and its Impact*. Sydney: University of New South Wales Press.

Cochrane, Allan, Peck, Jamie, and Tickell, Adam 1996. "Manchester Plays Games: Exploring the Local Politics of Globalization," *Urban Studies*, 33 (8): 1319–1336.

Dauncey, Hugh and Hare, Geoff (eds.), 1999, *France and the 1998 World Cup: The National Impact of a World Sporting Event*. London: Frank Cass.

Dick, H. W. and Rimmer, P. J. 1998. "Beyond the Third World City: The New Urban Geography of South-East Asia," *Urban Studies*, 35 (12): 2303–2321.

Duke, Vic and Crolley, Liz 1996. *Football, Nationality and the State*, Harlow: Longman.

Dunn, Kevin M. and McGuirk, Pauline M. 1999. "Hallmark Events," in Richard Cashman and Anthony Hughes (eds.), *Staging the Olympics: The Event and its Impact*, Sydney: University of New South Wales Press, pp. 18–32.

Economist 1996. "Penalty Zone," 8 June, pp. 38–39.

2000a. "Cities and the Olympics: Make or Break," 16 September, pp. 27–32.

2000b. "Unlucky Jin," 15 July, p. 42.

French, Steven P. and Disher, Mike E. 1997. "Atlanta and the Olympics: A One-Year Retrospective," *Journal of the American Planning Association*, 63 (3): 379–393.

Friedmann, John. 1995. "Where We Stand: A Decade of World City Research," in Paul L. Knox and Peter J. Taylor (eds.), *World Cities in a World System*. Cambridge: Cambridge University Press, pp. 21–47.

Godfrey, Brian J. and Zhou, Yu 1999. "Ranking World Cities: Multinational Corporations and the Global Urban Hierarchy," *Urban Geography*, 20 (3): 268–281.

Harvey, David. 1989. "From Managerialism to Entrepreneurialism: The Transformation of Governance in Late Capitalism," *Geografiska Annaler*, 71B: 3–17.

Hill, Christopher R. 1996. *Olympic Politics*. Manchester: Manchester University Press.

Hill, Richard Child and Kim, June Woo 2000. "Global Cities and Developmental States: New York, Tokyo and Seoul," *Urban Studies*, 37 (12): 2167–2195.

Hiller, Harry H. 2000. "Mega-Events, Urban Boosterism and Growth Strategies: An Analysis of the Objectives and Legitimations of the Cape Town 2004 Olympic Bid," *International Journal of Urban and Regional Research*, 24 (2): 439–458.

Hong, Sung Woong 1996. "A Global City in a Nation of Rapid Growth," in Fu-chen Lo and Yue-man Yeung (eds.), *Emerging World Cities in Pacific Asia*. Tokyo: United Nations University Press, pp. 144–178.

Hong Kong Special Administrative Region of the People's Republic of China, 2000, "Hong Kong: The Facts" (http://www.info.gov.hk/hkar99/eng/hkfacts/hkfacts.htm).

Hubbard, Phil. 1996. "Urban Design and City Regeneration: Social Representations of Entrepreneurial Landscapes," *Urban Studies*, 33 (8): 1441–1461.

John, Peter and Cole, Alistair 1998. "Urban Regimes and Local Governance in Britain and France: Policy Adaptation and Coordination in Leeds and Lille," *Urban Affairs Review*, 33 (3): 382–404.

Kim, J., Rhee, S., Yu, J., Ku, K., and Hong, J. 1989. *The Impact of the Seoul Olympic Games on National Development*. Seoul: Korea Development Institute, Seoul (in Korean).

Kim, Joochul and Choe, Sang-Chuel 1997. *Seoul: The Making of a Metropolis*. Chichester: John Wiley and Sons.

Kim, Won Bae 1998. "National Competitiveness and Governance of Seoul, Korea," in John Friedmann (ed.), *Urban and Regional Governance in the Asia Pacific*. Vancouver: University of British Columbia, pp. 33–50.

Kim, Yeong-Hyun 1997. "Interpreting the Olympic Landscape in Seoul – the Politics of Sports, Spectacle and Landscape," *Journal of the Korean Geographical Society*, 32 (3): 387–402.

1998. "Globalization, Urban Changes and Seoul's Dreams: A Global Perspective on Contemporary Seoul," Ph.D. dissertation, Syracuse University.

Kim, Yong-Woong 1995. "Spatial Changes and Regional Development," in Gun Young Lee and Hyun Sik Kim (eds.), *Cities and Nation: Planning Issues and Policies of Korea*. Seoul: Korea Research Institute for Human Settlements, pp. 53–78.

Korea National Tourism Organization 2000. "Visitor Arrivals, Korean Departures, International Tourism Receipts and Expenditures, 1961–1999" (http://www.knto.or.kr/index_1.html).

Korean Organizing Committee for the 2000 FIFA World Cup Korea/Japan (KOWOC) 2000. "2000 FIFA World Cup Korea/Japan" (http://www.2002worldcupkorea.org/hearhee/index.htm).

Kwon, Won-Yong 1995. "Seoul: Mega-City Problems in Korea," in Gun Young Lee and Hyun Sik Kim (eds.), *Cities and Nation: Planning Issues and Policies of Korea*. Seoul: Korea Research Institute for Human Settlements, pp. 177–204.

Larson, James F. and Park, Heung-Soo 1993. *Global Television and the Politics of the Seoul Olympics*. Boulder: Westview Press.

Ley, D and Olds, K. 1988, "Landscape as Spectacle: World's Fairs and the Culture of Heroic Consumption," *Environment and Planning D*, 6: 191–212.

Lo, Fu-chen and Yeung Yue-man (eds.), 1996. *Emerging World Cities in Pacific Asia*. Tokyo: United Nations University Press.

Loftman, Patrick and Nevin, Brendan 1996. "Going for Growth: Prestige Projects in Three British Cities," *Urban Studies*, 33 (6): 991–1019.

1998. "Pro-Growth Local Economic Development Strategies: Civic Promotion and Local Needs in Britain's Second City, 1981–1996," in Tim Hall and Phillip Hubbard (eds.), *The Entrepreneurial City: Geographies of Politics, Regime and Representation*. Chichester: John Wiley and Sons, pp. 129–148.

Machimura, T. 1998. "Symbolic Use of Globalization in Urban Politics in Tokyo," *International Journal of Urban and Regional Research*, 22: 183–194.

Ministry of Labor, Republic of Korea 1997. "Rapid Rise of Foreign Workers' Remittances" (http://www.molab.go.kr).

Monaco, Michael S. 2000. "The Olympic Almanac" (http://www.olympalmanac.org/).

National Statistical Office, South Korea 2001. "Population" (www.nso.go.kr).

Olds, K. 1995. "Globalization and the Production of New Urban Spaces: Pacific Rim Megaprojects in the Late 20th Century," *Environment and Planning A*, 27 (11): 1713–1743.

Öncü, Ayşe and Weyland, Peter (eds.), 1997. *Space, Culture and Power: New Identities in Globalizing Cities*. London: Zed Books.

Park, Soo-Young 1995. "Managing the Growth of the Seoul Metropolitan Area," in Gun Young Lee and Hyun Sik Kim (eds.), *Cities and Nation: Planning Issues and Policies of Korea*. Seoul: Korea Research Institute for Human Settlements, pp. 205–232.

Pound, Richard W. 1994. *Five Rings over Korea: The Secret Negotiations behind the 1988 Olympic Games in Seoul*. Boston: Little, Brown and Company.

Rimmer, Peter J. 1999. "The Asia-Pacific Rim's Transport and Telecommunications Systems: Spatial Structure and Corporate Control since the Mid-1980s," *GeoJournal*, 48: 43–65.

Rowe, David and McGuirk, Pauline 1999. "Drunk for Three Weeks: Sporting Success and City Image," *International Review for the Sociology of Sport*, 34 (2): 125–141.

Rutheiser, Charles 1996. *Imagineering Atlanta: The Politics of Place in the City of Dreams*. London: Verso.

Sassen, Saskia 1991. *The Global City: New York, London*. Tokyo, Princeton, NJ: Princeton University Press.

Schuster, J. Mark 1999. "Temporary Urbanism, Cultural Policy, and the Image of the City" (http://www.tc.columbia.edu/academic/arad/pages/Ephemera.html).

Seoul Metropolitan Government 2000a. "2002 World Cup Seoul" (http://smg.metro.seoul.kr:8000/).
2000b. "One Day in Seoul" (http://www.metro.seoul.kr/eng/smg/index_mun.html).
Seoul Olympic Organizing Committee 1989. *Games of the 24th Olympiad Seoul 1988*. Seoul: Korea Textbook.
Short, John Rennie, Breitbach, Carrie, Buckman, Steven, and Essex, Jamey 2000. "From World Cities to Gateway Cities: Extending the Boundaries of Globalization Theory," *City*, 4 (3): pp. 317–340.
Short, John Rennie and Kim, Yeong-Hyun 1998. "Urban Crises/Urban Representations: Selling the City in Difficult Times," in Tim Hall and Phillip Hubbard (eds.), *The Entrepreneurial City: Geographies of Politics, Regime and Representation*. Chichester: John Wiley and Sons, pp. 55–75.
1999. *Globalization and the City*. New York: Longman.
Singapore Department of Statistics 2000. "Latest Annual Indicators" (http://www.singstat.gov.sg/FACT/KEYIND/keyind.html).
Sugden, John and Tomlinson, Alan 1998. *FIFA and the Contest for World Football: Who Rules the Peoples' Game?*. Cambridge: Polity Press.
Syme, Geoffrey J., Shaw, B. J., Fenton, D. Mark, and Mueller, Walter S. (eds.), 1989. *The Planning and Evaluation of Hallmark Events*. Aldershot: Avebury.
Taylor, Peter J. 2000. "World Cities and Territorial States under Conditions of Contemporary Globalization," *Political Geography*, 19 (1): 5–32.
Thrift, Nigel 1994. "On the Social and Cultural Determinants of International Financial Centers: The Case of the City of London," in Stuart Corbridge, Ron Martin, and Nigel Thrift (eds.), *Money, Power and Space*. Oxford: Blackwell, pp. 327–355.
Todd, Graham 1995. "'Going Global' in the Semi-Periphery: World Cities as Political Projects: The Case of Toronto," in Paul L. Knox and Peter J. Taylor (eds.), *World Cities in a World System*. Cambridge: Cambridge University Press, pp. 192–212.
United Nations Conference on Trade and Development (UNCTAD) 1999. *World Investment Report 1999: Foreign Direct Investment and the Challenge of Development*. New York: United Nations Publications.
Weisenhaus, Doreen and Mustain, Gene 2000. "The Laid-Back Olympics," *New York Times*, 6 August, pp. TR11 and 18.
Whitson, K. and MacIntosh, Donald 1993. "Becoming a 'World-Class' City: Hallmark Events and Sport Franchises in the Growth Strategies of Western Canadian Cities," *Sociology of Sport Journal*, 10 (3): 221–240.
Wilson, Helen 1996. "What Is an Olympic City? Visions of Sydney 2000," *Media, Culture and Society*, 18: 603–618.
Yeoh, Brenda S. A. 1999. "Global/Globalizing Cities," *Progress in Human Geography*, 23 (4): 607–616.
Yeung, Yue-man 1996. "An Asian Perspective on the Global City," *International Social Science Journal*, 147: 25–32.
Zincone, G. 1989. "1988 Welcome to Seoul," *Abitare*, 273: 218–227.

3 Bangkok: evolution and adaptation under stress

Douglas Webster

Bangkok, the dominant city in Southeast Asia by 2003, and the political capital of Thailand has experienced high levels of stress since the early 1980s, associated both with periods of very rapid economic growth, and economic crisis. This assessment focuses on the adaptive behavior of key stakeholders that significantly influenced the economic, social, and environmental performance of the Bangkok urban region over that period.

Bangkok was at the center of a severe recession in Thailand in the early 1980s, peaking in 1984, that forced the national government completely to reorient its closed, import-substitution development strategy to one of openness and export-oriented manufacturing. Yet by the late 1980s and early 1990s, Bangkok was one of the fastest growing urban economies in the world, growing at an annualized rate of 17.2% between 1990 and 1996, a rate surpassed during that period only by coastal Chinese cities.[1] The Extended Bangkok Region (EBR) became the engine of the post-1984 boom, known as the "Golden Age of Manufacturing," driven to a considerable extent by foreign direct investment (FDI). But, domestic financial mismanagement, in the context of rapidly changing and volatile conditions associated with rapid liberalization of global economic, financial, and trading systems, resulted in Bangkok being ground zero in the Asian economic crisis that started in July 1997. By 1999, Bangkok's economy had returned to positive growth but at a much lower rate – approximately 3 to 5% (annually) from 1999 to 2000 (World Bank 2001, fig. 3, p. 3). However, in 2001, Bangkok's economy was again being challenged as a result of the slowdown in the economy of the United States. Nonetheless, by mid-2002, Bangkok's economy was growing in excess of 5% annually, supported by high levels of consumer spending. Bangkok appeared less vulnerable than cities such as Manila and Singapore that

[1] The economic growth figure refers to the Bangkok Metropolitan Administration (BMA) area, and is based on gross regional domestic product (GRDP) data published by the National Economic and Social Development Board (NESDB).

are more highly dependent on electronics,[2] or cities such as Jakarta that are perceived to be less stable and safe than Bangkok.

The stress experienced by the EBR from the early 1980s to the present was largely the product of alternating economic crises and "hyper growth". As an open economy, swings in Bangkok's fortunes were closely related to changing global conditions.

Analyzing the evolution of the Bangkok region, assessing adaptive responses, and relating outcomes of these adjustment processes to Bangkok's role in the Southeast Asian urban system are the foci of the discussion that follows.[3]

Themes

Key themes to be explored, in the context of the Bangkok case, are:

(i) Key drivers such as FDI, major changes in national economic policy or conditions, and large-scale infrastructure investments set off chains of entrepreneurial, social, and governance behavior that significantly determine an urban region's social and economic performance. The evolution of the Bangkok region in the 1984–2001 period in response to such drivers is a key focus of the analysis. It is the adaptation process that significantly determines the actual impacts of major drivers, be they international or domestic. Different urban regions, through their institutions, interpret and process ostensibly similar driving forces differently producing a wide range of, often unpredictable, outcomes.[4]

(ii) Because urban regions, such as Bangkok, are embedded in larger systems, e.g., the Southeast Asian urban system, local performance is constantly being tested against the performance of competing urban systems. Over time, differential performance, based on the cumulative impact of incremental decision making (public and private) in regard to key functions, relative to other major urban regions, repositions a major urban region, such as Bangkok, in terms of its regional, and even global, role.

The author's hypotheses, to be argued, are that:

[2] For example, 60% of the Philippines exports, and even a higher percentage from the extended Manila region, are electronics (by value).

[3] This chapter does not attempt comprehensively to inventory Bangkok's development history, its urban geography, or even its present functions and roles in an age of globalization – much has already been written on these topics. See, for example: Askew 1994a, 1994b; Kaothien and Webster 1995, 2000a, 2000b; Ruland and Ladavalya 1996.

[4] Dick and Rimmer (1998) argue that similar driving forces will result in increased convergence of urban characteristics in Southeast Asia.

(i) Bangkok is a flexible and dynamic urban system that makes adjustments quickly – when forced to do so. This quality has enabled the Bangkok urban region to play a high-profile role in Southeast Asia over the last twenty years, and to deliver expanded social and economic opportunities to its citizens, generally outperforming other Southeast Asian urban regions in this regard.

(ii) Stress accentuates both weaknesses and strengths in urban systems, often reinforcing ongoing dynamics; in this regard, Bangkok is no exception. For example, the 1997–1999 economic crisis accelerated the ongoing deindustrialization of core Bangkok, while strengthening "third-generation" manufacturing activity in the peri-urban area.

(iii) Stress, frequently precipitated by external drivers, often tests all cities in a region simultaneously. For example, the early 1980s and 1997–1999 economic crises were experienced throughout Southeast Asia (and beyond). As a regional system of cities is tested – some rise and some fall. Thus urban regions reposition themselves most during periods of stress, especially periods of significant economic downturn. It will be argued that the Bangkok region has gained in relative position from the recent (1997–1999) Asian economic crisis.

History

Bangkok has been the capital of Thailand since 1767 when the seat of royal power was shifted from Ayutthaya, which had served as the capital of Siam, as Thailand was known until 1939, for over 400 years (Map 3.1). The new capital was originally situated in Thonburi,[5] but in 1782 was moved across the Chao Praya River by King Rama I to its present site. The Chao Praya River is the key physical feature defining Bangkok's flat, sea-level, site.[6]

Thailand has been an open trading nation, except for short periods when external contacts were discouraged. As early as the fourteenth century, China, and states in present-day Japan and Vietnam, had significant trading relationships with Ayutthaya. By the seventeenth and eighteenth centuries many Asian and Western countries had embassies at Ayutthaya to represent their commercial interests.

The development of nineteenth- and early twentieth-century Bangkok was based on outward expansion from three nodes: (i) the royal/official city, (ii) Chinatown, and (iii) the International Quarter (Map 3.2). The original *raison d'être* of the city was the Royal Palace and surrounding

[5] Thonburi is currently part of the BMA, which governs the core city.

[6] For details on Bangkok's historical development, see Smithies 1986.

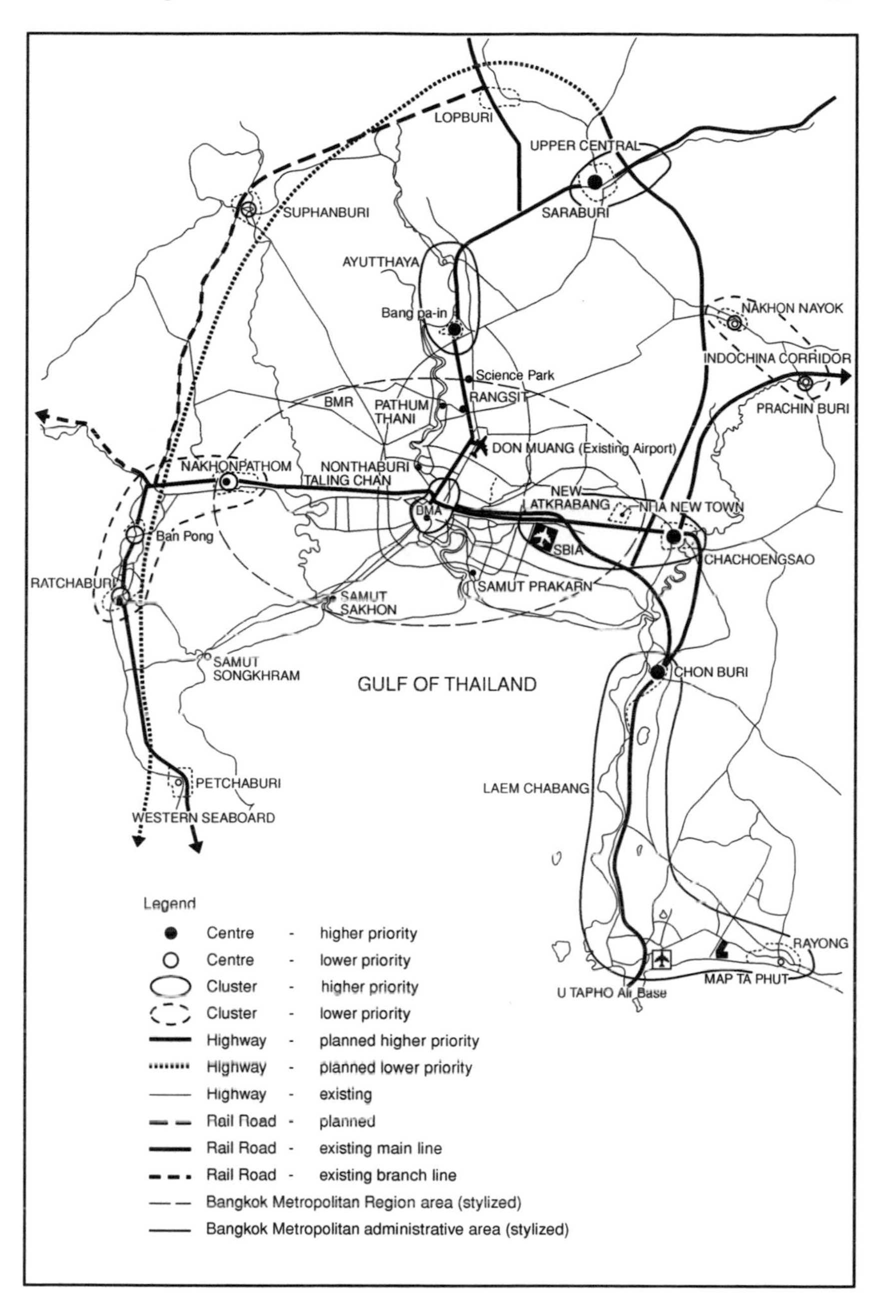

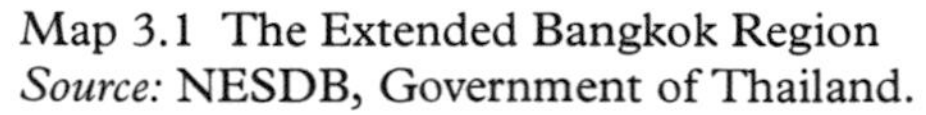
Map 3.1 The Extended Bangkok Region
Source: NESDB, Government of Thailand.

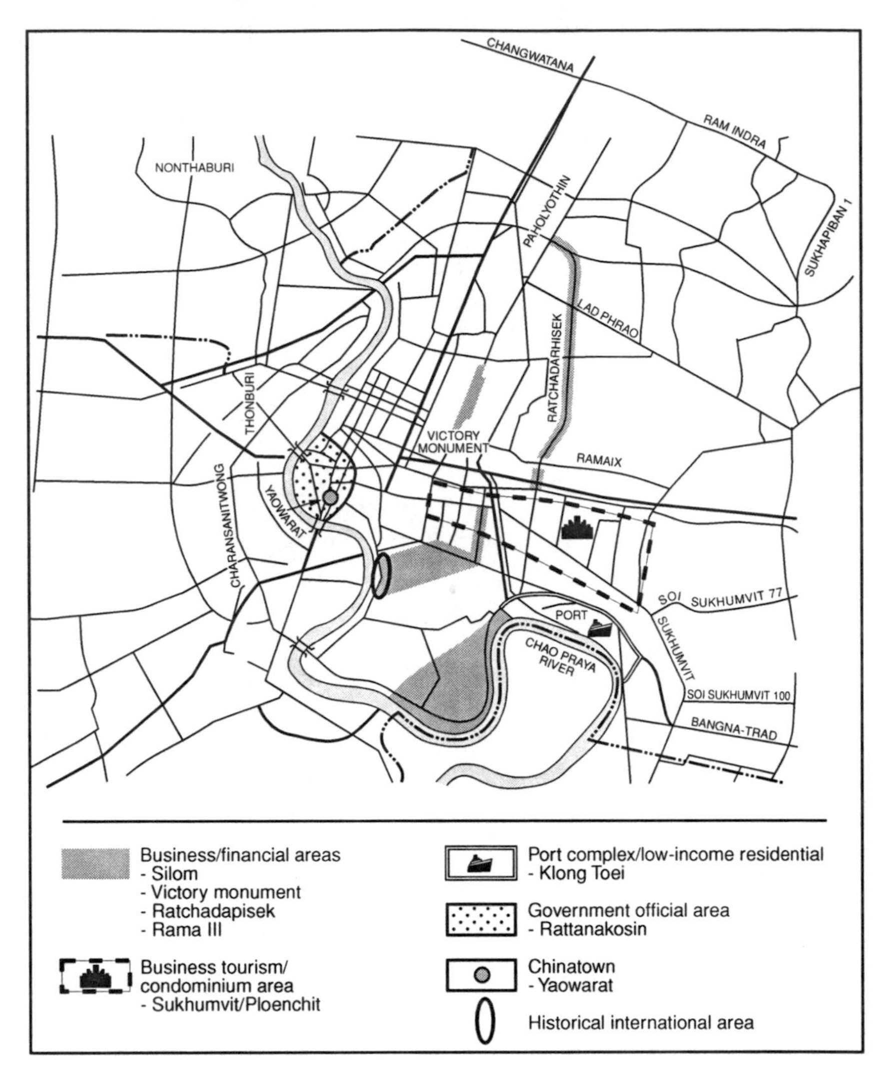

Map 3.2 Specialized nodes/corridors: Bangkok's core
Source: D. Webster.

government buildings that administered the Kingdom. This area, known as Rattanakosin, was carefully planned in terms of street layout, buildings, parks, and monuments; it is currently protected by height restrictions, and still contains a large number of inspiring government, religious, and royal buildings. Chinatown sprung up along the river downstream from Rattanakosin. It was populated through large-scale immigration from China for approximately 100 years starting in the mid-1800s.[7] A large percentage of Bangkok's population can trace roots to this migration. Chinatown served the official city, as well as the overall urban area and its hinterland, providing goods (retail and wholesale) and services. In addition, Chinatown's population played an important role in import and export of goods to/from Bangkok's hinterland, in particular, the export of rice from the agriculturally fertile Central Plain upon which Bangkok is located. The third early development node was the International Quarter yet further downstream. The International Quarter resulted from the reopening of Siam to foreign trade in 1855 under the terms of the Bowring Treaty. Bangkok's first road was built here (New Road, now named Charoen Krung) parallel to the river, in an area where international trade, particularly with European powers, was conducted. Although Thailand was never colonized, Western powers, such as the United Kingdom, had special rights in the International Quarter, e.g., courts to try their own citizens. At the end of the Second World War, Bangkok was a relatively small city, containing no more than 1 million people. It was an administrative and political capital, and the gateway to a rich agricultural hinterland.

Bangkok was known as the Venice of the East because of the city's extensive canal system that had been the prime means of transportation until early in the twentieth century. The Indo-China war in the 1960s unleashed dynamics that set the city on its current developmental pathway. In the 1950s and 1960s many canals were filled in to create an arterial road network, and motor vehicles became the dominant mode of transportation. Motorization, in turn, drove substantial suburbanization from the 1960s onward, and traffic jams in the core city became commonplace by the 1970s. Bangkok's notorious traffic jams (which peaked in the early 1990s) are largely a product of motorization combined with very limited land area devoted to roads and parking, 6–7% of the surface area of the Bangkok Metropolitan Administration (BMA). (By 1993, there were 220 vehicles and 179 motorbikes per thousand people in the BMA.[8]) The situation is exacerbated by the fact that side roads (*sois*) generally dead end at a canal or in the middle of "superblocks" (Figure 3.1), rather than serving as efficient feeder or connector roads.

Thailand has traditionally been highly centralized politically and administratively. Bangkok thus was the seat of very substantial political

[7] For more detail on the economic history of Bangkok and its hinterland, see Phongpaichit and Baker 1995, chs. 1 and 2.

[8] Road accidents in the BMA peaked in 1994 at 72,358 and 1,290 fatalities but the respective numbers had fallen to 42,032 and 673 by 2000 thanks to better traffic management and safety measures. Safety measures included greater use (mandated) of seat belts and motorcycle helmets. Data source: BMA (Office of Policy and Planning) 2001.

Figure 3.1 The superblock road network phenomenon
Source: Archer 1996.

and administrative power, while the city's government was under the control of the national government, with local government possessing limited powers.[9] Prior to 1972, the present area of the BMA consisted of

[9] For more detail on the development of local government in Bangkok, see Ruland and Ladavalya 1996.

twelve local governments. The two municipalities in the urbanized area (Bangkok and Thonburi) had elected mayors who often quarreled with centrally appointed governors who held considerable powers. In 1972, the military junta of Thanon/Praphat abolished local self-government in the metropolitan area and established the BMA. By 1974, the governor of the BMA became an elected official; in 1985 the BMA Act was passed which significantly extended the powers of the BMA government and established parliamentary procedures for it. Since then, the BMA has acquired further powers, particularly related to physical development.[10] A decentralization process, now underway, driven by the Constitution of 1997 and the National Decentralization Act of 1999, may deliver more powers and fiscal resources to the BMA. The BMA acts as pioneer in accepting new local government functions/responsibilities in Thailand which are often replicated in other larger cities in the nation.

Contemporary Bangkok

Population

The Bangkok metropolitan area contains about 8 million people (2002); the adjacent five provinces, which together with the BMA constitute the Bangkok Metropolitan Region (BMR),[11] are home to about 3.5 million more people, yielding a total of 11.5 million people in the BMR.[12] Areas of the EBR (Map 3.1 corresponds with this region) outside the BMR, where major peri-urban industrial clusters are located, contain about 6 million additional people (the vast majority of whom are engaged in non-agricultural pursuits). In sum, about 17.5 million people live in the EBR. Since Thailand's current population is 62 million, about 13% of Thais live in core Bangkok (BMA), 19% in the BMR, and 29% in the EBR.

According to the official statistics, core Bangkok (BMA) is growing slowly (at under 0.5% annually) while suburban Bangkok (BMR minus BMA) and the peri-urban Eastern Seaboard (ESB) are growing considerably faster at about 2% annually.[13] (These rates of population growth are very low for developing East Asian urban centers. For example, the real rate of urbanization in Indonesia is currently approximately 5% per

[10] For an official description of the BMA's powers, see BMA 2001, pp. 22–31.

[11] The BMR consists of the BMA plus five adjacent provinces, namely: Nonthaburi, Samut Prakarn, Pathum Thani, Nakon Pathom, and Samut Sakhon.

[12] Population figures have been rounded off to the nearest .5 million, to reflect the low degree of accuracy of urban demographic data in Thailand.

[13] Thai urban area growth rates are for the period 1997–2000.

Table 3.1 *The Extended Bangkok Region: emerging extended urban form in Southeast Asia*

	Key characteristics	Built form	Drivers	Population	Major threat
Core	• Knowledge/tertiary economy	• Poly nuclear • Mixed land use • Hotels, offices, and condominiums • Mass rail transit	• Global/national fusion and synergy	• Increasingly 2nd/3rd generation – slowing in-migration	• Too rapid deconcentration
Suburbs	• Residential (commuters) • Retailing • Mature (lower-value) industry	• Suburban villages ("muban") • Gated communities • Mega malls • Expressways • Radial development (primarily north and east)	• Thai property developers • Roads/expressways	• Households from core seeking space at affordable price • Some worker housing	• Mature industry threatened by international competition, e.g, Samut Prakam, Pathum Thani
Peri-Urban	• Industrial estates • Industrial support infrastructure	• Industrial estates • Ports • Spontaneous (squatter) worker settlements • Scattered factories • Scattered public institution compounds	• Exogenous • FDI driven • Infrastructure loan driven, e.g, OECF • Just-in-time production processes	• Rural migrants – Primarily from the northeast	• Overtly dependent on exogenous drivers

Source: Kaothien and Webster 1998.

year, while China is now urbanizing at close to 4% per year.[14]) However, real population growth is higher in all three jurisdictions, and especially the peri-urban area, because the population numeration system significantly under-counts in-migrants to urban areas.[15] The National Economic and Social Development Board (NESDB) estimates 51% of incremental population growth in the EBR will occur outside the BMA over the next twenty years (NESDB/Norconsult 1997, ch. 4 ["National Parameters"]). The fact that the core city (BMA) has added only 76,000 residents (officially) since 1997 means that there are virtually no demographic pressures on the city. This enables the BMA to focus on improving the quality, rather than quantity, of services.

Urban form and infrastructure

I distinguish three areas in the EBR: the core, i.e., the BMA area; the suburbs, i.e., the BMR minus the BMA;[16] and peri-urban areas, as described in Map 3.1.[17] Table 3.1 identifies typical characteristics (e.g., built form, population), drivers, and threats, associated with these three settlement types in the EBR.

The core The economy of the core has been propelled by service activity since the early 1990s, including producer, personal, retailing, aviation, tourism, hospitality, international governance, media, and health services. In 2001 the service sector accounted for 47% of core Bangkok's economic output (GRDP) compared with only 13% in the peri-urban ESB (Figure 3.2). Conversely, manufacturing accounts for 67% of economic output in the ESB, versus 33% in the core. The economic dominance of manufacturing in peri-urban (and suburban) Bangkok is among the highest in the world.

The growing importance of service activity in the core, and the ex-urbanization of industry, is mostly the result of market forces that have made the core city too expensive for manufacturers because of high land prices associated with the economic advantages of agglomeration.[18] This is reinforced by the lack of large spaces for factories in core areas. Official

[14] Based on data for 1995–2000 presented in Webster 2003, Table 1.

[15] The foregoing population growth rates are based on registration data of the Ministry of Interior. Since there is little incentive for individuals to reregister after moving, the system consistently undercounts urban populations, especially in rapidly growing areas such as the EBS.

[16] Nonthaburi, Samut Prakarn, Pathum Thani, Nakon Pathom, and Samut Sakhon Provinces.

[17] The area described on Map 1 minus the BMR (including the BMA).

[18] For a description of Bangkok's land market, see Dowall 1992.

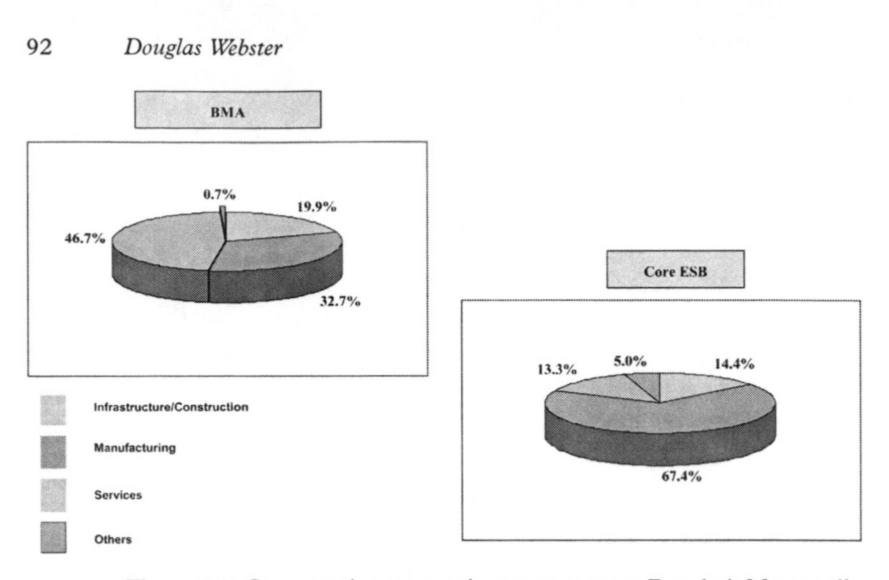

Figure 3.2 Comparative economic structure: core Bangkok Metropolitan Area, core Eastern Seaboard, 2001
Source: Gross Provincial Domestic Product Accounts, NESDB, Government of Thailand.

discouragement of industry in the city (as in other large East Asian cities such as Shanghai and Beijing) in part to minimize pollution, reinforced by other concerns such as truck traffic, has also contributed to the centrifugal movement of industry. Tax, tariff, and other spatially targeted investment incentives, administered by the Board of Investment (BOI) have, until recently, been used to encourage manufacturers to locate or expand in peri-urban areas. The shift of Thailand's flagship container seaport to Laem Chabang near Chon Buri in the ESB has also reinforced this dynamic (Map 3.1).

Some areas in the inner core are experiencing declines in residential population – young families have abandoned shop houses for the suburbs; in addition residential structures have been demolished for office and retail complexes, as well as transportation infrastructure such as elevated freeways. Over 100,000 people have been displaced through such displacement processes.

The rise of several business districts in the core has resulted in a multinodal structure. Over time, some business districts decline in importance, while others rise. This process, along with strong centrifugal development forces, accounts for disinvestment and deterioration in some formerly vital business areas in the core. However, this effect is relatively muted compared to other East Asian cities, e.g., Manila,[19] partly because rapid economic growth has generated enough domestic and foreign capital inflows to fund both rapid peripheral growth and investment in the core. Recent improved transportation access to/in the core, three expressways now serve the inner city, and a mass transit system serving all but one of the major core business districts is now operating, may slow centrifugal forces. This would limit any threatened "hollowing out" of Bangkok's core, even given the slow economic growth experienced since 1997. These new transportation systems, rather than encouraging flight to the periphery, seem to be strengthening the core by making it more accessible – it was literally choked by congestion in the early 1990s.

Bangkok's inner core is composed of tourist/hospitality/retail zones, financial districts, the government area (Rattanakosin), and Chinatown, in an overall environment of mixed land uses (Map 3.2). At a finer scale, areas of functional specialization can readily be identified, e.g., the jewelry district,[20] centered on Silom/Charoen Krung. Modern and postmodernist artifacts are everywhere: condominiums, hotels, office and retailing complexes, served by a 23 kilometer elevated rail mass transit system operated by the Bangkok Transit System (BTS) which is connected by a system of skypaths to most important venues along its route. Visitors from Japan comment on the diverse architecture of new buildings in Bangkok, compared with Tokyo.

Complementing the BTS system, in early 2004 a subway system began servicing the perimeter of Bangkok's inner core. These new mass transit systems are having a profound impact on the core's physical form. New high-density multiple-use complexes, directly linked to the mass transit systems, are already materializing around key transit stations.

Given the current low in-migration to the core, the city is increasingly populated by second- and third-generation migrants rather than recent arrivals. Different ethnic groups tend to cluster in different areas of the city, e.g., Chinese in Chinatown, South Asians at the foot of Silom, Westerners and Japanese along Sukumvit, and Islamic groups in Ban Khru. It is unclear whether ethnically defined areas are becoming more distinct or blurred in Bangkok as globalization forces become stronger – probably the latter.

The core is a vital place to work and play. Street life is exciting and varied; cuisine, ranging from street vendors selling noodles to elegant

[19] For a description of strong centrifugal forces creating disinvestment backlash effects in Manila, see Connell 1999.

[20] The jewelry industry employs over 100,000 people in Thailand, most working in the EBR.

restaurants, is superb. The city never sleeps. Traffic jams occur after midnight, as people travel to a variety of entertainment venues or return home – especially near the end of the month when they are paid. Like most cities, the daytime population of the inner core is much higher, expanding by about 1 million people during the working day.

The core is cosmopolitan, hundreds of thousands of expatriates work there, resulting in a creative fusion work culture that benefits from the combination of Thai and expatriate values, approaches, and skills. The advertising industry epitomizes this style, with Thai creative directors regularly winning international awards.[21] At the peak of the boom, the EBR contained 800,000 expatriate workers and their dependants, not counting a similar number of illegal workers from Burma and elsewhere.

The suburbs There are two dominant images, both grounded in reality, of Bangkok's suburbs. One is residential – of suburban villages, *mubans*, varying from "no frills" row housing developments to luxurious gated communities containing golf courses, swimming pools, country clubs, etc. In many ways the more expensive of these *mubans* are similar to gated communities in suburban Manila and "new towns" near Jakarta.[22] The other image is of non-competitive (increasingly closed or closing) labor-intensive factories. Interspersed are slum communities, particularly in low-lying areas, along canals and rail lines, and near factories.

The population of suburban Bangkok has grown rapidly since the 1970s, fueled by the desire of a middle class, which ballooned during the 1984–1997 period, for more living space, larger lots, and lower community densities, at affordable prices. The typical Thai suburban development is now sizeable, containing hundreds of housing units, constructed by a property development company. Developers built about 80% of housing in Bangkok's suburbs by 1997, the reverse was true in the 1970s when developers accounted for only about 20% of new housing constructed.[23] However, since the 1997–1999 economic crisis, the percentage of new housing constructed by individuals has been rising again, related to easier access to low-interest credit by individuals relative to heavily indebted property development companies.

Another major artifact of suburbia is the regional shopping mall, such as "Future Park" in the Rangsit area. These giant malls tend to lag residential population growth in suburban areas. The outward expansion

[21] For an analysis of Bangkok's advertising industry, see Muller 2002.
[22] See Connell 1999 for detail concerning Manila, and for the case of Jakarta, see Leaf 1996.
[23] For details, see Webster 2000.

of Bangkok enveloped existing service towns, such as Rangsit.[24] These former free-standing towns often continue to play a role as shopping and service centers within the suburban fabric, although the new regional malls increasingly threaten their vitality.

Significant industrial development came first to suburbia (e.g., Samut Prakarn, Pathum Thani), driven by import substitution in the 1970s, and even earlier. Thus the most globally uncompetitive industries, e.g., textiles, footwear, as well as heavy, polluting industries, are often found in suburban areas. The result is a growing "rust belt" phenomenon, both in physical and socioeconomic terms. Industrial layoffs during the recent economic crisis were much more prevalent in suburbia than in peri-urban areas, as were labor disputes.

Suburbia is linked to the core of the city and peri-urban areas, by extensive toll freeway systems. There is considerable open land in suburbia because development tends to leap-frog, especially along major roads. Thus narrow built-up tentacles reach out as far as 80 kilometers from the core. Because the spoke-like roads emanating from central Bangkok are limited in number, the interstices between these major transportation corridors are often rural-like in outer suburbia, punctuated by almost randomly located residential villages. This pattern is largely a reflection of the fact that there are no incentives for developers to build first in particular places, e.g., in areas with serviced land or closer to the core of the urban region. Local service infrastructure that would shape an area, i.e., feeder/connector roads, local drainage, social facilities such as schools and health centers, is often put in place later, after considerable development has occurred. This situation creates the type of haphazard suburban development illustrated by Figure 3.1.[25]

Construction of a commuter rail system by Hopewell that would have served the northern and eastern suburbs, the directions in which most suburban development is occurring, was abandoned when about 25% completed because the developer had financial problems. Means to restart the project are under consideration. Of particular concern is that the BTS and the Metropolitan Rapid Transit Authority (MRTA) subway systems, both serving the core were designed to connect with the Hopewell suburban rail routes. The failure to complete the Hopewell

[24] Envelopment of existing towns accounts for a considerable degree of urbanization in Southeast Asia where rural hinterlands tend to be densely populated. For example, in Indonesia one third of urbanization gains are the result of envelopment. Although data are not available for EBR, the corresponding figure would appear to be between 20 and 30%.

[25] For more information on the problems of "super block" development, and proposed solutions, see Archer 1996.

project may help to account for the fact that the BTS system is serving approximately 330,000 riders a day rather than the 600,000 forecast.[26]

Local governments responsible for suburban areas are often unprepared to cope with the combined stresses of rapid residential/ demographic growth, leap-frogging development patterns, and local economies under strong competitive pressures. Frequently, authorities in Bangkok's suburban areas express concern that new and vibrant economic activity is bypassing them, either moving out to green field sites in peri-urban areas, in the case of high-value manufacturing activities, or concentrating in the core, as do most high-value producer services and tourism activities. In effect, suburban Bangkok is caught between a dynamic core energized by rapid growth of producer services and peri-urban areas characterized by just-in-time firms linked to multilocational global production systems.

Peri-urban areas Peri-urban, in the Bangkok context, refers to areas beyond suburbia where industrialization is occurring rapidly, yet agriculture and other rural activities co-exist with this modern economy. Large-scale peri-urbanization, which took off in the mid to late 1980s, is found in the ESB, and in the Ayutthaya area, to the north of the BMR. Still, the three provinces that constitute the ESB special economic zone south east of core Bangkok's suburbs already contain close to three million people.[27]

The ESB is a public sector led regional development initiative planned in the 1970s and largely implemented in the 1980s and 1990s. Government decisions to develop two large ports in the ESB, Map Ta Phut and Laem Chabang (Map 3.1), and heavily invest in other infrastructure such as expressways, has further encouraged peri-urbanization. Much of this infrastructure development has been financed by international borrowing, particularly from the Japanese government's "soft loan" Overseas Economic Cooperation Fund (OECF).[28] Approved OECF lending for infrastructure spending in the ESB area totals 178,768 million yen.[29] Cumulative lending by OECF in the EBR totals 328 billion yen (to 1997), highest for any city in the world followed in East Asia by Jakarta (259 billion yen) and Manila (146 billion yen) (OECF 1997, fig. 14–1).

[26] As of October 2003.
[27] For more detail on Thailand's ESB, see Webster 2002.
[28] On 1 October 1999, OECF and the Japanese Export–Import Bank (JEXIM) were merged to create the Japan Bank for International Cooperation (JBIC).
[29] Source: OECF to 1997. OECF was the Major lender supporting development of the ESB special economic zone. The World Bank decided not to fund the program.

Most land in the peri-urban areas is not built up. Rather, the peri-urban landscape is best understood as a set of high investment clusters, that significantly impact the surrounding area through commuting, inter-industry linkages, flows of goods to ports, etc. The landscape itself is a patchwork encompassing green fields, factories; criss-crossed by freeways, arterial roads, and rail lines; and punctuated by small- and medium-sized long-established settlements. It would be a mistake to perceive the peri-urban area as a suburban or urban landscape in the making, the amount of land involved is too large, and, as noted, demographic growth which would feed such an outcome is slow in Thailand. Much of the peri-urban area is likely to remain a synthesis of rural and urban.

The lead artifact of peri-urban development is the industrial estate. Increasingly, Thailand has attracted major firms to locate in industrial estates. Industrial estates are attractive to investors, foreigners in particular, because the industrial estate's management acts as a buffer between local governments and the firm.

Large-scale FDI flows to Thailand since the mid-1980s have been the underlying driver of industrialization. Approximately 90% of Thailand's FDI went to the EBR during the 1990s, much of it to peri-urban areas, where virtually all new foreign-funded manufacturing facilities located. Most of this FDI was Japanese in origin. A variety of factors explain Thailand's success in attracting large-scale FDI including relatively low cost labor, a favorable business climate, and geo-strategic position. Public policy inducements include a clear commitment by the Thai government to freer trade, tax and tariff incentives administered by the BOI, and large-scale public sector championing and coordination of infrastructure investment in ports, roads, industrial estates, rail links, and other "productive" infrastructure. A recent study by A. T. Kearney (2000, p. 59) indicates that Thailand is the third most preferred location of Japanese investors, after the United States and China.

FDI to Thailand increased from an average annual inflow of US$1,656 million in the 1987–92 period to a peak of US$6,969 million in 1998 (Table 3.2). However, the share of the Association of Southeast Asian Nations's (ASEAN) FDI inflow relative to Asia and developing countries as a whole has been falling, especially relative to China. ASEAN's share of incoming FDI peaked in 1990 when it represented 35.5% of the developing world's total. By 1995, ASEAN's share had fallen to 19.6%, and by 1998 to 13.2%. Three sectors received the bulk of the inflow, namely manufacturing, trade, and real estate. In the early 1990s, FDI to Thailand was dominantly in manufacturing (48% of FDI, 1990), trade (20%), and real estate (12%); however, by the latter part of the decade,

Table 3.2 *FDI inflow to ASEAN (million dollars), 1987–1998*

	1987	1990	1991	1992	1996	1997	1998
			(annual average)				
Brunei	1	3	1	4	11	5	4
Indonesia	999	1,093	1,482	1,777	6,194	4,673	−356
Malaysia	2,387	2,333	3,998	5,183	5,078	5,106	3,727
Philippines	518	530	544	228	1,517	1,222	1,713
Singapore	3,674	5,575	4,879	2,351	7,884	9,710	7,218
Thailand	1,656	2,444	2,014	2,116	2,336	3,733	6,969
Vietnam	206	16	32	24	2,500	2,950	1,900
Total ASEAN	9,441	11,994	12,950	11,683	25,520	27,399	21,175
As % of developing countries	26.7	35.5	31.3	23.2	24.0	15.9	13.2

Source: United Nations Centre for Trade and Investment 2000, Annex Table 2, B.1.

the composition had shifted toward real estate and away from manufacturing.[30] This shift contributed to a property glut; approximately 300,000 housing units in the BMR remain vacant (2002).[31]

Inflows of highly mobile and volatile private debt capital, loaned short term, e.g., for six months; and portfolio capital used to purchase Thai equities also fueled the urban boom. As in the case of FDI, the vast majority of such flows went to the EBR. This capital fueled the property market in the region, and financed stock purchases. The rapid rise in capitalization of the Stock Exchange of Thailand (SET) fueled unrealistically ambitious real estate development due to the heavy weighting of property development companies on the SET. Because private debt capital provided low-cost loans to purchase vehicles, it encouraged and supported motorization, one of the key drivers of suburbanization and peri-urbanization.

Urban governance

A wide variety of agencies are responsible for delivery of services in the EBR (Table 3.3). Although core Bangkok's 8 million people are governed as one unit, the official local government, the BMA, has limited powers,

[30] Comparable figures for 1995 are: manufacturing: 28%, trade: 22%, and real estate: 42%.
[31] For details on FDI and portfolio capital flows into the EBR, see Kaothien and Webster 1998.

Table 3.3 *Functional responsibilities in the Bangkok region*

	Core city (BMA)	Bangkok Metropolitan Region (BMR)	Extended Bangkok Region (EBR)
Infrastructure development and management			
Water	▲	▲ ▲ ✖	▲ ❑ ✖
Sewage	(■) •	(▲) ❑	▲ ■ ❑
Highways/roads	▲ ▲ ■ ❑ •	▲ ■ ❑ ✖	■ ❑ ✖
Mass/public transit	▲ ▲ ❑ ❑(•)	▲ ▲ ❑ ✖	❑
Telecommunications	▲ ❑ ❑	▲ ▲ ❑	▲ ▲ ❑
Public housing/slum upgrading	▲ (■) •	▲ (■)	▲ (■)
Electrical power	▲ ▲ ❑	▲ ▲ ▲ ❑	▲ ▲ ❑
Social services			
Primary education	❑ •	■ ❑ ✖	■ ❑ ✖
Health	■ ❑ •	■ ❑ ✖	■ ❑ ✖
General urban services			
Refuse collection	•	✖	✖
Parks and recreation	•	✖	■ ✖
Fire protection	■ •	■ ✖	■ ✖
Law enforcement	■ •	■	■

KEY TO SYMBOLS
▲ State enterprise
■ National government
• BMA
❑ Private corporation or service provider
✖ Local government

Source: James Raphael and Douglas Webster, in Webster 2002.

and limited revenues. Many of the key functions of the city such as water and electricity service, expressways, public housing, public buses, commuter rail, are under the control of national state enterprises.[32] Because of a lack of horizontal coordination among these agencies, and the BMA's lack of significant influence over their activities, Bangkok lacks an overall capital budgeting, prioritizing, and coordinating process.

Outside the BMA, the situation becomes more complex and governance even more difficult. Although the BMA and its five adjacent provinces have been grouped to form the BMR, this is little more than a statistical entity. There is no structural or investment plan for the BMR,

[32] For details see Webster 2000.

and physical plans for the separate BMR provinces sometimes literally do not match at borders between provinces. Below the provincial level, there are hundreds of local governments in the BMR provinces outside the BMA. These entities are municipalities, including former Sanitary Districts recently upgraded to *Tambon Municipalities*, as well as small units of local government, with very limited capabilities, known as *Tambon Administrative Organizations*, in the least-developed areas. Problems include: (i) Fragmentation – cooperation among jurisdictions in delivering services best handled at larger spatial scales is lacking. (ii) Lack of capacity – technical and personnel capabilities are often not adequate effectively to manage rapidly developing suburban areas. (iii) Limited financial resources. With increased decentralization in Thailand, local governments are being devolved additional functions that require that they mobilize additional revenue, and understand and utilize innovative financing measures, such as responsible use of credit. By Fiscal Year (FY) 2006, 35% of public expenditure in Thailand will be by local governments, up from 8% in FY 2000. Obviously, this dynamic will have enormous impacts on local governments in the BMR.

The governance situation in peri-urban areas is similar to that in the BMR. There are 474 local governments in the three core ESB provinces of Chon Buri, Chachoengsao, and Rayong (Map 3.3), and over 2,000 in the EBR as a whole. Their capacities are frequently even less than local governments in the BMR. On the other hand, because of the national economic and strategic importance of special economic zones such as the ESB, the national government plays a stronger and more direct role in such peri-urban areas than in suburbia. For example, as noted, the national government has invested substantially in industrial support infrastructure. Public investment and regional development planning/programing in the ESB is coordinated by the NESDB. The ESB has also been the venue for innovative institution building. For example, East Water, a privatized entity, started by the Provincial Water Authority, a state enterprise, is responsible for trunk water supply to industrial estates and municipalities in the ESB.

Bangkok as a global-local mediating system

Early boom period urban development dynamics

In the early boom period (1980s), investment tended to be in lower-value activities such as textiles, tires, extruded plastics, footwear, and assembly of automobiles from knocked down kits. These industries needed the urban region primarily for its labor and basic infrastructure, and in many

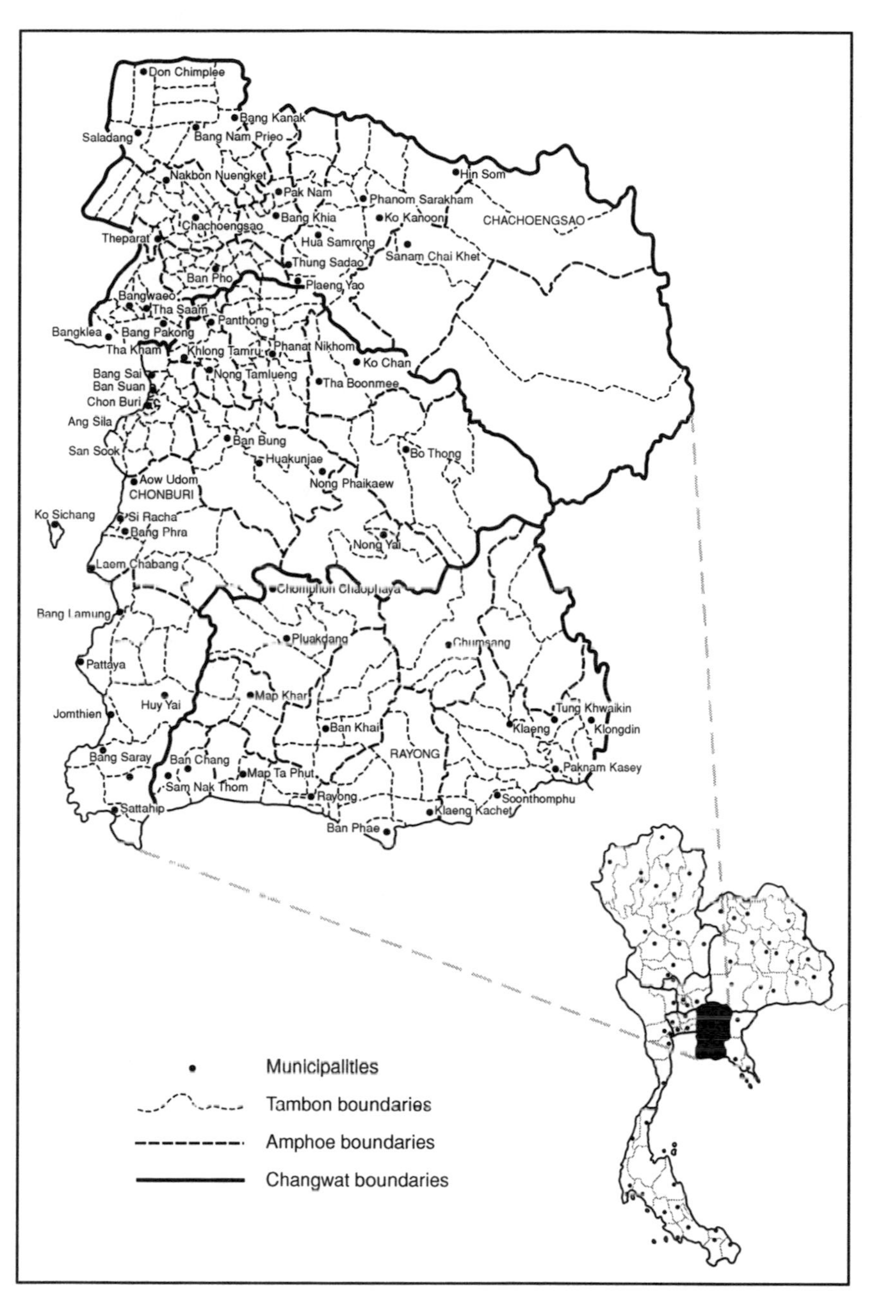

Map 3.3 Local government boundaries: core Eastern Seaboard
Source: NESDB, Government of Thailand.

cases, also for its market. Thus these "early" industries tended to locate on the major routes into Bangkok from the northeast region that supplied most of the migrant labor, i.e., along the northern corridor. At the same time, heavy industry, often funded from domestic public (state enterprises) and private sources, tended to locate to the southeast of the city, in Samut Prakan Province, partly because such industries often required a coastal location. These early boom period industrialists purchased basic business services, e.g., accounting, in the core of the city; and intermediate goods or raw materials from other local firms or from Bangkok's hinterland, e.g., petrochemicals, cotton, rubber. Because the inputs (raw materials or intermediate goods) needed were not particularly sophisticated, industrial clusters characterized by elaborate supply chains did not develop.

Early boom period industries tended to be located close enough to the city's core (generally within 50 kilometers) that executives and technical personnel, and their families, could live in the core of the city or in nearby suburbs. This was particularly important to expatriate personnel during this period because the national government licensed a very limited number of international schools – virtually all in Bangkok. Unskilled and semi-skilled labor tended to live near the factories, either in dormitories provided by the firms and industrial estates, or, more frequently, in rented worker apartments (shared by two, three, or sometimes more, workers) delivered by a reasonably efficient private housing market. In addition, buses chartered by factories (and suburban service institutions, such as the Asian Institute of Technology) provided inexpensive transportation to many areas, both in the core and in other suburban areas. (At the beginning and end of each shift, hundreds of buses streamed on to/from the freeway system, carrying thousands of workers.) This bussing enabled workers to live with relatives or rent housing on the private market in locations considerably remote from their work, including, in some cases, slum settlements.

Early foreign investors tended to rely on international Chambers of Commerce based in Bangkok, personnel of other firms (meeting on golf courses, etc.), the Thai government's Board of Investment, and their senior Thai employees, for advice on how to operate in the local environment. Since sophisticated technical suppliers or producer services were usually not needed, this network sufficed. In terms of business services, local firms, or local-international hybrid firms (in fields such as accounting, law, advertising, computing services, design), usually located in Bangkok's core, met their needs. One of the prime reasons for foreign firms using these core-based service providers was their knowledge of the Thai language, Thai government regulations, and their contacts with the bureaucracy.

Manufacturers frequently located in Sanitary Districts of the BMR, units of local government that were responsible for basic services such as garbage pickup, local roads, drainage, etc.[33] These local governments were not strong in terms of service delivery or enforcement, but the industries involved did not require high levels of amenity to attract labor or suppliers. Furthermore, a significant percentage of these "early" firms located within first-generation industrial estates such as Navanakorn (a large, industrial estate in the northern corridor about 55 kilometers north of core Bangkok). These estates provided services (e.g., water supply, solid waste, wastewater treatment, worker housing) that one would normally expect a local government to provide. Inadequacies in local environmental management result in free-standing industrial plants (outside industrial estates) often disposing of industrial untreated wastes into local fields, air, and waterways. For example, barrels of liquid waste are strewn in rice fields north of Bangkok.

During this period, tourism in the Bangkok region grew steadily; 1990 was "Visit Thailand Year" – approximately 3.5 million visitors came, most of whom passed through core Bangkok, although many did not stay long in the city – they were en route to beaches and hill areas. Bangkok catered to a wide spectrum of tourists, developing specialized functions. For example, during this period Bangkok solidified its position as "the main node of the international backpacker's circuit" (McLane 2000, p. 8).

Although the agricultural and natural resource components of the economy declined in relative importance, e.g., logging was banned in 1998 after disastrous flooding, Bangkok continued to serve as the main port, and business mediation center for export of natural resources and agricultural commodities (particularly rice). Import of capital and consumer goods, and export of manufactured goods, increased substantially as the economy's production and consumer economies boomed, adding to port activity.

As the country's dominant urban region, Bangkok (particularly its core) served as the main center for growing retail, wholesale, and financial functions serving the increasingly affluent Thai population, as well, importantly, as the center of national governance. However, the key economic driver of change during this period, as described above, was investment in manufacturing.

[33] In 1999 all Sanitary Districts in Thailand were upgraded to municipal status. Thus all large urban regions in Thailand contain several municipalities.

Late boom period urban development dynamics

By the mid-1990s, the labor-intensive, relatively low-value industries described above were under threat from lower-cost producers in places such as Indonesia, Bangladesh, Vietnam, and China. At the same time, higher-value industry in sectors such as autos, computer components, and appliances/consumer electronics began to play a much more important role. Much of this higher-value industry located outside Bangkok's daily commuter radius, in the ESB and to the north in the Ayutthaya area. These peri-urban industrial areas extended considerable distance from the core, 190 kilometers in the case of the ESB. By 1997, this peri-urban arc beyond the eastern and northern suburbs was known as the Industrial Heartland (Map 3.1). This appellation is not a misnomer; by the mid-1990s, EBR, led by the ESB, was the most important industrial area in Southeast Asia.

Preexisting communities, especially smaller ones, are generally not drivers of this peri-urban development process; industrial estate developers prefer "green field" sites,[34] but these communities experience significant impacts. In part this is because workers often choose to reside in established communities because of their relative vibrancy and existing social facilities, particularly higher-quality elementary and secondary education, even if these communities are under stress. Existing larger urban centers in peri-urban areas often see certain functions grow rapidly, e.g., Chon Buri is the most important banking center in Thailand outside the BMA.

The types of industry locating in peri-urban Bangkok are substantially different from those that drove suburban industrialization during the early stages of the boom. Second-phase industry is networked into complex multilocational global production processes. Although inputs are obtained worldwide, lead firms utilize numerous locally based suppliers, usually domestically or internationally owned small and medium enterprises (SMEs). Thus the new industrial estates tend to be focused around one industry, e.g., the ESB Industrial Estate is an automobile cluster, Ayutthaya is known for electronics clusters (Map 3.4).[35]

The new peri-urban industrial economy is essentially outside Bangkok's daily commuting area. Thus executives and skilled personnel (Thai or expatriate) cannot easily live in Bangkok's core or suburbs – yet attracting skilled labor who demand urban amenities is critical to the

[34] Especially sites where land holdings have not been fragmented, thus former agricultural plantations are favorite sites for industrial estates throughout Southeast Asia, including peri-urban Bangkok.

[35] Electronics industries prefer to be further away from the corrosive effects of sea air.

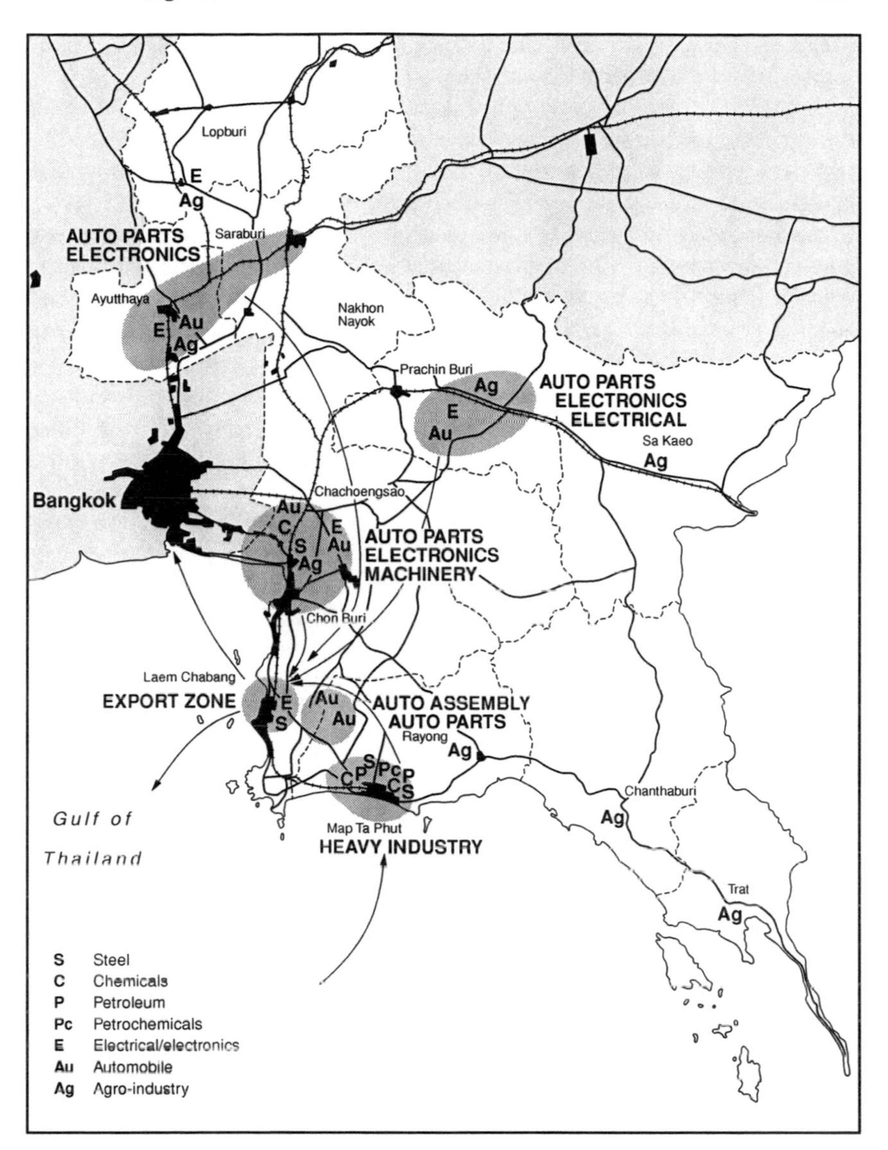

Map 3.4 Industrial clusters: peri-urban Bangkok
Source: NESDB, Government of Thailand.

success of these industries. The result has been the growth of "high end" residential enclaves throughout the peri-urban areas.

Route 331 is the new axis of industrial estate development in the ESB, the result of government–private sector consensus, but there are no substantive existing communities in this inland area (Map 3.4). Japanese skilled labor resides primarily in the existing coastal city of Sri Ratcha, while American skilled labor often resides on nearby golf course anchored gated communities. The influence of these exapatriate groups is readily apparent, e.g., the small city of Sri Ratcha is dotted with Japanese and Korean restaurants. Thai professional, semi-skilled and unskilled labor meanwhile is choosing to live in existing, primarily coastal, communities. Workers often live in informal settlements (slums) in communities such as Chon Buri and Rayong, despite the existence of nearer new and functional worker housing, to access the vibrancy and social facilities found in existing communities.[36]

The stresses on preexisting communities that are attractive to peri-urban workers can be enormous. For example, the mayor of Rayong indicates that approximately 40% of the residents of his city are unregistered, many living in sub-standard housing.[37] The fact that major firms run free buses for their employees throughout the peri-urban region (as far as 70 kilometers) partly accounts for the separation of places of work and residence.[38]

The growth of peri-urban manufacturing clusters has created new migration options for residents of poor, rural northeast region communities. Little is known about how this changing migration pattern will affect social support systems, learning, family life, cyclical migration, etc. Core Bangkok has been a very effective learning environment and urban staging area, supporting in-migrants in their efforts to take advantage of its diverse opportunities. Of particular concern is the lack of social capital in peri-urban areas. Unlike in core Bangkok, there do not exist generations of migrants from the same rural communities who can provide support and access to networks, particularly in "settling in" and emergencies. Furthermore, although wages are relatively attractive, income in kind, e.g., family-owned housing and child care from relatives, found

[36] Personal communication, Khamholung Ratsamany, manager, Eastern Seaboard Estate (Hemeraj Land and Development), 5 December 1999. For more information on worker residential choices and community impacts of these choices, see Muller 2000.

[37] Personal communication, mayor of Rayong.

[38] From the point of view of the firms, one of the advantages is that workers are on time for work and do not go home for long lunch breaks, etc., because they are dependent on the buses.

in the rural community or even core Bangkok, is often very limited in peri-urban Bangkok.

Local governance represents a major challenge. Many of the key industrial clusters are located not in municipalities but in *Tambon Administrative Organizations*, the least sophisticated level of government in Thailand. Thus essentially rural-oriented local governments with rudimentary capacities host sophisticated industrial clusters anchored by large multinational corporations.

The urban core, it too, has significantly changed during the latter stages of the boom period. The core developed a wider range of, and more sophisticated, financial and producer services, at the same time as its share of retailing was reduced by suburban competition. The financial function expanded as institutions developed to serve both producers and consumers benefiting from the boom. Bangkok became the financial center of the "Baht Zone" which included Laos, Cambodia, and Burma. Other services grew rapidly such as advertising, design and architecture,[39] fashion, media and journalism. Such services were overlaid on a long tradition of international governance in Bangkok that predated the boom. Bangkok is the most important center for international governance in Asia, hosting the headquarters of the United Nations' Economic and Social Commission for Asia and the Pacific (ESCAP), the International Air Transport Organization (IATO), regional offices of many United Nations (UN) agencies (e.g., UNICEF, UNESCO), the Asian Institute of Technology, etc. In all, sixty-six international organizations are represented in Bangkok. Equally important, the diplomatic community is extensive in Bangkok (123 countries are currently represented), largely in response to the history of conflict in the immediate region, Bangkok's geo-strategic position, and the existence of a large number of international agencies. For example, the United States embassy in Bangkok is that country's second largest worldwide.

Personal services also proliferated. International health care became more important, serving South Asia and Indochina, including alternative/traditional treatments. However, Bangkok's tourism performance can be described as mixed. Although tourist visits to Thailand increased dramatically to over 10 million in 2001, the average stay in Bangkok has decreased steadily to just over one day. This may be a result of perception of congestion even though traffic congestion and air pollution have actually decreased since the mid-1990s (Crispin 2001).

[39] For example, for a description of the growth and development of the architecture profession during this period, see Eckardt 1999.

Nevertheless, Bangkok remains a very important tourist, and related, business meeting/convention center; there are ninety-four quality hotels in the city (at least three stars), and seventy-nine airlines maintain offices. Bangkok recently overtook Singapore in international air passenger movements, becoming the leading aviation hub in Southeast Asia.

The core has benefited from more professional and higher-quality governance than exists in peripheral areas. The result is a considerable list of achievements during the 1990s including improved traffic flows, cleaner streets, and an operating mass transit system.[40] The ability of the BMA and the national government to improve Bangkok's environment after its nadir in the late 1980s/early 1990s accounts for some of the success of the service sector.

The workers in the core either commute from the suburbs or live downtown – the latter in apartments, condominiums, and traditional shop houses; in addition, a stock of detached homes still exists in the outer core, e.g., the Paholythin and Sukhumvit areas. The middle class tend to choose suburban housing (detached or row houses) because of a desire for additional space and less congestion at affordable prices, while some higher-income households choose to live in the core itself. About 20% of the BMA's residents lived in sub-standard housing during the latter phases of the boom. Increasingly slums are being found in suburban and peri-urban areas as manufacturing moved steadily outward during the post-1984 period – the new geography of urban poverty.

Adjustment processes in the extended region urban system

The economic crisis

When the economic crisis occurred in July 1997,[41] new types of stresses appeared, including increased unemployment, higher costs of many imported goods, and lower informal sector incomes.[42] Yet to a significant extent, Bangkok's residents, whether living in the core or periphery, were able to adjust. Most of the forecasts regarding expected unemployment, growth in incidence of poverty, social disruption, and unrest, issued at the beginning of the crisis, by agencies such as the World Bank, proved

[40] For details, see Webster 2000.

[41] Much has been written on the causes of the 1997–1999 East Asian economic crisis. For a concise economic interpretation, see Krugman 1999, ch. 5.

[42] For indicators on sectoral, employment, and income impacts of the economic crisis in Thailand and Bangkok, see World Bank 2000a; see also "How Much Did Thailand Suffer?", *Economist*, 22 January, 2000, p. 41.

unduly alarmist. Why? To a large extent because the adjustment capabilities of Bangkok residents and businesses were underestimated.

The economic crisis that hit Bangkok in July 1997 immediately put stress on the EBR, the flagship of Thailand's march to NIC ("newly industrialized country") status. Just as Bangkok had led the boom, it suffered most from the economic crisis. For example, the official unemployment rate in Bangkok (BMA) increased from 1.4% in early 1997 to 5.1% in 1999.[43] But many of the most negative effects were not the result of unemployment but income losses and sharp changes in the prices of essential imported goods. In terms of the income effect, the informal sector was affected most. The impact was very significant, for example, Bangkok's taxi drivers (numbering over 70,000), although not unemployed, saw their net incomes drop from approximately 700 Baht per day to 200 Baht or less as a result of both less business and no barriers to entry.[44] Informal food sellers were faced with growing competition as those laid off in the formal sector entered the informal sector, e.g., selling sandwiches in office buildings. But a countervailing force, not to be ignored, was the fact that many former middle-class people consumed more of the lower-cost food, and other services, sold in the informal sector as their incomes dropped.

Because of increases in prices of imported goods, significant negative impacts were experienced by persons dependent on petroleum products, e.g., truckers, commuters, taxi drivers, and/or dependent on imported (or licensed) medicines, e.g., the HIV positive population. As in any urban economic crisis, the construction sector was hard hit; 103,000 jobs were lost in core Bangkok (BMA) and real wages fell 3.7% for those who remained employed. But manufacturing in core Bangkok was hit even harder; 120,000 jobs were lost, although the real wage decline was only 2.2% in this sector. But to concentrate only on the poor and working class would be to bias description of the crisis. Over 100,000 individuals were laid off in the financial sector,[45] many of them "yuppies" who had become middle class during the boom period.[46]

[43] Based on third quarter labor surveys (1997 and 1999), Ministry of Labor, Royal Thai Government.

[44] The number of taxis increased from 18,000 in 1992 to 70,000 in 2000; their numbers increased sharply after the onset of the economic crisis.

[45] It is difficult statistically to track losses in the financial and other business/producer services employment occupations, because there were more than compensating gains in informal employment, which is also included in the service category. Overall, core Bangkok (BMA) gained 182,000 service jobs between 1997 and 1999.

[46] For details on the employment and income impacts of the crisis, see Thailand Development Research Institute, 1999.

The economic crisis exposed both weaknesses and strengths in the EBR. The crisis speeded up the ongoing process of deindustrialization in the core (BMA), weeding out uncompetitive firms. However, during the crisis, the peri-urban area gained 57,000 manufacturing jobs, indicating that the FDI-driven industrial structure now located in peri-urban areas is more globally competitive and resilient. The devalued Baht made many export-oriented industries more competitive.

At no time during the crisis did unemployment exceed 5.1% in Bangkok; however, this was among the highest unemployment rates in Thailand, exceeded only by the poor rural northeast where unemployment, which is consistently high, peaked at 9%. The economic crisis was centered in core Bangkok; regional cities (outer Thailand) did not develop high unemployment, nor did the peri-urban area.[47] Peri-urban unemployment peaked at 2.6%, and unemployment in cities of the north at 2.6%, the northeast at 4.2%, and the south at 3.8%.

Based on official statistics, which significantly undercount urban poverty, poverty remained low in Bangkok during the crisis, even though the national poverty incidence increased from 11.4% in 1996 to 15.9% in 1999. In fact the percentage of the population classified as poor in Bangkok (BMR) fell from 1.3% in 1996 (pre-crisis) to 0.2% in 1999. The BMR contained 1.8% of Thailand's poor people in 1996, but only 0.2% in 1999 (data source: World Bank 2000b, table 1.1). It is difficult to explain this data, but it is clear that the urban area provided significant opportunities for people to adjust rapidly, e.g., earning incomes above the poverty line in the informal sector, although often accepting lower income, after being laid off from formal sector employment. Another factor at play was that many of the poor left Bangkok for their rural or small-town roots, lowering poverty rates in the urban area, but increasing them in rural areas. The very low rate of growth of the BMA's population since 1997 indicates that out-migration has been occurring since the onset of the financial crisis. Predictions of social unrest in EBR proved to be completely unfounded. By way of contrast, in May 1992, during the height of the economic boom, mass violence erupted in the city with over fifty persons killed – this middle-class urban movement, coordinated over cell phones, demanded, and achieved, more participatory, decentralized, democratic government.

Why was Bangkok able to cope so well with a crisis that halved the value of the city's output (in US dollar terms) over a one-year period? Why was there no massive social disruption? Why did Bangkok emerge a stronger

[47] Real wages in agriculture fell by 14.4% between August 1997 and August 1999, the highest decline in any major sector. However, this can be explained more by physical conditions and world food markets, which were not favorable during the latter part of the recession.

player in the Southeast Asian system of cities? It is because households, workplace communities, and corporations in the EBR constitute a very adaptable, flexible system, even though Thai governments were slow to adapt.

Key adjustment mechanisms were as follows:

(i) Thai families proved very resilient. Bangkok, like most East Asian cities has seen the extended family, and even the nuclear family, weaken significantly over the last twenty years. Nevertheless, when the crisis occurred, the unemployed, and those who experienced dramatic declines in income, were supported by relatives either in Bangkok or in outer Thailand. Families or individuals were able to "double up" in housing units, pool incomes, etc. The World Bank estimates that transfers (including remittances), mainly private, as discussed above, resulted in the national poverty peaking at 15.9% during the crisis rather than at 18%, which would have otherwise been the case. In other words, household-based adaptation mechanisms saved 2.1% of Thailand's population from poverty during the crisis.

Similar dynamics occurred in workplace communities, where voluntary arrangements were made to share employment (less hours) or accept lower wages so that there would be no, or fewer, layoffs.

This does not mean that there were not serious ramifications from the crisis. The BMA's slum population increased from 1,247,000 in 1996 (it had been falling since the early 1990s) to 1,512,000 in 1998 (an increase of 21% over the two-year economic crisis period), according to BMA data.[48] However, the most recent data suggest that the slum population has returned to close to pre-crisis levels (1,255,330 in 2000). This may be because some of the poor left Bangkok after the economy failed to revive vigorously, and the collapse of the Bangkok property market made housing more affordable than ever before in the modern era.

(ii) Multinational corporations in the EBR were, and are, dominantly Japanese owned. Traditional Japanese business culture prevailed and persons were not laid off, rather year-end bonuses were cut.[49] This still led to some conflict. Also, the dramatically lower Baht improved the performance of many export-oriented industries, sparing many jobs.[50]

[48] BMA (Office of Policy and Planning) 2002, 2001, 2000, 1999, 1995.

[49] Japanese business culture is changing as a result of globalization pressures – this behavior is unlikely to be the norm in the next severe Southeast Asian recession.

[50] The Baht plunged from 25 Baht per US dollar to 57 in 1998, recovered to 36–38 Baht by early 1999, and then fell again to 44 by late 2000. By late 2003 it had partially recovered

(iii) Because many construction workers were Burmese, and the construction sector was hard hit in the EBR, it was possible to repatriate, or at least lay off, many Burmese workers without the social consequences being directly experienced in Bangkok. (At the height of the boom, there were approximately 750,000 illegal Burmese immigrants in Thailand – several hundred thousands left during the recession as a result of government policies, and perhaps because of fewer employment opportunities.)

(iv) Market dynamics created opportunities for the population of Bangkok, as well as suffering. For example, housing prices in Bangkok in 2002 were approximately half what they were in 1997 – the speculators have been driven out of the market. Combined with lower interest rates (7% now instead of +15% rates before the crisis), the result is greater housing affordability and a considerably higher home ownership rate than in 1997. New entrants to the housing market, particularly the young, have been net beneficiaries of the economic crisis in this regard. Housing prices fell much faster than wages, and have yet to turn up significantly.

(v) The Thai government was stable during the crisis period; the Democrat party government put together a strong economic team and worked closely with the International Monetary Fund (IMF) and World Bank. However, less structural and public sector reform occurred than would have been desirable to make the system less vulnerable to future economic crises. Thus the national government was less adaptive than individuals, households, and the corporate sector. A new majority government, Thai Rak Thai (Thais Love Thais) took power in late 2000, running on a populist platform, with strong support in the Bangkok region.

(vi) Through short-term labor-intensive employment creation, rural areas received more assistance than the EBR. However, there was also employment creation activity in the Bangkok region, particularly in core Bangkok, resulting in new sidewalks, landscaping of major corridors (including planting of hundreds of thousands of trees), etc., organized by the BMA. As well, individual citizens with time on their hands, or taking advantage of lower-priced labor, undertook considerable renovation at the neighborhood level. The result of these two dynamics was that Bangkok became a much more livable city as a result of the crisis.

to 40. The policy of the government of Thailand is to keep the value of the Baht relatively low in support of exports.

Bangkok's repositioning

Southeast urban system dynamics

To a significant extent, Bangkok's role in the Southeast Asian system of cities has been enhanced since 1997. The fact that Bangkok's peri-urban manufacturing and core service economies are in relatively healthy shape are part of the story. But, of equal importance is the decline of competitor cities.

Only Singapore and Kuala Lumpur, and to a lesser extent Penang, remain strong competitors to Bangkok in Southeast Asia.[51] Penang's economy has been significantly weakened by the recession in the electronics industry which started in 2001. Since urban systems compete in terms of activities rather than as cities, Singapore is not really a direct competitor of Bangkok – it competes with Hong Kong in areas such as finance, corporate headquarters and research and development. However, Bangkok competes more directly with Jakarta and Kuala Lumpur for firms seeking lower costs, typified by aviation and retailing companies. (Based on the Economist Intelligence Unit data (1999), of twenty-five major global urban regions monitored, Bangkok has the third lowest cost of living while Kuala Lumpur has the fourth lowest. Bangkok and Kuala Lumpur have costs of living about 55% of New York City while Singapore has a cost of living about the same as New York.) For example, Air France and Makro (retailing) have established regional headquarters in Bangkok.

In terms of quality of life, Bangkok benefited from the crisis (as is often the case) in a number of ways. Much-needed urban infrastructure started during the boom period (as is typical), e.g., the first mass transit system came on stream during the economic crisis. Traffic declined 13% (vehicle kilometers traveled in the BMA) lessening congestion and air pollution. As noted, public works and neighborhood initiatives flourished. Furthermore, accelerated deindustrialization in the core reduced air and water pollutants, truck traffic, etc. In fact, in the annual *Asiaweek* poll of the best cities in Asia, Bangkok improved its rank from twenty-sixth to thirteenth during the crisis period, i.e., from 1998 to 1999 (Sieu 1999). Because amenity is such a critical factor in attracting investment

[51] Malaysia adopted a very different macro-economic approach from Thailand in addressing the Asian economic crisis, but the results have broadly been the same. This outcome can be interpreted in two ways. To Malaysians, the fact that their exchange and capital flows control approach did not lead to disaster is a victory; to Thais the fact that the IMF approach led to equally good results without the risk of imposing controls indicates the vindication of the approach taken by Thailand.

and skilled labor to knowledge functions and high-value industry, these dynamics, if they can be maintained, will play an important role in helping the urban region to reposition itself upward. The improvements in Bangkok's physical attractiveness during the crisis are particularly important as Bangkok was known as a polluted, congested city in the early 1990s, when the negative impacts of the boom period had cumulatively reached alarming levels.

Challenges

Bangkok has coped reasonably well with the stresses of the last seventeen years and appears well positioned for future development. But what are the challenges that the region will encounter and how is it likely to fare?

(i) One challenge is accelerating globalization, in particular the increasing impact of the World Trade Organization (WTO) on national policies. In Southeast Asia, the WTO process is basically overtaking the continually delayed implementation of the ASEAN Free Trade Area (AFTA), which was supposed to have ushered in substantially free trade in ASEAN by 2003. Overall, WTO mandated changes should be good for the Bangkok region, as increased economic openness will play to the region's strengths. For example, the protected Malaysian auto industry may not be able to withstand international competition, whereas automobile clusters in the EBR are anchored by leading world vehicle manufacturers. On the other hand, a more open economy is threatening many domestic SMEs who are being outcompeted by off-shore suppliers to major industries, who are able to import components freely. The rapid rise of China as "factory of the world" and leading global recipient of FDI (2002) threatens exports from the EBR, unless the region can move up the value change quickly. On the other hand, trade data from 2002–2003 indicates increasing opportunities to export specialized manufactured products to China.

(ii) It is unlikely that the Bangkok region will develop a significant software development industry, as opposed to high levels of use of new software by firms and households. There does not seem to be a critical mass of professionals in computer software or hardware developing in Bangkok. (On the other hand, significant competency is emerging in areas such as website development, related to the core's strengths in advertising, marketing, and design.)

(iii) Another challenge is the shortage of technically trained workers. The number of Thai students enrolled in post-secondary technical education programs has recently climbed rapidly (from 325,000 students in 1994 to 454,000 students in 1998 – a gain of 28% over four years).

These students will be essential to fueling upward restructuring of the EBR's economy. However, questions persist concerning the quality and relevance of technical education in the EBR.

(iv) Lesser English language competence compared with Manila, Singapore, Hong Kong, and major Malaysian and Indian cities constrains developmental options. Although this may not seem like a serious disadvantage in terms of manufacturing, the next phase of off-shore investment will increasingly involve service industries, e.g., investment in call centers, off-shore data, and accounting centers, etc. (For example, routine accounting and transcribing of medical records for North American companies and professionals is now done in Manila.[52]) English is the working language of the international service sector, representing a real threat to the EBR.

How might challenges, such as those identified above, play out in the EBR over the next twenty years? One outcome may be that the peri-urban areas will become less important relative to the core, as high-level services continue to gain in importance while, at the same time, the proportion of FDI to Thailand continues to decline relative to emerging East Asian nations, particularly China. If energy prices significantly increase, centrifugal development forces within the extended urban region could slow. On the other hand, Thailand's peri-urban areas may develop synergistically in tandem with the companies located there, becoming real communities with high-value economies, similar, for example, to the Jurong industrial area of Singapore.

An optimistic future can be painted for core Bangkok, provided that decision makers in the private and public sectors focus on competitive niches such as tourism, health, media, design, cultural industries, international governance, producer services, etc. Enhancing competitiveness in these areas will require increased attention to language skills, amenity (quality of the environment), appropriate technical education, competitiveness assessment, image enhancement, promotion and marketing, etc.

Suburbia remains a big question mark. Brown field sites will need to be redeveloped – this will require public sector intervention. What is needed is a better match between the residential populations of suburban Bangkok and employment opportunities, perhaps "edge city" service activities, located in suburban satellite business centers, both to reinvigorate these areas and to reduce wasteful (of energy and time) commuting.

[52] Credit card companies are using Indian and Philippine locations to staff call centers to handle consumer inquiries and follow up on delinquent accounts; Manila is a major center for transcribing records of American physicians.

Conclusion

Bangkok has experienced two very severe recessions since the early 1980s, and very rapid economic growth in the intervening period. During the study period, except 1999–2002, it has never experienced moderate economic growth, say, 2–5% per year. The recent economic history of the EBR over the last two decades means that governments in the region have almost constantly been off balance. Yet, co-adaptation by millions of actors that constitute the region has resulted in a resiliency that has enabled the EBR to outperform many of its international competitors. This adaptation has taken a variety of forms, e.g., peri-urban workers commuting long distances daily to access better social services in established communities, corporations limiting layoffs during recessions, families doubling up in housing units during tough times.

If the past is any indication, the EBR will continue to enjoy strength in terms of resiliency and adaptability, based in its people, households, and workplaces. Adaptability and adjustment are likely to become even more important traits in urban East Asia as globalization creates opportunities, but also tears down the "fire walls", such as national tariff barriers and constraints on flows of capital, that "protected" urban systems, such as Bangkok, in the past. The result is likely to be both more opportunities and more threats. Urban regions that can anticipate, cope with, and quickly recover from shocks, the unexpected, and unanticipated reversals are likely to be the most successful, and the best places to live.

REFERENCES

Archer, R. 1996. *Network Infrastructure for Sustainable Development: Implementing the Formula L + P + F + NI = SUD*. Human Settlements Development Program Working Paper 53. Bangkok: Asian Institute of Technology.

Askew, M. 1994a. *Interpreting Bangkok: The Urban Question in Thai Studies*. Bangkok: Chulalongkhorn University.

1994b. "Transformation of the Thai City," in M. Askew and W. S. Logan (eds.), *Cultural Identity and Urban Change in Southeast Asia: Interpretative Essays*. Victoria: Deaking University Press.

BMA 2001. *Bangkok Metropolitan Administration*. Bangkok: Thammasat University Press.

BMA (Office of Policy and Planning) 2002. *Statistical Profile of BMA*. Bangkok: BMA. Note: statistical profiles of BMA for 2001, 2000, 1999, 1998, 1995, 1994 also consulted.

Connell, J. 1999. "Beyond Manila: Walls, Malls, and Private Spaces," *Environment and Planning A*, 31: 417–439.

Crispin, S. W. 2001. "Breathtaking Results in Bangkok," *Far Eastern Economic Review*, 25 October: 44–46.

Dick, H. W. and Rimmer, P. J. 1998. "Beyond the Third World City," *Urban Studies*, 35 (12): 2303–2321.

Dowall, D. 1992. "A Second Look at the Bangkok Land and Housing Market," *Urban Studies*, 29 (1): 25–38.

Eckardt, J. 1999. "The Good, the Bad, and the Ugly: The Architects," in J. Eckardt (ed.), *Bangkok People*. Bangkok: Asia Books.

Economist Intelligence Unit 1999. *City Costs of Living 1999*. London: Economist Intelligence Unit.

Kaothien, U. and Webster, D. 1995. "Thai City Regions: The Stage for Thailand's Involvement in the New Global Economy," in *Cities and the New Global Economy*. Canberra: OECD and Australian Government.

1998. *Globalization and Urbanization: The Case of Thailand*, Input Paper to World Development Report 2000. Washington, DC: World Bank.

2000a. "The Bangkok Region," in R. Simmonds and G. Hack (eds.), *Global City Regions*. London: Routledge.

2000b. "Globalization and Urbanization: The Case of Thailand," in S. Yusuf, W. Wu, and S. Everett (eds.), *Local Dynamics in an Era of Globalization*. Oxford: Oxford University Press.

Kearney, A. T. 2000. "Where Japanese Firms Prefer to Invest," *Far Eastern Economic Review*, 17 February.

Krugman, P. 1999. *The Return of Depression Economics*. New York: Norton.

Leaf, M. 1996. "Building the Road for the BMW: Culture, Vision, and the Extended Metropolitan Region of Jakarta," *Environment and Planning A*, 28: 1617–1635.

McLane, D. 2000. "A Road Less Travelled Leads through Laos." *International Herald Tribune*, 11 February.

Muller, L. 2000. *Automobiles from Pineapple Fields: Adaptation to Rapid Industrialization in Peri-Urban Thailand and the Philippines*. Paper presented at the 42nd Conference of the Association of Collegiate Schools of Planning, Atlanta, USA, 2–5 November.

2002. *Advanced Business services in Southeast Asia: An Opportunity for Localizing Investment*. Working Paper on Services, Space, Society. Birmingham: Service Sector Research Unit, University of Birmingham.

NESDB, *GRDP Accounts*. Bangkok: Government of Thailand.

NESDB/Norconsult 1997. *A Spatial Development Framework for Thailand*. Bangkok: NESDB.

OECF 1997. "Supporting Urban Infrastructure in Developing Countries," *OECF Annual Report 1997*. Tokyo: OECF.

Phongpaichit, P. and Baker, C. 1995. *Thailand: Economy and Politics*. Oxford: Oxford University Press.

Ruland, J. and Ladavalya, B. 1996. "Managing Metropolitan Bangkok: Power Contest or Public Service," in J. Ruland (ed.), *The Dynamics of Metropolitan Management in Southeast Asia*, Singapore: ISEAS.

Sieu, C. T. 1999. "Asia's Best Cities," *Asia Week*, 17 December, pp. 44–46.

Smithies, M. 1986. *Old Bangkok*, New York and Singapore: Oxford University Press.

Thailand Development Research Institute 1999. *Social Impacts of the Asian Economic Crisis in Thailand, Indonesia, Melaysia, and the Philippines*. Bangkok: Thailand Development Research Institute.

United Nations Centre for Trade and Investment 2000. *UNCTAD World Investment 1999*. Geneva: United Nations.

Webster, D. 2000. *Financing City Building: The Bangkok Case*. Urban Dynamics of East Asia Series, Asia/Pacific Research Center. Stanford: Stanford University.

2002. *On the Edge: Shaping the Future of Peri-Urban Asia*. Urban Dynamics of East Asia Series, Asia/Pacific Research Center. Stanford: Stanford University.

2003. *Urbanization Dynamics and Policy Frameworks in Developing East Asia*. Washington: World Bank (Best Practice Dissemination Paper).

World Bank 2000a. *Thailand Country Dialogue Monitor*. Bangkok: World Bank.

2000b. *Thailand Economic Monitor 2000*. Bangkok: World Bank.

2001. *Thailand Economic Monitor 2001*. Bangkok: World Bank.

4 Cairo: too many people, not enough land, too few resources

Janet L. Abu-Lughod

It is ironic that many of the mega-cities in the non-Western world today, now noted chiefly for their high rates of poverty and their intractable problems of inadequate infrastructure and ineffectual administration, were once counted among the world's outstandingly prosperous and highly cultivated centers of civilization.

As late as the thirteenth century AD, a time I have referred to as "before European hegemony" (Abu-Lughod 1989), half of the dozen largest cities in the world were located in the Far East, three were in North Africa (including Cairo, which was then the third largest city in the world), two were in Andalusia (Muslim-ruled Spain), and one, Constantinople (which ranked just below Cairo in size), lay at the bridge between the Christian and Muslim worlds (Chandler and Fox 1974).[1]

By 1500 little had changed. Of the top twelve cities, eight were located in the Far East and three were in the Muslim Middle East (including Cairo, still at third rank, and the newly conquered Constantinople, renamed Istanbul by the Ottomans, ranking ninth). At that time Paris was the only European city to appear on the list.

By 1700, however, Istanbul, which served as the imperial center for an extensive Ottoman Empire, may have become the most populous city in the world with some 700,000 inhabitants, followed by seven cities in Asia and two others (Isfahan and Cairo) in the Middle East. But by then, London and Paris, each with more than half a million residents, had joined the list as the fourth and fifth largest cities of the world.

One hundred years later, however, the balance between East and West was already beginning to change. In 1800, although Beijing was the largest city in the world with over a million inhabitants and seven other cities in the top dozen were also located in Asia, London, by then the second ranking city, had begun to catch up with close to 900,000. Istanbul, the only Muslim city left on the list, ranked fourth, and Paris fifth, each with

[1] These figures appear in a table entitled "Top 12 Cities, with Suburbs": Chandler and Fox 1974, p. 367.

well over half a million inhabitants. But Cairo was no longer included among the dozen largest cities in the world.

Although one can certainly question these estimates of city size for early centuries, the preponderance of evidence suggests that it was not until 1850, or even more clearly by 1900,[2] that "Western" cities began to dominate the list of the world's largest cities. In 1850, six of the dozen largest cities were still located in Asia, while the rest were to be found in "the West." But by 1900, Tokyo (Edo) was the only non-European city that remained on the top twelve list. These changes were clearly linked to larger forces of relative power and prosperity.

The demotion (creation) of the Third World

The story of how "the West rose"[3] is too familiar to be recounted here. The usual explanation put forth from a eurocentric view is that it was the peculiar genius of Western society – manifested in technological (the industrial revolution), institutional (modern capitalism), and sociopolitical (democracy) inventiveness – that propelled "the West" to the forefront of the modern world system, leaving "the Rest" in the dust. Told from a Third World perspective, however, it was the capacity (and/or rapacity) of certain Western European states to impose their dominion over large portions of, at first, the new world (North and South America) and then large portions of the old (Africa, the Middle East, and, to a lesser extent, Asia) that reversed the positions of the first and third worlds.[4]

Whatever its actual causation, Egypt and its capital city of Cairo, among other important entrepôts in formerly thriving zones, had declined precipitously by the eighteenth century. When Napoleon invaded Egypt in 1798, his savants placed the total population of the country at under 3 million and the population of Cairo at only 200,000. Both had declined from the 9 million and half a million, respectively, that they exhibited in the thirteenth century when Egypt commanded an extensive empire and was strategically positioned at the core of a wide trading circuit (Abu-Lughod 1971, 1989).

Therefore, long before the imposition of British colonial rule in 1881–1882, Egypt and Cairo had already lost their preeminence. The country had been weakened by the high mortalities it sustained in the so-called Black Death that began in the middle of the fourteenth century. These

[2] The rapid urbanization that occurred in Western Europe over the course of the nineteenth century is well documented in Weber 1967.

[3] The phrase derives from William McNeill's classic work, *The Rise of the West* (1963), although in recent years McNeill (1991) has modified his earlier position.

[4] See the radical critiques of conventional western history by James Blaut (1993, 2000).

high mortalities also facilitated the conquest of Constantinople by the Ottoman Turks in 1453 and, eventually, of Cairo in 1516. The Ottomans relocated many of Cairo's talented artisans and professionals to their capital and deflected trade and other economic/administrative functions to Istanbul. These reorganizations precipitated a further depopulation of Egypt.

Egypt's recovery began early in the nineteenth century, especially after her reentry into the world system through the introduction, under the semi-autonomous ruler Muhammad Ali, of long-staple cotton which would feed the textile mills of England and then, during the Civil War, the US. Modernizing efforts by his successors gradually wrested greater autonomy from the Ottomans and brought greater prosperity. Between 1800 and 1900, Egypt's population tripled, reaching 10 million by the end of the century. Cairo's population increased at a similar rate, reaching some 600,000 at the opening of the twentieth century.

But the nineteenth-century modernizing efforts of Muhammad Ali and his successors led to dependency. Egypt reentered the world system but on very different terms. No longer an imperial center of control, as it had been in medieval times, over the course of the nineteenth century the country gradually came under the control of Western powers, in part because of debts to European bankers incurred to fund development projects. The most important of these projects was the Suez Canal, opened with great ceremony in 1869. It had been constructed according to French engineering designs but with borrowed foreign capital and forced Egyptian labor. The Canal enhanced Egypt's strategic location, especially for England because it served as an indispensable link between the "mother country" and her Asian/Indian colonies. France and England used the pretext of Egypt's foreign debts to their bankers to declare the country bankrupt and by the 1870s had imposed a joint commission to supervise income and expenditures.

At that time the British government took advantage of the insolvency to "buy" Egypt's shares in the Canal at a bargain price, making the zone adjacent to the Canal an extraterritorial concession, which it remained long after Egypt had regained her formal independence in 1923.[5] Finally, Great Britain invaded the country in 1881 and, with the sufferance of the French (who in return were offered a "free hand" over other North African countries), reduced it to a semi-colony under a compliant monarch.

The history of the first half of the twentieth century was a struggle for increased Egyptian self-rule, gradually wrested from Great Britain. Three

[5] The fuller story is told in Abu-Lughod 1971.

critical moments in this struggle can be singled out: the establishment of Egypt's hollow independence in the 1920s under a figurehead king; the revolution by the Free Officers in 1952 which deposed the monarchy and established a republic; and the nationalization of the Suez Canal in 1956 which, despite a concerted attack by the combined forces of England, France, and Israel, led eventually to a negotiated withdrawal of all foreign troops.

Autonomy was not the only goal of the post-1952 government, however. Political and economic development were equally emphasized. President Gamal Abdul Nasser had been one of the important organizers of the Bandung Conference of 1955, which officially declared the unity of purpose of formerly colonized or subordinate countries – a unity captured in the term "the Third World."[6] Land reforms that redistributed the excessive holdings of a feudal class to the peasants who worked them and a socialist plan of state-led industrialization, along the import-substitution model so favored by the non-aligned states in those years, were all instituted by the new government. One unintended consequence of development, however, was a population explosion that impacted with particular vigor on the city of Cairo, the undisputed center of power and thus also a magnet for migrants.

Whatever progress in economic growth had been achieved by 1967, however, was abruptly aborted by an Israeli invasion during which Egypt lost control over her Sinai Peninsula and the Suez Canal zone. Nasser died in 1970 a broken man. In 1973, under his hand-picked successor, Anwar Sadat, Egyptian forces successfully crossed the Canal to dislodge the Israeli occupying forces along it but failed in their ultimate goal to reconquer all the lost territories (Israeli forces remained on Sinai until 1978.) However, the Canal was reopened for passage and Egypt once again received income from transit fees. But so long a closing of the Canal had encouraged a reorganization of world shipping routes and, by the time the Canal was reopened, traffic was lighter and tolls less lucrative, due to the introduction of supertankers.

Strengthened in office by his military success and reading the Cold War international balance of power differently, President Sadat soon afterward placed all of his hopes in the US and began to reverse the policies of nationalization and state-sponsored industrialization. He inaugurated a new policy of "opening" (*infitah*) the Egyptian economy to foreign investments. The so-called "open door" policy initiated in 1974[7] (that

[6] The original term was "non-aligned nations," only later changed to "Third World."

[7] For details on the various early legal changes from 1974 onward that constitute the "opening" of the Egyptian economy to privatization and foreign investments, see Yousry *et al.* 1998, pp. 272–275.

would eventually introduce relatively unregulated capitalist investments, foreign-guided production in joint ventures, tax-free export industrial zones along the Canal, and growing dependence upon remittances and tourism) has resulted in the greater income inequalities that often accompany such policies in semi-peripheral Third World countries.

During the final quarter of the twentieth century, all pretenses at political neutrality and economic autarchy were abandoned. A "cold peace" was concluded with Israel in 1978 under the auspices of the United States, in return for regaining lost territory and substantial American economic assistance. In addition, other means for generating foreign exchange were sought, primarily in the tourism sector but later in exploiting Egypt's modest petroleum resources. Furthermore, high demand for labor attracted Egyptians to the wealthier oil states; their remittances added to the foreign reserves.

These new policies were gradually reflected in the capital city. Long-neglected quarters of downtown Cairo were spruced up to attract wealthier consumers, as were some formerly middle-class residential zones. The Ministry of Tourism oversaw the construction of first-class hotels on prime real estate along the Nile, indicating how important for foreign exchange this industry had become, not only at the Pharaonic sites in Upper Egypt but in Cairo and two "resort" developments along the Mediterranean coast and the Red Sea. Clearly, these developments have provided much-needed employment, even though tourism can sometimes be a fragile base that fluctuates with external events.

The downside of these developments, however, has been the neglect and the deterioration of Cairo districts occupied by the poor, especially those zones unconnected to either tourism or the new industrialization. In those areas, street paving has gradually disappeared due to lack of maintenance, only modest attempts have been made to repair or extend water and sewer lines, and densely occupied older housing has begun to crumble. While land along the eastern bank of the Nile has been cleared of "unsightly" lower-income uses and replaced by showy office complexes, hotels, a World Trade Center, a new central library, etc., this new façade conceals the poorer zones of Bulaq and Rod Al-Farag that have slipped backward. The physical contrasts between wealthy and poor districts in the city have grown increasingly stark – rivaling the "dual city" of colonial and "native" quarters that made its appearance in the closing years of the nineteenth century (Abu-Lughod 1965).

I have stressed this historical development because, all too often, analysts attribute poverty in non-Western cities only to internal factors, such as deficient entrepreneurial and management skills and overpopulation. It is important, therefore, to bear in mind that poverty is relative and that a significant component of it is caused not by internal social dynamics but by larger military and economic forces in the world. Policies to ameliorate urban problems in poor countries tend to focus exclusively on "local" solutions, while ignoring their interaction with larger forces generating inequalities – both between nations and within countries and their cities. We return to this theme at the end of this chapter.

The following sections examine the state of Cairo today, show how population clearly outstripped land in the twentieth century, and describe planning processes and policies that have sought to alleviate the pressing problems of the city. We end with the issues of external debt and the influence of the International Monetary Fund (IMF) and the World Bank on national policies. To foreshadow our conclusions, it is the interaction between the local and the global that is yielding increased inequality in the city.

Cairo's population growth

The Greater Cairo Metropolitan Region[8] is currently estimated to house some 14–16 million residents or between one fifth to one fourth of the total population of the country.[9] In the past, Egypt boasted two "primate" cities: Alexandria on the Mediterranean coast and Cairo upstream on the Nile. However, over the past few decades, the proportion of Egypt's population living in the "second city" of Alexandria has fallen considerably behind. Its rate of growth has failed to keep pace with that of the capital city, thus increasing Cairo's primacy.[10]

A generation ago, analysts would have diagnosed Egypt's situation as one of "overurbanization" or "excessive primacy." However, these terms subsequently dropped out of the vocabulary, not only because they proved highly contingent measures (dependent upon the size of the country and its geographic constraints, inter alia) but also because the world has become more accustomed to mega-cities. Statisticians have increasingly acknowledged the failure of legal boundaries to contain the evolving urban forms generated by massive conurbations. Less and less do total populations within official boundaries (even when those are expanded to

[8] This includes large contiguous areas within the Giza Governorate on the west bank of the Nile as well as the entire population of Cairo Governorate, as far south as Helwan and as far north as Qanatar. Increasingly, the metropolitan area extends northward into the lower part of the Qalyubiya Governorate, planting urban industrial and residential uses on formerly productive agricultural land of the Delta.

[9] Some sources claim only one fifth. Much depends upon how the boundaries of the metropolitan region are drawn.

[10] Most recently, elaborate plans to revive Alexandria have been put forth, and significant vacation colonies are being constructed along the Mediterranean coast west of the city.

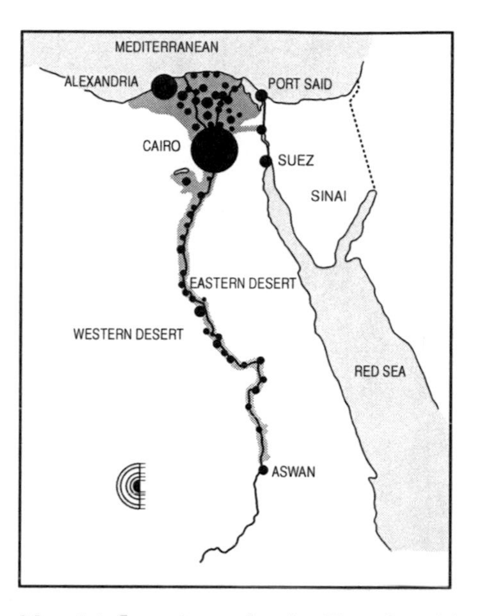

Map 4.1 Locations of major Egyptian cities

metropolitan regions) capture either the true demographic "realities" of a country or predict the kinds of urban problems that will be encountered in any given mega-city.

Egypt is a particularly apt case in point. Land shortages and geographic constraints, arising from the peculiar desert character of its terrain where almost all of the population has always had to live on a tiny fraction of the land dependent upon Nile water, have always meant that densities in the settled areas have run high. Old estimates were that only between 3 to 5% of the total land area of Egypt was inhabitable, and this has not increased very much although, as we shall see, there has been some building out on to desert fringes and a generation-old scheme to create a parallel "valley" in the western desert is once again being attempted.

Given this shortage of land on which to expand, it was inevitable that densities in both rural and urban areas of the country would increase, once death rates began to drop, at first slowly in the early part of the twentieth century and then precipitously after mid-century. Prior to the beginning of the so-called demographic transition, Egypt's crude birth rate had been high and relatively stable at about forty-three births per thousand; the moderate increase in the total population was due almost exclusively to the gradual decline of the crude death rate. Furthermore, the demographic system was a relatively closed one, since Egyptians were

Table 4.1 *Total and urban population of Egypt, 1900–2000 (millions)*

Year	Egypt	Urban	% urban
1900	10	1	10
1920	13	3	23
1940	16	5	31
1960	26	10	38
1980	42	18	43
2000	65	32	49

Note: I have left these figures very rough because of variations in the dates and reliability of various censuses.

notorious for remaining at home. Unlike the earlier European case, emigration did not siphon off "excessive" growth during the early stages of the transition.

But once the death rate began to decline sharply in the 1950s and 1960s, as it did elsewhere in the Third World, total population increased dramatically – doubling in just thirty years between 1950 and 1980. Here indeed was the "nightmare" Malthus had predicted, but in even more extreme form. Not only was the population increasing "geometrically," but given the desert constraints that pressed sharply along the borders of arable land, it was not even possible for land to expand "arithmetically." There was, in short, little alternative to rapid urbanization. By now, half of Egypt's population lives in cities and almost half of that urban population lives in the Greater Cairo Region (Table 4.1).

But this chapter will not be the usual one of hand wringing. There is much to be optimistic about the future of the man/land ratio of urban Egypt, even though, as we shall conclude, this optimism is tempered by a concern that the country's uneven "dependent" economic development and the increasingly unequal distribution of its income and its wealth will generate the persistence of the same types of urban problems for which, in the past, general poverty and overcrowding were responsible.

Two reasons for optimism

Intrinsic population growth has slowed The crude death rate in Egypt began to decline in the aftermath of the Second World War. This drop was particularly evident among infants and children but also more generally, as the population was better protected from malaria and other

Table 4.2 *Fertility and mortality, Cairo, 1965–1985, with a projection to 2000*

	Fertility		Mortality	
Period	Crude birth rate	Total fertility rate[a]	Crude death rate	Infant mortality rate
1960–1965	43.1	5.72	16.9	160.9
1965–1970	37.1	4.81	14.2	152.3
1970–1975	34.6	4.33	12.8	137.6
1975–1980	35.6	4.15	10.4	102.8
1980–1985	32.5	3.79	8.8	76.8
Projections:				
1985–1990	28.1	3.37	7.3	57.6
1990–1995	23.7	3.02	6.6	43.2
1995–2000	20.9	2.68	6.2	32.4
2000	20.3	2.53	6.0	28.4

[a] The total fertility rate is the most sensitive way to measure real change. It is defined as the "sum of children that women of different ages are bearing currently, summing across women of all child-bearing ages" (Shorter 1989, p. 12).
Source: Shorter 1989, p. 11.

infections by the availability of DDT and antibiotics. The positive effect was a significant rise in the life expectancy at birth.

The crude birth rate remained high, however, which caused a period of explosive population increase. Between 1947 and 1966, the total population of Egypt increased from under 19 million to almost 30 million. And during that period, population pressure was not yet relieved by significant emigration, nor were densities held in check by any appreciable expansion of habitable land. From the late 1960s on, however, the government abandoned its pro-natalist position and instituted measures for encouraging more widespread use of birth control. The total fertility rate (per woman in the childbearing ages) began to drop. However, given a continuing decline in death rates and the youthful age structure of the country, the total population continued to increase at about 2.5% per year.

Nowhere were birth control measures more effective than in the major cities, although continuing net in-migration from the countryside continued to fuel high urban growth rates. In just the past generation, the crude birth rate in Cairo dropped precipitously – from about forty-three births per thousand at the beginning of the 1960s to thirty per thousand in 1986 and was projected to approach twenty per thousand by the year 2000 (Shorter 1989) (see Table 4.2). These trends are gradually spreading to other parts of the country. Thus, the "demographic transition" should soon be virtually completed, as the gap between births and deaths grows smaller and the population begins to age.

Changing patterns of migration For several decades during the past half century, the population growth rate for the Greater Cairo Region ran considerably above that for the country as a whole, fueled by a massive movement of population to it from overcrowded farms and villages in the Delta and Upper Egypt.[11] Such internal migration from the countryside to urban areas was perhaps inevitable, given the preexisting rural overcrowding, the tiny size of most agricultural plots, and technological trends toward less labor-intensive farming and agribusiness. Furthermore, the fabled fertility of the Delta land had also begun to decline, due to the elevation of the high dam at Aswan which reduced the deposit of fresh silt, and the shift in housing construction from degradable sun-baked mud brick to fired bricks made from topsoil.[12] This internal migration from rural to urban areas more than compensated for Cairo's lowered rate of natural increase.

Most recently, however, the pace of rural to Cairo migration has slackened. Many existing villages have now grown to urban stature and medium-sized cities are among the fastest growing in the country, as road improvements and the proliferation of public services, such as hospitals, schools, and universities, have enhanced their attraction as less expensive alternatives to a move to Cairo. The good news, then, is that other cities of Egypt have begun to absorb an enlarged share of rural–to–urban migrants, thus deflecting some of the pressures that otherwise would have concentrated on the capital.[13]

Consequently, the proportion of Cairo's population born outside the Greater Cairo Region has declined – from its high of 36% in 1937 to only 18% by 1986 (General Organization for Physical Planning 2000, p. 24).[14]

[11] See Abu-Lughod 1961, which chronicles the ruralization of Cairo under the impact of rural to urban migration.

[12] This transformation seems to have begun in earnest as money from the Gulf workers flowed in and was invested in new housing and a preference for second stories that mud brick could not support. The practice of using topsoil for fired brick was quickly outlawed by the government!

[13] Not only have the three cities along the Suez Canal (Port Said, Ismailiya, and Suez) recovered from their evacuations during the war, but industrialization, encouraged by the establishment of free export zones, has fueled their attractiveness. According to maps in the *2000 Greater Cairo Atlas* (General Organization for Physical Planning 2000), the fastest-growing towns and cities are in the Delta and along the Canal Zone.

[14] These figures may be deceptive. To some extent, as the urbanized region has expanded to incorporate peripheral rural zones, persons born in the latter zones who earlier might have been classified as migrants if they crossed the city limits are now classified as non-migrants.

Furthermore, as one might expect from the heightened urbanization of the country, these migrants have been drawn increasingly from urban rather than rural areas.

In addition, ever since the boom in labor demand in the Gulf oil states in the 1970s and 1980s, a certain "shaking loose" of land-attached Egyptians has been occurring, directing them abroad. Many men became "guest workers," leaving their wives and children behind (one factor that may have inhibited birth rates). Some of these guest workers undoubtedly returned during the Gulf war of 1991, but they have not necessarily headed for Cairo. Increasingly, more permanent relocations have occurred, especially as the internal economy involuted or improved opportunities targeted only special subgroups.

Fertility declines, emigration, and the deflection of urban growth to alternative outlets have, however, waved no magic wands. They have not offered a simple panacea for the capital city's problems. Only faster and more even rates of economic development and better controls over the environment can hope to accomplish this.

Land shortages and Cairo's new pattern of spatial extension

The result of these demographic trends has been a gentler slope of population increase in Cairo over the most recent decades. Portions of the city within the Governorate of Cairo itself are no longer growing at explosive levels, and some centrally located older zones are actually losing residents. Nevertheless, the urbanized peripheral areas of the Greater Cairo Region have continued to expand, despite job and housing shortages, feeble attempts by the government to limit geographic spread and to control and channel its outlets, and the many hardships experienced by poorer Cairenes in the sheer mechanics of finding and/or making shelters for themselves, moving about, obtaining water, and disposing of wastes.

Expanding to the Greater Cairo Region

Cairo, like almost every other city, has grown physically by spreading into its environs. Even before the mid-1960s it was evident that the urbanized area was extending well beyond the limits of the Cairo Governorate,[15] whose legal jurisdiction covered only the eastern bank of the Nile, the

[15] The country of Egypt is divided into twenty-six provinces or states, each with its own governor. Four of these are urban provinces, of which Cairo is the largest.

two inhabited islands in the middle of the river, and the long southern "tail" of fertile land hugging the eastern Nile shore all the way to Helwan (where a new steel mill and associated industries were newly located). The town of Giza on the western bank (administratively part of the separate Governorate of Giza) was already absorbing a significant overflow, and developments, planned and unplanned, were spreading into the rural fringes of that town. North of the city urbanization was reaching deep into the fertile Delta, encroaching on the southern portion of the adjacent Governorate of Qalyubiya. This zone, called Shubra al-Khayma, which in 1976 still housed only a small fraction of the metropolitan region's population, continues to urbanize at a rapid clip and is now the fastest growing section of the Greater Cairo Region, in part because its development did not face the elsewhere intractable problem of a water supply. (For locations of expansion and relative growth rates of the three administrative components of this region, see Maps 4.1 and 4.3 and Tables 4.3, 4.4 and 4.5.)

The need to coordinate planning for the contiguous urbanizing zones that now reach into three Governorates led in 1965 to the delineation of a generously bounded Greater Cairo Region and to the appointment of special planning agencies – at first a high executive committee and then "The General Organization for Physical Planning of the Greater Cairo Region," (1997, p. 1), charged in 1973 with responsibility for drawing up long-range plans for the region.

The goals of successive plans have been to improve mass transit and circulation throughout the metropolitan region, to encourage construction out on to the desert fringes rather than remove any more fertile agricultural land from farming, and to gain some small measure of control over the "informal"[16] settlements that some suggest now number over a hundred (Bayat 1997).

To improve transportation, a new subway system was designed, flyovers were cut through populous quarters, and bypass highways were built. (More are under construction, as well as new bridges and tunnels.) To encourage formal settlements in the desert, satellite cities were designed, anticipating that these would be relatively self-sufficient mixes

[16] I use the term "informal" in a rather specific way. It is housing constructed without a building permit, whether on land owned by the government, purchased from private owners, or located in districts (mostly agricultural) in which the government, in order to preserve fertile land, has forbidden construction of urban dwellings. As such, the term denotes a wide range of actual types, everything from the stereotypical shack town (uncommon in Cairo) to well-laid-out five- to seven-story apartment buildings made of fired brick, a form that is springing up on the agricultural fringe.

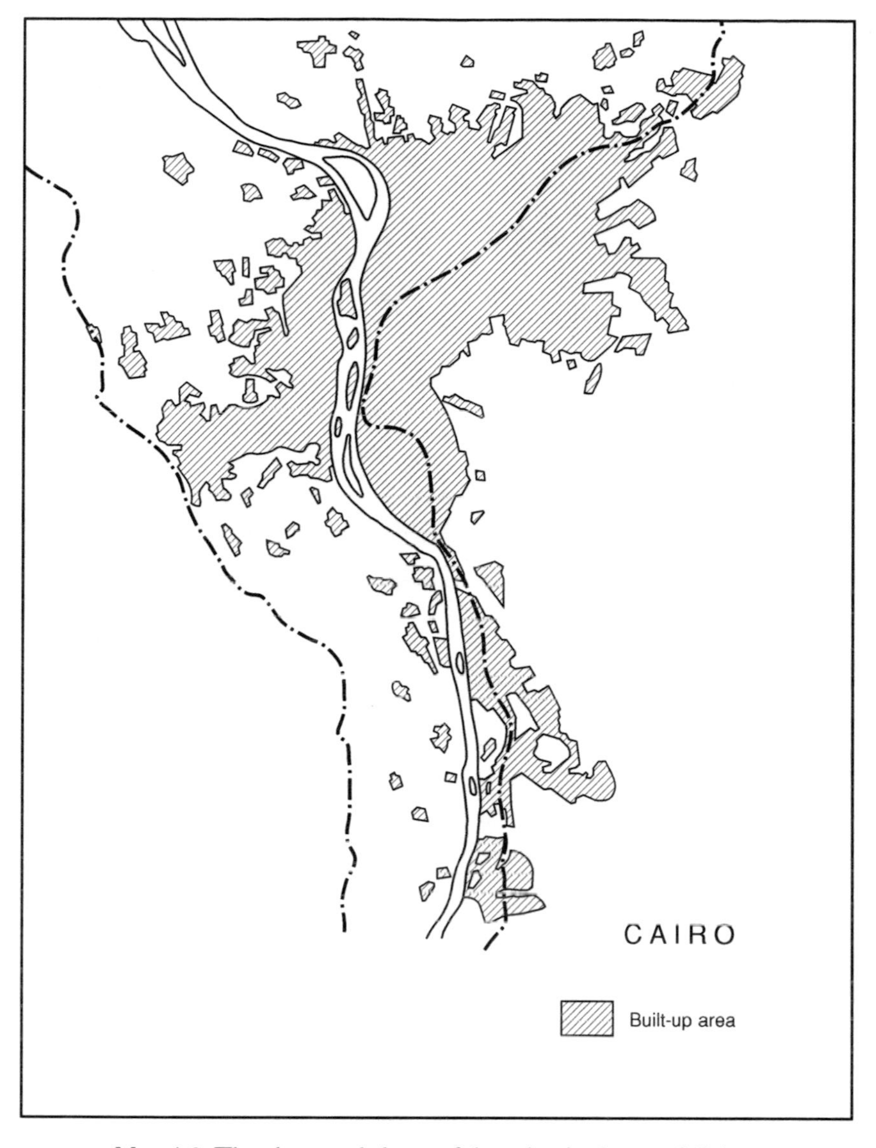

Map 4.2 The elongated shape of the urbanized area of Cairo
Source: General Organization for Physical Planning 1992.

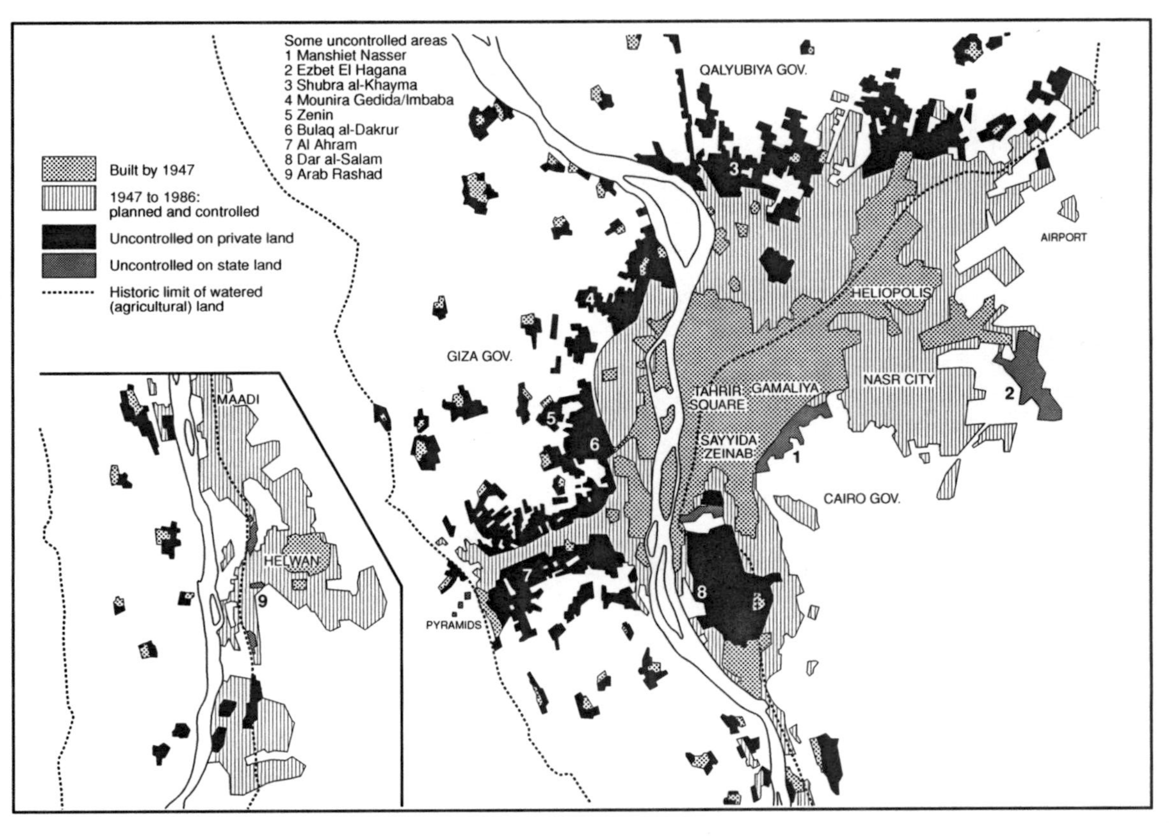

Map 4.3 The expansion of the built-up area of Cairo between 1947 and 1986
Source: Researched and drafted by David Sims. Personal copy provided by David Sims.

Table 4.3 *Population in the current agglomeration of the Greater Cairo Region by census years, 1947–1996, for the urban Governorate of Cairo and portions of Greater Cairo in the Governorates of Giza and Qalyubiya (thousands)*

Census year	Cairo proper	Giza portion	Qalyubiya portion	Greater Cairo Region[a]
1947	2,064	668	281	3,013
1960	3,358	1,118	434	4,910
1966	4,232	1,420	560	6,211
1976	5,074	2,137	879	8,090
1986	6,069	3,332	1,460	10,860
1996	6,789	4,273	2,081	13,144
2000 (est.)	7,012	4,720	2,398	14,130

[a] Do not add exactly due to rounding.
[b] The figures in this table end with the findings of the census of 1996. I have projected the components to the year 2000 by applying the average annual percentage increases which prevailed in each area between 1986 and 1996. The results indicate that the total of 16 million, widely circulated in literature and common conversation, is unlikely to have been reached.
Source: General Organization for Physical Planning 2000, table 4.2, p. 57.

Table 4.4 *Average annual intercensal growth rates for components in the current agglomeration of the Greater Cairo Region between census years, 1947–1996*

Period	Cairo proper	Giza portion	Qalyubiya portion	Greater Cairo Region
1947–1960	1.80	1.85	1.97	1.83
1960–1966	3.07	7.06	7.80	4.50
1976–1986	1.81	4.54	5.20	2.99
1986–1996	1.13	2.52	3.61	1.93

Source: General Organization for Physical Planning 2000, table 4.2, p. 57. The growth rates for the period 1966–1976 are omitted from the original source and I have not sought to compute them, although they appear to have been somewhere between the two periods that flank them.

Table 4.5 *Greater Cairo Region: changing relative weight of components, 1960–1996*

	% of Greater Cairo's population				
Urban unit	1960	1966	1976	1986	1996
In Cairo proper	68.4	68.1	62.3	55.9	51.7
In Giza Province	22.8	22.9	26.4	30.7	32.5
In Qalyubiya Province	8.8	9.0	10.9	13.4	15.8

Source: General Organization for Physical Planning 2000, Table 4.2, p. 57, my calculations.

of residences and work rather than commuter suburbs. To discourage the conversion of rich agricultural land to urban uses, laws were passed declaring such zones ineligible for construction. And finally, feeble attempts are belatedly being made to upgrade those informal settlements that could not be removed.

These four goals are not necessarily consistent and, indeed, often contradict each other. The first subway line intensified the longitudinal axis of Cairo and served primarily to connect higher-income areas to the south (Maadi) and to the northeast (Heliopolis) with the center. A second line similarly connected a high-income area (Muhandisin) on the west bank of the Nile with the north–south line on the east bank. While these lines offer choices for those with cars, they have done little to reduce the mounting automobile congestion, and thus far the poorer quarters have not been integrated into the network. Those without cars must still depend upon outdated, slow, and very crowded buses.

In a similar paradox, the bypass highways have not only diverted traffic and served the satellite towns (again, for those with cars) but have facilitated development of more informal settlements by both middle and lower classes along their routes. For example, the construction of the bypass route (Salah Salem) just east of the city proper led almost immediately to the development of informal settlements beyond it. The new parallel autostradt built just east of it is encouraging further informal settlements, even though these, such as Manshiet Nasser, are perched precariously on the sharp slopes of a dry limestone promontory (General Organization for Physical Planning n.d. but probably 1999). The new ring road designed to encircle much of the west bank and connect the city to the new town of 6th of October has encouraged commutation and the suburbanization of the middle and upper classes, often by making second homes available to them. This highway has also increased the accessibility of the still underdeveloped agricultural land on the west bank and has thus undermined the prohibition against building on it.[17]

New towns in the desert

As early as the Master Plan of 1969/1970, recommendations were made to transform the elongated shape of the city into a more circular pattern by building out into the desert. This was adopted as official policy after 1974. Such an approach had precedents. Early in the twentieth century, a Belgian entrepreneur had built a train line and extended water lines to a vast zone of desert land just northeast of the city, thus opening up for settlement the new (but contiguous) suburban town of Heliopolis (Ilbert 1981). During the post-revolution era, this feat was duplicated. By the early 1960s, Nasr City, an ambitious "new town," was being built on the intervening desert land just south of Heliopolis, and the construction of Muqattam City, a less successful venture on a high desert plateau overlooking the city, had begun. Across the river, albeit not in the desert but on sparsely settled agricultural land along and behind the northern Nile front, Medina Muhandisin (the "City of Engineers") was also being undertaken as part of a policy to build "new towns." (For details, see Abu-Lughod 1971.) None of these, however, were more than extensions of the built-up zones.

For many years Egyptian planners had also been advocating a more drastic solution to the space constraints: a series of satellite cities that would be far enough removed from the center to discourage their use as mere dormitory suburbs; that would contain factories and other employment opportunities; and that would, in addition to government-subsidized apartment complexes, provide large areas equipped with sites and services, so that poorer new residents could construct their own homes.

Shortly after the reopening of the Suez Canal in 1973, then-President Anwar Sadat announced the enactment of the "October Working Paper" calling for a drastic redistribution of Egyptian population according to a new plan for urbanization in the country. As described by Hegab (1985, p. 172), comprehensive plans were drawn up for Ramadan 10th City on the Cairo–Ismailia desert road, Sadat City on the Cairo–Alexandria desert

[17] Many of the so-called "squatter" settlements in the city, or, rather, illegal communities, consist of relatively tall apartment structures that, save for the fact that they have been built on agricultural land in defiance of this prohibition, appear little different from other more "legal" developments. In the 1980s, according to Hegab (1985, p. 172), some 1,500 acres of the most fertile fields located in the Greater Cairo region were being lost each year to urban construction.

road, 15th of May City on the southern Cairo–Helwan road, and the 6th of October City on the Cairo–Fayoum desert road. In addition, the plans were also implemented for Al-Obour on the northeastern Cairo–Bilbeiss road, Badr City on the Cairo–Suez road, and Al–Ammal City on the Cairo–Kattamiya–Ain Sukhna road.

The close-in satellite cities were designed to "round out" the formerly elongated shape of the city (compare Map 4.2 above with Map 4.4). These changes were intended to improve the circulation pattern, forestall further incursions on to fertile agricultural lands, and deflect population growth from overcrowded quarters of the city to cleaner, healthier, and better-serviced communities where new industrial development on a modern scale could provide jobs.

The other more distant self-contained towns along the highways between Cairo and other major population centers were intended to achieve an even more radical solution to the persisting problem of Cairo's primacy, by creating "growth poles" capable of totally reorganizing urban distribution in the country. The problem of course, as elsewhere, has been how to make the growth poles grow. Thus far, despite bargain land prices, tax incentives to industry, and provision of subsidized public utilities such as wide paved roads, water, and sewers, increases in population have fallen below expectations. For example, in February 2000, many apartments in Sadat City (between Cairo and Alexandria at the edge of the Delta) appeared to be unoccupied, despite the presence of scattered new factories.

In addition, the development of workers' housing in the more highly industrialized sections of the 6th of October has lagged behind, requiring some workers to commute long distances by infrequent buses, while the burgeoning "gated" subdivisions either remain vacant or contain elegant "second homes" that are occupied only intermittently. The wholesale produce market relocated from Cairo to Al-Obour is functioning, even though the residential population is mostly unconnected to it.

Clearly, the start-up of several new satellite projects has been fraught with difficulties. The meshing of job creation and local labor force skills, the provision of adequate public transportation access to the new towns, the premature and/or insufficient installation of sites and services, the lagging appearance of related commercial facilities, schools, and other municipal services, etc., have all proved challenging.

As of the year 2000, these problems had not been solved in time to accomplish the radical goals intended by the planners. However, their psychological success in redefining the desert as an attractive possibility for housing cannot be questioned. In recent years, upper- and

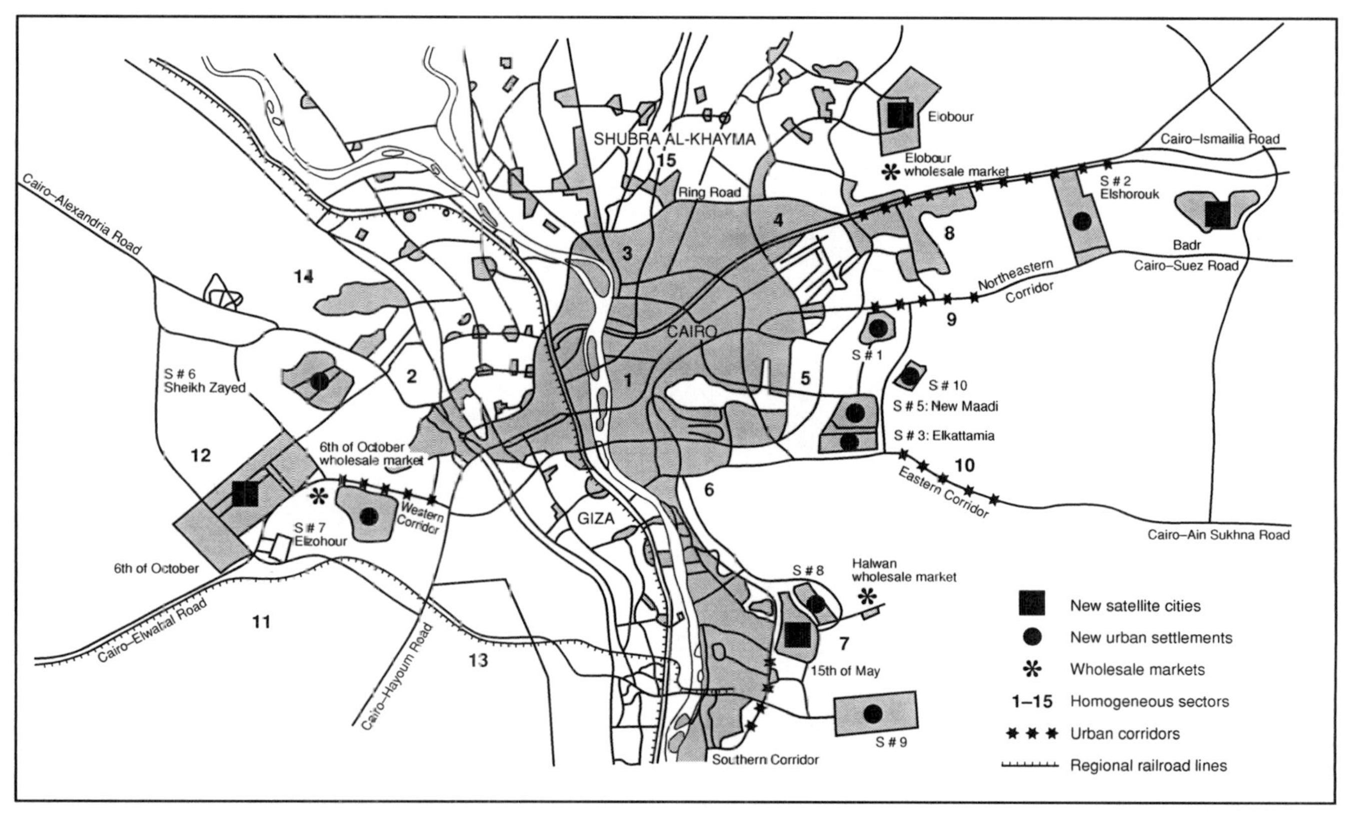

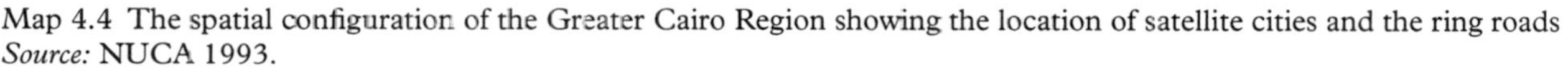

Map 4.4 The spatial configuration of the Greater Cairo Region showing the location of satellite cities and the ring roads
Source: NUCA 1993.

upper-middle-class Egyptians have begun to build walled compounds of houses and surrounding gardens (and even swimming pools) in the eastern desert zone beyond the airport. Although these remain scattered in isolated splendor, they indicate a new valuation of ex-urban desert space.

Unplanned expansions

Most expansions (and even satellite developments), however, have been unplanned – although they have probably been both forbidden and tolerated. The two ring roads around the already built-up portions of the urbanized region, intended to relieve traffic congestion at the center, have had the unintended – but not unexpected – consequence of "opening up" to housing developments the lands just outside their perimeters. A brief visit I made to the city in December 1998 revealed that portions of the "Khalifa City of the Dead," just inside the Salah Salem ring road, had been demolished to accommodate road widening. By then, orderly housing developments, complete with markets, shops, and other amenities, were already firmly entrenched east of the bypass route. These developments are part of the "informal" sector, although the city later assisted by installing utilities.

But the most "successful" of the expansions beyond the alluvial plain, at least in terms of accommodating a large number of Cairo's poor, was never part of the plan to conquer the desert. It is the "informal" settlement of Manshiet Nasser (one of the largest informal quarters in the city), which is reputed to house a population of between 450,000 and half a million persons. The evolution of this community over the past twenty years illustrates quite dramatically the thesis of Asef Bayat (1997, p. 2) who argues that

> The dearth of cooperative and contentious collective action on the part of the Egyptian urban poor by no means implies a lack of grassroots activism. Conditioned by political and cultural constraints, the poor instead resort to an alternative strategy – that of quiet encroachment. Qualitatively different from defensive measures or coping mechanisms, this strategy represents a silent, protracted, pervasive advancement of ordinary people – through open-ended and fleeting struggles without clear leadership, ideology or structured organization – on the propertied and powerful in order to survive.

More than two decades ago, migrants from Upper Egypt began to encroach illegally on government-owned land that climbed up the sharp slopes of the Muqattam desert limestone cliffs well east of the "old city," even though this area was not served by transportation or any urban utilities. By now, the structures are multistory, built of crude brick, and organized spatially on a rough plan of wide streets from which branch narrow alleys and even dead-ends. There are tiny shops and small industrial workshops, and an informal minibus system links the community(ies) to Cairo. The government itself contributed to further populating the zone, by building public housing projects and locating "emergency housing" there to accommodate families displaced by improvements elsewhere[18] or made homeless by the 1991 earthquake.

The 450,000 to 500,000 current residents of Manshiet Nasser can neither be removed nor more than a handful relocated to the small but elegant housing project, sponsored by Mrs. Mubarak, constructed on vacant flat land in the vicinity. The only available alternative is to accept the existence of this unplanned extrusion into non-agricultural land and try to upgrade conditions.

The first project designed to upgrade a portion of this vast area has been undertaken by the government (Governorate of Cairo 1998) in cooperation with a German non-governmental organization (NGO) which is providing financial and planning assistance. The goal is to regularize streets, to give existing residents legal title to their lots and buildings, and to install a sanitation system.[19] (Electrical service has already been extended.) But this upgrading project is only a drop in the bucket of need.

Bayat (1997, p. 3) claims that the estimated 6 million Cairenes who live in squatter settlements like Manshiet Nasser signify "only one, but perhaps the starkest, component of the growing socioeconomic disparity in Cairo since Sadat's *infitah* ('opening up' or economic liberalization) in 1974 and the more recent implementation of the IMF's structural adjustment program." We return to this issue at the end of this chapter.

Expanding alternatives to Cairo

In the last analysis, reducing pressures on the Cairo region can only be achieved by improving conditions in the communities from which migrants have been coming and/or deflecting some of the migrant streams to newer zones of attraction. The most promising growth pole lies along

[18] For example, the community engaged in garbage collection and recycling (the *Zaballin*) were relocated *en masse* from gentrifying Embaba along the shore of the Nile to a mountainous area east of medieval Cairo.

[19] I visited the site in February 2000 with David Sims, the chief planner of a portion of Manshiyet Nasser. We were accompanied by several planners/engineers who were designing the sewerage system that was to be installed there. The sight of men in bureaucratic dress (jackets!) walking the streets, carrying their maps, triggered high anxiety among all we passed.

the axis between Cairo and Alexandria. Middle-sized towns along this axis have grown faster than those off, aided especially by road improvements.

Two other areas have also served as new growth poles: those depending on the tourism sector, the others in free export industrial zones set up along the Canal. The former have been growing along the Mediterranean coast as tourist villages have spread westward from Alexandria. Along the Red Sea is a similar thrust to create new resort communities. Neither of these locations, however, has yet succeeded in attracting many permanent residents, since development has favored hotels for foreigner visitors or second homes for the new elite. Nor are they able to offer significant non-seasonal employment to service personnel.

The free export manufacturing zones are concentrated along the Suez Canal, both as part of efforts to rebuild cities that had been depopulated in the wake of the 1967 Israeli invasion and to harness the cheap labor of Egypt to the demands of the global market. Population in the governorates of the Canal Zone grew fastest between 1976 and 1986, but since that time increases have tapered off, suggesting that the success of these export zone platforms, if any, has already peaked.

Finally, there is the possibility of expanding the agricultural sector to desert regions of Egypt that were formerly devoid of habitation. Nasser's New Valley was perhaps a too-ambitious scheme to utilize an underwater course running parallel to the Nile and surfacing at several oases to open the western desert to agriculture. An abortive attempt was made in the 1960s, but the so-called Liberation Province never attracted as many farmers from the overcrowded Delta as had been hoped. More recently, plans exist to deflect water from Lake Nasser, the vast reservoir behind the High Dam at Aswan, to create additional space for irrigated agriculture. All of these projects require modern technology to conserve and recycle water and are therefore more suitable for specialty than subsistence crops. With the recapture of the Sinai, experiments have been initiated to grow high-value crops (strawberries, flowers) for export, utilizing the same advanced methods of plastic covers to recycle condensation that are also in evidence at other desert developments on the western edge of the Delta. They should contribute to foreign exchange but cannot be expected to support a large resident population.

Conserving the architectural heritage of "medieval" Cairo

Coping with the rapid growth of the Cairo region has been only part of the city's problems. A second pressing issue has been how to preserve the world's architectural heritage that is concentrated in the rectangular zone of the formerly walled city founded in AD 969. Within these few square miles just east of the modern downtown, together with their modest extensions south and north of the still-standing medieval gateways of Bab Nasr and Bab Zuwayla, are to be found the world's largest collection of historically significant Islamic mosques and monuments. Equally irreplaceable are the reminders of the medieval period still inscribed in typical street patterns and urban textures (Abu-Lughod 1978) (see Map 4.5). The dilemma is this: how shall competing interests in the zone be adjudicated and resolved? Must there be an inevitable zero-sum game in which the gains of one claimant destroy the lives and livelihoods of others?

The three major "interests" are (1) claims of the world to its cultural heritage (medieval Cairo has been declared a World Heritage site by UNESCO); (2) claims of the Egyptian state, with its legitimate interest in reaping maximum benefits from tourists attracted by the city's older bazaars; and (3) claims of current residents, many of them poor and living in "substandard" housing, who depend on jobs in the production and vending of handicraft items that appeal primarily to tourists.

Initially, the three claimants to the zone had little relationship to one another. Residents resisted (fairly ineffectually) the neglect of their living environment, due either to unrestrained clearance and replacement (for properties in private ownership) or to lack of funds for repair (for properties in religious trusts). Moisture spills from a deteriorated (leaking) water system, compounded by a rising water table, have weakened the structures, causing many buildings to collapse without warning. Upper stories crumbled and were not replaced. And some years ago an earthquake destroyed even more structures, causing residents to take temporary refuge in local mosques. The net effect of these "natural" changes has been a steady erosion of the number of residents in the area from a peak population that earlier approached half a million, to under 300,000 today (United Nations Development Program 1997).

But some of this decline in resident population has also been due to clearances arising out of real conflicts of interest. In order to widen the east–west thoroughfare (Sharia al-Azhar) that bisects the quarter, flanking shops and houses were demolished and a new tunnel connecting the modern downtown with the eastern ring roads has been constructed. In connection with the renovation of major mosques along the main north–south street (Mu'izz al-Din Allah), structures that were obstructing the approach views have also been removed. The major bazaar area of Khan al-Khalili has been "gentrified" and cleared of residual residents. In short, the tendency has been for all improvements to the

Map 4.5 The urban fabric of the medieval core
Source: Aga Khan Foundation 1984, p. 81. Reproduced by courtesy of the Aga Khan Foundation.

area, whether undertaken by the Egyptian government or the United Nations/UNESCO, to reduce the spaces available for informal production and low-cost housing.[20]

Fewer and fewer pockets of the traditional work-cum-residence neighborhoods, with their strong social and economic ties, remain. These are now to be found almost exclusively in the southern portions in Darb al-Ahmar, off the beaten paths, where a promising NGO project is working to preserve and reconstruct the area without displacing either the occupants or the small industrial workshops that offer them a livelihood. More projects of this type are sorely needed.

Poverty, inequality, and present policies

Measuring poverty and inequality

The bad news is that Egypt remains a poor country. Assaad and Rouchdy (1999; see also Korayem 1995/1996) have carefully reviewed the findings from a series of official sample studies of household consumption made in 1977, 1990/1991, and 1995/1996. Their disturbing conclusions are that the proportion of the population suffering from poverty and precarious status has changed little over time and remains high: "at least a quarter of Egyptians are poor by any standards and another quarter lives on the margins of poverty" (Assaad and Rouchdy 1999, p. 1).

Furthermore, there is considerable support for their view that the income gap between rich and poor Egyptians has grown greater in the last thirty years, especially in urban areas. Based on the evidence from these studies, Assaad and Rouchdy (1999, p. 14) conclude that

> the incidence of poverty has indeed increased in Egypt from the early 1980's to the mid 1990's. The rate of increase was greatest in the 1980's, but the increase continued into the 1990's, albeit at a slower rate, with the depth of poverty remaining roughly the same over this latter period. According to [one source], urban poverty appears to have increased more rapidly than rural poverty, although the rural poverty rate is still higher than the urban rate.

Their conclusions are confirmed in a new book by Saad Nagi (2001) which reported that income inequality continued to increase between the 1991 World Bank study and his new data collected in 1995. The increase was particularly marked in urban areas where the very rich's share of

[20] Not all changes have been to the detriment of residents and shopkeepers. The recent installation of new sewer lines along Mu'izz al-Din Street is certainly a welcomed improvement.

income rose significantly in the interim while that of the very poorest declined.

The gini coefficient is the conventional way to measure income inequality (expressed as a deviation from 0, which would imply absolute equality). The 1991 World Bank study (cited in Nagi 2001) computed a gini coefficient for Egypt of 32 whereas Nagi found inequality to have risen to 34 by 1995. The coefficient in urban areas (34.6) was higher than in rural areas (29.1).

Unfortunately, none of these studies reports a separate analysis for the Greater Cairo Region as a unit. However, the 1995/1996 gini coefficient for the Cairo Governorate, as reported in the Institute of National Planning, *Egypt: Human Development Report 1997/98*, stood at 33.7, which tends to confirm Nagi's results. If all portions of the Greater Cairo Region were included, I suspect the gini coefficient would be even higher, since the wealthy have gravitated to zones such as Dokki and Muhandisin on the west bank of the Nile, which fall within the Governorate of Giza and are therefore not included. (See Map 4.6 which shows that the most "degraded" sections of the Greater Cairo Region are located in the Cairo Governorate portion.)

Physical observations confirm these statistical findings. Cairo, despite its superficial new glitter and its rising number of *nouveaux riches*, remains the home of a very large number of poor persons (Bayat 1997 claims 50%). And even though absolute income figures suggest relatively less poverty in Cairo than in rural areas, the differences in their poverty rates are much reduced when one takes into consideration the higher cost of living in Cairo.

It is hard to escape the conclusion that the autarkic development and greater equality that were the aims and accomplishments of the early Nasser period of Arab socialism are now being reversed. One must ask why the concerted efforts at economic modernization under conditions of the *infitah* have not only failed to reduce the proportion of Egyptians and Cairenes living in poverty, but have actually contributed to greater inequality in the country and the city. The only reasonable interpretation is that the new policies are conferring substantial benefits on the few while ignoring the needs of the many. While the "floor" has undoubtedly risen, the ceiling has exploded once again, a situation quite comparable to what has been happening in the developed regions of the first world with deregulation and globalization.

But it would be mystical to consider "globalization" or "the world system" as *dei ex machinas* for producing these results. Nineteenth-century colonialism took place through real bankers and their political agents. At least for many parts of the residual Third World, including Egypt, today's

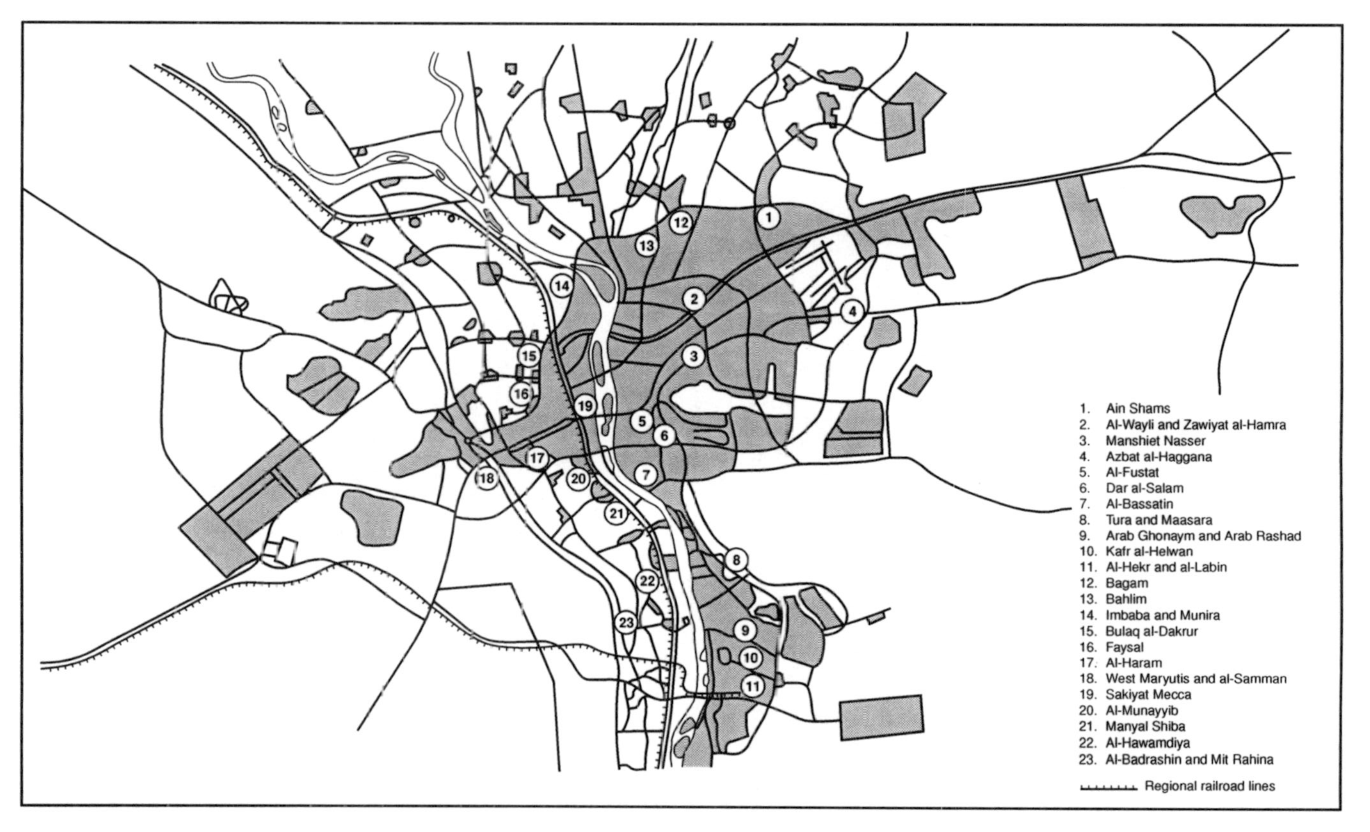

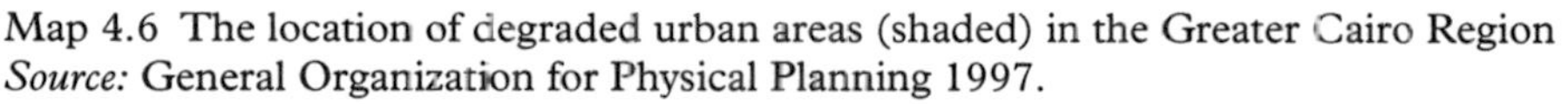

Map 4.6 The location of degraded urban areas (shaded) in the Greater Cairo Region
Source: General Organization for Physical Planning 1997.

agents, such as the World Bank and the IMF, similarly utilize loans, and the threat to call them in, as ways to influence national policies.[21] In the final section of this chapter we trace how structural adjustment and stabilization policies have combined with the open door policy to widen the gap between rich and poor in Egypt and between rich and poor areas of Cairo.

National and international factors contributing to inequality

Indebtedness, the growing influence of international lenders on national policies, and the not unrelated open door policy instituted from 1974 onward and periodically "liberalized" thereafter, have all been defended as means for modernizing Egypt and solving, inter alia, the pressing problems in Cairo. The question is whether Cairo's current position as a *dependent* world city may be contributing to heightened inequalities and adversely affecting the poor, rather than ameliorating their conditions. Yousry *et al.* (1998, p. 292) are unequivocal in concluding that "the implementation of the open-door policy within a Western economic dependency framework has led to large inequalities in the socio-economic structure of Egyptian society. It has also led to the emergence of parasite classes who benefited from the new economic dependency by linking their interests to the West."

Certainly, some of the recent unrest in Cairo – not only the "bread riots" that ensued after the World Bank first initiated its restructuring policies, but the rising support for Islamic movements among the middle and lower classes who have been suffering from the inflation that followed the open door policy – can be traced, in part at least, to the reappearance of what could easily be identified as both neo-colonialism and internal colonialism. High debts have been incurred and, with them, the cost of servicing them. As Nagi (2001) reminds us, Egypt's external debt increased from US$19 billion in 1980 to US$34 billion in 1995. Between 1991 and 1995, the average annual percentage of the government's total expenditures taken up by interest on debts was almost 19%. Much of this borrowed money has been spent on improving roads, communications, and other infrastructure required by Cairo's attempts to enter the global system. But these investments have not improved the living environments

[21] There are interesting parallels to the "joint control" exercised by French and British agents who were put in charge of supervising Egyptian finances in the 1870s; they too had to work through the national government (then a monarchy rather than a republic and in collusion with an oligarchic class of large land owners), rather than with today's urban class of government officials in collaboration with politically empowered entrepreneurial operators and builders.

of poorer Cairenes since, as we have seen, they have favored the wealthiest districts.

Indeed, they have differentially aided or harmed whole classes of residents. The deregulation of exchange rates and the attractive incentives to private entrepreneurs have spawned new fortunes in construction and capital-intensive production. At the same time, they have taken scarce resources away from the poor. Decontrol and inflation have eroded the buying power of the poor and of middle-class workers with fixed salaries.[22] Furthermore, World Bank recommendations to reduce subsidies on electric rates and basic food commodities have raised the costs of living for those at or below the margin of poverty who spend most of their income on necessities. Social services have also been deprived of needed resources for which substitutes, such as the new compensatory "Social Fund," have proven sorely inadequate.[23]

But it is not only the international system that has altered the distribution of wealth in Cairo and contributed to the growing disparities between quarters. The reversals of other national policies, on the advice of foreign advisors, have also played their part. Of these, the decisions to "privatize" the formerly very large government-enterprise sector, to reverse the guarantee of employment in the public sector (formerly granted to graduates of secondary schools and universities), and to encourage growth in two extreme directions – the high-level private industrial sector, often through partnerships with transnational firms, and the poorly remunerated informal sector – have also contributed to the growing economic disparities in the city.

Certain anomalies have resulted. Because mandatory schooling enlarged enrollments without increasing the resources available for education, most public schools are severely underfunded and understaffed and operate on multiple shifts. The wealthy can afford to enroll their children in better private schools and, despite the financial strain, many of the middle class and near-poor hire private tutors to give the remedial instruction their children need if they are to pass the national examinations. For

22 A detailed analysis of these factors, although taking a less critical position than my own, can be found in the excellent collection edited by Handoussa and Potter (1991) which analyzes the situation in Egypt between the 1960s and about 1985–1990, i.e., at the end of what they call the boom of the 1980s.

23 For a critical appraisal of these negative effects, see Korayem (1995/1996). Assaad and Rouchdy (1999, pp. 45–47) also express concern over these issues, although they temper their critique by acknowledging that the Social Fund for Development, established in 1990 by the World Bank and the United Nations Development Program, in cooperation with the Egyptian government, could serve to reduce some of the negative effects of restructuring and stabilization. However, the funding is channeled "around" the government and into NGOs, and the modest budget and small staff are insufficient really to effect major improvements.

the poor, functional illiteracy persists and children are withdrawn from school to help support the family (Nassar 1999, pp. 89 *et seq.*).

Even those students who meet the exacting standards required to enter the free public universities are less likely to advance these days. The universities are very overcrowded and the education they provide does not prepare their graduates to enter the new "global" economy. One of the most interesting anomalies is that the highest rates of undisguised unemployment in Cairo now are among younger high school and college graduates, unable to find jobs in the formal sector, either private or public, and unwilling to stoop to insecure and lower-status positions in the informal economy. One cannot blame them, for the informal sector is associated with underemployment, casual or temporary work, and low income (Assaad and Rouchdy 1999, pp. 27–8).

The informal sector in Cairo is very large and growing. Even though foreign advisors argue that it could offer a promising solution to Cairo's glut of labor, particularly if technical and credit assistance can be given to encourage micro-enterprises, expansion of this already overcrowded niche can scarcely absorb the educated group and will only intensify the class cleavages already evident in the Cairo region. (See the inconsistencies between the empirical findings of a study of the labor force in the Greater Cairo Region [Mahdi and Powell 1999] and the advice given by foreign agencies such as the World Bank.)

In short, the combined effects of international loans and advice and compliant local policies have failed to solve problems in Cairo and have often had the (unintended?) consequence of rewarding those groups that cooperate most closely with the government and the international bankers. The other side of that equation, however, has been persistent poverty for many Cairo households and growing pressures on the groups in the middle.

In this, Cairo is not atypical of many other examples of world cities in poor (and, we might add, dependent) countries in the semi-periphery of the world system. This is a class of very large "global" cities that warrants more detailed and comparative study. Hitherto, studies of global cities have focused almost exclusively on the "winners" in developed countries. It is time to pay attention to the "losers" – the underside of global change.

REFERENCES

Abu-Lughod, Janet 1961. "Migrant Adjustment to City Life: The Egyptian Case," *American Journal of Sociology*, 67: 127–136.

1965. "Tale of Two Cities: The Origins of Modern Cairo," *Comparative Studies in Society and History*, 2 (4): 429–457.

1971. *Cairo: 1001 Years of the City Victorious*. Princeton: Princeton University Press.

1978. "Preserving the Living Heritage of Islamic Cities," in Renata Holod (ed.), *Toward an Architecture in the Spirit of Islam*. Philadelphia: Aga Khan Foundation, pp. 27–35.

1989. *Before European Hegemony: The World System A.D. 1250–1350*. New York: Oxford University Press.

Aga Khan Award for Architecture 1985. *The Expanding Metropolis: Coping with the Urban Growth of Cairo: Proceedings of Seminar Nine, Held in Cairo, Egypt, November 11–15, 1984*. Singapore: Concept Media Pte Ltd.

Assaad, Ragui and Rouchdy, Malak 1999. "Poverty and Poverty Alleviation Strategies in Egypt." Entire issue of *Cairo Papers in Social Science*, 22 (1).

Bayat, Asef 1997. "Cairo's Poor: Dilemmas of Survival and Solidarity," *Middle East Report* (Winter):1, 3–6, 12.

Blaut, James 1993. *The Colonizer's Model of the World: Geographical Diffusionism and Eurocentric History*. New York: Guilford Press.

2000. *Eight Eurocentric Historians*. New York: Guilford Press.

Chandler, Tertius and Fox, Gerald 1974. *3000 Years of Urban Growth*. New York and London: Academic Press.

General Organization for Physical Planning, Ministry of Housing, Utilities and Urban Communities 1992. *The Greater Cairo Plan*. Cairo.

1997. "Summary of the Long-Range Urban Development Plan of The Greater Cairo Region." Typed reproduction, August.

n.d. but probably 1999. "Planning and Upgrading of Informal Settlements, Manshiet Nasser: Pilot Project, First Phase."

2000. *2000 Greater Cairo Atlas*.

Governorate of Cairo 1998. Working Group for the Development of Ezbet Bekhit. "Participatory Urban Development of Manshiet Nasser: Ezbet Bekhit." Cairo: Bureau for Urban Management and Environmental Planning, MS.

Handoussa, Heba and Potter, Gillian (eds.) 1991. *Employment and Structural Adjustment: Egypt in the 1990s*. Geneva: International Labor Organization.

Hegab, Mohammed Salah-Eddin 1985. "New Towns Policy," in Aga Khan Award for Architecture, *The Expanding Metropolis: Coping with the Urban Growth of Cairo: Proceedings of Seminar Nine, Held in Cairo, Egypt, November 11–15, 1984*. Singapore Concept Media Pte Ltd., pp. 171–174.

Ilbert, Robert 1981. *Heliopolis: 1905–1922. Génèse d'une ville*. Paris: Centre National de la Recherche Scientifique.

Institute of National Planning 1998. *Egypt: Human Development Report 1997/98*. Cairo: Arab Republic of Egypt: Institute of National Planning.

Korayem, Karima 1995/1996. "Structural Adjustment, Stabilization Policies, and the Poor in Egypt." Entire issue of *Cairo Papers in Social Sciences*, 18 (4).

McNeill, William 1963. *The Rise of the West*. Chicago: University of Chicago Press.

1991. *The Rise of the West: A History of the Human Community with a Retrospective Essay*. Chicago: University of Chicago Press.

Mahdi, Alia El and Powell, Kathy 1999. *Preliminary Report: "Small Entrepreneurs in Greater Cairo Community."* Cairo: Social Research Center, American University in Cairo.

Nagi, Saad 2001. *Poverty in Egypt: Human Needs and Institutional Capacities.* Latham: Lexington Books.

Nassar, Heba 1999. *Survey on "Socio Economic Conditions of Work in Greater Cairo:" Preliminary Report.* Cairo: Social Research Center, American University in Cairo.

Shorter, Frederic 1989. "Cairo's Leap Forward: People, Households, and Dwelling Spaces," *Cairo Papers in Social Science*, 12, Monograph 1, Spring: 1–60.

United Nations Development Program and (Egyptian) Supreme Council for Antiquities, Technical Cooperation Office 1997. *Final Report: Rehabilitation of Historic Cairo.* UNDP, December.

Weber, Adna 1967. *The Growth of Cities in the Nineteenth Century: A Study in Statistics.* Repr., Ithaca, NY: Cornell University Press.

Yousry, Mahmoud, Abu-Zekry, Tarek, and Yousry, Ahmed M. 1998. "Cairo as a World City: The Impact of Cairo's Orientation towards Globalization," in Fu-Chen Lo and Yue-Man Yeung (eds.), *Globalization and the World of Large Cities.* Tokyo: United Nations University Press, pp. 270–313.

5 Mexico City in an era of globalization and demographic downturn

Peter M. Ward

Recent political and economic changes, both in Latin America and beyond, demand that we take a fresh view at the way in which we view mega-city development, particularly within an increasingly globalized environment. There are several intellectual imperatives to confront. First, the democratization process in Latin America has required that governments take a fresh look at the way in which cities are governed. Also, the growing disenchantment that some Latin American populations feel towards their national leaders has led to a resurgence of interest in local government, and has quickened pressures for a "new federalism" that shifts the locus of power, away from central government, towards greater state and city autonomy (Rodríguez 1997).

A second imperative to emerge is the significant shift towards decentralization and devolution. This can occur at the national level as regional and city governments have greater aegis with respect to central government. This process has found quickening support among international agencies such as the World Bank (Jones and Ward 1994b; Rodríguez 1997). In Mexico, for example, austerity measures introduced during the 1980s, along with economic restructuring and political reform, have intensified the need for the local authorities to do more with less. A greater willingness to embrace decentralization and administrative reorganization has been a direct outcome of this process (Morris and Lowder 1992; Rodríguez and Ward 1992, 1995). But decentralization and devolution also occur *within* cities, as population moves outwards, as activities are reorganized, and as sub-city governments play a greater role in local city affairs (Ward 1999). Throughout Latin America, city and metropolitan authorities have had to confront cuts in public expenditure, declining subsidies, and often growing pressure to privatize a range of public utilities. Greater fiscal responsibility is being placed at the local level, municipal and state governments are required to raise more of their own revenues (Cabrero 1996). Not surprisingly, people have become more concerned about how their local taxes are spent.

Third, many countries are experiencing a technocratization of administrative and governmental procedures which is bringing greater transparency to city budgeting and increased efficiency to the delivery of urban services. This obliges us to consider issues of devolution, empowerment, and accountability, since city administrators today recognize the political benefits of accounting more openly to those they serve, as well as to explore areas of administrative innovation and so-called best practices (Cabrero 1995; Wilson and Cramer 1995).

Fourth, as democracy has been extended to formerly authoritarian or one-party regimes, new governance institutions have had to be forged predicated upon representational democracy. This has meant experimentation in recasting traditional state–society relations, whether these were patrimonial, corporatist, or dominated by party political machines. It has also invoked a need to consider how civic structures of participation can be created that will change the political (civic) culture of dependency. Whether at the national or city level, there is an intensification of civic participation in governance. In short, we have begun to observe the emergence of a more genuine civic culture in a number of world cities – even the poor ones.

Fifth, and particularly germane to this chapter, is the changing population structure and demographic transition that many countries are beginning to experience (especially in metropolitan areas). As Josef Gugler notes in his Introduction, the rate of growth is beginning to slow in many world cities: indeed, as I will show here, some world cities appear to have stopped growing and may even be losing population – at least from certain areas of city, most notably the central core. This is demanding new government approaches as governments seek to expand their capacity to absorb young-middle-aged populations, and as they begin to anticipate and plan for an aging population structure early in the new millennium. This changing demographic scenario throws into even sharper relief current strategies to reduce the burden upon the state by privatization of pension schemes and social welfare benefits. It also means that cities, or parts of cities, are no longer growing: indeed they may be in decline. While few cities in less-developed countries appear to be experiencing absolute population decline, we have begun to see an inner-city "problem" emerging in Latin America, albeit little studied to date (Ward 1993, 1998b).

My aim in this chapter is to review the case that I know best: Mexico City's Metropolitan Area. But before proceeding, let me raise a concern that I have – which may not be shared by my fellow authors in this volume – regarding what I see as an intellectual inebriation with globalization theory.

Globalization or "glocalization"?

Typically, globalization theses assert a number of common features, inter alia: the growing internationalization of trade and foreign investment; the rise of multinational and transnational corporations; a new international division of labor; intensified competition associated with new industrializing countries; the emergence and changing functions of so-called world cities; the hyper-mobility of capital, and the existence of twenty-four-hour financial markets, and so on. It is argued that these processes lead to a loss of sovereignty on the part of nation-states, and to a convergence process whereby social and cultural relations increasingly conform to a common global culture, manifest through globally recognized icons. In turn, this leads to increasing divergence: between regions, sectors, and social classes that are not so effectively tied into the global. Thus regions and social groups are left behind. So pervasive are these arguments that we often tend to take them for granted, without question.

However, there are several problems with the globalization thesis. First, much of it is far from new – we can see clear echoes of dependency theory here – and much denies the existence of important spatial, social, and political configurations which make for important geographical differentiation between one place and another (Roberts 1978, 1994). In short, cities are not becoming all the same. Second, nations, regions, and governments are not helpless within this process, even if the macro-economic freedom for maneuver is often constrained.[1] Nor is the significance of local territorial arrangements and meanings being set aside: rather they are being reconstituted as the local engages with the national and with the global.[2] Interactions between and within areas of activity can

[1] It is important to distinguish between globalization on the one hand, and internationalization on the other, particularly in so far as the latter is embedded in development philosophy as embraced by many international organizations. While I would wish to play down the deterministic aspects of globalization and the loss of sovereignty this might entail, it is necessary to recognize the important influence that international espousal of conventional wisdoms has in determining "strategic perspectives in administrative modernization of large metropoli" and upon contemporary state–society relations. This internationalization of macro-economic strategy and of new patterns of government and governance philosophy is highly influential – ranging from structural adjustment policies and loans (International Monetary Fund, etc.), to more micro-strategies of urban administration, "New Urban Management" (the World Bank), privatization, and so on. This international "convergence" of what are considered to be good institutional practices, do, in my view, require careful consideration and adaptation rather than whole-scale adoption (see Jones and Ward 1994a, 1995; cf. Cohen and Leitmann 1995).

[2] In short, by focusing overly upon the economic dimension and upon globalization we are in danger of reproducing the same mistakes of dependency theory of the 1970s. By that I mean looking overly much at the originating processes at the center (new rationale of technologies and of flexible production systems, the dynamics of capital markets and

be defined in scale terms, and there is a rescaling of regulatory practices which sees interventions of the nation-state being scaled downwards to the level of the city or region on the one hand, and upwards to the new institutional structures of global and economic cooperation on the other (European Union, NAFTA, MERCOSUR, G-8). Global or local, and less of the national, hence the term that has been coined: "glocalization" (Swyngedouw 1997).

This "glocalization" is nowhere better exemplified than in the paradox of the United States itself: although the principal global power and economic force, outside of the Washington beltway its people are extraordinarily locally oriented. One only has to look at the news; with the exception of CNN (Cable News Network), news broadcasts quickly cut to local news stories. At least until the September 11th Terrorist Attacks, for most North Americans the (immediate) local was more important than the global, prompting some social scientists in the past to encourage people to "Think Global: Act Local"; and to develop "Municipal Foreign Policies" (nuclear free zones; anti-apartheid or anti-regime consumer purchasing practices etc.).[3]

I hope that these comments regarding globalization will urge caution when we analyze world cities. Specifically, that we do not assume macro-economic processes and sociocultural convergence, but focus, instead, upon the local, and at local population dynamics as these increasingly become "glocalized" as the local intersects with the global. As Parnell and Wongsuphasawat (1997, p. 137) argue in the case of the economic development of the Greater Bangkok Metropolitan Area in Thailand, "What unfolds at the interface between the global and the local is of just as much significance to our understanding of the true meaning of the globalization phenomenon as the wider processes that are driving it."

Mexico City's economy: a global, regional or national powerhouse?

A number of indicators give pause for thought if not skepticism about Mexico and Mexico City's true insertion into the global economy. Comparing either the flow of international resources or stock market

their flows, and so on), all of which allegedly reduce national sovereignty (see Sassen 1996); rather than looking at the ways in which these processes impact and *engage* with nation-states, and give rise to the many different policy responses in which governments assert their sovereignty within a particular development paradigm. Fortunately, I am not alone in making such assertions; this also forms the principal argument of the authors in an important anthology by Cox (1997).

[3] See for example the papers by Smith and Timberlake, and Kirby and Marston in Knox and Taylor 1995.

investments and activity in major cities such as New York, London, Paris, Hong Kong, Tokyo, Los Angeles, Frankfurt, and so on, one immediately observes Mexico's relatively modest role. For example the level of capitalization of the respective national stock markets (enterprises registered and share activities) ranges from 16 trillion dollars (US definition) for the USA in 2000, compared with 4.55 and 2.9 trillion for Japan and the UK respectively. In contrast Mexico's stock market capitalization was a relatively paltry 0.126 trillion dollars; indeed, Brazil, Korea, and India show greater weight than does Mexico (Table 5.1). Nevertheless, regionally Mexico City does play a more important economic role alongside São Paulo (Brazil), Buenos Aires (Argentina), and Santiago (Chile).

And while Mexico City's economic profile has changed dramatically during the past thirty years, it has also undergone particular changes during the past decade, not least since NAFTA ratified the city's importance within North America. According to the National Economics' Secretariat, in 2000 the Federal District (DF – approximately half of the total metropolitan population and the locus of most investment) comprised 55% of direct foreign investment compared with the next highest – 10% – to the State of Nuevo León (in effect read "Monterrey"). Of all direct foreign investment 50% comes from the USA with Spain in second place (7%). My point is that however one looks at it, globalization has not significantly impacted nor raised Mexico City's eminence.

Nationally, however, the city continues to be preeminent, albeit not so much as in the past in certain specified activities. From a position of national preeminence at the principal generator of gross domestic product (GDP) associated primarily with ISI (Import-Substituting Industrialization), the ZMCM (Metropolitan Zone of Mexico City) was harder hit than most other Mexican cities as the nation retooled to export-oriented growth. Its total share of national GDP declined from 36 to 32% in only five years (1980–1985). Due mainly to a breakdown in the manufacturing arena (−5.8% per annum during that period) the DF was especially badly affected as big companies decentralized their productive capacity either to nearby states or to the north of Mexico. The DF declined as the overarching center for economic decision making, such that while in 1982, 287 of Mexico's "Top 500 Companies" were located there, this had declined to 145 by 1989 (Parnreiter 2002). Briefly, the city has declined from around 43% of total industrial GDP to less than 30%, although the city continues to be very important for manufacturing activities, notwithstanding a decline in total numbers employed from around 1 million in 1980 to 750,000 in 1988 (Garza 1987). Mexico City's share of manufacturing employment fell from around 45% in 1980 to 33% in 1990 (Aguilar 1996), as did overall employment, although it did so to a lesser extent. Outside of Mexico City, the metropolitan areas

Table 5.1 *Stock markets as indicators of global insertion*

Country	Market capitalization				Value traded % of GDP		Turnover ratio value of shares traded as % of capitalization		Listed domestic companies	
	$million		% of GDP							
	1990	2000	1990	1999	1990	1999	1990	2000	1990	2000
United States	3,059,434	16,635,114	53.2	181.8	30.5	202.9	53.4	123.5	6,599	7,651
Japan	2,917,679	4,546,937	98.2	104.6	5.4	42.5	43.8	52.5	2,071	2,470
United Kingdom	848,866	2,933,280	85.9	203.4	28.2	95.6	33.4	51.9	1,701	1,945
France	314,384	1,475,457	25.9	103.0	9.6	53.8	–	62.4	578	968
Germany	355,073	1,432,190	22.2	67.8	21.4	64.3	139.3	107.5	413	933
Canada	241,920	800,914	42.2	126.1	12.4	57.4	26.7	54.2	1,144	3,767
Switzerland	160,044	693,127	70.1	268.1	29.6	208.5	–	78.0	182	239
Hong Kong	83,397	609,090	111.5	383.2	46.3	154.1	43.1	51.4	284	695
Brazil	16,354	226,152	3.5	30.3	1.2	11.6	23.6	43.5	581	459
Argentina	3,268	166,068	2.3	29.6	0.6	2.7	33.6	4.8	179	127
Korea, Rep.	110,584	148,649	43.8	75.8	30.1	180.3	61.3	233.2	669	704
India	38,567	148,064	12.2	41.3	6.9	27.3	65.9	133.6	2,435	5,937
Mexico	32,725	125,204	12.5	31.8	4.6	7.5	4.4	32.3	199	179
Chile	13,645	60,401	4.5	101.1	2.6	10.2	6.3	9.4	215	258

Source: World Bank group. Data by topic. International Economics. Web page: www.worldbank.org/data/databytopic.

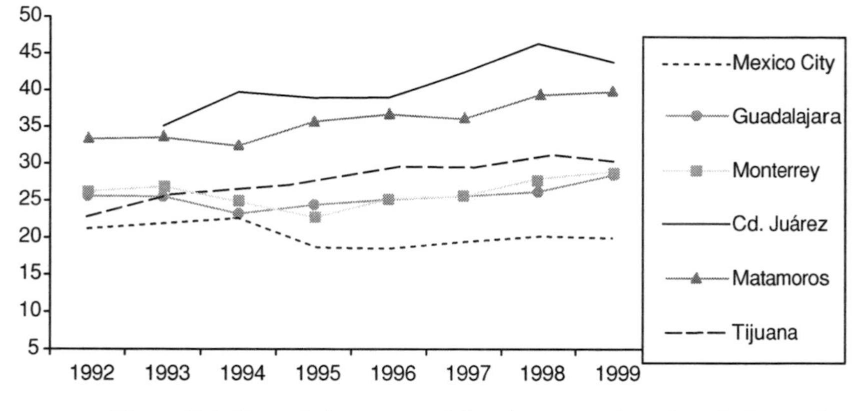

Figure 5.1 Occupied personnel in the manufacturing industry by city (%)
Source: INEGI. Banco de Información Económica.

of Guadalajara and Monterrey, and border cities in particular (Ciudad Juárez, Matamoros, Tijuana), have increased employment in industrial activities (see Figure 5.1).

Somewhat paradoxically Mexico City's economy has recovered considerably, both from the crisis of the 1980s as well as since the 1995 economic meltdown. National GDP generated by the DF rose from 21 to 23% between 1988 and 1996, and it is one of the few states where GDP per capita was higher in 1995 than in 1980 (in part, of course, because its population has not increased in absolute terms [Parnreiter 2002]). In 2000 the DF's share had increased further to 25%, and together with the surrounding State of Mexico, together contributed over one third of the national total. In the DF the manufacturing industry's share of GDP has also grown from 17.24% in 1993 to 19.61% in 1999.

Economic recovery since 1994–1995 appears to have come from two principal sources. First, from restructuring which led to a more efficient manufacturing sector with growth rates of nearly 3% 1993–1997.[4] And second, Mexico City's service sector has grown impressively and is the most important sector both in terms of GDP and in employment. This expansion includes both advanced producer services as well as a shift towards services in general. Employment in "real estate, financial and professional services" grew very fast – by 60% between 1990 and 1997 (Parnreiter 2002). Reflecting this trend, the DF's share of the "Top 500

[4] Although some of this apparent increase may be attributed to internal reorganization of firms and reclassification of former workers into the services sector as well as to some "hiving-off" of manufacturing workers into the informal sector.

Table 5.2 *Offices and commercial banking indicators, Federal District and other states combined, 2000 (% of national total)*

Item	DF	Other states
Number of offices	19.28	80.72
Total amount in national currency	49.84	50.16
Checking accounts	36.10	63.90
Savings accounts	48.33	51.67
Set term deposits for withdrawal on fixed dates	79.21	20.79
Fixed rate deposits	76.96	23.04
Others	96.02	3.98
Capture of foreign exchange	56.01	43.99
Investment Bank and turnover	75.48	24.52
Number of exchanges in national and foreign currency		
Checking accounts	27.26	72.74
Savings accounts	70.10	29.90
Short-term deposits	27.94	72.06

Source: BANXICO (Banco de México), Dirección General de Investigación Económica, Indicadores Económicos, abril 2001. Reproduced from Parnreiter 2002.

Companies" in the country began to rise again (from 145 to 213). In terms of share of total savings and investment banking Mexico City's DF remains highly concentrated with 75% of the national total, 56% of the external investment, and 70% of all savings accounts (Table 5.2). In this sense Mexico City is a financial powerhouse, and it is one that has undoubtedly grown through globalization.

However, this recovery had only a limited effect upon employment, with Mexico's economically active population growing more slowly than the nation as a whole, and with severe constraints upon employment creation in manufacturing. Whereas industry provided for 50% of formal employment in 1980, it gave jobs to only 20% of the total in 1999 (Cárdenas Solórzano 1999). Manufacturing has risen dramatically in the border region, such that in some cities (Ciudad Acuña for example) where it represents almost 55% of all employment (see also Ciudad Juárez, Table 5.3). Comparing the distribution of jobs across Mexico's principal metropolitan areas one sees immediately two features: first the absolute importance of the city in terms of numbers employed – in large part of course a reflection of its much larger size; and second, the relative importance of service activities in Mexico City (39% of all employment).

However, wage rates have declined in real terms, and the wage differential advantage that the Federal District has traditionally enjoyed

Table 5.3 *Economically active population by sector for different metropolitan areas and border cities*

	Manufacturing		Services		Government		Others	
City	Total	%	Total	%	Total	%	Total	%
ZM Ciudad de México[a]	951,873	17.60	2,112,046	39.06	334,474	6.19	2,009,417	37.16
ZM Guadalajara[b]	362,932	25.99	456,243	32.67	50,053	3.58	527,193	37.75
ZM Monterrey[c]	369,405	29.15	408,323	32.22	35,693	2.82	453,805	35.81
Nuevo Laredo	27,292	23.59	34,912	30.18	4,151	3.59	49,314	42.63
Tijuana	145,128	32.52	129,737	29.07	11,245	2.52	160,229	35.90
Chihuahua	79,427	29.49	77,125	28.64	13,198	4.90	99,572	36.97
Mexicali	72,481	25.44	81,550	28.63	11,489	4.03	119,364	41.90
Piedras Negras	16,479	35.82	12,440	27.04	1,599	3.48	15,492	33.67
Reynosa	60,839	36.40	42,890	25.66	4,285	2.56	59,124	35.37
Matamoros	65,141	39.80	39,988	24.43	4,922	3.01	53,629	32.76
Nogales	28,200	43.68	15,066	23.34	2,122	3.29	19,175	29.70
Ciudad Juárez	222,042	46.28	110,066	22.94	10,866	2.26	136,797	28.51
Ciudad Acuña	24,660	54.54	9,561	21.15	933	2.06	10,060	22.25

Notes:
ZM = Metropolitan Zone
[a] Includes the Federal District, Netzahualcóyotl, Naucalpan, Tlalnepantla, Tecamac, Chalco, Cuatitlán and Ecatepec.
[b] Includes Guadalajara, Zapopan, Tonalá, and Tlaquepaque.
[c] Includes Monterrey, General Escobedo, Apodaca, Juárez, Guadalupe, San Nicolas de los Garza, San Pedro Garza García, and Santa Catarina.
Source: Own elaboration with data from INEGI (Instituto Nacional de Estadística e Informática). Census 2000.

relative to other parts of the country had almost disappeared by the end of the 1990s. In seems likely, too, that there has been a trend towards wage polarization in recent years. Certainly, in terms of migration, Mexico City was always seen as a recipient and end-stage for internal mobility. Increasingly, however, limited employment opportunities, low wages, and rising expectations are leading to an export of labor from the DF to other cities, as well as to the United States. The DF has now become an important and notable source of transnational migration (Cornelius 1992). Understanding this apparent paradox of growth yet intensifying crisis helps to nuance an understanding of the backdrop to demographic change in the Metropolitan Area of Mexico City.

But before turning to these demographic impacts I wish to make a brief evaluation of how the toppling of the Institutional Revolutionary Party (PRI) from its seventy-year dominance of federal government is likely to shape this economic scenario. President Fox is certainly highly tuned to raise Mexico's role in international affairs, just as he was with his own State of Guanajuato when he was governor (1995–1999), but is his party, the Partido de Acción Nacional, likely significantly to change Mexico City's role? It seems unlikely for two principal reasons. First, despite his best efforts, recession is impacting negatively upon Mexico generally, requiring a downward revision of anticipated growth rates from around 5% at the beginning of 2000 to around 1% at year's end. Second, Fox is committed to trying to strengthen the state's capacities relative to the center. Moreover, since 1997 the Federal District government has been in the hands of the leftist Partido de la Revolución Democrática (PRD), and there is little love lost between President Fox and the *Jefe de Gobierno* Andres Manuel López Obrador. Although Congress is unlikely to purposively to hurt the Federal District, Fox will probably ensure that neither does it get special treatment.

Mexico City: anticipating the population downturn

Demography and politics

Rightly or wrongly Mexico City has the image as being one of the least attractive world cities or large metroplex areas of the Americas in which to live. Unlike New York or Los Angeles, its nearest world city neighbors, many inhabitants – with the exception, perhaps, of the *Chilango* city born – find little to commend permanent residence in the city. And even these local die-hards have become nervous about the apparent intractability of problems such as traffic congestion, increased pollution levels, and a crime wave that in 1997 threatened to engulf the city. While not wishing to

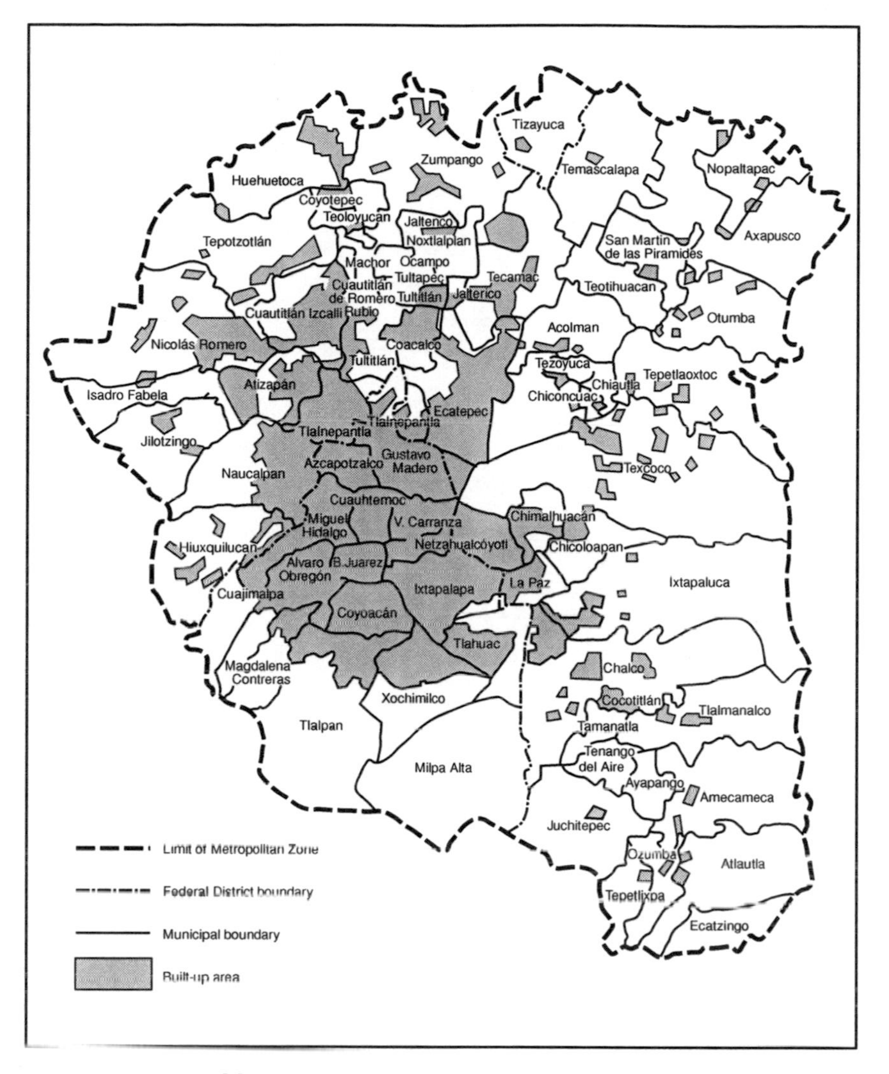

Map 5.1 Metropolitan Area of Mexico City

trivialize these problems which are very real, one must ask the question – are they palpably worse than ten, twenty, or even thirty years ago? In some respects they are; yet in other ways, perhaps, they are no worse, and may even be considerably better. Any long-term observer knows that writers have complained about life in Mexico City quite literally for centuries, and that since the 1970s in particular, doom-mongers have predicted the

Table 5.4 *Mexico: national population increase and demographic indicators, 1930–2000*

	1930	1940	1950	1960	1970	1980	1990	2000
Total national population (millions)	16,553	19,653	25,791	34,293	48,225	66,847	81,141	98,872
Population growth:								
% annual increase[a]	1.6	1.7	2.8	3.1	3.3	3.3	1.9	1.4
Birth rate[b]	49.5	48.1	45.6	46.1	44.2	35.0	29.0	24.6
Mortality[c]	26.7	22.8	16.2	11.5	10.1	6.2	6.0	5.02
Natural increase[d]	n.a.	25.3	29.4	34.6	34.1	28.8	n.a.	n.a.
Net migration[e]	n.a.	−3.7	−4.7	−4.1	−3.7	−1.2	n.a.	−2.77
Growth rate[f]	n.a.	21.6	24.7	30.5	30.4	27.6	22.0	n.a.
Population dispersion								
Density[g]	8.4	10.0	13.1	17.8	24.5	34.0	43.6	50.0
% rural[h]	66.5	64.9	57.4	49.3	41.3	33.7	27.5	26.0
% urban[i]	33.5	35.1	42.6	50.7	58.7	66.3	72.5	74.0
% small city[j]	n.a.	8.1	9.3	10.8	9.4	10.0	n.a.	n.a.
% middle city[k]	n.a.	4.0	7.5	11.6	13.3	16.5	n.a.	n.a.
% large city[l]	n.a.	7.9	11.1	14.9	22.9	26.2	n.a.	n.a.

Demographic indicators of quality of life								
% illiterate	n.a.	37.21	30.38	34.67	19.81	13.88	9.65	6.6 males 10.5 females
Life expectancy (years)								
average	36.1	40.4	50.6	58.6	61.5	66.8	n.a.	72.2
males	n.a.	39.5	49.1	57.1	59.5	63.7	n.a.	69.5
females	n.a.	41.5	52.1	60.1	63.6	69.9	n.a.	75.5
Fertility[m]	n.a.	n.a.	6.87	6.82	6.52	4.24	3.12	2.62
Infant mortality[n]	131.64	125.69	96.2	74.19	68.46	46.6	34.0	31.0

Notes:

[a] Average annual percent increase for the decade.
[b] Average annual number of live births per 1,000 inhabitants.
[c] Average annual number of deaths per 1,000 inhabitants.
[d] Average annual population increase per 1,000 due to births minus deaths.
[e] Average annual population increase per 1,000 due to migration (negative figures = emigration)
[f] Total average population increase per 1,000 inhabitants.
[g] Average population density in inhabitants/sq.km.
Per cent population in localities with:
[h] less than 2,500 inhabitants
[i] more than 2,500 inhabitants
[j] 15,000–99,999 inhabitants
[k] 100,000–999,999 inhabitants
[l] more than 1 million inhabitants.
[m] Number of registered births per 1,000 women aged 15–49.
[n] Number of deaths within the first year of birth per 1,000 live births.
Source: Various population censuses.

implosion of the city as its population was expected to grow to a predicted 26–28 million by the year 2000, and as its inhabitants became asphyxiated in an "ecological Hiroshima" (*Time*, 2 January 1989).

Like almost all large metropolitan cities in Latin America, the area comprising Mexico City transcends more than one jurisdiction (Ward 1999), spreading as it does across sixteen *delegaciones* in the Federal District and into no less than thirty-eight municipalities all but one of which lies in the surrounding State of Mexico. To my knowledge, no other world cities including Buenos Aires and São Paulo show this degree of atomization, and there is no tradition of a metropolitan tier of executive government in Latin American cities that might help to integrate this complexity (Iracheta 2004; Pírez 2002). In Mexico City we have a patchwork of local governments. Moreover, there are additional tiers of government with which to contend – Federal, State, or Federal District – which while offering the potential for some level of coordination and "big-picture" planning, also pose problems of intergovernmental relations and rivalry, especially where different political parties are juxtaposed.

The national scene: a late demographic transition Mexico's demography is both fairly typical of middle-income developing countries, and it is also encouraging. Much of the data profiles demonstrated clearly in Table 5.4 are typical: (1) high national population growth rates from 13.6 million at the turn of the twentieth century to 16.5 million in 1930, 48 million in 1970 and over 80 million in 1990; (2) high birth rates and annual rates of increase 1950s–1970s; (3) a fast decline in the death rate and rising life expectancy at birth; and (4), a switch in the population from being rural to predominantly urban (cf. 1930 and 1980). As well as being encouraged by improving survival rates of infants and life expectancy, one of the most significant features of Mexico's recent demographic trends is the fast-declining rate of natural increase – from 3.3% per annum during the 1960s and 1970s, to less than 2% since 1980 (Benítez Zenteno 1995). It is expected to get close to the replacement rate by 2010.

In terms of urbanization, by 1970 Mexico was already an urbanized country. However, the distribution of the urban population was extremely skewed, with the "primate city" of Mexico City dominating the next largest two cities of Guadalajara and Monterrey respectively. Since the late 1970s National Urban Development Plans have identified the magnitude of the problem more in terms of the extremes in urban population distribution rather than in city size *per se*. On the one hand there was 20% of the national population living in a single city; while on the other, over 95,000 population centers had less than 2,500 people. The challenge, therefore, has been to develop an urban policy that might begin to integrate population centers into a more structured and efficient system and sub-system of centers. Thus Mexican urban policy since 1978 has sought to control and consolidate the process of development in the largest metropolitan centers, and to encourage and promote the development of so-called "intermediate" (sized) cities within a series of regional urban systems (Aguilar *et al.* 1996; Castro Castro 1995). Intercensal data showing the growth rates indicate that the fastest-growing cities during the 1980s were those of 50,000–100,000 (5.0% per annum), whereas the large metropolitan areas of over 1 million grew at only 1.2% during the same period. Cities of 250,000–500,000 grew second fastest – at 4.3% per annum (Aguilar and Graizbord 1992). The latest Mexican version of urban development policy in Mexico was published in 1996 and was developed in a context of growing deregulation and insertion into the global economy, as well as the concerted efforts to reinforce federalist structures through decentralization focusing upon the "100 (intermediate size) cities" (Mexico 1996).

Mexico City: mega-city In 1996 Mexico City with just over 16 million inhabitants ranked as the fourth largest city in the world after New York/Jersey and Tokyo/Yokohama, and São Paulo (Gilbert 1996, p. 2).[5] Unlike two of its slightly larger counterparts, however, it is a single city rather than two or more large urban centers which merge into a single Metropolitan Area. But league tables based upon city size do not mean very much. More important are the processes and dynamics of city growth and the effects that these have upon the quality of life of its citizens.

Nowhere has the demographic transition been more apparent than in Mexico City. While the 1980 census indicated a significant slowing in city growth, that particular census is widely regarded as being seriously flawed, and overestimated the Metropolitan Area's population by almost 1 million. Between 1970 and 1990 the rate of increase declined to an average of 6.0% (Table 5.5), giving 1990 total population of 14.7 million.[6] Since 1990 the growth rate has been around 1.7% (CONAPO 1996, p. 1; Rowland and Gordon 1996). This means that all of the projections for Mexico City's population by the year 2000 and beyond had to be drastically revised downwards. Scenarios of 26–30 million which seemed not unrealistic in the 1980s, were gross overestimations. If we take the baseline figure of 14.7 in 1990 and 15.64 in 1995, then the total population in

[5] Today it vies with São Paulo as the world's single largest city entity, but both are behind New York and Tokyo if the wider agglomeration is included.

[6] Analysts offer different figures from the official census: showing a range from 14.7 to 15.8, although these higher figures may include population from the metropolitan zone and not just the Metropolitan (built-up) Area, see for example Camposortega 1992.

Table 5.5 *Mexico City's population growth, 1940–2000, for different "rings" of expansion*

	Total population (millions) and decennial growth rates										
	1940	%	1950	%	1960	%	1970	%	1990	%	2000
Metropolitan Area	1.64	9.2	3.14	7.3	5.4	7.0	9.2	6.0	14.7	1.7	17.3
% in DF	107[a]		103[a]		96		80		56		50
Central-city area	1.44	5.5	2.2	2.3	2.8	−0.6	2.7	−2.1	2.7	−3.7	−1.69
First "ring" areas[b]	0.18	34.4	0.8	17.5	2.2	12.3	4.9	5.5	7.6	1.9	9.05
Second "ring" areas[c]	0.01	–	0.05	–	0.4	22.5	1.3	15.3	3.3	4.2	4.7
Third "ring" areas[d]	–	–	–	–		–	0.1	7.0	0.8	7.5	1.4

Notes:

[a] 1940 and 1950 figures exceed 100% because some population centers within the Federal District were located outside the built-up area of Mexico city.

[b] Includes the following *delegaciones/municipios*: Alvaro Obregón, Azcapotzalco, Coyoacán, Gustavo Madero, Iztacalco, Ixtapalapa, Cuajimalpa, Naucalpan, Netzahualcóyotl.

[c] Includes the following *delegaciones/municipios*: Magdalena Contreras, Tlalpan, Xochimilco, Tlahuac, Tlalnepantla, Chimalhuacán, Ecatepec, Atizapán, Coacalco, Huixquilucan, La Paz, Tultitlán, Atenco, Cuautitlán Izcalli.

[d] Includes the following *delegaciones/municipios*: Milpa Alta, Cuautitlán de Romero Rubio, Chalco, Chiautla, Chicoloapan, Chiconcuac, Ixtapaluca, Nicolás Romero, Tecamac, Texcoco.

Source: Adapted from Negrete and Salazar 1987, p. 28; and Rowland and Gordon 1996, p. 179. 1980 data excluded because of misleading growth rate information.

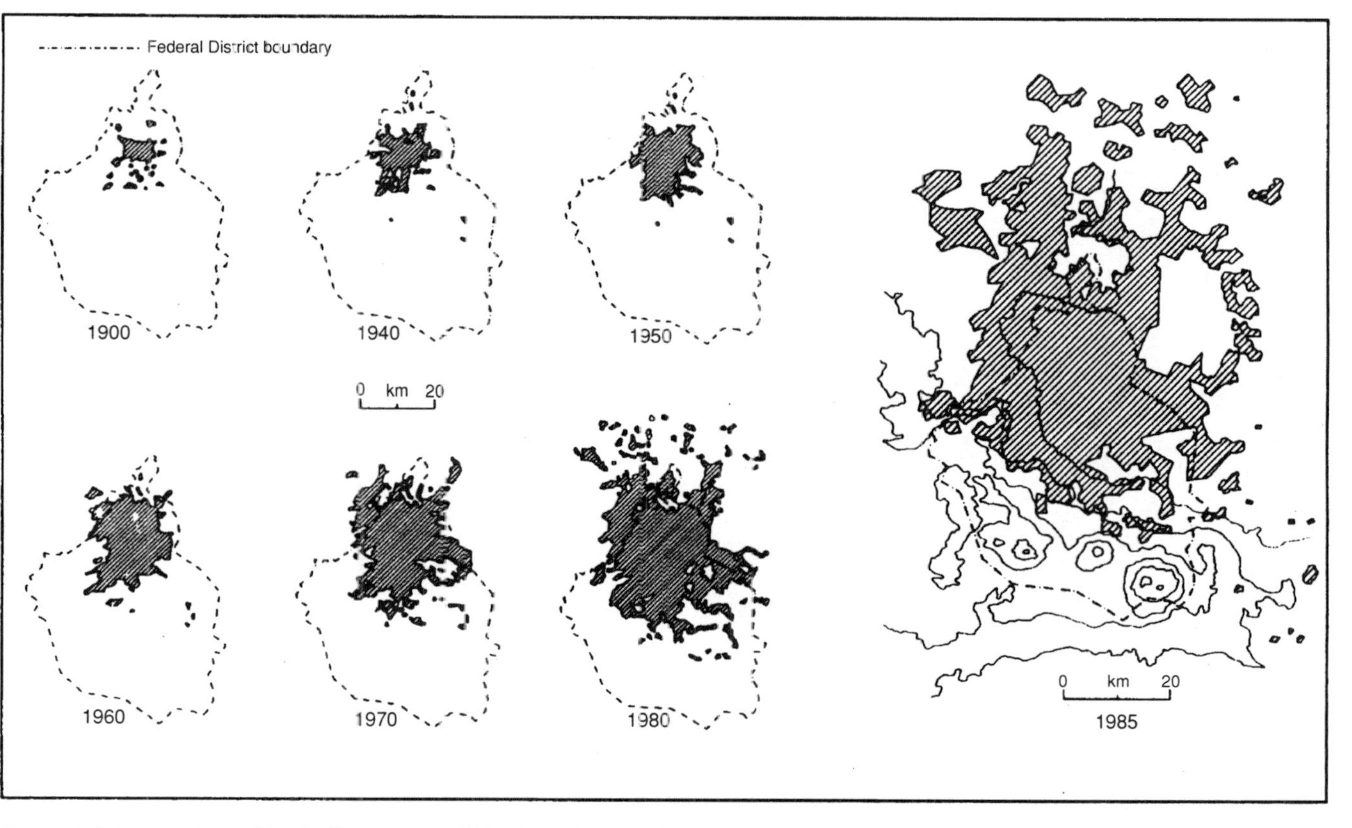

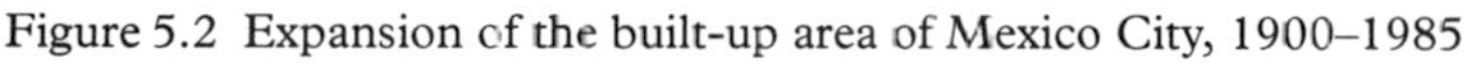

Figure 5.2 Expansion of the built-up area of Mexico City, 1900–1985

the year 2000 was expected to be 18 million or thereabouts (CONAPO 1996), and so the census ultimately confirmed.

The dynamics of city growth derive from provincial migration and from natural increase. The latter are the most important, and while birth rates have traditionally been lower in the Metropolitan Area than elsewhere in Mexico, they remained high until the late 1970s, after which they experienced a sharp decline. Crude birth rates for the city have declined from 44.7/000 inhabitants in 1950–1960 to 37/000 1970–1980, to 26/000 in 1990. Death rates have declined from 12.9/000 to 7.3/000 to 4.6/000 during the same period (CONAPO 1996; Partida 1987a). Mortality and morbidity rates for the city appear higher than for many areas of Mexico, but this may reflect more assiduous reporting and the higher level of treatment available in the capital (Fox 1972).

In-bound migration is an important factor in city growth although its relative weight is often overstated. During the early decades of the city's expansion, when the demand from industry for labor was high, migration flows accounted for around 60% of population expansion, with the remainder the result of natural increase. But, in the absence of a sharp decline in the birth rate achieved nationally or locally until the late 1970s, natural increase quickly took over as the principal component of city growth. For example, at the metropolitan level decennial rates of annual natural increase declined from 3.18% to 2.97% between 1950–1960 and 1970–1980 respectively; while the proportion attributed to migration fell from 1.66% to 1.09%, to 0.1% 1980–1990 (Camposortega, 1992, p. 8). Indeed, as I will explain later, some downtown areas of the Federal District have been losing population through out-migration to the suburbs. Nevertheless, city-ward migration added an estimated 38% to the city's net population between 1950 and 1980 (Partida 1987b), but according to Mexico's National Population Council (CONAPO 1996, p. 16) it has begun to show a net negative balance as population decentralization overtakes in-migration to the outlying areas of the metropolitan zone (Aguilar and Ward 2003).

Spatially this population growth has led to a "wave" of rapid population expansion moving outwards, first through the DF and then into the surrounding State of Mexico (Tables 5.2 and 5.3). Prior to 1940, the central area of the city absorbed most of the population increase until rapid suburbanization processes began to take over during the 1940s. Thereafter, as the population began to soar, many city center residents began to move out to the intermediate ring *delegaciones* (boroughs), several of which tripled or quadrupled their population between 1940 and 1950 and doubled it further during the 1950s (see Table 5.5 and Figure 5.2). A ban imposed in 1954 upon the authorization of low-income subdivisions in the DF also led to some premature movement into adjacent State of Mexico municipalities of Netzahualcóyotl and Naucalpan where the law did not apply.[7] This process was accentuated later once the wave spread out further into other municipalities during the 1960s and 1970s. In addition to those municipalities already mentioned, Tlalnepantla and Ecatepec expanded greatly at this time as did some southern *delegaciones* of the Federal District. Since the 1980s the "wave" of growth has run into the more distant municipalities of Cuautitlán, Tecamac, and Chalco: today's rapid-growth areas. For every immigrant that the DF receives, six migrants leave to municipalities in the State of Mexico (Graizbord and Mina 1995, p. 107). It was predicted that the population of Tecamac would grow from around 156,000 in 1987 to over 1 million by the turn of the century (Delgado 1988). However, this population count was reduced in the 1990 census (to 123,000), and while Tecamac (173,000 in 2000) remains one of the few "hot spots" in Mexico City's contemporary growth, it never came close to Delgado's earlier predicted figure (Aguilar and Ward 2003).

If, as it appears, migration is to play a relatively minor role in Mexico City's future growth, then the age/sex population pyramids can help us to understand the future principal demographic challenge (Figure 5.3). Notice how the city's equivalent of the babyboomers of the past two decades are now being "flushed" through the pyramid, and how the most youthful cohorts have narrowed or shrunk. This has several important implications for the nature of population change through to 2025. First, that the population will continue to grow as these babyboomers have their own children (i.e. a minimum of 2.1 children per family to replace themselves). But it also underscores just how significant both the introduction and relative effectiveness of birth control policies have become in stemming Mexico City's overall growth.

The second implication is that we are increasingly dealing with a population that will be predominantly middle-aged. There will also be an increase in the aged population and a slowly rising death rate. This brings me to the third implication – one that is already familiar in Western Europe – and that is the need to restructure social welfare and education facilities in order to take account of the changing structure. I believe that Mexico City will be able to achieve such an adjustment process, since generally its record on education and health care in the past has been

[7] A similar injunction was approved by the new PRD administration in 2001 – called Bando 2 – which has raised new specters of further forced shifts of new working-class housing out of the DF into the neighboring State of Mexico. This contradicts, somewhat, other policies in the same plan seeking to densify the existing built-up area of the Federal District.

Table 5.6 *Population and built-up area: past trends and short-term future scenario*

Part AMCM	1970	1980	1990	2000 trend	2000 target	2010 trend	2010 target	2025
DF population	6.9	8.8	8.2	–	7.9	–	7.5	9
DF area km^2	461	549	662	742	661	806	661	800
Municipio population	1.8	4.9	6.9	–	10.0	–	12.3	16
Municipio km^2	261	343	633	1,000	910	1,407	912	1,400
Metropolitan population	8.7	13.7	15.1	–	17.9	–	19.8	25
Metropolitan area km^2	722	891	1,295	1,743	1,574	2,214	1,574	2,200

Notes: 1980 data are adjusted (down) figures. 2025 estimates are the author's. Population in millions. Area in square km.
Source: 1970–2010: CONAPO 1996.

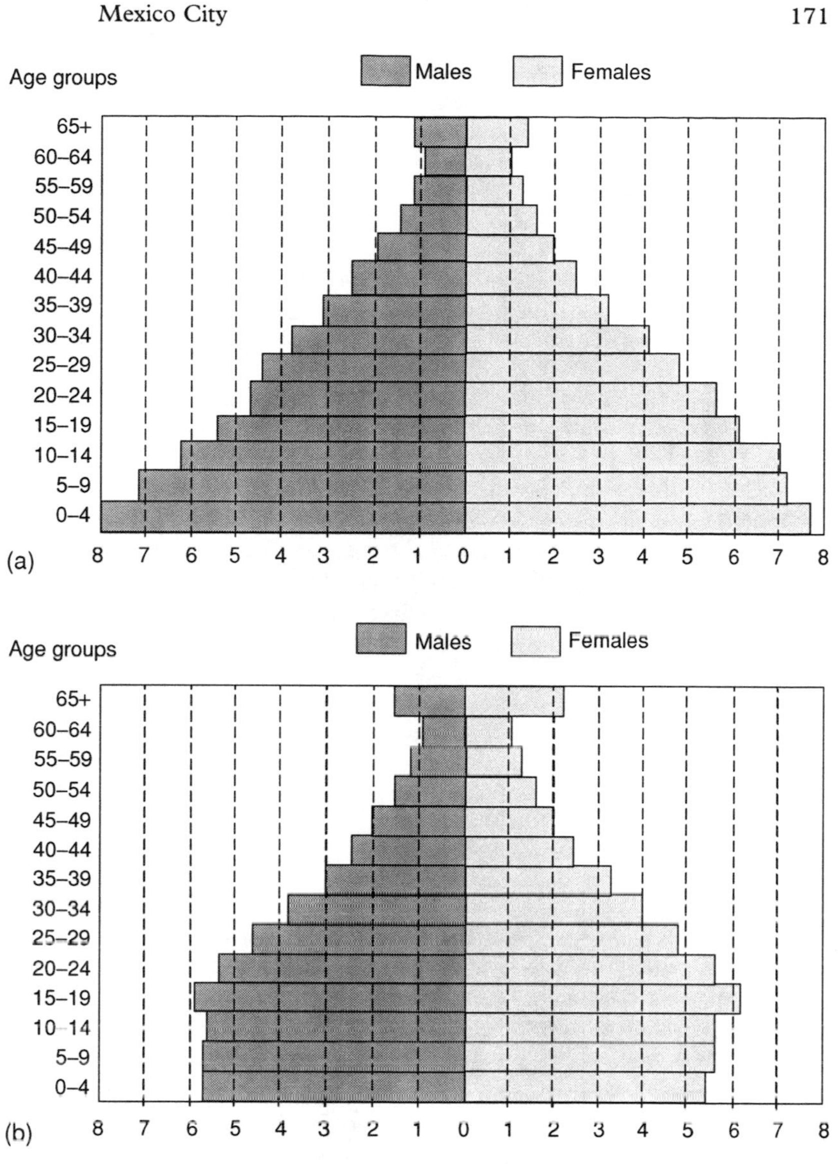

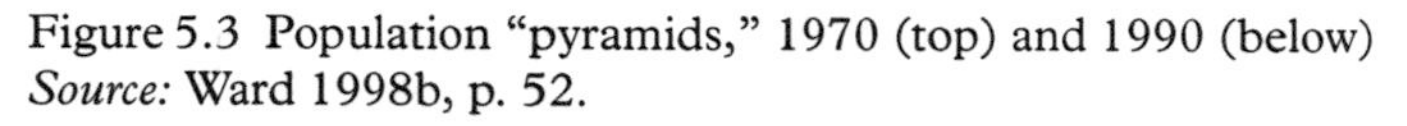

Figure 5.3 Population "pyramids," 1970 (top) and 1990 (below)
Source: Ward 1998b, p. 52.

quite good, and it has improved. The question will be whether it will able to afford that coverage given the current trend towards withdrawing some of the preferential budgetary allocations and favored status of the capital, as the federation seeks to develop more equitable resource-sharing with the states (Rodríguez 1997).

Mexico City's demographic future: the debate

Looking beyond the 17.3 million for 2000, and estimating to the year 2010 and 2025, the figures one arrives at depend largely upon the assumptions made about the dynamics of the two principal variables discussed above: the rate of natural increase, and net migration. As observed above, the National Population Council's projections estimated a total population of 18 million in the year 2000 and 20 millions a decade later in 2010. This halving of projected decennial increase 1990–2000, 2001–2010 is predicated upon natural increase declining from 2.1 to 1.1% 1990–2010, and that the average fertility rate of 2.8 children per woman in her fertile years will decline early in the twenty-first century to 2.1 (i.e. the intergenerational replacement rate), and drop further to a negative replacement rate of 1.9 by 2010. Given the age/sex pyramids already described, and the high potential for growth, then notwithstanding the achievement of intergeneration replacement rate, it seems to me inevitable that the overall population will be considerably higher than that envisaged by CONAPO.

Of course the other size of the coin is net migration and here, too, CONAPO anticipates an overall net loss for the Metropolitan Area. Although the Commission recognizes that some of the flow outwards from the DF is into the State of Mexico, and that there is also a minor flow of province to peripheral municipalities, it argues that this is offset by the decentralization of population out of the metropolitan region altogether. They estimate a small net loss of 6 out of every 10,000 inhabitants each year (0.006%). While I agree that the new inflow into the conurbation will be modest, I am less convinced about the extent to which such a large population is actively decanting out of the region through a process of decentralization. There is some decentralization from the DF to surrounding municipalities, but until we have fully analyzed data from the 2000 census, it is probably premature to be too "bullish" about active out-migration from the region, "new federalism" and political decentralization notwithstanding.

I suspect that achieving the next 1% decline in natural increase among Mexico City's parent population cohorts (i.e., from the 2.1% in 1990) is not going to be quite so easy. My informed guess is that the population in 2010 will be considerably closer to 22 million than the 20 million predicted by CONAPO (see Table 5.6). Whatever and whoever is proven correct, these are nevertheless dramatic reductions on previous forecasts, and Mexico should be congratulated for having achieved a demographic transition in a single generation. In less than two decades Mexico City has lost the dubious demographic honor of being the leading mega-city in the world, and it may be thankful for that (Rowland and Gordon 1996).

Quality of life issues in poor world cities

Here I propose to outline possible quality of life scenarios for cities like Mexico City. I see little prospect of dramatic changes in the economic/wage structure of the city population, which will continue severely to constrain the life chances for too many citizens, so that many of the social costs of underdevelopment will fall upon their shoulders. But as I have argued elsewhere, in the case of this particular world city, I do not anticipate the demise of the city by asphyxiation or awash in its own sewage such that anyone should begin to write its epilogue (Ward 1998b). Horror stories about the dangers of city growth abound from previous decades, and even from previous centuries, and all have proven to be grossly exaggerated.[8]

Granted, *ecologically* the system is fragile, but successive administrations are taking firm action to reduce contamination levels, tightening transportation emissions; and closing noxious fume-emitting factories (Rowland and Gordon 1996). Moreover, the population is becoming increasingly environment conscious, and the "Green Ecology" party has begun to win a consistent slice of the city vote (around 8%), winning several proportional representation seats in national Congress and in the Legislative Assembly of the DF. Provided that progress continues to be made, then ecological meltdown has probably been averted, and the movement to a more steady-state demographic situation makes the crisis of water supply and wastewater removal less insuperable than it once appeared (Castillo *et al.* 1995; Ward and Durden 2002).

Transportation networks and systems may be expected to improve, although much still needs to be done in the short term to achieve better planning at the whole metropolitan level (Navarro Benítez 1993). Moreover, there is an ongoing need to broaden the ridership of public transport, especially among the middle classes. Approximately 70% of the pollution derives from vehicles – mostly private cars, and governments for the past ten years have sought to take measures to reduce car circulation

[8] Elsewhere (Ward 1998a) I have tentatively sought to examine Mexico City in the *longue durée* – looking through to 2075.

and contamination (including the one-day-a-week ban, use of catalytic converters, low lead fuels, etc.). Between 1997 and 2000 elected government intensified these requirements with a six-monthly check for all cars over two years old, if users wish to avoid the one-day ban.

Culturally we must anticipate some convergence of practices as media and information flows become more internationalized. But as I argued earlier, it is important not to overstate this convergence process. It is the manner in which supra-local influences *engage* with local structures and belief systems and shape the production of culture that is important, and we may expect to observe significant differences from one place to the next. Culture is dynamic and evolves: it is the evolutionary outcomes and their local meanings that should most occupy our attention, and not simply the originating global images (Garciá Canclini 1990, 1993). Moreover, it is important not to dismiss cultural hybridization as a process, since this reflects real "meaning" for communities.

Mexico City is fortunate, indeed, to have a rich cultural patrimony and there is the real possibility (and opportunity) that people will value what is real and genuine in the past rather than creating a post-modern pastiche. The Historic Core of Mexico City is a UNESCO World Heritage Site. Thus far, at least, Mexican architects have largely avoided trivializing their buildings with superficial post-modern elements, relying instead upon indigenous and vernacular inspiration and applying it to modernist and international *genre*.

Greater *gender equity* is another important quality of life outcome of these demographic and economic changes. While it remains a male-dominated society, Mexico (and Mexico City especially) is fast opening up political and economic opportunities to women. The same liberalization is true in other respects – homosexuality for example; but it remains a fact that with the exception of artists and intellectual cosmopolitan groups in Mexico, few publicly acknowledge being "gay" (Gutmann 1996). One may reasonably expect that over the next quarter of a century the levels of prejudice will decline, as Mexico becomes a much more "liberal" society.

Most analysts consider democracy and opportunities for *self-governance* to be an important criterion in any assessment of the quality of life. In the past decade and a half, many countries have moved from being authoritarian and totalitarian regimes. Mexico, dominated by a single party for over seventy years, is experiencing political opening and greater pluralism of "opposition" parties in government. In July 1997 for the first time since 1928, citizens in the Federal District of Mexico City were able directly to elect their chief executive officer (formerly an appointee or "Regent" of the President), and by a large majority elected the leftist PRD candidate Cuauhtémoc Cárdenas as the governor (Ward and Durden 2002). Now, also for the first time, urban development policy in Mexico City will be tied firmly and directly to electoral politics and quality of local governance. Already many of the local mayors in the twenty-eight surrounding municipalities that form the Metropolitan Area and who are elected, are governed by opposition (non-PRI) parties (Ward 1998b).

Moreover, attempts are being made to decentralize away from the political center and Mexico City, giving greater power to the states (Rodríguez 1997). This "New Federalism" as it is called, is seen by many as an imperative for democracy and for improved governance at the local level (Ward and Rodríguez 1999). The goal is to reduce dependence and to strengthen the opportunities for greater self-governance.

Governance in Mexico City is already becoming more localized. So long as some level of balance of subsidiarity is achieved between those activities that are best organized locally and those which, by their nature, are more efficiently achieved at a larger metropolitan scale (transport for example), then the shift towards greater local governance is likely to be positive. A danger, however, is the other extreme of centralism – that of a "balkanization" of mini-republics. This may work for the local level, but it is no way to run a mega-city. The present challenge for Mexico City is to achieve a blend of local and strategic metropolitan planning, but this process is still being worked out (Ward 1999; Ward and Durden 2002).

The urban structure: the inner city and the segregated city

The neglected inner city

While there is a wealth of material written on the inner-city processes in advanced countries, there is virtually nothing on population and change in the inner cities of poor countries. Most of the attention has focused upon sub-urbanization at the periphery. Few analysts have sought to look systematically at Latin American inner-city areas. Important exceptions are Hardoy and Dos Santos's early work (1983), and more recently, Scarpaci and Gutman's inventory and analysis of land uses and building structures in a number of Latin American and Caribbean cities (Scarpaci and Gutman 1995). The latter body of work suggests that while many cities are valued for their inner-city cultural patrimony, and some – like Mexico City – have been designated as UNESCO World Heritage

Sites, it is the constellation of intervening variables such as governmental (national and municipal) and private sector commitment and support for renovation projects that is most important. Those cities that have assiduously sought to renovate (e.g., Cartegena) have often been highly successful; whereas those cities where urban revitalization has been largely ignored are terribly run-down (Havanna and Trinidad – both in Cuba and both UNESCO heritage sites). Nor do Scarpaci and Gutman see mixed commercial and residential functions as incompatible in historic centers: quite the opposite, such a mixture bodes well for revitalization efforts, they argue.

Similarly, evidence from Quito suggests that renovated properties are more usually associated with mixed land uses and that the impetus is motivated more by economic than by residential criteria. This is leading to some reduction of the residential opportunities in the historic core – both through declining densities and through change of building functions (Jones and Bromley 1996). Most of the few studies to date suggest an evolutionary trajectory that is markedly different from West European and North American historic centers (Scarpaci and Gutman 1995; Ward 1993). Scarpaci and Gutman correctly argue that most Latin American central core areas have low skylines and remain anchored to historic plazas (see also Herzog 1995, 1999).

Thus, for the most part while they show many similarities in overall processes of urbanization, Latin American inner cities have not shown the same level of decline and population loss as their European or North American counterparts. Nor have they experienced the same upswing or resurgence of reinvestment and back-to-the-city movement associated with classic 'gentrifiers' (Hamnett 1991; Smith 1996). It is probably fair, therefore, to characterize Latin American inner cities as being different in kind rather than in degree, certainly when compared with their European counterparts.

As outlined above, in Mexico City the four central *delegaciones* began to experience a net loss of population to surrounding areas from 1970 onwards (−2.1% per annum between 1970 and 1990), resulting in a total population decline of 1 million (approximately one third of the total, see Table 5.5). This is a substantial loss, but it is not a "gutting" of the heart and soul of the city, and notwithstanding the damage wrought by the 1985 earthquakes, the central-city *delegaciones* are still home to almost 2 million citizens, the large majority of them working class. Moreover, these are areas with strong traditions of popular culture (Eckstein 1990b; García Canclini 1993). Similarly they have had long traditions of political organization, not least since the 1985 earthquakes which proved crucial in fomenting inner-city social movements that, in some cases at least, have developed into constituency bases for contemporary leaders in the Legislative Assembly (Eckstein 1990a; Ward and Durden 2002).

Similarly, the inner area of Mexico City was never the location of new industries established during the 1950s and 1960s. These went instead to the first and second "rings", so there was never the same level of job loss associated with industrial dereliction and job relocation to the periphery associated with new more modern branch plants and factories. In Mexico City these new industries *began* in the (then) periphery. This is not to suggest that there have not been significant job losses, but these have neither been wholesale nor without some level of compensatory job creation, especially in services.

Commenting upon these processes in a nuanced way is rather difficult given the lack of detailed analyses about Mexico City's inner city on the one hand, and the lack of good disaggregated data on the other. The data in Table 5.5 provide some insight into what is going on, but each of these four inner-city *delegaciones* has a population of over 400,000 and many processes vary internally in important ways.

Monnet's (1995) excellent study helps us to overcome some of these data analysis problems, since while he compares 1970 and 1990 census data he focuses almost exclusively upon the 1990 material. Moreover, these data are disaggregated at a much smaller AGEB level (Basic Geo-Statistical Areas). And although the study is not comprehensive of the full inner city, and does not adequately capture *change* (given that it is almost exclusively draws upon the 1990 data), it is nevertheless the first of its kind to effectively get a handle on the highly heterogeneous nature of the area. Thus, at least in the case of Mexico we are slowly beginning to develop a more satisfactory and nuanced socioeconomic understanding of the characteristics of Mexico's inner-city area. Other cities, particularly Islamic ones with their traditional economic and population concentrations around the Medina, may not show the same lack of attention as is the case in Latin America. But in studying world cities in poor countries we need to ensure that we do not ignore what is going on in the center for it is here that urban *restructuring* will be the focus. And it is here that we should seek to learn the lessons of inner-city redevelopment in developed countries, thereby avoiding displacement of marginal populations, and inequity born of "gentrification"-type processes whether these be residential or commercial (Ward 1998b).

Residential segregation in poor cities

A common assumption is that poor cities are highly segregated cities. In some cases segregation is quite dramatic – under former apartheid rules in South Africa, for example. But elsewhere it is less obvious whether the levels of residential segregation in Latin American cities are greater than those of developed cities; or that they are becoming more or less segregated over time. Mexico City affords some interesting, and, perhaps, counter-intuitive insights.

From the outset we must recognize that residential segregation is not a new phenomenon. In pre-industrial and nineteenth-century Mexico City, while the rich and poor resided in close proximity and rubbed shoulders in the streets, they did not live cheek-by-jowl. The poor lived apart in discrete *barrio* areas at the then northern and eastern edges of what came to be the city's core or the *Primer Cuadro*, as it was then known. Perhaps the principal difference today is that sub-urbanization has reproduced neighborhoods and social segregation over a much larger area.

The existing pattern of social segregation is readily demonstrated when one maps the distribution of population according to income levels (Ward 1998b, p. 75, not reproduced here; see also Rubalcava and Schteingart, 2000, p. 287). The highest income areas of Jardines de San Angel, Las Lomas (de Chapultepec, de Reforma, and de Tecamachalco) are all clearly differentiated as are the more numerous second category of areas such as Napoles, Polanco, Satélite, etc. In contrast, the poorest areas are to be found in the eastern and northern peripheries. The greater heterogeneity in the inner city leads to more mixed income distribution, and there is also evidence that low-income groups living in and around the city center are significantly better off than their counterparts who live at the periphery.

This spatial distribution may be depicted as a series of zones, sectors, and nuclei that form the broad pattern of the city's ecology (Ward 1998b, p. 76). Poorer areas have developed as a series of concentric zones in the east and north. As one moves outwards, so the settlements become poorer and more recently established. Hence their level of physical integration is lower (measured in terms of levels of urban infrastructure, residential consolidation, population densities, etc.). Generally speaking, these zones expand through new housing production at the periphery with increasing densities in the inner and intermediate zones. Those groups in the upper-income bands also provide a *leitmotif* for urban expansion, creating new areas of exclusivity in which symbols of wealth and "cachet" may be displayed. However, the desirability for clearly defined neighborhoods that may be protected against encroachment from other groups has led to the emergence of wedge-shaped sectors following the contours of the land and using natural barriers as divides. Some "elite" residential development is also occurring through the gentrification and in-fill in the more attractive ex-*pueblo* cores such as San Angel and Tlalpan. Gentrification of the inner city is relatively unusual compared with that observed in Europe and in some North American cities (Jones 2000; Ward 1993). Some formerly exclusive elite areas (like Polanco and Lomas de Chapultepec) have moved slightly down-market as upper-middle-income groups "filtered" into residences and plots that were vacated by their would-be elite peers who have moved out to more recently developed and ever-more "exclusive" areas.

By far the most systematic attempt to analyze these processes of social differentiation in the case of Mexico City between 1970 and 1980 was made by Rubacalva and Schteingart (1987), using census data and factor analysis of some eighteen variables (subsequently reduced to seven). This analysis was later extended (2000) to include data for 1990. In the first two decades, two broad factors of differentiation emerged: (a) "urban consolidation" associated with variables such as levels of home ownership; dwellings with water service; persons per room; and (b) "socioeconomic development" linked with the proportion of economically active persons; proportion with primary education; proportion earning more than six times the minimum salary. Between them these two "factors" explained almost three-quarters of the total variation, with urban consolidation emerging as the most important way of differentiating sociospatial patterns in the city. Unfortunately, in their earlier analysis the data were aggregated and displayed at the level of *delegación* and municipality so that the resulting patterns were rather generalized (Rubacalva and Schteingart 1987). Nevertheless, the factor "urban consolidation" did show a sharp differentiation between the better-off levels recorded in the three western downtown *delegaciones* of Miguel Hidalgo, Cuauhtémoc, and Benito Juárez, but was lower across a broad west–east divide. Factor 2 (socioeconomic development) showed even more clearly the sharp divide between western political entities and those of the north and especially the eastern municipalities. More significant, perhaps, was the finding that up until 1970 there was a tendency towards greater polarization between social areas, but that the evolution of the urban area during the 1970s and 1980s had begun to reverse this process. In particular they noted a tendency for the position of middle-income groups to improve between 1970 and 1980 at the expense of the upper-income and lower-income groups. They concluded that there had been "a decline in the spatial and social differences, despite the fact that extreme disparities remain for important indicators between the zones" (Rubacalva and Schteingart 1987, p. 114; but cf. Esquivel Hernández 1995).

While the later study of 1990 data used the same factor analysis methodology, it revealed important differences to the previous runs. Moreover, it was a much more nuanced analysis since the data were disaggregated at the AGEB (neighborhood) level (Rubacalva and Schteingart 2000). However, although the resulting analysis is much more informative, the authors draw no conclusions about the direction that segregation is taking. Their analysis shows that the former twofold factor analysis explanation has been reduced to one covering five variables that are more associated with the urban fabric ("consolidation") and less with factors emphasizing socioeconomic differentiation particularly those weighted to the high end of the income spectrum (Rubacalva and Schteingart 2000, p. 288). The overall spatial depiction of sociospatial stratification patterns is a very broad brush since the unit of analysis is the *delegación* and municipality, but the authors do conclude that there *has* been a intensification of the differentiation between the east (poorer) and west (richer) sides of the city. But they are also the first to emphasize that these differences mask greater internal heterogeneity – as the AGEB analysis demonstrates. While their map confirms the broad east–west divide, its true significance is that it also reveals the enormous mixing of socioeconomic levels that occur within individual sections of the city. Moreover, it is important to appreciate that these AGEB data portray the stratum selected for that individual unit, and that covering as it does several thousand people, the portrayal may gloss over important internal variations. Indeed, their analysis of the three highest socioeconomic stratum *delegaciones* of the center (Benito Juárez, Miguel Hidalgo, and Cuauhtémoc) reveal major internal variations when broken down at the AGEB level (Rubacalva and Schteingart 2000, p. 295). And knowing these *delegaciones* well, as I do, it is important to appreciate that even individual AGEB units are far from internally homogeneous. The study further confirms this and shows that the level of internal homogeneity/heterogeneity that can be observed, whether within the *delegación*/municipality or within AGEBs, is more pronounced in the "very poor" and "poor" strata units of analysis: "In the highest [income] *delegaciones* considerable gradations of socioeconomic variation are to be found. On the other hand, those zones with AGEBs in the very poorest category, only very exceptionally include other income groups that are not either poor or very poor" (Rubacalva and Schteingart 2000, p. 294, my translation). This distinction between richer zones of the city in which there is considerable internal variation, versus poor zones that are more homogeneous, helps to explain the apparent paradox of no significant overall increase in segregation at the macro level, yet a sharper division and differentiation between neighborhoods at the micro level. In short, it points to the paradox of intensifying sociospatial segregation locally, and yet little apparent change in segregation at the broader (macro) metropolitan level.

How to explain this apparent paradox? There are a number of factors that help to explain greater or lesser segregation. State intervention to screen out certain groups and to designate them to certain areas may further polarize spatial segregation (as in Santiago, Chile, under the military [Sabatini 1998]). Local (city) fiscal policy may also lead to the intensification of exclusive elite enclaves as it did in Chacao, Caracas (Mitchell 1998). On the other hand, state policies to build working-class housing in certain parts of the city, or to permit illegal land occupancy, etc., can also serve to reduce polarization. In the aforementioned analysis of Mexico City the authors also tentatively explain the changing significance of the variables selected as being due to the withdrawal of the state during the 1980s, reinforcing inequalities in the role of the market place. However, while theoretically this should lead to greater segregation, such a trend is not yet observable.

Moreover, even if left to the private sector and the market place, decisions by realtors and developers do not make greater polarization axiomatic, as Sabatini (1998) shows for Santiago, Chile. There, as elsewhere, land is socially produced by agents and is not a simple outcome of supply and demand. Thus, in Santiago since the late 1970s upper-income groups have been moving to ex-urban places (farms, leisure homes, etc.) while developers have promoted middle-income housing projects in the south and west of the city – areas formerly given over to low-income housing. The decentralization of commercial sub-centers is further adding to the heterogeneity of the city. As we will observe below, my own work tracking land prices and residential land market behavior in Mexican cities also suggests that prices follow economic cycles and that it is social actors (realtors, developers, low-income land invaders and sub-dividers) that produce urban space, in ways that are not axiomatic for social segregation. In short, perhaps the most surprising feature is that Latin American large cities are not actually much *more* highly segregated.

In Mexico City one of the most important reasons why social areas are not so sharply polarized is the existence of social property (*ejidal*) land to which middle-income groups have had limited access (since its development would be illegal). This is largely (although not exclusively) a preserve of low-income housing development, and has allowed for incursions of working-class populations into the south, west, and northwest, balancing, at least modestly, the expansion of irregular settlements to the east. Even the fact that since 1992 *ejidal* land may be sold legally, it does not seem to have led to greater incursion of better-off groups into that part of the land market (Jones and Ward 1998). Our data for other cities suggest that, thus far at least, there is little evidence of higher-income or other sector "raiding" of *ejido* lands (Jones and Ward 1998). Nor is the new legislation likely to make a dramatic difference in the Federal District, since much of it has already been urbanized.

In analyzing social segregation, scale is an important consideration. While the *overall* level of residential segregation in poor cities may not be increasing significantly, the segmentation, separation, and dividing line (barriers) between rich and working-class neighborhoods does appear to be increasing. Mexico City, like many Latin American cities, has seen a dramatic rise in violence levels in the 1990s (Alvarado 2000; Briceño León 1999). Private security firms are increasingly being hired to secure the perimeters of upper- and middle-income residential neighborhoods, making them in effect no-entry zones for working-class and outsider populations (Caldeira 2000; see also Blakely and Snyder 1997). Moreover, as a growing number of urban services are contracted out to private operators, this serves to segment still further the transactional separation of rich and poor.

Nevertheless, the finding that there has been no detectable increase in sociospatial differentiation is important because it underlines the fact that conditions in Mexico City may not be deteriorating inevitably and inexorably in the manner often claimed by Marxist theorists (Esquivel Hernández 1995). In making this point, I am not seeking to extenuate the existence of the clear disparities that exist. Nor am I suggesting that, left to their own devices and market mechanisms, these spatial inequalities will gradually be resolved. But it does underscore two points: first, the need to take account both of the complexities of the processes involved in the evolution of the large cities, and to analyze the social production of urban space; and secondly, the need to disaggregate the scale at which one is seeking to make generalizations about the processes that lead to intersettlement segregation, as well as internal heterogeneity or homogeneity of individual neighborhoods themselves.

Conclusion: futures or epitaphs?

In this chapter I have argued that it is misleading to equate globalization processes as driving urbanization in less-developed countries in the direction of spatial and social convergence process – a kind of "race to the bottom" for world cities. Just like dependency theory of yesteryear, we must analyze how the global *engages* with the national, the regional, and, above all, with the local. Places are different, and those differences make for alternative development scenarios and opportunities. Cities – world cities in this case – do have considerable room for maneuver, and are much more masters of their own destinies than proponents of globalization would often have us believe. In part this helps to explain the trend towards decentralization and devolution that so many countries and regions are seeking today, both as a symptom of globalization (cultural differentiation) as well as a means to cope with responding to locally defined needs and priorities. In short, how best to balance the advantages of autonomy of local governance on the one hand, with the need to compete and participate in the global on the other. It is the epitome of the now three-decade old adage: "think global – act local." Many, if not all, of the case studies in this volume reflect this capacity for innovation and experimentation. My hope is that my co-authors, even if they have not assiduously done so already, will examine the processes that they are describing, particularly the origins and synergies of those processes and their interface with globally driven processes, rather than simply accepting broad-brush convergence hypotheses. Having said that, one area where there is a convergence is in the promotion and adoption of *international* conventional wisdoms, not least within the policy arena. While often positive, these normative approaches, in my view, also need to be carefully nuanced to local conditions.

I have sought to show how one of the leading world cities is responding to economic change and international opening, and how it is adjusting and compensating to both the endogenous as well as the exogenous constraints Mexico City has had to confront. My reading of Mexico City's development in the second half of the twentieth century, and especially since 1970, is essentially a positive one that persuades me that it would be premature to write the city's epitaph. Notwithstanding this reluctance, the proliferation of dramatic signals of economic, political, and social crisis have appeared in less than a decade (Ward 1998b). Many people accuse me of being overly optimistic in painting Mexico City's future. However, I believe that the responses already entrained – spontaneous as well as planned – auger quite well for the city specifically, and for the country at large. However, getting "there" from "here" will not be an even process; nor is it likely to be conflict free. But I firmly believe the prospects for Mexico City are probably better than for most world cities in the less-developed countries, and may even prove to be less conflict ridden, less revanchist, and less implosive than either New York or Los Angeles – its two nearest mega-city neighbors.[9]

[9] Smith 1996.

REFERENCES

Aguliar A. and Graizbord, B. 1992. "Las ciudades medias y la pol'itica urbano-regional: experiencias recientes en México," *Boletín del Instituto de Geografía*. Mexico DF: Universidad Nacional Autónoma de México (UNAM).

Aguilar, A. G., Graizbord, B., and Sánchez Crispín, A. 1996. *Las ciudades intermedias y el desarrollo regional en México*. Mexico: Consejo Nacional para la Cultura y las Artes.

Aguilar, A. G. and Ward, Peter M. 2003. "Globalization, Regional Development, and Mega-city Expansion in Latin America: Analyzing Mexico City's Peri-urban Hinterland," *Cities*, 20 (1): 3–21.

Aguilar, Adrián Guillermo. 1996. "Reestructuración económica y costo social en la Ciudad de México. Una metropóli periférica en la escena global." Presentation at the seminar "Economía y urbanización: problemas y retos del nuevo siglo", UNAM, 20–22 de mayo 1996.

Alvarado, Arturo 2000. "La Seguridad Pública," in G. Garza (ed.), *La Ciudad de México en el Fin del Segundo Mileno*. Mexico DF: Departamento del Distrito Federal and Colegio de México, pp. 410–419.

Benítez Zenteno, R. 1995. "Distribución de la población y desarrollo urbano," in A. G. Aguilar (ed.), *Desarrollo regional y urbano: tendencias y alternativas*, tomo I. Mexico, UNAM, and Universidad de Guadalajara: Juan Pablos Editor, SA, pp. 165–198.

Blakely, Edward J. and Snyder, Mary Gail 1995. *Fortress America: Gated Communities in the United States*. Washington DC: Brookings Institution Press.

Briceño León, R. 1999. "Violence and the Right to Kill: Public Perceptions from Latin América." Paper presented at the International Research Workshop "Rising Violence and the Criminal Justice Response in Latin America: Towards an Agenda for Collaborative Research in the 21st Century" held at the University of Texas at Austin, 6–9 May.

Cabrero Mendoza, E. 1995. *La nueva gestión municipal en México: analisis de experiencias innovadoras en gobiernos locales*. Mexico DF: Miguel Angel Porrua.

Cabrero Mendoza, E. (ed.) 1996. *Los dilemas de la modernización municipal: estudios sobre la gestión hacendaria en municipios urbanos de México*. Mexico DF: Miguel Angel Porrua.

Caldeira, Teresa Pires del Rio 2000. *City of Walls: Crime, Segregation and Citizenship in São Paulo.* Berkeley: University of California Press.

Camposortega Cruz, S. 1992. "Evolución y tendencias demográficas de la ZMCM," in Consejo Nacional de Población, *La Zona metropolitana de la ciudad de México: problemática actual y perspectivas demográficas y urbanas*. Mexico DF: CONAPO, pp. 3–16.

Cárdenas Solórzano, C. 1999. *Segundo Informe de Gobierno. Anexo Estadístico*. Gobierno del Distrito Federal.

Castillo, H., Navarro, B., Perló, M., Plaza, I., Wilk, D. and Ziccardi, A. 1995. *Ciudad de México: retos y propuestas para la coordinación metropolitana*. Mexico DF: Universidad Autónomoa Metropolitana, Unidad Xochimilco.

Castro Castro, J. L. 1995. "El programa de 100 ciudades de la Secretaría de Desarrollo Social," in A. Aguilar, L. J. Castro Castro, and E. Juárez Aguirre (eds.), *El desarrollo urbano de México a fines del siglo XX*. Mexico, Nuevo León: Instituto de Estudios Urbanos de Nuevo León, pp. 1117–1126.

Cohen, M. and Leitmann, J. 1995. "Will the World Bank's 'New Urban Policy' Please Stand Up?," *Habitat International*, 19 (1): 117–126.

CONAPO 1996. *Escenarios demográficos y urbanos de la zona metropolitana de la Cd. de México, 1999–2010*. Internal document prepared for a meeting in Toluca, April 1996.

Cornelius, W. 1992. "From Soujourners to Settlers: The Changing Profile of Mexican Immigration to the United States," in J. Bustamante, C. Reynolds, and R. Hinojosa Ojeda (eds.), *U.S.–Mexico Relations: Labor Market Interdependence*. Stanford: Stanford University Press, pp.155–195.

Cox, K. (ed.) 1997. *Spaces of Globalization: Reasserting the Power of the Local*. New York: Guilford Press.

Eckstein, Susan 1990a. "Poor People versus the State and Capital: Anatomy of a Successful Community Mobilization for Housing in Mexico City," *International Journal for Urban and Regional Research*, 14 (2): 274–296.

1990b. "Urbanisation Revisited: Inner-City Slum of Hope and Squatter Settlement of Despair," *World Development*, 18 (2): 165–181.

Esquivel Hernández, M. T. 1995. "Dinámica sociospacial de la zona metropolitana de la Cd. de México y patrones de segregación 1980–1990," *Anuario de Estudios Urbanos*, 2: 297–315.

Delgado, J. 1988. "El patrón de ocupacional territorial de la Ciudad de México al año 2000," in O. Terrazas and E. Preciat (eds.), *Estructura territorial de la Ciudad de Mexico*. Mexico City: Plaza y Janes and Departamento del Distrito Federal, pp. 101–141.

Fox, D. 1972. "Patterns of Morbidity and Mortality in Mexico City," *Geographical Review*, 62: 151–186.

García Canclini, N. 1990. *Culturas híbridas*. Mexico DF: Grijalbo.

1993. *Transforming Modernity: Popular Culture in Mexico*. Austin: University of Texas Press.

García Canclini, N. (ed.) 1994. *Los nuevos espectadores: cine, televisión y video en México*. Mexico DF: Instituto Mexicano de Cinematografía and Consejo Nacional para la Cultura y las Artes.

Garza, G. 1987. "Distribución de la industria en la Ciudad de México," in G. Garza (ed.), El atlas de la Ciudad de México, Mexico DF: Departmento del Distrito Federal and Colegio de México, pp. 102–7.

Gilbert, A. (ed.) 1996. *The Mega-City in Latin America*. New York: United Nations University

Graizbord, B. and Mina, A. 1995. "La geografía de la decentralización demográfica de la ciudad de México," in A. Aguilar, L. J. Castro Castro, and E. Juárez Aguirre (eds.), *El desarrollo urbano de México a fines del siglo XX*. Mexico, Nuevo León: Instituto de Estudios Urbanos de Nuevo León, pp. 101–114.

Gutmann, M. 1996. *The Meanings of Macho: Being a Man in Mexico City*. Berkeley: University of California Press.

Hamnett, C. 1991. "The Blind Man and the Elephant: The Explanation of Gentrification," *Transactions of the Institute of British Geographers*, 16 (2): 173–89.

Hardoy, J. and Dos Santos, M. 1983. *El centro de Cusco: introducción al problema de su preservación y desarrollo*. UNESCO.

Herzog, L. 1995. "Rethinking Public Space in Mexico City's Historic Core." Paper presented at the International Research Workshop "The Cultural Patrimony of Mexican Inner-Cities: Towards Equitable Conservation Policies and Practices." The Mexican Center, University of Texas at Austin, 8–9 December.

1999. *From Aztec to High Tech*. Baltimore, MD: Johns Hopkins Press.

Iracheta, Alfonso 2004. "El Estado de México–La Estado de México: la otra cara de la Megacíudad. Un epilogo al libro de Peter Ward," in Peter Ward (ed.), *México megacíudad: desarrollo y política, 1970–2000*. Mexico DF: Miguel Angel Porrúa and El Colegio Mexiquense.

Jones, G. and Bromely, R. 1996. "The Relationship between Urban Conservation Programmes and Property Renovation: Evidence from Quito, Ecuador," *Cities*, 13 (6): 373–375.

Jones, G. and Ward, P. 1994a. "The World Bank's 'New' Urban Management Programme: Pardigm Shift or Policy Continuity?," *Habitat International*, 18 (3): 33–51.

1995. "The Blind Men and the Elephant: A Critics Reply," *Habitat International*, 19 (1): 61–72.

1998. "The Privatization of the Commons: Reforming the Ejido and Urban Development in Mexico," *International Journal of Urban and Regional Research*, 22 (1): 76–93.

Jones, G. and Ward, P. (eds.) 1994b. *Methodology for Land and Housing Market Analysis*. London: University College London Press.

Knox, P. and Taylor, P. (eds.) 1995. *World Cities in a World System*. New York: Cambridge University Press.

Mexico 1996. *Programa Nacional de Desarrollo Urbano 1995–2000*. Mexico DF: SEDESOL publication.

Mitchell, Jeffrey 1998. "Political Decentralization: A New Tool for the Segregation of Urban Space? The Case of Chacao in Caracas, Venezuela." Paper presented to the 1998 meeting of the Latin American Studies Association, Congress, 24–26 September, the Palmer House Hilton Hotel, Chicago.

Monnet, J. 1995. *Usos e ímagenes del centro histórico de la Ciudad de México*. Mexico DF: Departamento del Distrito Federal and the Centro de Estudios Mexicanos y Centroamericanos.

Morris, A. and Lowder, S. (eds.) 1992. *Decentralization in Latin America: An Evaluation*. New York: Praeger.

Navarro, Benítez, B. 1993. "Dialéctica contradictoria del transporte," in A. Bassols Batalla, G. González Salazar and J. Delgodillo Macías (eds.), *Zona metropolitana de la ciudad de México, complejo geográfico, socioeconómico y politico: qué es y qué pasa*. Mexico DF: IIS–UNAM, pp. 175–191.

Negrete, and Salazar, 1987. "Dinámica de crecimiento de la población de la ciudad de México," in G. Garza (ed.), *El las de la Ciudad de México*. Mexico DF: Departmento del Distrito Federal and Colegio México.

Parnreiter, Cristof 2002. "Mexico City: The Making of a Global City?," in S. Sassen (ed.), *Global Networks*. New York and London: Routledge, pp. 145–182.
Parnwell, M. and Wongsuphasawat, L. 1997. "Between the Global and the Local: Extended Metropolitanisation and Industrial Location Decision Making in Thailand," *Third World Planning Review*, 19 (2): 119–138.
Partida, V. 1987a. "El proceso de migración a la ciudad de México," in G. Garza (ed.), *El atlas de la Ciudad de México*. Mexico DF: Departamento del Distrito Federal and Colegio de México, pp. 134–140.
1987b. "Proyecciones de la población de la zona metropolitana de la Ciudad de México," in G. Garza (ed.), *El atlas de la Ciudad de México*. Mexico DF: Departamento del Distrito Federal and Colegio de México, pp. 410–414.
Pírez, Pedro 2002, "Buenos Aires: Fragmentation and Privatization of the Metropolitan City," *Environment and Urbanization*, 14 (1): 145–158.
Roberts, B. 1978. *Cities of Peasants: The Political Economy of Urbanization*. London: Edward Arnold.
1994. *The Making of Citizens: Cities of Peasants Revisited*. London: Edward Arnold.
Rodríguez, V. 1997. *Decentralization in Mexico: From* Reforma Municipal *to* Solidaridad *to* Nuevo Federalismo. Boulder: Westview Press.
Rodríguez, V. and Ward, P. 1992. *Policymaking, Politics, and Urban Governance in Chihuahua*. Austin: LBJ School of Public Affairs, University of Texas.
Rodríguez, V. and Ward, P. (eds.) 1995. *Opposition Government in Mexico*. Albuquerque: University of New Mexico Press.
Rowland, A. and Gordon, P. 1996. "Mexico City: No Longer a Leviathan?," in A. Gilbert (ed.), *The Mega-City in Latin America*. Tokyo: United Nations University Press, pp. 173–202.
Rubacalva, R. M. and Schteingart, M. 1987. "Estructura urbana y diferenciación socioespacial en la zona metropolitana de la ciudad de México (1970–80)," in G. Garza (ed.), *El atlas de la Ciudad de México*. Mexico DF: Departamento del Distrito Federal and Colegio de México, pp. 108–115.
2000. "Segregación socioespacial," in G. Garza (ed.), *La Ciudad de México en el fin del segundo mileno*. Mexico DF: Departamento del Distrito Federal and Colegio de México, pp. 287–96.
Sabatini, F. 1998. "Urban Land Prices and Spatial Segregation: The Case of Santiago, Chile." Paper presented to the 1998 meeting of the Latin American Studies Association, Congress, 24–26 September, the Palmer House Hilton Hotel, Chicago.
Sassen, S. 1996. *Losing Control? Sovereignty in an Age of Globalization*. New York: Columbia University Press.
Scarpaci, J. and Gutman, M. 1995. "Buscando lo común: Land Use Patterns in Seven Latin American *cascos históricos*." Paper presented at the International Research Workshop "The Cutural Patrimony of Mexican Inner-Cities: Towards Equitable Conservation Policies and Practices." The Mexican Center, University of Texas at Austin, 8–9 December.
Smith, N. 1996. *The New Urban Frontier: Gentrification and the Revanchist City*. London: Routledge.

Swyngedouw, E. 1997. "Neither Global nor Local: 'Glocalization' and the Politics of Scale," in K. Cox (ed.), *Spaces of Globalization: Reasserting the Power of the Local.* New York: Guilford Press, pp. 137–66.

Ward, Peter M. 1993. "The Latin American Inner City: Differences of Degree or of Kind?," *Environment and Planning A*, 25: 1131–1160.

1998a. "Future Livelihoods in Mexico City: A Glimpse into the New Millennium," *Cities*, 15 (2): 63–74.

1998b. *Mexico City*. 2nd edn. Chichester and New York: John Wiley & Sons. 1st ed. published in 1990 and, in Spanish, 1991 as *México: una megaciudad.* Mexico DF: Consejo Nacional para la Cultura y las Artes.

1999. "Creating a Metropolitan Tier of Government in Federal Systems: – Getting 'There' from 'Here' in Mexico City and in Other Latin American Megacities," *South Texas Law Review Journal*, 40: 603–623.

Ward, P. and Durden, E. 2002. "Government and Democracy in Mexico's Federal District, 1997–2001: Cárdenas, the PRD and the Curate's Egg," *Bulletin of Latin American* Research, 21 (1): 1–39.

Ward, P. and Rodríguez, V. 1999. "New Federalism, Intra-Governmental Relations, and Co-Governance in Mexico," *Journal of Latin American Studies*, 31 (3): 673–710.

Wilson, R. and Cramer R. (eds.) 1995. *International Workshop on Good Local Government.* Austin: LBJ School of Public Affairs, University of Texas.

Part 2

The impact of the state

6 Moscow's changing fortunes under three regimes

James H. Bater

Three distinctly different cultural, economic, and political epochs have characterized Moscow's role as a world city. The first was that of imperial Russia. This epoch lasted several centuries until internal social, political, and economic dysfunctional conditions combined to set the stage for the Russian revolution of 1917. This event of global significance ushered in Soviet socialism, a theoretically egalitarian system which lasted until its own internal inconsistencies caused it to implode in 1991. Since then a new political order of fifteen independent countries has arisen from the ashes of the former Soviet empire. In 1991 Russia was launched on the road to liberal democracy and a market economy, or what passes for both in this new epoch. Contemporary Moscow retains its historical role of capital city. It still retains claim, albeit presently somewhat diminished, to world city status.

Tsarist-era Moscow

Founded in the middle of the twelfth century, Moscow's early history was defined first and foremost by its role as a military outpost. By the mid-fifteenth century it had emerged as the center of Russian Orthodoxy. Barely two centuries later Moscow was celebrating its role as the "third Rome," a place where liturgy would never be compromised by the politics of religion as had occurred in both Rome and Constantinople. Although over time trade and commerce figured ever more prominently in Moscow's economic base, the major economic, political, and social developments which helped to define the evolution of neighboring European cities and states seldom penetrated far into the Russian Empire. Moscow was the seat of administrative authority of the Russian Empire until 1712, at which date St. Petersburg was assigned the role of capital. St. Petersburg, a planned city, was founded in 1703 by Peter I as Russia's "window on the west," a tangible expression of his wish to modernize his Empire (Bater 1976). Yet little in Russia changed very much in consequence. Technological backwardness not innovation characterized

Russia's industry and its military. Enterprise was stifled because of the social class structure and the imperial bureaucracy which underpinned it (Owen 1983). Trade in human capital continued until Alexander II introduced the Emancipation Act of 1861. Prior to that date wealth was as often defined by how many serfs one owned as it was by one's financial capital or extent of business holdings. At the end of the nineteenth century, business in Moscow was little integrated with, and therefore little influenced by, the rest of the world. The culture of Moscow's business community was still very much shaped by the values and behavior of the traditional merchant classes. Russia's importance amongst European states was more a function of the size of its territory and population, and presumed directly related military prowess, than of the modernity of its industry or commerce.

Moscow was Russia's largest city until late in the nineteenth century, at which time it was overtaken by St. Petersburg. On the eve of the First World War Moscow's population was a shade less than 2 million, St. Petersburg's a shade more. But in the shadow of Moscow, in contrast to St. Petersburg, was a densely populated hinterland. Moscow and its hinterland, dominated by traditional manufacturing of textiles and foodstuffs, was the Empire's most important commercial and industrial region for virtually all of the Tsarist period. Notwithstanding its large population, to many European visitors, and not a few Russians as well, Moscow had very much the appearance of a vast network of villages bound together by industry and commerce of mostly traditional types. That the vast majority of Moscow's inhabitants in 1914 were recently arrived, mostly illiterate peasants, simply served to underscore the village atmosphere and image. Thus, in the eyes of many people, Moscow lacked the seeming urbanity of such European centers as London, Paris, Berlin, or Vienna. Nonetheless, over the hotchpotch of unplanned urban-industrial development that characterized much of turn of the century Moscow there lay a thin veneer of modernity. There was a vibrant intellectual and artistic life in the city, even if it was often overshadowed by that of the imperial capital St. Petersburg. Outside the salons, theatres, and lecture rooms, a few streets had gas or electric lighting, electric trams plied a number of Moscow's central thoroughfares, and some buildings were noteworthy architecturally (Colton 1995). But in general most of the city's inhabitants were obliged to endure poor housing and deficient essential city services. Sewage and water supply systems were wholly inadequate, and infectious disease was endemic in consequence. That the burden of infectious disease fell most heavily on Moscow's burgeoning underclass is no surprise. No surprise either is the fact that the imperial regime sought to maintain social stratification as represented by the official *sosloviye* or estates. Modernization and such an antiquated form of enforced social stratification were clearly incompatible. The abysmal conditions of daily life and labor for the majority of the urban masses in the early years of the twentieth century figured prominently in the demise of the autocracy and the emergence of the new political regime (Bater 1976).

Other than its near 2 million population, Moscow in the late imperial era had few attributes of a world city. It was not capital, it was a laggard not a leader in civic administration and urban infrastructure, its economic base was dominated by traditional forms of manufacturing and commerce, it stood on the sidelines of the most important political, intellectual, and ideological movements of the times. It did retain its central place in the world of Russian Orthodoxy, but the church was scarcely an agent of change, of modernization of state and society. All of this was to be transformed in the ensuing epoch, however.

Moscow in the Soviet era

In the immediate aftermath of the Russian revolution Moscow, like Petrograd (as St. Petersburg had been renamed in August 1914 in deference to anti-German sentiment), experienced a substantial reduction in population following the disintegration of the national economy and the resultant acute food shortage. Fully 40% of Muscovites departed for the countryside to villages where they had retained a formal link even if having been resident in the city for years (Lorimer 1946, p. 33). Moscow was designated capital of the new socialist state in 1918 and its economic base was bolstered accordingly. As home to an ever-expanding, and before long, bloated central administrative bureaucracy, Moscow's population grew rapidly and by 1926 exceeded 2 million. It was now the largest city in the Soviet Union, a primacy it retains in present-day Russia. The urban-industrialization drive unleashed with the adoption of the first Soviet-era Five Year Plan in 1929 further spurred growth. Indeed, industrialization transformed Moscow's economic role within the country just as profoundly as being named capital had transformed its administrative functions. The Communist Party, and its attendant agencies of state propaganda, soon supplanted the city's historic role as the center of the Russian Orthodoxy. Indeed, all forms of traditional religious belief and practice steadily withered under the heavy hand of a state which sought to create both a new society and a new morality based on scientific atheism.

Moscow as a model Soviet socialist city – ideal and reality[1]

The concept of a distinctly socialist urban form soon emerged as an important part of state ideology in the early years of Soviet socialism. What its specific features should be was the subject of much debate during the 1920s (Bater 1980). While debate continued, the first steps towards the goal of creating a socialist urban environment were being taken. The first step involved municipalization, or from the point of view of owners, confiscation of the housing stock. Thereafter, the reassignment of housing on ostensibly egalitarian principles, the construction of enterprise housing for workers, the demise of private sector activities, and the intrusion of the state into all aspects of daily life, changed the geography of the city. After more than a decade of increasingly contentious debate over the most appropriate spatial form for the future socialist city, further discussion was terminated by decree in 1931. A plan for the redevelopment of Moscow, adopted by the Soviet government in 1935, embodied principles which were soon applied in the planned development of cities across the Soviet Union. During the debate over the future Soviet socialist city in the 1920s, the notion that there would be no distinguishable city center was embraced by those proposing a radical departure from past, and indeed contemporary, trends. For them the only acceptable design solution was to create an entirely new urban environment consistent with the ideals of the society being forged. Taken to its logical conclusion, all vestiges of the pre-Soviet city would eventually be erased.

The 1935 Moscow Plan, however, did not endorse such a radical departure from the reality of the existing urban form. Nonetheless, the conviction that human behavior could be modified by the built environment, and therefore by the design process, remained firmly entrenched. There would be a city center, but it was to be the nucleus of urban social and political life not of commerce. By means of unified and uniform architectural ensembles, thoroughfares, and squares, the city center was to cater to massive public demonstrations (Map 6.1). Thus, unified and uniform architectural ensembles and thoroughfares were imposed on central cities throughout the Soviet Union in order to accommodate periodic mass demonstrations. Such orchestrated public events were deemed to be of great importance in inculcating values consistent with the state ideology. In further contrast with Western market economy cities, the Soviet central city would retain a substantial residential population. This objective was easily realized since the state controlled the construction and allocation

[1] Material in this and the following sections has been drawn from Bater *et al.* 1998, and Bater 2001.

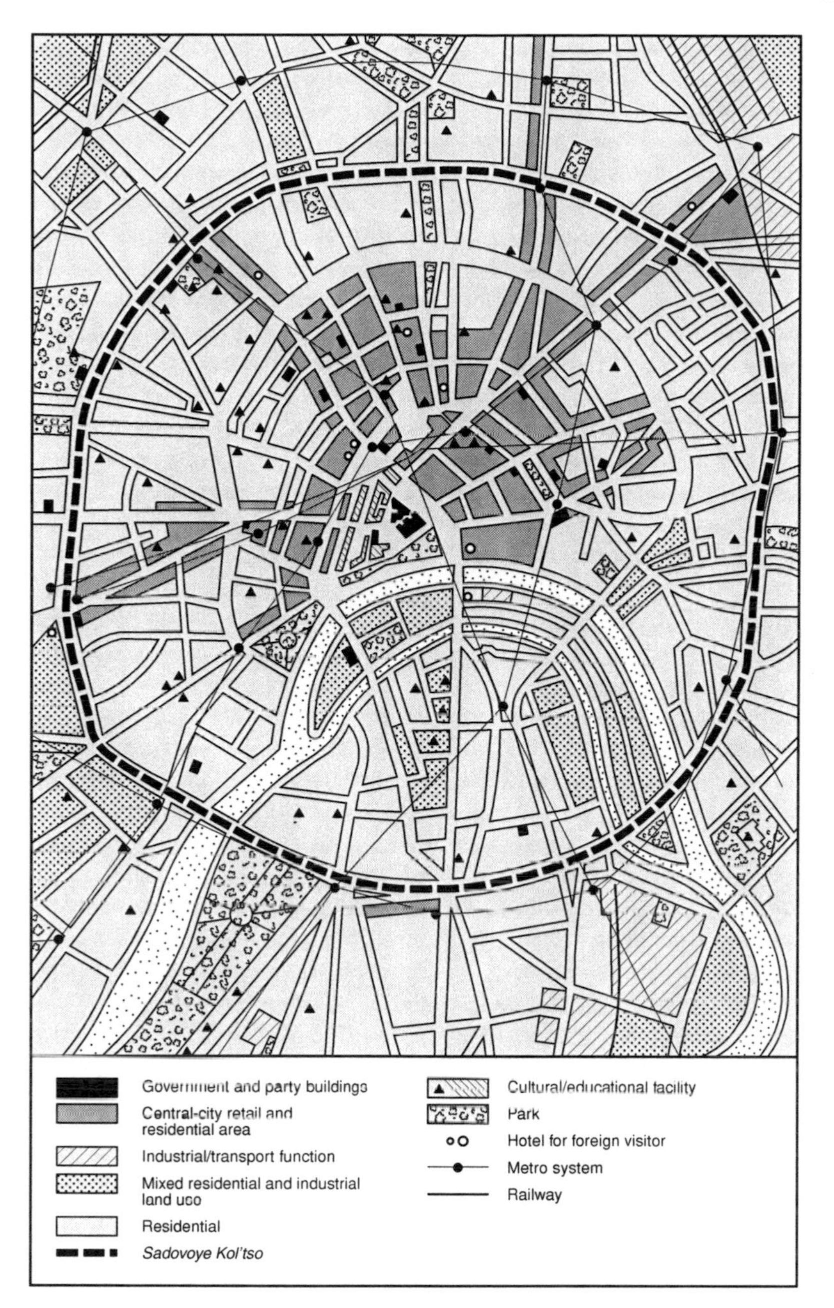

Map 6.1 Central Moscow – land use in the Soviet era
Source: Based on *Deirke Weltatlas* 1978, p. 123.

of housing. The design problem was one of striking a reasonable balance between occasional public functions and the day-to-day purposes that these same thoroughfares, squares, and buildings had to serve. Notwithstanding the intentional decentralization of a wide array of consumer services, central cities in general and Moscow's in particular were well provisioned in comparison with peripheral, suburban areas. This spatial concentration of consumer services enterprises further enhanced Soviet central city's role as the locus of political and cultural life. It is therefore scarcely surprising that in the "deficit culture" created by the failure of the state to meet planning norms, the comparatively well-off central city was frequently a preferred residential location amongst elites. Thus, beneath the surface of socialist town planning principles, and ample evidence of their implementation in the case of Moscow, there was a world in which public values and private values and activities were increasingly divergent.

To co-opt the managerial class, the Soviet system early on in Stalin's era offered rewards and privileges. This obviously influenced how people lived, and to some degree where they lived as well. Historically, the western part of the city was a preferred residential location in comparison to the heavily industrialized eastern and southern regions, and a residence in the central city was preferred over one on the periphery (Trushchenko 1993). Since the Soviet state determined what type of housing was to be constructed, where it was to be built, and to whom it would be allocated, the social class composition of specific city district populations could be easily influenced. For instance, the 1971 General Plan for the Development of Moscow pronounced the central-city area bounded by the *Sadovoye Kol'tso*, or Garden Ring, which includes the Kremlin (Map 6.1), to be a cultural center. The population living in this part of the central city peaked in 1940 at more than 1 million. Population density then was approximately 51,000 per square kilometer. Most residents were *rabochiye*, or blue-collar workers, a great many of whom were obliged to live in communal housing. Single persons and families alike who were assigned a communal apartment typically occupied just one room of a multiroom apartment, the toilet, bath, and kitchen facilities being shared by all occupants. While such apartments often were located in poorly maintained buildings dating from the Tsarist era, Soviet-era apartment buildings were by no means spared such intensive use.

By 1980 the number of people living within the area delimited by the *Sadovoye Kol'tso* had declined to about 300,000, and the population density to 16,000 per square kilometer. In the early 1990s there were fewer than one quarter of a million people living there (*Nezavisimaya gazeta*, 10 March 1994, p. 6). In the re-development of the area within the *Sadovoye Kol'tso*, unskilled and skilled workers alike were displaced by the tens of thousands. The total housing stock within the *Sadovoye Kol'tso* shrank by nearly 50% between 1960 and 1988. At the same time, new and refurbished apartments in this area were allocated to elites (Trushchenko 1995). The privileged as a proportion of the total population in central Moscow increased substantially as a result of the implementation of the 1971 General Plan. Social stratification which the state implicitly supported through its policies embedding privilege and its perpetuation, thus had a distinctly geographical dimension in the 1971 General Plan.

Even though the population density in central Moscow declined after the 1940s, by the end of the Soviet period it was still higher than in many western cities in which business dominated central-city land use. Moreover, the typical density gradient of the Western European city, and most especially the North American city, which declined with distance from center, differed from that of the Soviet city. In the latter case, outside the high population density central city was a band of mixed land uses in which industry figured prominently. Here the population density was generally lower than in the central city. But unlike Western cities which had comparatively low population density peripheral, suburban rings, in the Soviet era this was the zone in which high-rise housing was built on a massive scale after 1960, and thus it was often the case that toward the periphery of major Soviet cities, including Moscow, population density actually increased, sometimes to levels much higher than in the central city (Bertaud and Renaud 1995).

Having legal claim to residence in the Soviet capital was something to which most Soviet citizens aspired. Muscovites were spared the economic hardship visited upon most Soviet citizens because of the special treatment accorded Moscow within the Soviet economic system. As in the late imperial era, Moscow in the late Soviet era figured prominently in the list of world cities by virtue of its population of nearly 9 million. But as important as the sheer number of residents was, it paled in comparison with Moscow's importance as a center of political power, of an ideology which extended well beyond the borders of the Soviet Union, embracing at one point in time about a third of the world's population. Communism and Moscow were synonymous in the years immediately following the Second World War, and therefore the city played a dominant if not unique role in the global geopolitical system. While Moscow was truly a world city in terms of political ideology, it did not figure as prominently in the global economy. In principle, the Soviet economic system promoted autarchy, or self-sufficiency, often irrespective of cost, over international trade based on comparative advantage. In practice, after 1970 exports, especially of oil and natural gas, created an unwanted but necessary dependency on a foreign hard currency earnings, and therefore a dependence on the global economy. Income generated by exporting energy was used in a vain attempt to satisfy domestic demand for food, consumers goods, and technology. In terms of oil and natural gas exports, all the important decisions were taken in Moscow, just as was the case in every other sphere of the economy.

Post-Soviet Moscow

The collapse of the Soviet system in 1991 ushered in an entirely new political economy. Moscow is currently the hub of Russia's new economy simply because it is still the capital city and therefore is the place where political decisions which facilitate business get made. But Russia is not the Soviet Union. It is truncated territorially, its population has been reduced by nearly 50%, and it is by Western standards a poor country as measured by gross domestic product, per capita income, and overall quality of life as reflected in, for instance, life expectancy. While much reduced in territory, it nonetheless possesses a vast stock of the natural resources required by modern industry, a well-educated population, and therefore has considerable economic development potential. But the legacy of the Soviet system is both pervasive, and deeply engrained. Values and behavior patterns inculcated over more than seven decades constitute a real impediment to change. After years of state planning and centralized decision making, strict limitations on personal freedoms, including determining where one could live, and a communist political regime, democracy and a market economy have not always found Russian soil especially fertile. In post-Soviet Moscow there is evidence of integration into the world market economy, but that said principles and practices of the previous era persist.

Getting the ear of key decision makers whether in government, in the new economy, or in the burgeoning underworld of crime bosses spawned by the arrival of what passes for a market economy in Russia, is still easiest in places where they are located in greatest number. For example, in terms of the financial services industry the vast majority of head offices of Russian companies are, not surprisingly, located in Moscow. And foreign companies in this and other business sectors typically maintain an office in Moscow. In short, it is important for international and domestic business alike to have a presence in the capital. In this sense at least Moscow has lost none of its importance as a central place within Russia. In one respect, however, Moscow is now much less a world city than in the Soviet era. This is because the political ideology for which it was synonymous for so long has been discredited.

Within Russia, Moscow has the same political-administrative status as the other eighty-eight regions comprising the new post-Soviet Russian Federation. Because it is the seat of the federal government and by far the largest city in the country, it has traditionally been regarded very much as the first among equals. But in recent years its political and economic primacy has been eroded somewhat as Russia's regions wrest control over decisions impacting their political economies away from the bureaucrats and politicians in Moscow. Nowadays Moscow possesses a diminished economic base compared to what it had during the Soviet era. With the demise of the Soviet system much of Russian industry lies in ruin. Manufacturing industries which still function are, for the most part, not competitive in the global market place.

Moscow and Muscovites have both been profoundly affected by the changes introduced to date. This transformation of the urban economy is most evident in the central city where the "commodification" of space has proceeded apace. Land uses there are changing rapidly as Moscow's economy becomes more fully a part of the global economic system. For instance, the demand for office space to house both domestic and foreign businesses has brought market pressures to bear on a landscape shaped in large part by the principles of socialist town planning. As rents and lease rates have shot up since independence, residential use of central-city space for some segments of society has come under enormous market pressures. The central city is also where the conspicuous consumption of the market economy is vividly reflected in the proliferation of billboards advertising all manner of Western consumers goods and services. Less obvious are the changes in social structure and demography, but these are certainly more important than the bricks and mortar manifestations of the new economy. The implosion of the Soviet socialist system and the transition to a market economy has produced unprecedented opportunity and wealth for some people, but grinding poverty and hardship for a great many more. The following brief overview of population change patterns and social stratification in the central city during this transition period provides some clues as to the impact the changing role of Moscow as a world city increasingly integrated into the global market place has had on its citizenry.

In 1991 Moscow's total population was a shade less than 9 million. Ten years later the total population is not larger but smaller; indeed, there are now about 500,000 fewer inhabitants. This is the consequence of both demographic trends and Moscow city government policies. For instance, the rate of net natural increase of Moscow's population was −3.7 per 1,000 in 1991. From 1992 through 1995 inclusive it averaged −8.6 per 1,000 (*Moskva* 1997, p. 12). This substantial negative rate of net natural increase, which continues to the present, has not been offset through in-migration, though it could be. Instead, in deference to those already living in Moscow and the political importance of ensuring that Muscovites' comparatively high standard of living not be jeopardized, migration to Moscow remains restricted. To reside in Moscow legally requires possession of a residence permit, or *propiska*, notwithstanding federal legislation which supposedly ended such restrictions on freedom of movement in post-Soviet Russia. Tight control over the allocation of residence permits is intended to stem the flow of in-migration. Population decline has not occurred evenly across all of the city's ten prefectures, but nowhere has the relative change been as great as in the Central Prefecture, which for our purposes may be equated with the central city (Map 6.2). The Central Prefecture had nearly 9% of Moscow's total population in January 1992, but accounts barely for 6% now.

Following the market reform introduced in 1992 there was wholesale conversion of central-city housing space into other, mostly commercial, uses. In 1993, for instance, a million square meters of floor space were taken out of their various uses in the Central Prefecture for redevelopment. According to agreements between local government and firms engaged in building reconstruction, 50% of the refurbished floor space is supposed to be returned to the city for allocation as housing (*Moskovskiy komsomolets*, 16 February 1994, p. 4). By mid-1994, less than 10% of the one million square meters under redevelopment in the Central Prefecture in 1993 had been returned to the Prefecture housing stock. This figure was far below what the rate of construction project completion should have generated (*Tsentr plus*, 6, 1994, p. 1). Such 'losses' of housing space have characterized the property redevelopment process down to the present day. What is happening may be surmised. The return on investment in capital construction projects involving building redevelopment is clearly higher when refurbished floor space intended for housing is redirected to commercial uses. Local government also has a vested interest in turning a blind eye to violations of redevelopment agreements since city-owned housing is a drain on municipal budgets, whereas fees and taxes from commercial activities are increasingly important sources of revenue. Given the fact that tens of thousands of occupants of central-city apartments have been permanently displaced since 1991 (many unwillingly), the exact nature of the relationship between property developers and municipal officials is likely to remain rather murky. Data on Central Prefecture residential housing allocations in the 1990s go some way toward illuminating how people are faring in the new political economy.

Virtually all Muscovites live in apartments as opposed to detached houses of the European or North American type, therefore the size of

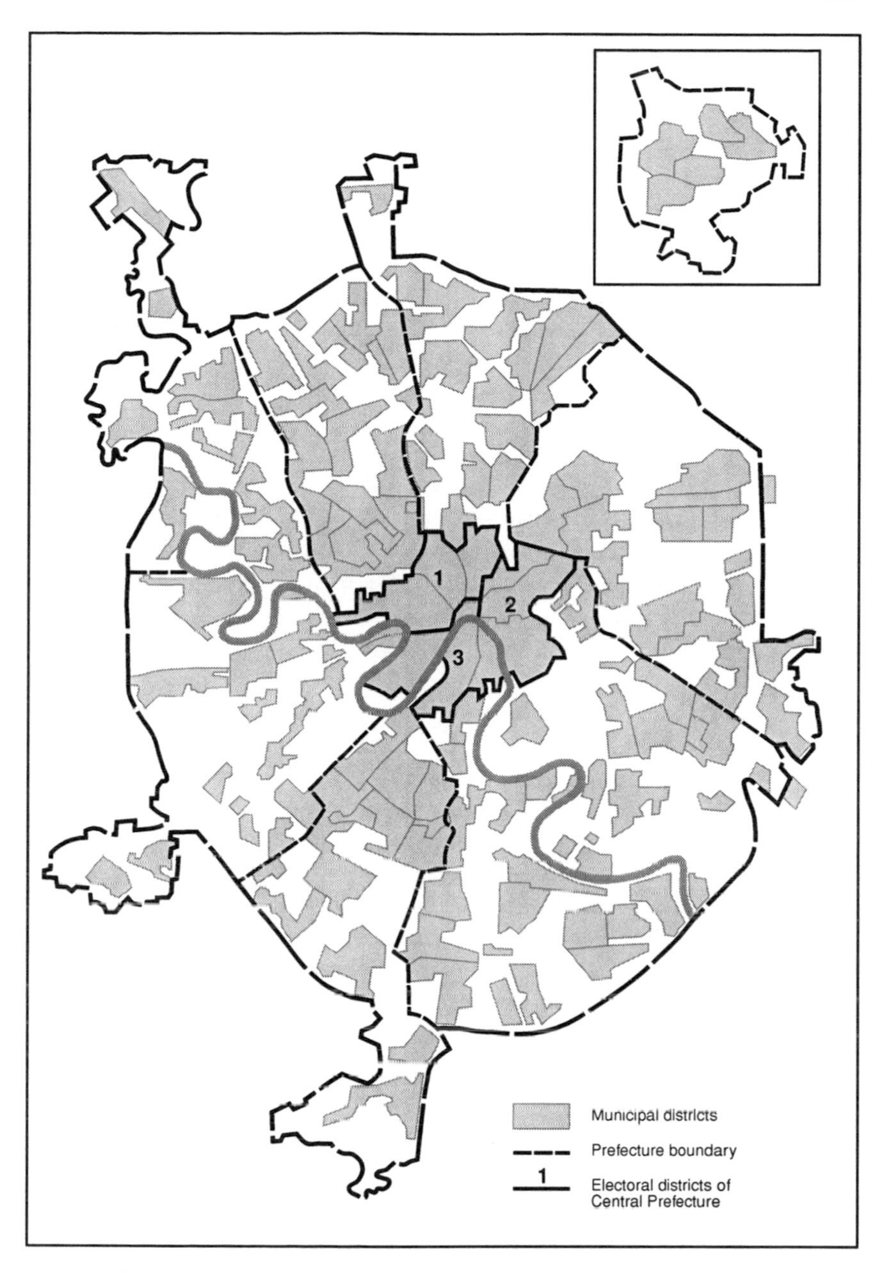

Map 6.2 Moscow – prefectures and central-city electoral districts
Source: Meriya, *Pravitel'stvo Moskvy* 1992.

apartment, its location, and the quality of the apartment building itself are the most important variables in differentiating who has what. The most readily available measure of housing is floor space per capita. In 1992 each Muscovite had, on average, 11.7 square meters of living space. Living space excludes the areas devoted to kitchen, corridors, toilet, bathroom, and storage in each apartment. At this date there was limited dispersion around the average of 11.7 square meters, save for Central Prefecture in which the average was 16.2. Given the Soviet-era prohibition of questionnaire surveys dealing with housing allocations by social class, there was no way of testing the popular perception that many elites occupied spacious apartments in the central city. The collapse of the Soviet system ushered in many changes, including a new attitude to public opinion polling and questionnaire surveys. Such surveys can shed some additional light on the process of social stratification in post-Soviet Moscow.

Surveys were conducted in October 1993 and in October 1997 by teams of professional interviewers. The October 1993 sample population of 308 respondents and the October 1997 sample population of 315 respondents were drawn from two electoral districts, which accounted for about two-thirds of the total Central Prefecture population (districts 1 and 2, see Map 6.2). The electoral rolls include all people legally resident in Moscow who have reached the age of majority, which in Russia is eighteen. The sample populations in both surveys are representative in terms of age, gender, education, and privatization of apartments. The margin of error for the sample populations is +/− 3.0% nineteen times out of twenty. Interviews were conducted in the subjects' apartments during the fourth week of October 1993 and during the third week of October 1997. A standard, pre-tested questionnaire with open and closed questions was used in both surveys. In order to ensure comparability, the questions addressing socioeconomic parameters posed in the 1997 survey replicated those used in the 1993 survey, adjusted to account for inflation during this period. Thus, all subsequent references to Russian roubles in 1993 are expressed in terms of their value in 1997.

By early 1997 per capita living space in Moscow averaged 13.5 square meters (*Moskva v Gody Reform (1992–1996)* 1997). The increase over the 1992 per capita average of 11.7 square meters resulted in part from the public and private sector housing construction programs expedited by Mayor Luzhkov's administration. All told, more than 11 million square meters were added to Moscow's housing stock during this five-year period. The reduction in Moscow's total population obviously helped to improve the per capita statistic as well. Central Prefecture residents remained the most spaciously housed, and by extension the most privileged. In 1997 living space there averaged more than 19 square meters per person (*Osnovnye* 1997). Not only had the per capita housing space average increased, there is also evidence of a qualitative improvement in housing conditions. Between 1993 and 1997 the share of the survey sample populations living in separate, as opposed to communal, apartments was similar (69.1 and 72.3% respectively). But more of them occupied separate apartments with three or more rooms in 1997 than in 1993, the proportion having risen to 35.7% from 23.4 (Survey Data Base 1993, 1997).

Not only did the Central Prefecture have a sizeable number of very well-housed residents, it also had a larger share of its population living in communal apartments than in any other Prefecture. The October 1997 questionnaire survey data reveal that nearly 28% of Central Prefecture respondents still lived in communal apartments, a figure little different from the share noted in the survey four years earlier (Survey Data Base 1993, 1997). Obviously there was a very wide variation in actual housing allocations. The reduction in total population, the improvement in the per capita allocation of living space, the increase in the size of the apartment occupied by some people, and the continuing importance of communal housing raise a number of questions regarding the Central Prefecture's social class structure. Survey data from 1993 and 1997 help to shed some light on the issues, who lives there, and whether there are any notable trends in terms of social stratification. Occupation, income, and level of education data are used as indicators of social class.

In 1997, 88.3% of the sample population of 315 respondents listed Russian as their nationality, up a percentage point from 1993 (n = 308). Jews, Ukrainians, and Tatars were the next most important nationality groups in 1997, but taken together they comprised 7.6% of respondents, about the same as in 1993. The only notable difference was that in 1997 the percentage declaring themselves to be Jewish had declined from 4.5 to 3.3%. While there were fewer people living in the Central Prefecture in 1997, they were younger, and more of them were divorced (Survey Data Base 1993, 1997).

In 1993, 62% of respondents were women. Nearly 37% of the total sample population were fifty-five years of age or older. This is a significant threshold for women especially since those who were part of the workforce, and nearly all were, are entitled to retire at that age. Men generally retire at sixty, but for some occupations the age for pension entitlement is lower. Clearly, pensioners were a numerically significant social group in central Moscow in 1993. By the time of the second survey in 1997 the demographics of the population had changed somewhat. As noted earlier, the Central Prefecture's total population had dropped quite substantially between 1993 and 1997. At the latter date, not only was the share of female respondents much lower, the proportion of the sample population of both sexes over age fifty-five was also smaller. Females now comprised 55% of the sample; men and women over age fifty-five, about 30%. A seemingly positive social change is the reduction in working pensioners (see Table 6.1). However, it is entirely possible that some of them had simply departed the Central Prefecture. Conventional wisdom has it that amongst those obliged to relocate when apartment buildings were redeveloped, a disproportionate number were elderly women. The changing proportions of women and especially those of pensionable age amongst the sample populations between 1993 and 1997 certainly support this supposition. Marital status data paint a less auspicious picture of social change. There was a smaller share of married respondents (56.1% as opposed to 60.3% in 1993), but a much larger proportion of divorced people (17.7% and 9.3% in 1997 and 1993 respectively). The rather substantial increase in the share of divorced respondents is not especially surprising in light of the turmoil the collapse of the Soviet system has visited upon the lives of ordinary people. Singles and those widowed comprised 12.5 and 13.7 respectively of the sample, not significantly different shares from 1993. All of these developments suggest some alteration in the social class fabric of the Central Prefecture. Occupational data provided by the survey respondents provide some insights into what is happening.

The changing proportions of the sample populations by occupational category are listed in Table 6.1. Several trends are apparent from these data. One of the most notable amongst them is the substantial reduction in the share of pensioners, from 36 to about 27% over the 1993–1997 time period. This is, of course, consistent with the demographic change observed for the sample populations. Another noteworthy change is the more than twofold increase in the share of business owners, from 3.9 to 9.4%. Clearly, the economic reform has taken root even if some people have become business owners less out of choice than necessity. For instance, in government white-collar occupations annual incomes have suffered since 1991. Not only has the traditional wage relationship between workers and the intelligentsia been disrupted by the market reform process, the bane of those dependent on salaries from government, irrespective of the importance of what they do, is simply their non-payment, often for months at a time. Going into business for one's self at least puts a measure of control over income. Based on responses to the surveys conducted, it is clear that some people in the business owner category are former government sector employees. These people are partly responsible for the diminution in the importance of the government employee occupational group between 1993 and 1997 (Table 6.1). There is also considerable anecdotal evidence of people having built up

Table 6.1 *Occupational structure: Central Prefecture electoral districts #1 and #2*

Occupation	1993 (%)	1997 (%)
Business owner	3.9	9.4
Office worker in state sector	10.5	11.5
Skilled worker or apprentice	10.2	5.9
Blue-collar worker (*rabochiye*)	9.2	10.6
Trade and service sector employee	4.6	5.8
Government employee	4.9	3.8
Member of profession (doctor, teacher, etc.)	5.9	7.6
Artistic professional	3.9	4.6
Student	5.3	6.7
Homemaker	5.6	7.2
Working pensioner	5.9	4.2
Non-working pensioner	30.1	22.7

Note: Margin of error is 3%.
Source: Compiled from Survey Data Base 1993 (n = 308); Survey Data Base 1997 (n = 315)

substantial private sector businesses while formally retaining their ostensibly full-time, but irregularly paid, government sector positions.

There is some suggestion of de-skilling amongst manual workers since the blue collar, or *rabochiye*, occupational category increased slightly its share of the sample, whereas the skilled worker or apprentice group had declined quite substantially by 1997 (Table 6.1). The apparent de-skilling does not necessarily mean that personal incomes for manual workers have declined, however. The demand for manual laborers in the Central Prefecture has surged because of the massive scale of urban re-development, and in the post-Soviet market economy so therefore have wages. The sizeable contingents of foreign workers on building sites in the Central Prefecture speaks to the shortage of Russian labor.

While the evidence of de-skilling amongst manual workers is only suggestive, it is consistent with the change in the level of education of the sample populations. In 1993, nearly two-thirds of all respondents had a higher or specialized education (64.6%). By 1997 this figure had dropped to 57.9%. While fewer of the Central Prefecture's working-age population had a higher or specialized education in 1997 compared to 1993, the reduction in the number of people over fifty-five played a part in this change as well. Many pensioners were well educated even if obliged to live in a communal apartment. The cultural attractions of the central city for the educated elderly were significant, especially during the Soviet era when being on a state pension did not preclude participation in cultural activities. Since 1991 the economic position of most pensioners has deteriorated drastically. Indeed, no longer are tickets to many cultural events and facilities even available for the official rouble price, such items now being part of the dollar-denominated world of the professional scalper.

The changes in occupational categories listed in Table 6.1 – the slight reduction in the share of working pensioners, the significant reduction in the percentage of people on pension, the increase in the percentage of homemakers and students, and the more than twofold increase in the business owner occupational group – taken together suggest something of an improvement in the overall financial well-being of the respondents. Survey data on monthly income confirm this to be the case.

After adjusting for inflation, the share of respondents with monthly incomes in excess of 500,000 roubles rose from 20.2 to 52% between 1993 and 1997. A monthly income of 500,000 roubles has been used as a rough dividing line between the better off and the less well off, between those who have benefited from the new economy and those who quite clearly have not. Of the 315 total sample population, there were 164 respondents who earned more than 500,000 roubles per month, and 151 who did not. Perhaps not surprisingly, the low income group was older, and females outnumbered males by a substantial margin. In terms of age, 42.6% were fifty-five or older compared to 30% for the sample population in total, and 64.2% were women compared to 55% for all respondents. Thus, higher income earners were both younger and there was a larger number of males amongst them. In terms of marital status there was a larger share of married and single respondents in the higher income category than in the lower. In the latter category, widows were more numerous than in the higher income group (24.7 as opposed to 4.4%). The share divorced was about the same in each income category. Slightly more of the low income group were Russian than in the higher income group (89% and 87.6% respectively), but neither group deviated very much from the figure for Moscow as a whole (90.5% in 1994) (*Moskva v Tsifrakh '95* 1996).

Nearly 24% of respondents in 1997 had monthly incomes of more than 1 million roubles, 9% more than 2 million, and roughly 7% more than 2.5 million. In post-Soviet Russia, defining the middle class has become an interesting sociological issue (*Noviye izvestiya* 12 March 1998). Few observers of the post-Soviet Moscow scene would dispute that anyone with an income in excess of 2 million roubles per month in 1997 would certainly qualify (*Noviye vremya* 22 March 1998).

At the other end of the income scale, the number of respondents declaring monthly incomes of less than 100,000 roubles dropped from 14.7 to

2.9%. The smaller share of pensioners amongst the respondents in 1997 compared to 1993 is at least partly responsible for the significant reduction in the number of people with a monthly income of less than 100,000 roubles. In 1997 people trying to live on this level of monthly income would be regarded as very poor indeed. The reduction in the number of the very poor living in the Central Prefecture was consistent with the trend in Moscow as a whole, but was of greater relative magnitude (*Segodnya* 22 September 1997). Moscow is in most respects a different economic and social world, however, and this relative change in the fortunes of the poor is a case in point. In most places in Russia during this period, the number of poor had increased, and rather substantially at that (*Nezavisimaya gazeta* 17 October 1997).

While social stratification increased over time during the Soviet period, notwithstanding official propaganda to the contrary, elites and manifestations of their privileges were seldom on public display. By way of contrast, since the collapse of the Soviet system the newly rich tend to be both lavish, and conspicuous, consumers. Social class standing is a function of many factors, but occupation, income, and level of education must figure prominently amongst them. Based on these criteria, there was clearly a much greater degree of social stratification in 1997 than in 1993 amongst Central Prefecture survey respondents. There was a sizeable contingent of quite well-off people in 1997, housing for some was much improved, those owning their apartments had increased from about 35 to nearly 55%, and business owners were fast becoming a numerically important occupational group. Despite these material improvements, as noted earlier, nearly 28% of the respondents still lived in a communal apartment in 1997, a figure little different from four years earlier. The very poor, while fewer in number in 1997, were probably worse off than in 1993 owing to the rapid inflation in the prices of many basic goods and services. Clearly, Central Prefecture society had changed in many tangible ways.

Moscow in a transitional and turbulent political economy

Moscow has had some claim to world city status during three eras – the imperial, the Soviet, and now the post-Soviet. Social class relations as well as the built environment were impacted differently in each of them. In imperial Russia, social class standing was very much determined by legal estates and ranks, and declaration of position in society was more often conveyed by how one dressed than by where one lived in the city (Bater 1984). Thus, residential segregation as one manifestation of social class stratification was little developed in comparison with the major cities of Europe or for that matter North America on the eve of the First World

War. While living in the central city even at this time afforded some obvious advantages, the rich and the very poor tended to live in close proximity, indeed, often living within the same building (Bater 1976). Grinding poverty was everywhere much in evidence in imperial urban Russia and Moscow was certainly no exception.

All such imperial Russia social class difference was to be erased in consequence of the revolution in 1917. Soviet socialism heralded a new society, and a new urban scene, both of which were to reflect egalitarian principles. As with most things Soviet, principle and practice were rarely congruent. An apartment in a good-quality building well located in central Moscow came to be associated in the mind of the general public with a privileged position in Soviet society. To be sure, manifestations of elite social standing were less conspicuous in Soviet-era Moscow than during the imperial era. But they existed nonetheless, as some of the data on housing allocations presented here indicate.

Post-Soviet Mosow is in an obvious state of transition. Within the Central Prefecture there is evidence of increasing social change and social stratification. The combined pressure of gentrification and needs of commerce is giving rise to a more stratified, a more polarized society. Central-city space is being rapidly commodified, as Russia's economy and hence Moscow's is becoming more integrated with the global market place (Kostinskiy 2001). However, vestiges of the former era do remain and do impact what is happening in Moscow. For instance, although rent and lease rates have increased dramatically during the 1990s, reaching and indeed sometimes exceeding those in Western cities long integrated in the world economy, in Moscow there is still no counterpart to the capitalist city real estate market. The sale of land is still resisted by Moscow city government. Land sales by means of auction do occur on occasion, but are rare, limited in terms of property involved, are restricted to the one Prefecture which sits 'outside' the city border (see Map 6.2), and consistently produce less income for the owner, in this case the city, than assumed (*Izvestiya* 10 January 2001). Unlike most other world cities, the mayor of Moscow, Yuri Luzhkov, has been able to hold some of the forces for change at bay. Restricting in-migration has obviously benefited the existing population in material terms since there are fewer people to place demands on the urban system. It does, however, exacerbate the natural process of aging since deaths exceed births and family formation dwindles. But in the quest for the higher standard of living promised by the post-Soviet new economy, personal material priorities rather than the well-being of society as a whole take precedence. In contemporary Moscow money talks, and the louder the better it would seem.

The changes set in motion by the advent of a market economy are not just affecting the social fabric of the central city, they are altering the built environment as well. But not all citizens are enamoured with the turn of events since 1991, irrespective of how they might have fared in a material sense. To be sure, there is ample evidence of the material aspects of a consumer society and some indications from employment data trends of a vigorous private sector. The majority of Muscovites now own their apartment, an important facet of the privatization process, but one that was stage-managed by the Moscow mayoralty in defiance of federal government legislative guidelines (Bater 1994). In a similar fashion, the "privatization" of Moscow's huge complement of industries initiated in 1992 did not follow federal legislative guidelines. In a deal made between Mayor Yuri Luzhkov and then-President Boris Yeltsin, the Moscow mayoralty enacted its own version of privatization, one in which the city did not lose control of the process, and therefore, as Luzhkov argued, lose out on any of the benefits. That a few well-placed people became exceedingly wealthy as a result of these mayoralty-managed transactions was a price the Moscow mayoralty was more than willing to pay it seems. Control of urban development by the mayoralty continues to be pervasive. For instance, it was not until January 1999 that a draft law was sent to the City *Duma* (Council) from a joint commission of the *Duma* and Moscow mayoralty to permit the sale of land. Up until that date, land could only be leased for up to forty-nine years. However, this legislation will not result in land being freely bought and sold, as it is just outside the city borders in Moscow *Oblast'* (district). The legislation will permit land within Moscow to be sold for the first time, but only for single-family housing for elites, and for special private enterprise projects which fit the criteria for urban economic development as determined by the Moscow mayoralty (*Kommersant-Daily* 11 December 1998, p. 2). In short, in Moscow, the privatization process is a very grey area, for little occurs which is not approved by the city administrative authorities, a decision-making process in which Mayor Yuri Luzhkov frequently figures very prominently (Chinayeva 1996).

Summary

The role of Moscow as a world city has been clearly and significantly diminished since 1991. Once the center of a political-economic system in which the center dominated all aspects of life everywhere in the state, it is now the seat of a federal government in a rump country beset with strong centrifugal tendencies. The federal government in Moscow must now deal with problems increasingly outside its political jurisdiction to resolve, even if the financial resources to do so were available, which they are not. The standard of living for most Russians has plummeted during the 1990s. Adapting to the changing material circumstances has been a necessary, and mostly unwelcome, development since in most cases this has meant getting by with much less. This has had direct and fundamental consequences in terms of how people view the future. Perhaps the most telling indication of how attitudes have shifted is in terms of the birth rate. Despite sizeable net in-migration since 1991, Russia's total population has contracted, and quite substantially. As the foregoing discussion has highlighted, Moscow's demographic situation is no different. Indeed, it has been exacerbated by the mayoralty's policy of limiting the number of new resident permits issued each year. While this policy eases the strain on city-supported social services, it contravenes individual rights to move freely within the country as enshrined in the federal constitution. Thus, living in Moscow is not a right but a privilege, just as it was in the Soviet era. The city's role within Russia in this regard has not changed even if the quality of life of its citizens has. Moscow's role as a world city may be diminished in the current post-Soviet epoch, but what goes on there doubtless will continue to be of consequence well beyond the confines of its official border.

REFERENCES

Bater, James H. 1976. *St Petersburg: Industrialization and Change*. London: Edward Arnold.

1980. *The Soviet City: Ideal and Reality*. London: Edward Arnold.

1984. "The Soviet City: Continuity and Change in Privilege and Place," in John Agnew, John Mercer, and David Sopher, *The City in Cultural Context*. Boston: Allen and Unwin, pp. 134–162.

1994. "Privatization in Moscow," *Geographical Review*, 84: 201–215.

2001. "Adjusting to Change: Privilege and Place in Post-Soviet Central Moscow," *Canadian Geographer*, 45 (3): 237–251.

Bater, James H., Amelin, Vladimir N. and Degtyarev, Andrei A. 1998. "Market Reform and the Central City: Moscow Revisited," *Post-Soviet Geography and Economics*, 39: 1–19.

Bertaud, Alain and Renaud, Bertrand 1995. *Cities without Land Markets: Location and Land Use in the Socialist City*. Washington, DC: World Bank. Policy Research Working Paper No. 1477.

Chinayeva, Elena 1996. "Yurii Luzhkov – the Man Who Runs Moscow," *Transition*, 2: 30–33.

Colton, Timothy J. 1995. *Moscow: Governing the Socialist Metropolis*. Cambridge, MA: Belknap Press of Harvard University Press.

Dierke Weltatlas 1978. Braunschweig: Georg Westermann Verlag.

Izvestiya 10 January 2001.

Kommersant-Daily 11 December 1998.
Kostinskiy, Grigoriy 2001. "Post-Socialist Moscow in Flux," in Ronan Paddison (ed.), *Handbook of Urban Studies*. Beverly Hills: Sage, pp. 450–465.
Lorimer, Frank 1946. *The Population of the Soviet Union: History and Prospects*. Geneva: League of Nations.
Meriya, *Pravitel'stvo Moskvy* 1992. Moscow: Department of Administrative Affairs, Information of the Moscow Mayoralty.
Moskovskiy komsomolets 16 February 1994.
Moskva v Gody Reform (1992–1996) 1997. Moscow: Moscow City Statistical Committee.
Moskva v Tsifrakh '95 1996. Moscow: Moscow City Statistical Committee.
Nezavisimaya gazeta 10 March 1994.
17 October 1997.
Noviye izvestiya 12 March 1998.
Noviye vremya 22 March 1998.
Osnovnye 1997. *Osnovnye Pokazateli Sotsial'no-Ekonomicheskogo Razvitiye Administrativnyy Okrugov g. Moskvy za Yanvar' – Dekabr' 1996 g.* 1997. Moscow: Moscow City Central Committee.
Owen, Thomas 1983. "Entrepreneurship and the Structure of Enterprise in Russia, 1800–1880," in Gregory Guroff and Fred V. Carstensen (eds.), *Entrpreneurship in Imperial Russia and the Soviet Union*. Princeton: Princeton University Press, pp. 59–83.
Segodnya 22 September 1997.
Survey Data Base 1993. Electoral districts #1 and #2, sample size 308, unpublished questionnaire results, October.
1997. Electoral districts #1 and #2, sample size 315, unpublished questionnaire results, October.
Trushchenko, O. E. 1993. "Akkumulyatsiya Simvolicheskogo Kapitala v Prostranstve Stolichnogo Tsentra," *Rossiyskiy Monitor: Arkhiv Sovremennoy Politiki*, 3: 145–165.
1995. *Prestizh Tsentra: Gorodskaya Sotsial'naya Segregatsiya v Moskve*. Moscow: Socio-Logos.
Tsentr plus 6, 1994.

7 Hong Kong's pathway to becoming a global city

Alvin Y. So

Hong Kong, like Singapore, seems to be quite different from the other cities that we discuss in this volume. This is because Hong Kong is not just a city, but also a quasi "city-state" (Kirby 1997, p. iii). Even in the colonial era, the Hong Kong government was highly autonomous in determining its own political, economic, and social affairs, and Hong Kong was an independent member in such a global organization as the Asia Pacific Economic Cooperation. In addition, Hong Kong is a rich city. Its gross domestic product (EDP) per capita of over US$24,211 in 2001 made it one of the richest territories in the Asian region. Furthermore, unlike the other cities in this volume that aspired to be a global city, Hong Kong has already attained the status of a global city. Hong Kong is ranked the ninth largest trading entity in the world. It operates the busiest container port in the world in terms of throughput, and it is the world's ninth largest banking center in terms of external banking transactions (Hong Kong Government 1999).

Hong Kong resembles Singapore in some aspects, but it had a different path of development. In Singapore, independence took place before development, and it was the independent city-state that elevated Singapore to the global city status. In Hong Kong, development took place before decolonization. It was the colonial government that elevated Hong Kong to the global city status in the 1980s and the 1990s. Moreover, Hong Kong just went through the historical process of national reunification and became a Special Administrative Region (SAR) of China on 1 July 1997. Thus, researchers would like to know in what ways China's resumption of sovereignty in 1997 has affected Hong Kong's global city status.

Singapore and Hong Kong also differ in spatial integration. Singapore acts as a regional center for Southeast Asia, and it has developed extensive economic networks with the Southeast Asian states. On the other hand, Hong Kong acts as a regional center for East Asia, and it is deeply embedded in the production and trading networks of the East Asian states. It will be shown that Hong Kong's embeddedness in the East Asian region

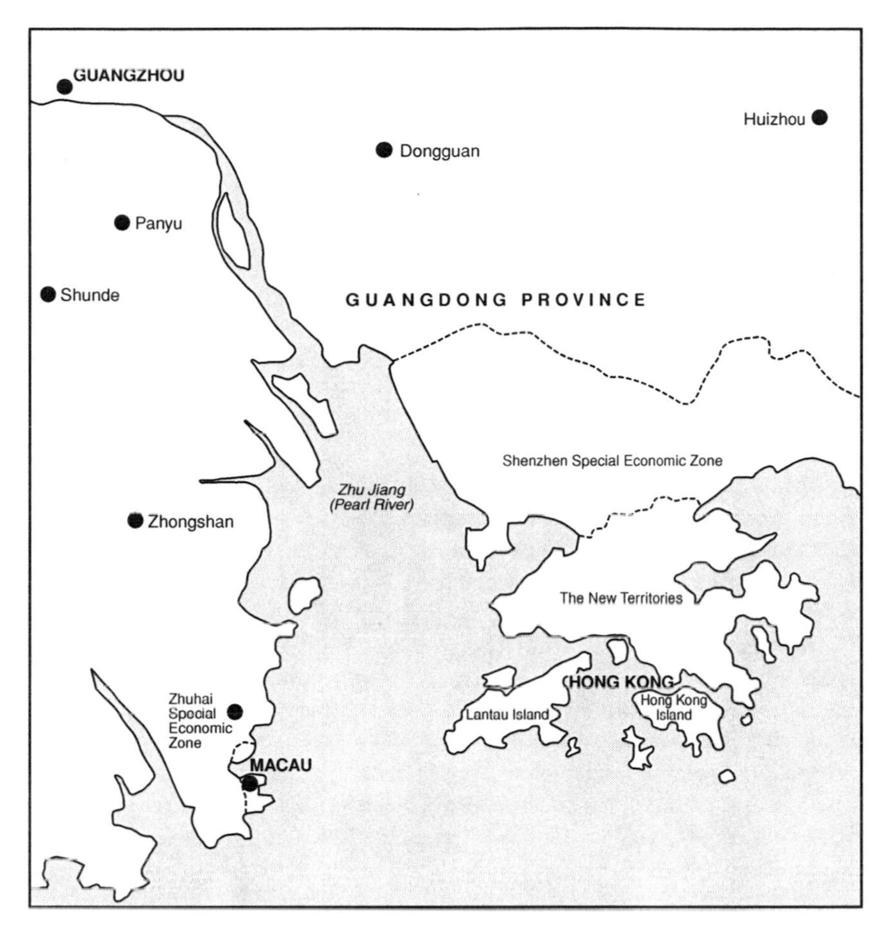

Map 7.1 "The Pearl City" in the Pearl River Delta

has been decisive in shaping its path of development in the second half of the twentieth century.

The literature on large cities focuses on either the global level or the local level. There are those who examine the role of large cities within the global economy, usually from the point of view of their importance as the sites of global and regional headquarters of transnational corporations as well as their specialization in business and financial services (Friedmann 1995; Sassen 1997). However, another group of researchers examines large cities from a local perspective, focusing upon city development and governance as well as the distribution of needs such as housing, health care, and clean environment to the urban population (Ward 1998).

Although this chapter will also deal with the global and the local, it will focus on the regional. In particular, this chapter will highlight the following regional dynamics in Asia: the Cold War between the US and China, the Chinese national reunification project, the Asian financial crisis, and the competition for a global metropolis status. This chapter will show that these regional dynamics have shaped three different phases in Hong Kong's development in the second half of the twentieth century. It will show how the Cold War in Asia in the post-Second World War era has transformed Hong Kong from an entrepôt to an industrial city in the 1970s, how the Chinese national reunification project has transformed Hong Kong into a service center in the early 1990s, and how the recent Asian financial crisis and the competition for a global metropolis have provided impetuses to transform Hong Kong into a high-tech center in the twenty-first century.

The emphasis on regional dynamics makes this study also different from much of the Hong Kong literature, which stresses either the role of the colonial state or the contribution of Hong Kong entrepreneurs. In the colonial state explanation, Hong Kong was often said to be only a place with barren rock when the British occupied it in 1842. Thus, it was the colonial state that was responsible for turning the "barren rock" into the "Pearl of the Orients." The colonial state instituted the rule of law, created an efficient bureaucracy free of corruption, set up a modern infrastructure, instituted a low tax system, and, most important, adopted a laissez-faire economic policy that attracted foreign investment and generated the spirit of capitalism in Hong Kong. As a result, Hong Kong was known to be a capitalist "paradise" that had the freest economy in the world (Tsang 1999).

Aside from the colonial state, another factor stressed by the Hong Kong literature is the Neo-Confucian spirit of Chinese entrepreneurs. Confucian familism has facilitated the pooling of capital among kin, the reliance on unpaid family labor, and the avoidance of bureaucratic rules among family members. The small family firm was said to be highly dynamic, able to adjust to work with the fluctuation of the business cycle. Confucian education was said to have generated an educated workforce highly committed to work and to the firm (Wong 1988).

As convincing as the statist and entrepreneurial arguments are, they are unable to explain the changing phases of the Hong Kong economy during the second half of the twentieth century. Given the laissez-faire colonial state and Neo-Confucian entrepreneurs, how can researchers explain Hong Kong's structural shift from an entrepôt to an industrial city, to a service center, and toward a high-tech city? As such, this chapter argues that regional dynamics have to be brought back in so as to explain the changing phases of Hong Kong's economy.

This chapter is divided into four main sections: (1) Hong Kong as an entrepôt (up to the late 1940s), (2) Hong Kong as an industrial city (the early 1950s to the late 1970s), (3) Hong Kong as a service city (the early 1980s to the mid-1990s), and (4) the impetus toward a high-tech city (since the late 1990s). Although the focus of this chapter will be on the impact of Asian regional dynamics on the political economy of Hong Kong, it will also discuss demography, labor market, and spatial development.

Hong Kong as an entrepôt

At the turn of the nineteenth century, China was still a powerful empire dominating the East Asian region. Since the Chinese state perceived trade as a favor granted to vassal states, foreign trade was tightly controlled and limited to take place only at Guangzhou (Canton). Thus, it took Great Britain to wage a war, the so-called "Opium War," to open up China for trade. Britain took the lead because it was the hegemonic power during this period, and because it was developing a highly profitable opium trade between China and its colonies in India.

After winning the Opium War in 1842, Britain took the island of Hong Kong as its colony in order to secure a base for the China trade. In 1860, Britain added the Kowloon peninsula to its territory after winning another war. Finally, in 1898, Britain leased the hinterland and the outer islands, the "New Territories," for ninety-nine years after China lost a war to Japan. Under the British, Hong Kong quickly became an entrepôt handling Anglo-Chinese trade because of its fine natural harbour and its strategic location in the south China coast. As an entrepôt port, Hong Kong was responsible for handling goods from China for reexport and importing goods for its hinterland of south China and Southeast Asia.

After losing many wars to foreign powers, the Chinese Empire finally crumbled, leading to the scramble for concessions, the opening of China to foreign trade and investment, and the partitioning of China by warlords at the turn of the twentieth century. Only in the late 1920s did the Nationalist government based in Nanjing begin to recover sovereignty over a number of foreign settlements and treaty ports in China. Hong Kong, however, remained a British colony. Britain was determined to hold on to this Far East colony because of the prosperous entrepôt trade with China and Southeast Asia. The Japanese wartime occupation (1941–1945) disrupted the Hong Kong economy momentarily, but the rehabilitation process was swift enough to allow normal entrepôt activities to recover in less than a year's time after the war ended.

As a result of a century of entrepôt development, Hong Kong had developed a sophisticated institutional framework of commerce and finance on the eve of the 1949 Communist Revolution. Major commercial shipping and insurance companies had established bases in Hong Kong and the port's success led to the development of shipbuilding and ship repairing industries (Chalkley 1997). Because of the rapid development in entrepôt trade and related industries, Hong Kong's population had expanded very rapidly, from about 5,000 in the 1840s to more than 500,000 by the 1940s. In Chalkley's (1997, p. 139) account, these newcomers were almost entirely from China. Mainland Chinese came and went freely across the border. They were attracted either by the opportunities for trade and employment or by Hong Kong's role as a refuge of political stability during wars and rebellions. However, they tended to return to China when the situation improved or they had amassed enough capital to retire or buy a business. Hong Kong had also been the center for overseas Chinese emigration. Many Chinese laborers and merchants immigrated via Hong Kong to other parts of Southeast Asia, the USA, Canada, and Australia. In this respect, Hong Kong was a place of transit and few felt that it was their home. The colony's rather few Europeans – government officials and traders – were transient as well (C. Speak 1997, p. 256).

Like other British colonies, the Hong Kong government failed to institute a competitive, electoral system to choose its governor and legislators. The governor of Hong Kong was appointed by the London government for a renewable term of five years. The governor, in turn, appointed senior government officials and "Unofficial Members" to the Executive Council (Exco) and the Legislative Council (Legco). There was a close expatriate business alliance between senior government officials and the British *hongs*, large traditional trading companies such as Jardine & Matheson, John Swire, and Hong Kong and Shanghai Bank formed during the mid-nineteenth century.

In short, up to the late 1940s, Hong Kong was a typical British colonial city. Its government was dominated by the expatriates. Its economy was dependent on entrepôt trade and had little manufacturing industry. And its residents were mostly immigrants. However, all of these changed in the early 1950s as a result of the changing dynamics in East Asia.

Hong Kong as an industrial city

After the Second World War, the US emerged as the new hegemonic power in the capitalist world economy. Under American leadership, the post-war world economy became much more liberal, multilateral, and interdependent, resulting in a global expansion in trade under the American free trade policy. These conditions provided an excellent opportunity for developing countries to strive for upward mobility in the world economy.

In response to the 1949 Chinese Communist Revolution in East Asia, the US initiated several actions, which indirectly fostered the economic development of what were to become the East Asian Newly Industrial Economies (NIEs). The United States sent warships to protect the defeated Guomintang (GMD) in Taiwan, dispatched soldiers to fight against the communists in Korea, supported counterrevolutionary activities in China, froze mainland Chinese assets in the United States, imposed an economic embargo on mainland Chinese products, prevented mainland China from gaining a seat in the United Nations, and waged ideological attacks on Chinese "communist totalitarianism" in the mass media.

In order to build up a strong capitalist Asia as a bulwark against the spread of communism, the US provided economic aid, industrial contracts, and open American markets to its East Asian allies (So and Chiu 1995).

As a result of American hegemony in East Asia, Hong Kong was gradually pulled into the new international division of labor in which the capitalist states in East Asia supplied consumer products to advanced industrial countries in exchange for technology, capital, and producers' goods. However, also behind the push for Hong Kong to enter the US-led world economy was the regional dynamics in East Asia, whereby the isolation of communist China from the capitalist world economy closed off possibilities of a regionalist development trajectory in East Asia. Furthermore, the process of decolonization in Southeast Asia brought into existence a number of nationalist regimes, which installed import barriers to protect their domestic markets. This closing off of Southeast Asian markets further pushed Hong Kong to search for new markets in the Western industrial states in the late 1950s.

The industrial revolution

The Korean War dealt a decisive blow to Hong Kong's entrepôt economy. In June 1951, the war prompted the United Nations to impose an embargo on Chinese trade, which crippled the Hong Kong economy, since China was the colony's largest trading partner. In 1954, Hong Kong's total value of trade was a meagre 60% of its 1948 level (Szczepanik 1958, p. 45). Apart from the embargo, entrepôt trade with China also declined in the 1950s because of the communist regime's rigid control of foreign investments, imports, and exports. Including the direct loss of both earnings from entrepôt trade and of indirect earnings through warehouses, transport, banking, and insurance services, Hong Kong's real GDP fell by 5.5% in 1951 (Ho 1979). As Hong Kong's trading houses and shipping companies were decimated, thousands of workers were displaced from employment. Added to this was the flow of refugees fleeing communist China. By 1952 unemployment was estimated between 15% and 34% (Henderson 1991, p. 170).

Fortunately, several "windfall profits" from the Chinese Communist Revolution enabled Hong Kong to start its industrial revolution. The "liberation" of Shanghai by the Chinese communists prompted a large number of Shanghainese textile firms to divert their production to Hong Kong (Wong 1988). In addition, the massive inflow of refugees from China, many of whom had industrial employment experience, created a pool of potential entrepreneurs willing to work hard and take the risk of setting up manufacturing firms. The result was a mushrooming of small firms with low-level capital investment and technology, firms which tapped into the extensive commercial networks established throughout Hong Kong's entrepôt history, as well as into the abundant supply of cheap and diligent refugee workers. This particular conjuncture of refugee capital, refugee labor, and preexisting entrepôt trading networks provided the impetus for Hong Kong's export-oriented industrialization in the early 1950s. In other words, a major part of socialist China's capital and labor assets suddenly was transplanted to Hong Kong to reap the benefits of the post-war economic upswing of the capitalist world economy.

The flight from socialism was only one consequence of the conflict between the US and the emergent Chinese socialist state. In the midst of the Cold War, US policy makers supported the Nationalist government in Taiwan, sent troops to Korea, and imposed an economic blockade on China. Such heightened hostility from the capitalist power bloc explains why China did not reclaim control of Hong Kong right after the Communist Revolution. Due to its colonial status, Hong Kong was the only port where China had access to foreign currency to buy necessary foreign equipment. As a result, China was quite willing to supply food, raw materials, and water to Hong Kong in exchange for foreign currency – earning an estimated 30 to 40% from its foreign currency from the Hong Kong trade (Pye 1983, p. 461). Observing this peculiar policy of China, Kraus (1979, p. 256) insightfully remarks: "geographical isolation permits the People's Republic of China to benefit from bourgeois skills [of Hong Kong] without sustaining the cost of internal capitalist institutions." The "unequal exchange" of low-priced food from socialist China for the Hong Kong currency also subsidized the Hong Kong economy, lowered Hong Kong's cost of living, and strengthened the competitive power of Hong Kong in the world market.

The liberal, laissez-faire state

Intense conflict between socialist China and the capitalist power bloc also explains the lack of political unrest in Hong Kong in the 1950s. The sudden influx of capitalists and laborers in this period did not arouse any tension between the Chinese population and the British ruling class in Hong Kong. As immigrants fleeing from communist rule, the new Chinese capitalists in Hong Kong tolerated the British monopoly of the state machinery in order not to create any political instability that would threaten the business environment.

Most of the members of the Hong Kong's working class were also immigrants who moved to the territory during the Second World War or during the Communist Revolution. These immigrants seemed generally satisfied with Hong Kong's labor situation. Although critics cited terrible working conditions in the colony, immigrant workers themselves perceived improved status compared to previous work conditions in China. Young female workers, bound by a set of patriarchal values, perceived factory work as a means of promoting the welfare of their families. Thus Lau (1982) proposes a "utilitarian familism" thesis: recent immigrant workers were more interested in making money for their families than in political participation. No state ideology of anti-communism was needed to dilute the class-consciousness and radicalism of the Hong Kong workers.

Of course, unions did exist, and strikes occurred. But unions tended to be small and ideologically divided between pro-socialist and pro-nationalist factions. Moreover, China is said to have held back the more radical demands of the pro-socialist trade unions so as not to risk disturbing China's substantial foreign exchange earnings. Strikes were few in number, serious strikes almost unknown (Levin and Chiu 1993). The absence of intensive class struggles further enhanced the industrialization process, with economic output, employment, and export receipts tripling within a few years in the 1950s (Youngson 1982).

The favorable world market situation and the lack of domestic class struggles partially explain the liberal, non-interventionist policy of the Hong Kong state. Unlike the Taiwanese and South Korean regimes, the colonial government in Hong Kong did not need to militarize or promote an anti-communist ideology to justify its colonial rule. Nor did the Hong Kong administration need to involve itself in the promotion of export industrialization because the Chinese colony had already gained a head start in exports by the early 1950s. The Hong Kong administration was further constrained from pursuing an active developmental strategy or embarking on financially risky intervention because of the colony's need to remain financially solvent and balance its budget lest the British home government step in. And Hong Kong did not benefit from the sort of geopolitical links with the US, which endowed the South Korea, and Taiwan states with large amounts of aid and loans. Hence, fears of the colonial state's "inability" to pay for any industrial assistance program largely shaped the policy discussions of the 1950s. Industrial land had to be sold to the capitalists at the going market price without any special allowances or concessions. Public money also could not be used to subsidize the cost of low-interest industrial loans (Chiu 1994).

British expatriates continued to dominate Hong Kong's senior state managers. The central organs of the Hong Kong government – the Executive Council (Exco) and the Legislative Council (Legco) – similarly fell under the control of British businessmen and bankers. The British business community in Hong Kong, the directors and top managers of giant corporations such as the Hong Kong and Shanghai Banking Corporation, monopolized the banking industry and the public utilities sector of Hong Kong. Their interests lay in the financial sector, and they did not want state interference in this sector limiting their freedom. They also were inclined to support the state's hands-off policy in the manufacturing sector (Chiu 1994). Subsequently, the state continued its laissez-faire policy despite Hong Kong's entrance into a new phase of export-industrialization in the 1950s.

New immigrants and the public housing program

In 1949, after the Chinese communists defeated the GMD and "liberated" the mainland, Hong Kong experienced a sudden influx of refugees. Hong Kong's population jumped from 1,600,000 in 1941 to more than 2,360,000 in 1950 as a result. Hambro (1955, p. 162) estimated that about 667,000 mainland refugees fled to Hong Kong for political and economic reasons in 1954. This massive population increase imposed a backbreaking burden on the colony in the early 1950s. Subsequently, the Hong Kong government set up border fences separating Hong Kong from mainland China in order to control the flow of immigrants to Hong Kong.

As the industrial revolution began to take off later in the 1950s, the manufacturing factor was able to absorb the fifties' immigrants into the workforce. In fact, by the late 1960s, despite another wave of about 120,000 Chinese immigrants during the early 1960s after the failure of the Great Leap Forward, Hong Kong had begun to transform from a labor surplus economy to a labor deficit economy. To meet the needs of the expanding manufacturing sector, the control over illegal immigration was relaxed until 1980. Before 1980 any illegal immigrants who were caught at the frontier were returned to mainland China, but those who succeeded in reaching the urban areas were permitted to stay. This "touch-base" concession encouraged illegal immigration. About 500,000 illegal or legal immigrants are estimated to have entered Hong Kong in the late 1970s. Like the previous waves, these migrants were dominated by young men who were absorbed primarily into the manufacturing sector and who helped to relieve upward pressure on wages in that key sector (Chalkley 1997, pp. 140, 144; Skeldon 1997, p. 266).

Christine Speak (1997, p. 257) explains that until 1954, the Hong Kong government believed that the immigrants would return to China, and the provision of houses was organized on an *ad hoc* basis. The huge influx of immigrants to Hong Kong, however, placed serious strains on Hong Kong's environment and infrastructure. Since the Hong Kong government generally adopted a laissez-faire policy, the newcomers were left to build squatters for themselves, and makeshift settlements spread over the hillsides. It took a disastrous fire which swept through a squatter area on Christmas Eve 1953, leaving 50,000 people homeless, to prompt the Hong Kong government to deal with the housing problem for the immigrants. After developing a few relatively small-scale projects on resettlement estates in the late 1950s and 1960s, the Hong Kong government in 1972 announced an ambitious plan to rehouse 1.8 million people in public housing in ten years to eliminate squatter huts clinging to the hillside. Public housing helped to lower the cost of labor and promote peaceful labor-management relationships, facilitating economic development. However, the massive population dislocation by the demolition of squatter huts and slums led to discontent among those affected, especially so since the public housing provided was of poor quality and did not meet their needs. Issues such as public housing management and allocation of public housing resources thus became catalysts for urban social conflict throughout the 1970s.

Faced with the constraint of limited space in the territory on the one hand, and increasing momentum of economic development on the other, the government devised various means to extract land for development. Large-scale reclamation from the sea and excavation from hillsides could not adequately resolve the problem. The government therefore resorted to the development of New Towns on the urban fringe. The first three New Towns were built around the urban fringe at Tsuen Wan, Sha Tin, and Tuen Mun in the 1970s. The New Towns were aimed to reduce central-area congestion, to reduce inner-city overcrowding, and to provide better housing and environmental conditions for the working class (Chalkley 1997, p. 145; C. Speak 1997, p. 257).

Hong Kong as a service center

The golden era of post-war economic expansion came to an end in the 1970s when, after the oil crisis of 1973, the world economy entered into a downward phase. In addition, the industrial, commercial, and financial supremacy of the US was increasingly challenged by rival core powers. As with other periods of global rivalry, the ideology of protectionism replaced the ideology of free trade. States tightened import restrictions and set up trade quotas. The new wave of protectionism posed a threat to the expanding export economy of Hong Kong.

Mirroring the decline of the US was the emergence of Japan as a regional power in East Asia. Hard-pressed by the rising cost of production, the Japanese small and medium-sized firms initiated a transborder expansion to the NIEs in the early 1970s (almost a decade earlier than the transborder expansion of the large Japanese firm to the US in the mid-1980s). These Japanese firms provided a significant portion of the machinery and components that NIE enterprises badly needed to turn out toys, bicycles, radios, television sets, and personal computer monitors. What emerged in East Asia since the 1970s, therefore, was an "organic division of labor" that married Japanese capital and technology to the cheap, relatively docile labor of the NIEs.

By the 1980s, East Asia became a new epicenter of capital accumulation in the world economy. Furthermore, due to Latin America's debt, Africa's poor record of governance, the Middle East's political instability, East Asia became the preferred destination for investment by financial giants from Japan and the United States. The lowering of profit rates in the core, and the relocation of their industries to the periphery, also called for a new financial center outside New York and London.

In the late 1970s, communist China was incorporated into the capitalist world system. China changed from self-reliance to an open-door policy, actively seeking to introduce foreign capital, technology, and expertise so as to achieve the "Four Modernizations." Thus, China used special economic zones and joint-venture oil field explorations to lure foreign investment. These new developments enhanced the possibility of establishing a new service center close to China's territory.

Economic integration with mainland China

Having been involved in international trade for over a century, Hong Kong was well known for its strength in entrepôt trade, financial connections, and other services. Hong Kong now became a facilitator or intermediary for mainland trade and investment, providing valuable channels of information to China, serving as a contact point for China's trade, financing China's modernization, acting as a conduit for China's technology transfer, and providing a training ground for China to learn and practice capitalist skills in a market environment (Sung 1992).

The growing importance of Hong Kong as a service center is evident from its reemergence as an entrepôt and transshipment center for trade with China and the East Asian region. Sung (1992, p. 25) estimates that 56% of China's total exports were consumed, reexported, or transshipped by Hong Kong. Reexports have to clear the customs of an entrepôt twice, whereas transshipped goods do not have to clear the customs of the entrepôt at all. Also, 49% of China's imports were from Hong Kong, in part, due to Hong Kong's investment in processing/assembling operations in China. Hong Kong firms supplied such operations with the required raw materials, components, part of which were made in Hong Kong.

Hong Kong also served as the financial center for mainland China. Of the total realized foreign capital investment received by China, 63% originated from Hong Kong between 1985 and 1993. The World Bank estimates that China will require some US$700 billion in infrastructure investment between 1995 and 2004, much of which will be obtained from, or be coordinated by, the Hong Kong offices of international institutions (Lin 1997, p. 260). Stephen Speak (1997, p. 262) points out that since the early days of the Chinese reforms, Hong Kong companies have been at the forefront of Chinese infrastructure and property development, initially in south China, but more widely throughout China in the 1990s. Of an estimated US$25 billion of foreign investment in China in 1995, more than half had been sourced from Hong Kong. At the end of June 1995, Hong Kong's cumulative direct investment in China totalled US$68 billion, with investments in Guangdong Province totalling US$25 billion. According to the World Investment Report 1996, Hong Kong was the fourth largest exporter of capital in the world, after the US, Britain, and Germany, with an outflow of US$25 billion in 1995 (Yeung 1997, p. 253).

Stephen Speak (1997, p. 262) contends that more than twenty enterprises owned by the Chinese state have been listed on the Hong Kong stock exchange. *Peoples' Daily* (20 September 1999) further reports that forty-five Chinese companies were listed in the stock exchanges in Hong Kong and other global cities. Since these are extremely large enterprises, they added substantially to the overall capitalization and liquidity of the Hong Kong stock market. While Hong Kong has served as China's primary channel for international fund raising, the territory has also long been the largest recipient of China's outward international investment, estimated at US$28 million by 1998 (Hong Kong Government 1999).

Serving as the "home" market for China-oriented investment, Hong Kong grew to become the financial capital of Asia and the third largest financial center of the world, exceeded only by New York and London. By the beginning of the 1980s, Hong Kong hosted scores of transnational banks, foreign exchange dealers, security houses, and other non-bank financial institutions conducting an entire range of retail and wholesale banking services. By the mid-1990s, Hong Kong had more than 170 foreign licensed banks and a thousand regional headquarters that represent business interests from around the world. It had received over US$14 billion of direct investment from the US alone (Ho 1992; Meyer 2000).

The status of a global financial center produced enormous effects on the Hong Kong economy. Investment capital flowing into Hong Kong became mostly invested in stocks and real estate, causing a sudden real estate boom at the end of the 1970s. With an excess of idle capital around, the banks in Hong Kong lent fuel to the real estate boom by instituting easy credit policies. A highly speculative property market resulted in the early 1980s (Haggard 1990).

The Hong Kong government did nothing to halt this land speculation. Rather, it exacerbated the problem by auctioning off the best crown land in the colony. The state released the crown land in intervals in order to create an artificial limited supply as well as to push up the auction price. The real estate boom provided the state with huge earnings revenues. In the late 1970s, they constituted one quarter to one third of the state's total revenues. They strengthened public finances and provided for massive infrastructure projects without raising taxes higher than 15% of income and corporate earnings. The Hong Kong state thus tried to "walk on two legs" in the 1980s: it promoted export industrialization by providing infrastructure, while promoting Hong Kong as a world financial center by pursuing laissez-faire policies.

However, this "two legs" policy created problems. The financial sector had expanded at the expense of the industrial sector. Rising land prices caused a chain effect of rising service and food prices, leading to higher inflation rates (with a double digit inflation rate in the late 1980s and the early 1990s) and a very high cost of living. High cost of living raised rent and the price of industrial sites, leading to high cost of industrial production. As a result, rising land prices eventually cut down the profit margin for the industrialists as well as decreasing their competitive edge in the global export market.

Small firms in the Hong Kong manufacturing sector did not have the capacity to engage in long-distance offshore production in other countries to reduce costs and remain competitive in the world market. Instead they relocated their labor-intensive industries to the nearby Pearl River Delta in Guangdong, only a couple of hours' drive from Hong Kong. The labor costs in the Delta region in the late 1980s are about one third of Hong Kong production at comparable skills and productivity levels (Ho and So 1997).

The major form of investment in the Delta is "outward processing," known locally as "projects of imported material processing" (Sit 1989). "Outward processing" involves a partnership between Hong Kong and Chinese capital. The Hong Kong investor supplies the machinery, material, technology, product design, and marketing services; the Chinese partner provides the plant, labor, water, electricity, and other basic facilities, and assembles the product according to the Hong Kong design. The Hong Kong investor pays the Chinese partner a "processing fee" which covers workers' wages and the facilities provided. Maruya (1992) estimates that by June 1991 there were 20,000 Hong Kong garment, plastic, textile, and electronic firms conducting "outward processing" in Guangdong. These Hong Kong firms in 1991 employed more than 2 million workers in Guangdong, about three times more than these firms employed in the colony itself. By 1999, more than 5 million workers are employed in Guangdong by industrial ventures with Hong Kong interests. This is about twenty times the size of Hong Kong's own manufacturing workforce (Hong Kong Government 1999).

After moving the labor-intensive processes across the Guangdong border, Hong Kong manufacturers next began to concentrate on trading. Thus the Hong Kong firms gradually transformed into modern trading houses focusing on marketing, product design, quality control, inventory control, management, and financial arrangements (Sit 1989).

Globalization of the Hong Kong population

In the transition to a global financial city and a service center, Hong Kong began to experience the problem of a "deindustrializing economy" in the early 1990s. The number of workers in the manufacturing sector dropped dramatically from 892,140 in 1980 to 375,766 in 1995 (see Table 7.1). On the other hand, the service sector grew at an average of 14% from 1980 to 1999, the number of service workers rising from 789,454 in 1980 to 2,648,600 in 1999. In 1999, the manufacturing sector occupied only 7%, while the service sector accounted for 82% of the workforce (Yeung 1997, p. 251). As a result of these sectoral changes, Hong Kong's class structure has become increasingly polarized over the last two decades. Although the professional middle class has expanded, skilled working-class segments

Table 7.1 *Indicators of Hong Kong's development, 1980–1999*[a]

	1980	1985	1990	1995	1999
Population (in millions)[b]	5.1	5.5	5.7	6.3	6.7
GDP[c]					
GDP at current market price (US$ million)	$14,485	$33,470	$71,649	$141,726	$158,093
GDP per capita (US$)	$2,875	$6,134	$12,560	$23,022	$23,523
EXTERNAL TRADE (US$ millions)					
Total	$26,909	$59,816	$144,646	$363,493	$351,502
Reexport	$3,855 (14%)	$13,496 (23%)	$53,076 (32%)	$142,624 (39%)	$151,076 (43%)
TRADE WITH CHINA (US$ millions)					
Total	$3,614	$15,407	$50,578	$126,548	$153,531
Reexport (destination)	$595 (17%)	$5,900 (38%)	$14,219 (28%)	$49,236 (39%)	$51,178 (38%)
WORKFORCE					
Total	2,268,700	2,540,000	2,800,000	2,905,100	3,230,000[d]
Manufacturing	892,140 (39%)	847,615 (33%)	715,597 (26%)	375,766 (33%)	244,720 (7%)
Services[e]	789,454 (35%)	1,082,011 (43%)	1,489,245 (53%)	2,104,100 (72%)	2,648,600 (82%)
TRAFFIC					
No. of tourists (in millions)	2.3	3.7	6.6	10.2	11.3
Air passengers (in millions)	6.2	8.6	14.8	21.3	21.3
No. of container handled (TEUs) (in millions)[f]	1.5	2.3	5.0	11.2	16.2

[a] The figures from 1980 to 1995 are from Yeung 1997, p. 252; the 1999 figures from "Hong Kong: The Facts: Statistics", available at http://www.gov.hk/hkfacts/.

[b] The population figures are from Siu 1996, p. 326.

[c] All figures are expenditure-based GDP.

[d] Figures for workforce are 2000 figures.

[e] Service sector includes four categories namely, wholesale, retail and import/export trades, restaurants and hotels; transport, storage, and communication services; financing, insurance, real estate, and business services; and finally community, social, and personal services.

[f] "TEUs" refers to Twenty-Foot Equivalent Units (based on a standardized container size of 20 ft × 8 ft × 8 ft).

have been squeezed and have declined, and the income distribution has become more skewed over the past three decades (Henderson 1991, p. 171). In 1971, the families in the lowest 10% income bracket accounted for 2.3% of total income earned, but their share decreased to 1.6% in 1986, 1.4% in 1991, and 1.1% in 1996. On the other hand, families in the highest 10% income bracket accounted for 34.6% of total income earned in 1971, and share increased to 35.5% in 1986, 37.3% in 1991, and 41.8% in 1996 (Yeung 1997, p. 253).

After the Hong Kong economy shifted to a service economy, there was also a change of policy toward illegal immigration. "Touch-based" migration was no longer allowed after 1979, and immigration from the mainland has been tightly controlled: from 1983 to the end of 1993 numbers were set at 75 a day, the intake was raised to 105 a day and eventually to 150 a day from 1 July 1995. The vast majority of this later wave of immigrants from China, who in 1995 numbered 45,986 persons, were dependants of Hong Kong residents and unlikely to be direct entrants into the labor force.

As Hong Kong became a regional hub and a global city, it experienced an internationalization of its labor force. The total number of foreign nationals (not counting the British) rose from 150,000 in 1982 to 438,200 in 1996. There was an influx of expatriate professionals, such as senior company executives, bankers, highly paid stockbrokers, and technicians, during the late 1980s and the 1990s. The annual inflow of professionals and managers with employment visas rose from around 2,000 in the mid-1980s to more than 7,000 in the peak year of 1994 (Skeldon 1997, p. 267).

Aside from the influx of foreign middle-class professionals, there was an inflow of foreign domestic workers (Skeldon 1997, p. 266). The vast majority are women from the Philippines, although more and more came from Thailand, Sri Lanka, and Indonesia. In the mid-1990s, they numbered in excess of 150,000. As Skeldon (1997, p. 266) remarks, the rise of a domestic servant class reflects the growing affluence of the Hong Kong population and the incorporation of the Hong Kong middle-class women workers into highly paid professional and managerial occupations in the service economy.

Along the influx of foreigners to Hong Kong, there was also massive emigration out of Hong Kong in the early 1990s as a result of the uncertainties arising from the 1997 transition. By 1990, the outflow of Hong Kong residents reached 62,000. It fluctuated at that level in the early 1990s, with 60,000 in 1991, 66,000 in 1992, 60,000 in 1993, and 62,000 in 1994. Most of the emigrants were middle-class professionals, and their most popular destinations were Canada, the United States, and Australia

(Asia Pacific Migration Research Network 1998). Close to 500,000 Hong Kong residents are thought to have left the territory between 1988 and 1998. By the late 1990s, the wave of emigration subsided. In 1998, only 19,300 left Hong Kong (hknews@ahkcus.org 29 July 1999).

Indeed, by the mid-1990s, the trend began to shift from emigration from Hong Kong to return-migration from overseas Hong Kong communities. The most conservative estimate was made by the Hong Kong government, which held that 10–12% of the emigrants had returned to Hong Kong. Other estimates range from more than 100,000 to 250,000 who returned to Hong Kong after they had secured citizenship in Canada, Australia, and the US (hknews@ahkcus.org 29 July 1999; Skeldon 1997, p. 269).

The rise of "the Pearl City"

As Hong Kong's manufacturing industry relocated to the Pearl River Delta, and as Hong Kong became the financial and service center for the South China region, new terms such as "the Pearl City," "a vast mega-urban region," "a unified Hong Kong-Guangdong megalopolis," or "the Hong Kong Bay Area" are invented to describe the economic integration between Hong Kong and its south China hinterland (Lin 1997; Yeung 1997; see Map 7.1). In Yeung's (1997, p. 249) conception, Pearl City is a visionary's megalopolis that connects Hong Kong to Guangzhou (Canton), with a constellation of smaller but economically vibrant and culturally varied cities such as Dongguan, Shunde, Zhuhai, and Macau, and Shenzhen Special Economic Zone in between (see Map 7.1). Pearl City spans more than 160 kilometers from north to south and has a population of more than 40 million. Mass transit rail systems and a network of highways, bridges, and tunnels enable residents to travel from Hong Kong to Guangzhou city center in less than ninety minutes. From a spatial viewpoint, this Pearl City is a functionally integrated economic system as well as a rapidly expanding urban region, with Hong Kong constituting the service and financial center linking the south China region to the global economy and society (Skeldon 1997, p. 265). Moreover, the massive relocation of industry from Hong Kong to the villages and market towns across the border has led to the rapid urbanization of the south China countryside, as peasants enter the factories without having to move into large cities. Lin (1997, p. 261) remarks that the pattern of land use in the south China countryside has been altered, as much farmland has been rapidly converted to non-agricultural use, mostly for the building of factories, workshops, highways, and the development of export-processing zones.

As the border between Hong Kong and China became "diluted" due to the intense economic integration through investment, trade, and service between Hong Kong and mainland China, a new kind of geopolitics of "national reunification" rose to the forefront.

National reunification, decolonization, and democratization

The New Territories and the outer islands of Hong Kong were only leased to Britain for ninety-nine years. Since this lease would expire in 1997, capitalists were reluctant to make long-term investments in the colony. The British government was therefore under pressure in the early 1980s to enter into negotiations with mainland China to renew the lease so as to boost business confidence in the colony. During these negotiations, Britain was shocked to find that China wanted to take back not just the New Territories but also Hong Kong as well. Since China had reentered the capitalist world economy in the late 1970s, it felt little need to maintain Hong Kong's "borderland" status.

Finally, the British government backed down on extending the lease because developing a long-term relationship with China had higher priority (Scott 1989). In 1984, Britain signed the Joint Declaration with mainland China, agreeing to return sovereignty over Hong Kong by 1 July 1997. At that date, Hong Kong became a SAR of China, with its social and economic system, its way of life, its status as a free port, and the convertibility of its currency to remain unchanged.

The Hong Kong colonial government responded by initiating a series of policy changes over the next decade. First, it accelerated democratization in Hong Kong, announcing successive plans to reform the political structure and broaden popular participation. These last-minute attempts at democratization could be interpreted as a means for the British government to rebut criticism that it sold Hong Kong out to the communists. After all, if democratization succeeded, the Hong Kong government would be run by the people of Hong Kong in 1997, and the British government could claim that it retreated in an honorable manner by returning sovereignty to the people of Hong Kong rather than to Beijing.

Second, in order to boost business confidence in Hong Kong, the colonial government unveiled a proposal for massive state expenditures in new infrastructure and social services projects, including an US$16 billion proposal to construct a new airport with subways, railways, and an expanded container port. In its quest for legitimacy, the colonial government also responded to popular demands regarding the addition of more social services and welfare provisions, such as a proposal in the late 1980s to foster higher education by adding a new Science and Technology

University and to double the enrolment of higher education. In the early 1990s, the colonial government further proposed a plan to arrest the rapid rise of property prices, an old age pension scheme, an Environmental and Conservation Fund, and a new middle-income housing scheme for the "sandwich" class.

Third, after the 1989 Tiananmen Incident, the British government proposed a nationality package to grant the right of abode in Britain to 50,000 Hong Kong families. The aim of the nationality package was to provide "insurance" to the bureaucrats in Hong Kong so that they would remain at their posts until 1997; it also aimed at attracting Hong Kong entrepreneurs and new middle-class professionals to Britain.

These decolonization policies failed to attain their goals. First, the democratization process was hampered. Faced with strong opposition from Hong Kong capitalists (who feared that democratization would bring about more taxes, more state regulation, and less business freedom) and the mainland Chinese government (which feared that democratization would lead to a truly autonomous local government that could not be controlled), the lame-duck colonial government suddenly withdrew its promise to conduct direct elections in 1988. This angered the new middle-class professionals who constituted the strongest supporters of the democracy movement, causing them to emigrate on a massive scale.

The proposed infrastructure and social services projects and the nationality package also ran into trouble. They were challenged by mainland China, which saw these policies as a British conspiracy to weaken mainland control after 1997. For instance, mainland China complained that the post-1997 Hong Kong government would be in deep financial straits if the British used up the Hong Kong government's monetary reserves on the expensive airport package and the old age pension scheme. Furthermore, China accused the British of attempting to extend its colonial influence in Hong Kong after 1997; the nationality package let most high-ranking officials in Hong Kong hold British passports after 1997, ensuring their loyalty to Britain rather than mainland China. As a result of these policy disputes, hostility between mainland China and Great Britain intensified in the 1990s (So 1999).

Hong Kong as a high-tech center

The Western mass media envisioned an authoritarian scenario in Hong Kong after the 1 July transition. Hong Kong's Democratic Party would be outlawed. There would be press censorship, the banning of "subversive" organizations, and political prisoners. Beijing would rely upon its "unholy alliance" with business people to rule Hong Kong without any input from the democrats.

However, contrary to the Western media's prediction, the authoritarian scenario has failed to materialize in Hong Kong so far. No violent political confrontation, no outright political repression, and little political censorship took place after mid-1997. Instead, a democratic compromise was achieved among Beijing, the Hong Kong SAR government, and the democracy camp during this critical political transition from British to Chinese rule. What explains this democratic compromise in mid-1997?

First, Beijing toned down its opposition to the Democratic Party after 1996. Beijing assured the democrats that they would be allowed to compete in elections in the post-1997 SAR government, and it tolerated political protests in Hong Kong. Beijing took no action even when protesters shouted offensive slogans against Beijing leaders. Beijing's moderate stand toward Hong Kong democrats was a result of the waning of the emotions triggered by the Tiananmen Incident, strategic considerations to lure Taiwan to the negotiation table, and intensive mass media exposure of the 1 July 1997 transition.

In return, Hong Kong's Democratic Party adopted a moderate stand toward Beijing. The Democratic Party staged only a peaceful protest during the 1 July 1997 transition. It was also willing to participate in the 1998 elections, even though the Chinese-appointed Provisional Legislature had so drastically changed the electoral rules that the Democratic Party would have little chance to gain a majority in the post-1997 Legislature. Furthermore, the Democratic Party diluted its anti-Beijing platform. Instead, the Democratic Party emphasized that it would always support Beijing's resumption of Hong Kong sovereignty and always hopes for Hong Kong's stability and prosperity. Their acceptance of "Beijing sovereignty" and "Hong Kong stability and prosperity" encouraged Beijing to think that it could work with the Hong Kong democrats in the post-1997 era.

This democratic compromise between the Beijing government and the Hong Kong democrats in 1997 has strengthened the Hong Kong SAR government and allowed it to deal with the changing regional dynamics in the Asian region.

Regional dynamics

In the late 1990s, Hong Kong's development was deeply affected by a series of events in the Asian region: the Asian financial crisis, the growing competition for a global metropolis status, and the increasing hostility between mainland China and Taiwan.

First of all, the Asian financial crisis spread from Thailand to Korea, Indonesia, Malaysia, Hong Kong SAR, and other countries in 1997. The key manifestations of the crisis were a wholesale flight of foreign capital, plummeting currencies and real estate prices, failing banks, massive layoffs, labor strikes, public demonstrations, and civil unrest. According to an estimate, an Asian asset worth 100 dollars in June 1997 was worth only 25 dollars in August 1998 (Wolf 1999).

At the height of the Asian crisis in 1998, Hong Kong's GDP contracted by about 5% (compared to a 5.2% real growth in 1997), property prices dropped by 50%, rents declined by about the same amount, and stock market prices and turnover rates dropped considerably. Unemployment hovered at a record high of 6%, wages had fallen, many small businesses had closed, and consumer demand remained weak (Sassen 1999, p. 85; Tsang 1999, p. 30).

Still, Hong Kong was fortunate because the Asian crisis arrived after China had successfully resumed sovereignty on 1 July 1997. Had the Asian crisis arrived a year or a few months earlier, it might have triggered not only an economic recession but a political confidence crisis as well. In addition, the Asian crisis reached Hong Kong at a time when the SAR had built up a strong economic basis to weather the economic turmoil. The Hong Kong government had accumulated substantial fiscal and foreign exchanges reserves by 1997, which allowed it to respond to the challenges of the Asian crisis.

Aside from the Asian financial crisis, Hong Kong's status as a global service center has been increasingly challenged by other cities in the region (Meyer 2000). Although Singapore was also heavily engaged in trading and financial activities, it suffered much less damage during the Asian crisis than Hong Kong. During the crisis, the Singapore government implemented policies such as reducing the salary of public employees by 10% in order to increase the competitiveness of its economy. In addition, Singapore opened a futures market which threatened to take away some of Hong Kong's business. More generally, the very rapid development of Shanghai threatened Hong Kong's status. Many analysts predicted that Shanghai would catch up with Hong Kong in the next decade because most exports of north and central China would pass through Shanghai rather than Hong Kong, and because more and more transnational corporations were setting up their headquarters in Shanghai. Finally, the success of Hong Kong reduced its competitiveness: it had become not only one of the richest per capita income, but it had also among the highest property prices and biggest salary packages in Asia.

Another significant event in the East Asian region is the rising tension between mainland China and Taiwan over the issue of national reunification. In mid-1995, mainland China and Taiwan already were on hostile terms when Taiwan President Teng-hui Lee visited the US. In early 1996, mainland China even fired some missiles across the Taiwan Strait during Taiwan's presidential election. Mainland China and Taiwan seemed to be on friendlier terms in early 1999, but the new "state to state" platform proposed by the Taiwan government in mid-1999 immediately drew a hostile reaction from mainland China, leading to the cancellation of the scheduled talk in the fall of 1999 as well as military exercises in Fujian Province.

The worsening of mainland China–Taiwan relations has helped to promote the autonomy of the Hong Kong SAR. Since 1997, the Chinese government has largely pursued a "hands off" policy, other than in its remit over foreign affairs and defence. The People's Liberation Army garrison has stayed nearly invisible. Chinese state leaders have paid only cursory visits to Hong Kong. The territory's democracy groups and dissidents survive without too much harassment from the mainland government. Hong Kong is used as a showcase for the Chinese government to entice Taiwan to come to the bargaining table. The more intense the hostility between mainland China and Taiwan, the more freedom and autonomy the Hong Kong government appears to have in formulating its policies in response to the Asian crisis and the competition for the global city status.

Promoting high-tech and cross-border joint-venture projects

After the 1997 transition, the Hong Kong government began to take a much more active role in managing the economy (Jessop and Sum 2000, p. 2305). At the height of the Asian financial crisis in August 1998, there was a concerted attack by some venture capitalists on Hong Kong's currency. In response, the Hong Kong government made an unprecedented decision to use around US$15 billion in foreign reserve to buy into the Hong Kong stock and futures markets in order to protect the integrity of the Hong Kong dollars' fixed exchange rate with the US dollar (Sassen 1999, p. 85; Tsang 1999, p. 31).

The blessing of the Asian crisis is that it showed how vulnerable financial services and dependency on property have made Hong Kong. Financial and real estate markets are very volatile, and Hong Kong's economy cannot be based solely on providing such services. In search of more balanced development, the Hong Kong government pursued a series of long-term plans to turn Hong Kong into an innovation and technology center in Asia as well as an information technology hub at the gateway to China. The aim is to promote the development of a new technology-based and high-value-added sector in order to strengthen the long-term competitiveness of Hong Kong's economy.

The Hong Kong government has set up a high-powered Commission on Innovation and Technology (CIT), chaired by Professor Tien

Chang-Lin of Berkeley, to develop Hong Kong into a high-tech center. In its first report, the CIT (1998, pp. 13–14) stated that Hong Kong would be an innovation-led, technology-intensive economy in the twentieth century. In this vision, Hong Kong will be a leading city in the world for information technology, a world center for health food and pharmaceuticals based on Chinese medicine, a leading supplier in the world of high-value-added components and products, a regional center for multimedia-based information and entertainment services, and a market place for technology transfer between mainland China and the rest of the world.

In March 1999, the Hong Kong government announced plans to build Cyberport, a US$1.7 billion technology park in Pokfulam (Jessop and Sum 2000, p. 2306). Cyberport is aimed to create a strategic cluster of leading IT and service companies in Hong Kong in the shortest possible time. It will concentrate on communication-oriented industries, calling for the building of telecommunications, network and wireless communications, optical electronics, and Internet appliances in Hong Kong. The giant project is supposed to serve as a multimedia and information technology hub, with state-of-the art wiring, room for 130 companies, and adjacent housing. The project is expected to generate more than 12,000 jobs in Hong Kong, while approximately 4,000 jobs will be created in the construction industry to build Cyberport. When completed, Cyberport will generate demands for support services such as accounting, legal, and other back office functions (hknews@ahkcus.org 26 July 1999; Pun and Lee 1999, p. 9).

In September 1999, the Hong Kong government accepted the recommendation of the CIT to merge the Science Park, Industrial Estate, and Industrial Technology Center, to phase out the Industry and Technology Development Council, and to expand the existing incubation program to assist small entrepreneurs undertaking commercial research and development (R&D) work at the pre-market launch stage.

In order to fill the high-tech personnel gap, the Hong Kong government accepted a proposal from the CIT to relax immigration restrictions in order to allow skilled mainland Chinese to work in Hong Kong. In fact, the CIT suggested that no quota be set on the mainland talents to be admitted, and mainland talents should be permitted to bring their family members along. They are allowed to move to another job after the first year's contract expired (hknews@ahkcus.org 17 June 1999). This policy should make Hong Kong truly a global city in terms of its recruitment of highly skilled workers. Not just expatriate professionals but also mainland Chinese professionals are now welcome.

Furthermore, in the early 2000s, the Hong Kong government actively pursued cross-border joint-venture projects with mainland local governments in order to develop the Pearl River Delta (Hong Kong's hinterland) into a more seamless supply chain to both its onshore as well as offshore customers.

The recently approved Shenzhen–Hong Kong corridor link via Shekou to the proposed Route 10, together with the proposals for a western link via Lantau Island, will put Hong Kong squarely in the "center" of the Pearl River Delta. Also, a proposed bridge linking Zhuhai and Macau on one end and Hong Kong's Chek Lap Kok Airport on the other will make Hong Kong the logistic nerve center of the Pearl River Delta for years to come.

In addition, the SAR state is working with local mainland customs on one common platform to process clearance electronically, on sharing common data bank whilst ensuring individual customs systems requirements are still maintained, and on establishing a joint SAR/mainland customs group at Chek Lap Kok Airport to expedite flow of goods between Hong Kong and the Pearl River Delta.

Still, the strong influence of real estate developers and bankers on government policy continues to haunt the development of Hong Kong into a high-tech center. Cyberport has been heavily criticized because the government awarded the project to Pacific Century Group, a company of Richard Li, the son of Hong Kong's richest real estate developer. Other Hong Kong property developers felt jilted, and issued a rare letter of protest complaining about the lack of public bidding for Cyberport (hknews@ahkcus.org 13 Sept. 1999; Jessop and Sum 2000, p. 2307). In addition, there is doubt whether Hong Kong has enough high-tech talent for all these projects. In the past the Hong Kong government was reluctant to invest in education and R&D. In 1995, total education expenditure as a percentage of GDP was 6 for Taiwan, 3.5 for Singapore, but only 2.5 for Hong Kong. The R&D expenditure was 1.4% for Taiwan, 1.2% for Singapore, but only 0.2% for Hong Kong (Lin 1999).

Conclusion: Hong Kong's pathways to a global city

Hong Kong's developmental trajectory has been greatly influenced by three events in the Asian region: the Cold War in the 1950, the economic integration with China in the 1980s, and the Asian crisis in the late 1990s. Although these events caused hardship for the Hong Kong population, they also opened up new paths and opportunities for Hong Kong's development.

This chapter argues that these three regional events help to explain Hong Kong's pathway to a global city in the second half of the twentieth century. Thus, it was the Cold War in the 1950s – with the fusion of refugee capital and refugee labor, the supply of cheap food and materials from mainland China, and the liberal US trade policy – that transformed Hong Kong from an entrepôt to an industrial city in the 1970s. The regional situation was so favorable that the Hong Kong government could afford to maintain liberal laissez-faire policies, saving itself from promoting exports or from exerting authoritarian rule to suppress labor unrest. It was only after the success of the industrial revolution was assured that the Hong Kong government initiated public housing and New Towns projects for mainland immigrants.

In the 1980s, it was the economic integration with mainland China – the relocation of labor-intensive industries across the border, the revival of the entrepôt trade, the opening of China for investment, the massive mainland investment in Hong Kong, and the emergence of "the Pearl City" – that transformed Hong Kong from an industrial city to a service center. By the 1990s, Hong Kong has become a financial center, a transshipment center, and a regional headquarters for transnational corporations in East Asia.

Finally, in the late 1990s, it was the democratic compromise between Beijing and the Hong Kong democrats and the rising hostility in the Taiwan Strait that laid the foundation for an autonomous Hong Kong government, and it was the Asian financial crisis and the regional competition for metropolis status that provided the impetus for the Hong Kong government to push for a series of high-tech projects (including Cyberport, Silicon Harbour, and Herbalport) and large-scale cross-border joint-venture projects.

In short, this chapter argues that Hong Kong's pathway to a global city was largely shaped by the regional dynamics since the 1950s. The Cold War in East Asia transformed Hong Kong into an industrial city in the 1970s. The economic integration with China transformed Hong Kong into a service center in the early 1990s. And the Asian financial crisis provided an impetus to a high-tech center in the twentieth-first century. This regional explanation is different from those in the literature, which stress the factors of globalization, the state, local city politics, and Confucian cultural values in explaining Hong Kong's development. Although these factors are important, this chapter has shown that it was through the regional contexts of the Cold War in the 1950s, mainland integration in the 1980s, and the Asian crisis in the late 1990s that these factors exercised their influences on Hong Kong's development.

Regional dynamics also help to explain the divergent path of development between Hong Kong and Singapore. The colonial government in Hong Kong could afford to continue its old laissez-faire policy because the Hong Kong economy was "blessed" by the Cold War and the economic integration with mainland China between the 1950s and the 1980s. On the other hand, without such "blessings", the Singaporean government had to adopt interventionist policies to promote industrialization and regional integration with Southeast Asian economies (Yeung 2000).

At the turn of the early twenty-first century, Hong Kong has beyond doubt become a global city by all standards. However, one thing that is uncertain is whether Hong Kong could be transformed into a high-tech city. Since the Hong Kong government has proposed the high-tech projects since 1997, it may be too early to predict their outcome. Moreover, having started late, Hong Kong will have to go a long way to catch up and grow into a global high-tech center.

REFERENCES

Asia Pacific Migration Research Network 1998. "Issues Paper from Hong Kong." http://www.unesco.org/most/apmrnwp7.htm.

Chalkley, Brian 1997. "Hong Kong: Colony at the Crossroads," *Geography*, 82: 139–147.

Chiu, Stephen W. K. 1994. "The Politics of Laissez-Faire: Hong Kong's Strategy of Industrialization in Historical Perspective." Hong Kong: Institute of Asia-Pacific Studies, Chinese University of Hong Kong, Occasional Paper No. 40.

Commission on Innovation and Technology (CIT) 1998. "First Report." Hong Kong: Hong Kong Government.

Friedmann, John 1995. "Where We Stand: A Decade of World City Research," in P. L. Knox and P. J. Taylor (eds.), *World Cities in a World-System*. Cambridge: Cambridge University Press, pp. 21–47.

Haggard, Stephan 1990. *Pathways from the Periphery: The Politics of Growth in the Newly Industrializing Countries*. Ithaca: Cornell University Press.

Hambro, Edward 1955. *The Problem of Chinese Refugees in Hong Kong*. Leyden: A. W. Sijthoff.

Henderson, Jeffrey 1991. 'Urbanization in the Hong Kong–South China Region: "An Introduction to Dynamics and Dilemmas," *International Journal of Urban and Regional Research*, 15: 169–181.

hknews@ahkcus.org (news distributed on the web).

Ho, H. C. Y. 1979. *The Fiscal System of Hong Kong*. London: Croom Helm.

Ho, K. C. and So, Alvin Y. 1997. "Borderland Integration of Singapore and Hong Kong: Origins, Characteristics, Conflicts, and Dynamics," *Political Geography*, 16 (3): 241–259.

Ho, Yin-Ping 1992. *Trade, Industrial Restructuring and Development in Hong Kong*. Honolulu: University of Hawaii Press.

Hong Kong Government 1999. *Hong Kong Annual Report*. Available at http://www.info.gov.hk/hkar99-.

Jessop, Bob and Sum, Ngai-Ling 2000. "An Entrepreneurial City in Action: Hong Kong's Emerging Strategies in and for (Inter) Urban Competition," *Urban Studies*, 37: 2287–2313.

Kirby, Andrew 1997. "Global Cities or City States?" *Cities*, 14 (5): iii.
Kraus, Richard C. 1979. "Withdrawing from the World-System: Self-Reliance and Class Structure in China," in Walter L. Goldfrank (ed.), *The World-System of Capitalism*. Beverly Hills: Sage, pp. 237–259.
Lau, Siu-kai 1982. *Society and Politics in Hong Kong*. Hong Kong: Chinese University of Hong Kong.
Levin, David and Chiu, Stephen 1993. "Dependent Capitalism, Colonial State and Marginal Unions: The Case of Hong Kong," in Stephen Frenkel (ed.), *Organized Labor in the Asian-Pacific Region*. Ithaca: ILR, pp. 187–222.
Lin, George 1997. "Economic Integration of Hong Kong and Guangdong Province, China," *Geography*, 82: 259–261.
Lin, Otto 1999. "Technology and Sustainability of Hong Kong." A talk given at the Asia Society Hong Kong Center, Hong Kong, 6 September.
Maruya, T. 1992. "Economic Relations between Hong Kong and Guangdong Province," in T. Maruya (ed.), *Guangdong*. Hong Kong: Center of Asian Studies, University of Hong Kong, pp. 126–147.
Meyer, David R. 2000. *Hong Kong as a Global Metropolis*. Cambridge: Cambridge University Press.
Pun, Ngai and Lee, Kim Ming 1999. "A New Age of Urban Imagineering: A Cyber Society without Its People." Paper presented at the Annual Meeting of the American Sociological Association, Chicago, August.
Pye, Lucian 1983. "The International Position of Hong Kong," *China Quarterly*, 95: 456–468.
Sassen, Saskia 1997. "City in the Global Economy," *International Journal of Urban Sciences*, 1: 1–31.
1999. "Global Financial Centers," *Foreign Affairs*, 78(1): 75–87.
Scott, Ian 1989. *Political Change and the Crisis of Legitimacy in Hong Kong*. Honolulu: University of Hawaii Press.
Sit, Victor F. S. 1989. "Industrial Out-Processing – Hong Kong's New Relationship with the Pearl River Delta," *Asian Profile*, 17: 1–13.
Siu, Yat-Ming 1996. "Population and Immigration," in Mee-Kau Nyaw and Si-Ming Li (eds.), *The Other Hong Kong Report 1996*. Hong Kong: Chinese University Press, pp. 326–347.
Skeldon, Ronald 1997. "Hong Kong: Colonial City to Global City to Provincial City?," *Cities*, 14: 265–271.
So, Alvin Y. 1999. *Hong Kong's Embattled Democracy: A Societal Analysis*. Baltimore: Johns Hopkins University Press.
So, Alvin Y. and Chiu, Stephen 1995. *East Asia and the World Economy*. Newbury Park: Sage.
Speak, Christine 1997. "Hong Kong 1949–83: An Economic Miracle," *Geography*, 82: 256–258.
Speak, Stephen 1997. "A Capital Location: Hong Kong's Emergence and Future as a Financial Center," *Geography*, 82: 261–263.
Sung, Yun-Wing 1992. *The China–Hong Kong Connection*. Cambridge: Cambridge University Press.
Szczepanik, Edward 1958. *The Economic Growth of Hong Kong*. Oxford: Oxford University Press.

Tsang, Donald 1999. "Tooting Our Horn: Hong Kong as an Engine of Development," *Harvard Asia-Pacific Review*, 3 (2): 28–31.
Ward, Peter 1998. "Administration and Modernization of Governance in Contemporary Latin American Metropolis: Making Good Cities Work." Papers presented at the "Good Cities, Good Buildings" Meeting, University of Texas at Austin, 1–3 April.
Wolf, Charles, Jr. 1999. "Three Systems Surrounded by Crisis," in Murray Weidenbaum and Harvey Sicherman (eds.), *The Chinese Economy: A New Scenario* (report). Philadelphia, PA: Foreign Policy Research Institute, pp. 7–14.
Wong, Siu-lun 1988. *Emigrant Entrepreneurs*. Hong Kong: Oxford University Press.
Yeung, Henry Wai-Chung 2000. "State Intervention and Neoliberalism in the Globalizing World Economy: Lessons from Singapore's Regionalization Programme," *Pacific Review*, 13: 133–162.
Yeung, Yue-Man 1997. "Planning for Pearl City: Hong Kong's Future, 1997 and Beyond," *Cities*, 14 (5): 249–256.
Youngson, A. J. 1982. *Hong Kong: Economic Growth and Policy*. Hong Kong: Oxford University Press.

8 Singapore: forming the family for a world city*

Janet Salaff

The Republic of Singapore is a premier example of a state whose developmental trajectory started by taking into account its international and regional location. The government explicitly repositioned the city-state to utilize its historical legacy, spatial location, economic heritage, political structure, and the demographic and ethnic constituency. Two decades after independence, Singapore already emerged as a global "city," a feat that took others a century to accomplish.

This chapter explores the use of the social services to promote Singapore's status as a world city. A hallmark of Singapore's policy making is the ongoing attention to the comparative advantages and disadvantages of a nation of the "South." The state applies social engineering to direct the economy and society to affect the nation's place in the global economy. To legitimize its programs, the populace is exhorted to see its fate linked to that of their country and its world status. There are ongoing efforts to anticipate change and adjust manpower policies. Integration into the world economy occasions immense social dislocations, which the social services continue to moderate. The policies at first fit a particular set of circumstances, but dynamically change with conditions (Ho 1995).

I focus on the government's molding a new family on behalf of its development program, the best-known example in a market economy of a society restructured by the state. Social policies shape people's goals as well as how they reach their objectives. The Singapore city-state early on offered a range of services in the realms of jobs and retirement, housing, education, health, and childbearing, among others. These "social goods" provide for major family needs. The social policies are not neutral, and convey social, economic, and political objectives. At the same time, families are not passive recipients of services. They rework these policies for their own ends. The specific policy goals and the means to achieve them

* This contribution draws on and up-dates research reported in Salaff 1988. The original research was generously supported by the International Development Research Centre and the Social Sciences and Humanities Research Council of Canada.

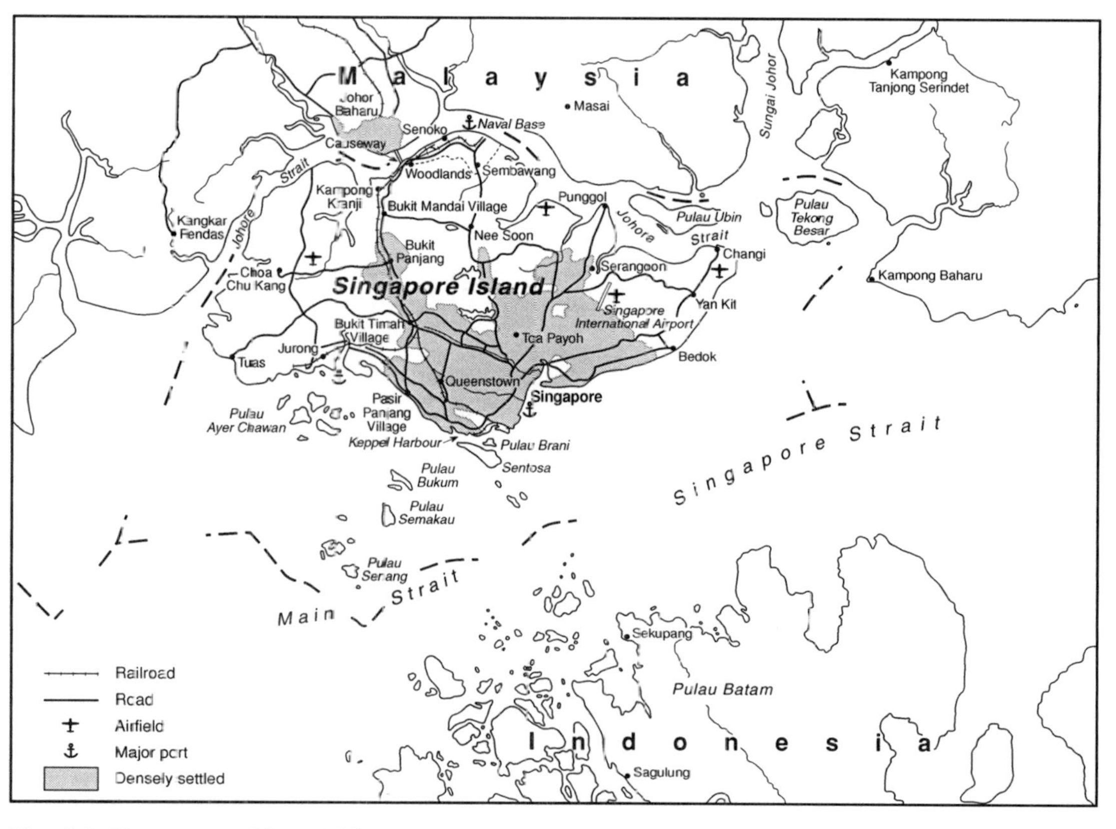

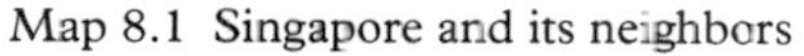

Map 8.1 Singapore and its neighbors

have been continuously modified to counter popular reactions and attain the new world city's needs.

This chapter devotes itself to the first decades of societal reforms, in which we identify two stages of development. The first of these two sets of programs, called here first-stage industrialization, refers to labor-intensive industrialization. At this stage, the social services provided rudimentary goods and a basic safety net. Second-stage industrialization describes more value-added knowledge-intensive manufacturing and services. Social services have improved in quality. The state's active stance in dealing with ongoing changes prompted by the global setting can still be seen in the social services after the main period of our study was concluded.

From the outset, the policies were bent on "modernizing" the family for market-oriented development. By closely associating needed social goods to the party-state development plan, the state not only won political support. These social policies also extended social control by forming a common core of family values that have taken root among families from a broad range of social classes and ethnic backgrounds. These social goods have narrowed obvious social class differences, as defined by poverty levels and possessions. However, differential access to these goods contribute to social stratification. More affluent families use different versions of the social services than the families of the poor. Although families of different statuses are assimilated into the new social order based on the international commodity economy, the social services convey variations in meaning. Social class differences in family interaction and achievement are carried forward.

These policies were also formulated to push ethnic tensions off the center of the political stage (Chua 1997a). Although each of the three main ethnic groups in Singapore is internally differentiated, ethnic groups are also stratified in relation to each other. If the state proffered social goods to everyone and broke the link between ethnicity and poverty, Chinese, Malays, and Indians would be less likely to mobilize their own members politically (Moore 2000; Wong 2000). An important aim is to negate the impoverished Malay "ethnoclass." Our study concerns itself with the Chinese of different social class groups, and hence a detailed study of ethnic integration is beyond our scope. Still it needs to be noted that while sheer access to political goods is not coterminous with ethnicity, Malays still live with different quality public sector services (Teo and Ooi 1996). Although everyone enjoys more, continuously rephrasing terms of access is an ongoing government project.

The social services directed toward raising family living standards are not social welfare or social security programs. Indeed, the Singapore government maintains that its limited resources should not undermine the work ethic. Instead, state services enmesh citizens in the money economy and speed the tempo of the industrial way of life. As services gradually reach all class levels, they provide new consumer goals that spur families to work harder to pay for them. Moreover, most of the social services help to accumulate investment capital.

The social services had become widely available when we ended our family study in 1986. But the success of these particular social policies changed their emphases. Rapid economic growth changes people's goals. When their basic needs are met, they demand higher quality. The social services become more expensive at the same time that the competitive global economy demands paring of state costs (Ho 1994; Yeung and Olds 1998). Among new issues were popular mobilization, status conflicts, and competitive individualism. The leadership, which constantly scans the Western world for an image of its future, sees the welfare state as a route to sloth. The party-state began to tie the services to the ethos of an "Asian value system," to use the services to make communities and families more cohesive and to counter alienation (Tu 2000). Since the services became the means by which the state rewards different class groups, they are still widely competed over as symbols of political access and of class achievement.

In this chapter, after a summary of the social policies, I note how the policies were implemented during the period of this study. I follow with a discussion of how families of different social groups used the policies. My research team studied these families during the mid-l970s and restudied them in the early 1980s. During this period these families moved from poverty to prosperity. I credit the social policies with much of these changes. I conclude by taking into account shifts in social policies as Singapore further adjusted to the world economy in the following decade.

The delivery of government social services

Singapore gained independence from Great Britain in l959. The world depression, Japanese occupation, and struggle against colonial rule bred poverty and immense social dislocation. The new government faced a weak economic infrastructure, high unemployment, inadequate housing, and rapid population growth. Active political opposition mobilized the populace for radical social change. Led by the People's Action Party (PAP), the government forged its social policies to cope with this heritage.

To restructure the political system, the party-state marginalized opposition political parties, and labor groups. Traditional quasi-political clan associations were curtailed. In the restructured social service delivery system, state organizations replaced the schools, health centers, and other services that local groups had previously offered (Chan 1976; Lee 1992). The statutory boards, new overarching state service organizations, had a great deal of resources and skillful leadership to carry forward social policy.

Services became a tool for development. As sole supplier of the desired social goods, the PAP gained an edge over opposition groups and parties. In a form of corporatism the government granted certain interest groups a monopoly to provide these services, in exchange for adhering to its developmental guidelines. This political system created the social policies that socialize and discipline the ethnically disparate and class-divided population. The PAP's legal and administrative measures effectively suppress opposition, by limiting the press, religious activism, and the functions of politically oriented civil society organizations (Chua 1997b). They offer political stability to foreign investment. This state-guided development model, which attempts growth with political stability and imposes political repression to accomplish economic development, has become known as "the Singapore model" (Jeon 1995). This corporate political structure is key to implementing the major social policies studied here.

Specific development programs

The first industrial stage was short lived. In the mid-1960s, these programs aimed to create a potentially skilled but labor-intensive and low-wage industrial sector, to help it compete in the world economy. Production for foreign corporations would absorb the many unemployed (Lee 1973; Yoshihara 1976). As the 1970s drew to a close, the leadership took an increasingly dim view of the country's future in the world order as a regional outpost for low-wage and low-skill manufacturing. Neither import substitution nor labor-intensive development could compete with the low-cost labor of Indonesia, Thailand, and other neighbors.

Singapore next actively solicited knowledge-based, capital-intensive industries from abroad and launched the New Economic Program, referred to here as the second industrial stage. Older heavy industries were joined by new firms that exploit advanced technology in chemical processing, machine tools, heavy engineering, computer micro-technology, technical services, and industrial research and product development. These mainly produce goods for export. The finance and banking industry, which includes off-shore fund management, is also a leading growth sector (Chong Yah Lim 1984; D. Lim 1984). In the second stage of its industrial program, the state courted higher technology, capital-intensive, mainly overseas, firms. The nation became a "client economy," producing technological products for foreign companies. It offered the internationally financed manufacturing sector many breaks. These, accompanied by considerable investment in labor, attracted multinational firms. A battery of programs raised workers' skills to meet the many new demands of second-stage industrialization. Human capital and labor discipline were central goals. Programs to train workers on the job were coupled with the expansion of polytechnic and diploma-conferring education. Companies agreed to accept a number of strictures. They committed to hefty pensions, recognized the main labor union, in exchange for a disciplined and compliant workforce.

Pensions

The government introduced the Central Provident Fund (CPF), a pension plan that is also a comprehensive social security savings scheme. Both employee and employer make deposits in the employee's CPF. That the social services have multiple functions can be seen in the functions of the CPF. They imply: (1) individual and family responsibility for their own social security needs; (2) forced income savings; (3) accumulated national savings resulting in long-term economic growth; and (4) the avoidance of welfare. The worker can draw on these funds not only to retire, but also to buy into the public housing sector. Once employees commit themselves to use their CPF to buy a family home, they have to keep working to continue their payments. In the future, the elderly that build up such funds will no longer depend on kin for support (Chan 1999). Their relatively loose social bonds seemed at the time to herald a modern lifestyle.

Housing

The construction of large blocks of rental housing and the Home Ownership for the People Scheme are designed to stimulate the market in construction and finance and to promote an industrial way of life. The statutory Housing Development Board (HDB) took charge of the ambitious state housing program. Many lived in settlements of Malay-type housing, called *kampung* villages, where they visited neighbors, raised barnyard animals, and grew tropical fruit. The HDB demolished these villages along with central-city slums and replaced them with high-rises. Those that objected were accused of opposing the future well-being of the nation by blocking its development plans.

The state housing program that propelled residents into the wage labor force and consumer economy was a drastic social policy with major consequences for social bonds. In the shift from *kampung* housing and farms to small HDB quarters, families lost their home garden plots, their food bills and outlays on utilities increased.[1] Many suburban bungalows and *kampung* houses that were torn down housed several married couples, both related and unrelated; few of the HDB flats do (Armunainathan 1973, Table 97, p. 208). Before resettlement, these family units often shared appliances. After relocation, they had to buy their own furnishings and other consumer durables. When they no longer needed to borrow these things from other people, their exchanges with kin and neighbors decreased. Deployment of women into the wage labor force, overtime work, and moonlighting help pay for a more costly HDB lifestyle.[2]

However, the first industrial stage, based on low-wage labor, could not guarantee a strong wage-earning position. Although many households moved into low-cost HDB units, and worked in nearby factories as wage earners, they often continued subsistence production and petty trading in their high-rise flats. Low-income families could not give up their exchanges within the community of the impoverished. Poverty was thus "modernized" into high-rise housing (Buchanan 1972, pp. 189–92; Hassan 1977, pp. 85, 145). Further, the labor market greatly affected a family's housing options. Families with below-average income occupied the smallest HDB flats after their relocation. Income in HDB households varied widely by housing development. Middle-class families, who applied for the more spacious and expensive Queenstown flats, earned twice as much as resettled slum dwellers in Bukit Ho Swee (Yeh 1975, Table 2, p. 352). Furthermore, families that purchased their own HDB flats earned more than the renters (Chua and Ho 1975, Tables 7, 8, pp. 71–2; Yeh 1975, p. 333 and Table 3).

By stage 2, however, a spurt in HDB construction, accumulation of CPF savings by maturing workers, secure employment, and higher average wages decreased visible class differences in housing. Parts of the poorest developments were demolished. The policy of mixing flats of various sizes in new developments further loosened the link between address and class position. By 1979–1980, 67% of all Singaporeans resided in HDB quarters, and 59% of these homes were their own. Singapore has become a society of home owners, or, more precisely, apartment owners (HDB 1980, p. 5).

Consumer financing of HDB housing through the CPF strengthens the involvement of families in the labor force over the entire life cycle

[1] Buchanan 1972, p. 242. With few legal utilities, slum dwellers paid only 13% of their household budgets on utilities; poor HDB dwellers had to spend much more.

[2] In a 1973 HDB survey, 52% of relocated families stated that they enjoyed increased employment opportunity for women in their new housing. Yeh 1975, p. 357.

as they committed themselves to regular monthly wage checkoffs. When they save enough for a down payment, couples improve their housing by buying their first public sector flat; later they may sell it and buy a larger one. In 1973, one-room, "one-room improved," and two-room dwellings accounted for 58% of all HDB households; few larger flats were built. By stage 2, only 31% of all HDB households lived in one or two rooms (HDB 1980, pp. 53, 55; Yeh 1975, Table 1, p. 331). It appeared that the occupants of the larger flats achieve greater earning power as they advance to later stages of their family cycle.[3] Provisions for moving from smaller to larger apartments and from renter to ownership status demarcate the Singapore proletariat from their counterparts in many older industrial cities with inadequate housing stock and weak home-financing arrangements.

Education

Schools loom in importance in this multiethnic nation. More schools were built, and tuition fees reduced. To mold a national ideology, principals, teachers, and Ministry of Education officials, all secular educated professionals, espoused the norms and values of the scientific-technological revolution, multiculturalism, and egalitarianism. The term *meritocracy* has gained currency. By this is meant that people have equal opportunities to advance through their abilities and training. To ensure this, the school system stresses testing at early ages. A complex balloting system gives families throughout the republic greater access, even to renowned schools that children with "school ties" attended.

A unified admissions policy, a common core curriculum, and a bilingual language system were introduced. All pupils chose either English or their native language as the primary school medium, and course work was also introduced in the second language. Increasingly, however, Chinese parents placed their children in English-medium, instead of Mandarin schools, recognizing it as the language of success in the international economy. Here, barely any Chinese studies are introduced, resulting in the desinicization of the educational system (Wong 2000). The proportion of primary school students enrolled in Chinese schools dropped from 50% in 1959 to 11% in 1978, although not all in the English stream performed well in their adopted language.

Entrance to schools is competitive, but the standards are multibranched. When the state aimed to reduce birth rates during

[3] HDB survey figures show the average number of income earners in resettled households increase with the size of the rented flat, a finding that suggests different stages in the family cycle. Yeh 1975, Tables 6–8, pp. 129–156.

second-stage development, family planning policies were linked to primary school admissions. Children in small families enjoyed priority in admission, especially if one parent was sterilized before age forty. Children whose parents or siblings attended the same school, and parental choice and neighborhood location, were considered next. Secondary school admission was accessed by choice and the pupil's scores on the primary school-leaving examination (PSLE). Further, candidates who attended feeder primary schools (a primary school attached to a secondary school) gained first priority. Youngsters who start their early childhood education in highly ranked schools have a good chance to progress through the grades. Parents with more education themselves are most likely to organize their offspring's future educational careers from the early years.

During the first industrial stage it was hard for children from lower-class backgrounds to finish high school. Out of a cohort of 1,000 first-grade pupils, only 440 graduated from secondary school ten years later. The rest repeated courses or dropped out of the academic stream without getting any of the skills required by the advanced hi-tech industries (Goh and Education Study Team 1979, p. 1). "Educational wastage" threatened to derail economic advancement.

Sweeping educational reforms have accompanied Singapore's second-stage economic program. Even more attention is paid to meritocracy. A revamped instructional system features continuous testing, starting with a language test in grade 3. Examination-based streaming within each grade separates students of different language, technical, and academic abilities (*Straits Times* (Singapore), 2 December 1982). The major change is that those who do not advance along the pre-university path do not have to drop out. They are eligible to attend the Vocational and Industrial Training Board's certificate- and diploma-conferring institutions, prepared for the new skilled industries.

While these reforms greatly reduced the role of class origins in educational advancement, the desired equality of opportunity was not achieved (Mukhopadhaya 2000). Middle-class parents still devote more time and money to preparing their children at home for success in school. Pupils in government-aided private schools, with higher social class backgrounds, do better on the key exams than their peers in state schools. Exams are as likely to measure pupils' familiarity with schoolroom concepts and techniques as their inherent intelligence. Streaming and early testing of students could not help the poor. The battery of tests designed to identify superior pupils gave rise to widespread tutoring to improve children's performance. Here, too, parents with money and knowledge have an edge. Tuition fees at the local university and polytechnic institutes are low, but degree-seeking students who failed to gain admission to the sole university, the National University of Singapore, could only go abroad, at great expense. When the government recognized these limitations to a knowledge-based economy, it further reformed the educational system, establishing additional universities.

Health and population policies

The health care delivery system, fundamental to the quality of labor needed for investment, was upgraded and centralized. The ratio of physicians and beds in government-run hospitals to population improved, and small clinics run by midwives for the poor were labeled "below standard" and closed. By the late 1970s, maternal and child health services were delivered by twenty-four hospitals, thirteen of them public, and an associated network of forty-six clinics. Over 80% of all registered births took place at public hospitals, and over 90% of all newborns were enroled for comprehensive post-natal care at a neighborhood clinic. This extension of state medical care enabled the public to enjoy a better quality of life and reduced occupational time lost to illness. It also laid the groundwork for what Foucault calls the medicalization of social control (Foucault 1973). The idiom of science legitimized the extension of state mechanisms of social control into society.

Rapid population growth appears to slow capital formation, and, by increasing the labor force, decreases the capital available to invest in each worker. In the late 1960s, the state overrode the opposition of the medical, religious, and professional communities, and liberalized abortion and sterilization laws. The Ministry of Health provided contraceptive services through this new network of public health facilities. The crude birth rate declined in response to fertility-limitation services and first-stage industrialization. From 44.4 births per 1,000 population in 1956, the crude birth rate fell to 21.8 in 1969, and bottomed at 16.6 per 1,000 population in 1977 (Chang 1974; Ministry of Health 1977, p. 11).

In the early 1970s, however, the government became alarmed at evidence of large families among the working poor (Family Planning and Population Board [FPPB] and National Statistical Commission 1973, pp. 16, 25, 54). The FPPB then vigorously popularized its tenet that numerous children undermine efforts to upgrade the family. Parents become too poor to afford their own flat, mothers cannot work, and children cannot receive a good education. Mass media presentations on population control created an atmosphere of crisis, and identified large families as an imminent threat to the limited resources of the city-state. Thus the national family-limitation campaign aimed to convince people that rapid population growth endangered both their present livelihood and their future prospects. Here, too, the populace was directed to see their fate linked to that of their country, and the country's fate was tied to its global status.

Amid much fanfare, the economic and social "Disincentives against Higher Order Births" were enacted in 1973, to attain zero population growth. The social services fell into line to support this program. Obstetrical fees, which had increased in public hospitals for mothers who had already given birth, were waived for the mother that sterilized within six months. While no child was denied schooling, the fourth child received lower priority in choice of elementary school than children of small families. Though public housing was available to all, large families no longer had priority in access to HDB flats as hardship cases. Nor could families with three or more children rent out one of their HDB rooms. A female civil servant or union member had two months of paid maternity leave for each of her first two deliveries, but not for subsequent births. She was, however, given paid medical leave for being sterilized. Finally, couples could claim only two children as income tax deductions (Saw 1980).

It is in the state's interest to expand public goods, and these measures did not actually deny services to citizens. They did, however, raise the price of needed social goods for parents of large families. The measures shored up the ideology of the Singapore meritocracy: only the diligent succeed in raising their families above poverty. Prime Minister Lee Kuan Yew explained that a system of disincentives was needed

> so that the irresponsible, the social delinquents, do not believe that all they have to do is to produce their children and the government then owes them and their children sufficient food, medicine, housing, education, and jobs . . . Until the less educated themselves concentrate their limited resources on one or two to give their children the maximum chance to climb up the educational ladder, their children will always be at the bottom of the economic scale. (cited in Thomson and Smith 1973, p. 249)

Lee's government justified the measures as a means of helping the poor help themselves, and of reducing conflicts engendered by competition over social services.

As the national birth rate declined in the 1970s, social class differences in family size narrowed. Zero population growth was attained on the eve of the new economic policy, and pressures on mothers to sterilize abated. Yet, those from different class backgrounds still held to different definitions of how children fit into their future. The poor wanted more children, if they only could afford to feed and clothe them. The better off did not want more children because they felt they could not educate them properly for the new competitive society.

The impact of government policy on poor and secure families: phase 1

The social services were interlaced with the new ideology of individual merit and responsibility for one's own poverty. They extolled self-help, individualism, and competition. The educational, family planning, and housing policies moved people around. Such mobility in living arrangements, social class, and the flow of ideas atomized people and devalued reliance on kin. These massive changes to a young society were intended to fit the new economic order, based on Singapore's position as a world city. The extent to which the social services affected family lives can be seen in the ways the services reshaped kin ties of the families I interviewed.

To understand how social services alter family lives while reproducing social class structure, I traced a panel of Chinese families with different class backgrounds from the mid-1970s to 1982.[4] They were young married adults, under age thirty. I grouped them based on scores derived from the occupational status of the parents of both husband and wife, and the average educational level, occupational status, and combined earnings of the husband and wife. I divided the couples into two main socioeconomic groups: the poor and the secure.

The lives of the poor were affected by the type of work they did, the past course of their family life, their material resources, and the presence or absence of wider kin ties. In the first development stage, poverty shaped the lives of many families. With limited education, having entered the labor force at an early age, and having contact mainly with other poor people, these men and women could not break out of their low job status. The highest wages accrued to men with a skill or entrepreneurial resource, and some capital. Wives who earned money helped their families eke out a minimal living, but they earned less than the men.

[4] I conducted this study with Dr. Aline Wong, then at the National University of Singapore, at two points in time. In the first period, we chose 100 young married Singapore Chinese couples. Over half came from the rosters of Maternal and Child Health Centers, located in the main HDB estates serving families from a range of class backgrounds. The remainder came from factories which employed married women. The period in which I first met these couples, mid-1974 to mid-1976, I designate as "phase 1." During the next few years the government elaborated many of the programs of the second development stage. In "phase 2," 1981–1982, we met for a second set of interviews with 45 of the original families. I call these 45 families the panel sample, and it is mainly from them that we learn how the development program affected family lives. The case studies are fully presented in Salaff 1988.

In the first industrial stage, many could not afford the social services. Poverty and their life-cycle stage placed families in close dependence on their relatives to make ends meet. Their dependence on help and handouts from kin placed most partly outside the market economy. Their marginal employment fostered closeness of poor adults to their families and with their peers, and competed with the husband–wife relationship. Most husbands spent their spare time with their buddies. Wives visited kin and neighbors. Since couples had to take into account the views of kin in many spheres of their family life, they were not independent decision makers. Their poverty and kinship ties limited access to the state-provided housing and educational services, and they could not plan far ahead. Although they were young, they expected to bear many children. They thought this would give them future security, but instead children hindered their ability to plan ahead. Only a few poor couples with hopes of advancing in their jobs, above-average schooling, or some unusual trait were not deeply integrated in their kin community. These husbands and wives tried to work out plans related to their family life. They tried to use the social services to a fuller extent.

In contrast, couples with above-average education, a skill, or another asset did far better under first-stage Singapore industrialism. As they held solid jobs and their futures seemed bright, I refer to them as secure, but they include couples of relatively modest means as well as the affluent. Secure couples were optimistic about the future. Though many lived with kin, few depended on them for daily support or finding jobs. The majority took steps to buy a home, set high standards for their children's education, and intended to have no more than three children. Most enjoyed close marriages, in which partners shared pastimes and talked things over. They were proud of their ability to plan their futures together. Most took advantage of Singapore's social services to advance their family's living standard. Secure folk expressed recognizably similar goals in the main spheres of their lives as they planned for the advancement of the small family in Singapore's industrial revolution.

The impact of government policy on poor and secure families: phase 2

Much had changed a few years later. I spoke with panel families of all skill levels and industrial sectors again in the early 1980s. I found them expressing increasingly similar goals as the social services society, the wage-earning and consuming and market economy took hold. Living standards have improved. Many that we dubbed "poor" in phase 1 earn enough to consider themselves secure, and the secure have become even better off. Nevertheless, within the narrowed limits of lifestyle, class, and employment sector, differences remain. Class position shapes diverse family styles and plans.[5]

Couples vary in their use of state programs and in the meaning of the policies to their way of life. Family relations are often negotiated, and public housing and other social services played a central part in this process. Favored under the terms of the state development program, able to maintain their position in the class order, secure families make even greater use of the state services than the formerly poor. State policy, with its emphasis on training and skills for the trend toward capital-intensive industrial work in foreign-financed firms, strengthened its grip on the secure families.

The gap between the secure and less affluent families in the use of the key institutions promoted in second-stage development has been reduced. All my interviewees have become wage workers. Deepening participation in wage labor has major ramifications for other spheres of their family life. Their commitment to the labor market determines how they exploited the social services. The development program most benefits new groups of workers with jobs in the key, mainly foreign-based, industries of the second stage. The program marginalized others who could not.

Because of economic improvements, nearly all families exploit the social services to a greater extent than before. Whereas in phase 1, the poor either could not afford any or only the most rudimentary public goods and services, by phase 2 all have bought into the public sector and enjoy a more stable lifestyle. Because no poor families were excluded from basic social services, and all used these services more than before, the outward class cleavage was less visible than in phase 1. Nevertheless, in phase 1 the affluent already received the best the public sector had to offer. In phase 2, some top up the public sector, which turns on income, education, and property. They pay for highly ranked private sector schools, buy unattached flats, and private health care. Secure families maintain a class lead. In these ways, while the social services shape the new and more uniform way of life throughout the class structure, the usage and meaning of these social services differ by class resources.

The Singapore development strategy has changed the outward appearances of family lifestyle. Reinterviews of panel families of different social classes reveal greater similarity in use of more readily available social

[5] I have not changed the ranking of the panel families in these broad categories so as to see more clearly the relative changes to the lifestyles of the class groups. Thus in the pages to follow, I still refer to these families as they were placed in the earlier categories of "poor" and "secure."

goods. However, since families retained their distinct positions in the class structure and in wage labor, class position shapes their interactions, concerns, fears, and hopes. Variations in goals and living standards remain.

A range of state policies aim at improving workers' skills. But these programs of job creation, job finding, and retraining carry forward the major class divisions and inequalities. The state's labor investment policies affected wage earners differentially depending on their place in the labor process and in the market economy at the time of industrial takeoff. Job training programs were highly selective. The poor, who received little education and possessed few skills, were least likely to get training. Either programs were absent in their trades, or people with low formal education lacked access to them. The secure, who already had certificates or diplomas in technical subjects, are most likely to upgrade skills. The secure families stay ahead of the mainstream.

Women are increasingly proletarianized. To add to the family purse, many work at part-time jobs. While lacking benefits and poorly paid, part-time jobs subject women to the demands of the market economy. Through their market commitment women help bring their families more deeply into the new structures of the second-stage economy. The state social services, such as birth control services and housing developments in areas where factories located, enable women to work. In turn, their wage labor increases their families' participation in the new state social services. Women's wages help furnish new public sector apartments and pay for tutors for their youngsters.

Women's position in economy and society reflects their early upbringing and further contributes to the class position of the families they form. Their educational level and social class background figured in their phase 1 jobs, which then leads to the work they do in phase 2. Women who were not working at the time the second-stage development program was launched find it hard to break into mainstream jobs. Since women contribute to their household budget, the size of their pay packet makes some difference to the quality of their family life, including the ability to buy more fully into the state services. Thus state programs that encourage women to work for a wage spread the new social institutions further among families of all class levels, while women's earnings differentiate their families.

Women's unpaid labor also reproduces the family, and they put even more energy into their family roles in phase 2. The nuclearization of their household places a greater burden on each housewife. These efforts limit their freedom to move ahead on the job. Many are informally excluded from the key jobs of the new economy. But many place their home roles in the forefront. The majority have to maintain the family domestically, and their family responsibilities limit alternatives. Indeed, the work of women at home also helps the families attain the new social benefits of the new economic order, such as their children's school performance, and hence a place in a good school. Even if they do struggle to overcome the gender barrier and advance in the job market, the social services themselves create barriers to women's advancement (Doran and Jin 2002; Luke 1998).

Because of the differential involvement of families, a class gap remains in the educational system. The school system not only divides families. The educational system adds to a common conceptual framework that helps legitimate the class-divided nation. The losers redefine their loss within the dominant ideological paradigm. The ideology of the meritocracy proclaims that children with talent face no real financial obstacle to advance in the school system. The cost of formal schooling is low, and children who do well in the national competitive exams are promised state support. Many poor parents point to these factors as evidence of an open school system. Few attribute their children's failure to their disadvantaged place in the class system. Adopting the terms of discourse of the meritocracy, they explain that their children do poorly on school tests because they lack merit or talent. Therefore, they cannot expect to get good jobs, and will remain poor.

Class differences in housing, the most equitable of all of Singapore's social policies, also remain. Three times as many poor as secure tenant couples lack plans to obtain a flat of their own, and the size of a flat varies by class, as does its cost in absolute terms. As well, housing takes a larger proportion of working-class earnings. They also mortgage their hard-gained pension funds, to fund a flat. Come a recession, the poor have more trouble making do.

Nevertheless, the Singapore public housing program further homogenizes the social structure. After resettlement, and with much movement from one apartment to another, the poor lose much of the help they once got from kin and neighbors who had once lived nearby. By buying new flats, families become further constrained by the money economy. They are involved in long-term work goals, mortgage payments, and indebtedness to their pension plans. Continued market activity is necessary for Singapore home owners, regardless of class position, even in the social service society. The Singapore housing transformation creates a society of home owners, in fact or in aspiration. This transformation greatly narrows differences in family lifestyles.

Families also come to think alike. A home of one's own provides the new measure of family achievement in the modern society. Turning to home ownership as their standard of well-being compensates for dashed job hopes. The poorest, without even such a social good as their own home, recognize they are socially disadvantaged and are embittered. Thus public housing joins jobs and the school system in the frame of discourse for assessing the new social order.

Phase 2 social and economic development programs that proletarianize the populace also increase the cost of raising children. Couples lower their actual family size below their phase 1 intentions. Poor parents have slightly more children than secure parents. As a result, the relative family size of poor and secure in phase 2 do not differ much from the ratio of their intended family size in phase 1. Their reasons for reducing fertility differ. Along with their distinct positions in the labor market, the groups also have their own views of the costs of raising children.

The nuclear family, structurally isolated from both close and distant kin, and with independent goals and obligations, has emerged as the capitalist market and the social services penetrated society. We saw the great economic and social cleavages in the first industrial stage. Poor couples then were tightly bound to their kin by poverty, uncertainty, and job links. Secure couples also depend on their kin for mutual help, especially in the early stages of their life cycle. Both groups nourish a sense of shared responsibility in the local community.

The state, through the social services it sponsors, pushes and even forces ties to the market and key social institutions, and families change. The transformation of family- and kin-based exchanges of services and goods into a way of life in which families buy what they need was largely completed during the period of study. Families can afford to buy the everyday items they once made by hand or exchanged with kin and neighbors, as well as many other things they did not dream of having. In these less intended ways, state policies that are embedded in the international market economy transform the society.

By altering the source as well as the distribution of resources, the state's economic and social policies restructure the fabric of community and family life. People are not only more closely integrated into an international market economy, they also deeply enter its culture. The social services play a major part in their integration. In both the economic and the ideological spheres, state services commit people to the new social order. Their involvement in the mainstream economic and social institutions can be seen in the dependence by families at all social class levels on the money economy, public housing, the school system, and family planning organizations. But since access to these social services and institutions varies across the class structure, the meaning of the new social order for individual families also differs by social class and industrial sector.

Families in both major class groups depend on state services materially and as a source of ideas about their place in the society. But the family's position in the labor market shapes the process. The motives and meaning of reciprocal involvement with kin vary with the economic status of the family. Few poor families are economically secure, and all have a history of uncertain income. Thus economic status, coupled with the lack of crucial family support services in the public sector (day care, homes for the elderly), shapes the structure and meaning of family life along class lines. Many poor families, unable to separate from their kin for economic reasons, make a virtue of long-term reciprocity.

In comparison with the past, however, reciprocity has narrowed. As sections of the formerly poor advance, with the meritocracy as the overarching ideology, the community of the poor is no longer cohesive. Families that bettered themselves contract their ties to a smaller circle. They recognize the uncertainty of their achievements and the continued need to help out those closest to them when called upon to do so. But as they no longer extend such help to wider circles of kin or neighbors, the very poor families lose their supportive community.

Secure couples, in contrast, keen on separating from their wider kin links from the day they marry, now attain this goal. They express their better living standard by living apart, while they continue to see relatives for emotional satisfaction. They can support their kin materially or emotionally while living apart. Their greater access to resources allows husband and wife to develop a strong marriage bond. As a result of real differences in freedom from dependence on relatives, higher incomes, and better prospects for the future, the nuclear family structure and close marital bonds are much more common among the secure than among the poor.

In both class groups, women's responsibilities for maintaining the family increase. Homemaking tends to become even more the sole work of the wife. Upkeep of their small apartments, their new consumer items, and raising children for the stringent educational system take time. Women's burdens increase as traditional helpers find other duties and employment, move elsewhere, or are aged and can no longer help.

In sum, in the first phase, social class cleavages were marked; in the second stage, industrialization narrows more visible gaps. Our findings suggest that differences in family opportunities are still associated with social class. Nevertheless, whereas poor and secure families form two types of Singapore families in phase 1, they become variations on a recognizable theme in phase 2. Similar economic and social institutions constrain families in the two class groups. They are still divided by their market positions, which affect their behavior and the meanings they assign to their actions, but the market claims a tighter hold on all of them. They aim for recognizably similar goals and attempt to use the same means to attain them: these are public services of the second development stage. The social services that invest in labor redraw the stratification system to bring more workers deeply into the market economy and subject them to its demands. The positions in the labor process differ, but the system offers the ideology that all have equal opportunity to advance. State-sponsored public services became means to alter family lives. They provide entrance into the market and the cultural categories that become the framework within which the public evaluates the state and its socioeconomic programs.

Moving into the new millennium

Whether the Singapore model will survive in Singapore itself, let alone apply elsewhere, is hotly debated (Clammer 1997; Thompson 1996; Thornton 1998; Yeung and Olds 1998). Like other affluent countries, Singapore's services face steeply rising costs. Health care costs are soaring, with a rapidly aging population and rising expectations. The heavy dependency on foreign investment and exports for economic stability constrain increases in tax revenue, making it hard to sustain comprehensive programs (Ramesh 1995). Challenged, policy makers have shifted toward pro-market objectives, structures, and ideologies (Haque 1998).

True to its own special path, Singapore social policy does not set market consumers free to buy the social services they can afford. Rather, the state tries to avoid individualism attendant on economic development while shifting the costs to the community. Policies encourage mutual care by family members, and minimize forms of care that divert funds from industrial growth to welfare. The government enforces intra-family transfers, drawing in a network of providers beyond employers and the state (Duff 1998; Low 1998). The challenge of a move "from authoritarianism to communitarianism" promotes an Asian value system that mobilizes a tradition of family loyalty and Asian values. The Asian value system legitimizes family and community responsibility for social services (Chua 1995 and 1999). It aims to minimize independence from family even under conditions of rapid economic change. These policies build mutual responsibility in the family to care for disadvantaged members, taking on some of the functions of state policies (Hill and Lian 1995, pp. 154–8; Chua 1999). Youth and their seniors have a chance to live near each other; the younger generation is legally bound to care for their elders. In the process, the state attempts to shore up or recreate such a tradition that may not have even existed in those terms. Yet filial piety in

Singapore is not so strong that the family care of the elderly can be taken for granted.

The economy and the state

The state bureaucracy still participates in the economic realm, directing its investment policy to meet Singapore's function as a second-order global city. Its place in the world capitalist system creates a demand for specific types of both highly skilled and unskilled labor. But orienting the economy towards the knowledge society creates conditions for a more open atmosphere.

Since the 1980s, the state encourages applied scientific and technological investments. Government and university research and development programs (e.g., the government-backed National Science and Technology Board, created in 1991, which supports several research centers and public funding for research efforts) still emphasize applied research.

Schooling access and types have broadened to meet the needs of global industry. The Nanyang Technological University and National University of Singapore together accept 14% of the college age group, two-thirds more than the previous decade. There are now four polytechnics, as against two a decade ago, and nearly twice as many youths take this route to University. Yet there are criticisms that the school system restructuring needs to go past expanding numbers. Educational changes are being introduced to anticipate the demand for creative and technical labor in the coming decades (Gopinathan 1999).

Economic development may transform the Singaporean state itself (Yun 1997). The passage to industrial capitalism and the restructuring of the national economy shifts the bases of capital accumulation towards technological capital. The professional, managerial, technical middle class asserts itself not only economically, but also culturally and socially. It is widely believed that expanding new middle classes and recomposition of capital challenge political hegemony in Asia. Some suggest that Singapore's new middle class similarly seeks greater autonomy. The middle class and intellectuals respond to these political constraints by espousing a more innovation-driven and less applied economy. By promoting creative intellectual capital, the leadership may open the political system to alternative viewpoints.

The reality may be greater incorporation of the middle, knowledge-based strata into the state. Those with professional backgrounds have increased their leadership role in the PAP, extending the party's control over the economy. The very terms of the meritocracy elevate middle-class status. The new middle class also expresses its interest as consumers not opponents (Rodan 1996). To appease them, the ruling PAP of the 1990s has opened the political atmosphere to greater discussion and commentary (Lim 1997). Censorship of the arts is softened. In another realm, when the state-controlled Internet carrier used its power to dragnet individual accounts searching for viruses it provoked a wide protest. However, there is considerable support for media censorship on "sensitive" TV content, because of its supposed bad moral influence (Arun and Yap 2000; Chua 1997b; Goh 1998; Gunther and Peng 1996).

The working class enjoys considerable material improvements, and working conditions are ameliorated, thereby absorbing complaints by low-income groups (Leung 1998). However, recent prosperity increases material disparities, especially between ethnic groups, challenging the state to compensate for these disparities without compromising its ideology of meritocracy (Teo and Ooi 1996).

With rapid economic growth, nearly all available adults have been drawn into the labor pool. The need for a wide range of labor for industry is pressing. Singapore's labor force grew annually by only 0.6% during the 1990s. By 1988, over four-fifths of women aged twenty to twenty-four were employed. The proportion is still low for older women (just over half of women aged forty are employed). One solution to the labor shortage is raising the age of retirement and improving their skills. But the more high-tech industrial segments eschew the elderly.

State bodies continue to regulate the labor market. Migration policy supplements the country's workforce with foreign labor, while stemming the social problems that this entails through strict limits on its rights. Unskilled foreign labor totals approximately 20% of the country's labor force (Findlay, Jones, and Davidson 1998). Low-cost foreign domestic workers release local women for industry. At the same time, since highly educated and skilled labor is more important, a more skilled foreign labor pool of computer programers from India and other technically skilled workers willing to work for lower wages have obtained work permits (Shadier 2001). New Hong Kong immigrants with capital or technical skills, who sought an escape from the reversion of the British colony to China in 1997, found it easy to enter.

Development policies address local firms. The National Wages Council encourages employers to retain professionals in its firms, as well as hire part-time staff, draw in housewives, and retire employees. There is more skills training (Chowdhury 1993).

Most significant is the reemergence of Singapore's hinterland and its expansion into the wider region (Chiu, Ho, and Lui 1997). With the absorption of unskilled labor, Singapore investors are moving their labor-intensive products to poorer neighboring nations. Increasing regionalization and the relocation of Singapore-based companies abroad alleviates the need for migrant labor. The state, for instance through the Economic Development Board, but joined by the Government Linked Companies or the Committee on Promoting Enterprises Overseas, helps small and medium enterprises to export capital and technical expertise to Indonesia, India, and other Asian countries (e.g., Goh 1993). At the same time, new government organizations support the role of multinational corporations in the economy.

Social services and change

The social services' functions meet new development needs, as well as pare and distribute costs among the population (Duff 1998). People are encouraged to save and manage their own health care, with a stress on self-reliance and mutual care.

The CPF is today treated more as a personal savings account for citizens than a uniform governmental pension support. The CPF can now be used for a wide range of investments, to buy shares, life insurance, and even gold. Parents can devote their CPF to pay for their children's tertiary education.

Similarly, Medisave calls for wage earners to save for their own and their dependants' health costs. Wage earners choose between buying health services in the present or saving for their future old age. Families are expected to draw on their CPF and Medisave to care for needy members, further promoting Asian family values (Shantakumar 1996).

Singapore has become the first newly industrialized economy to adopt a broad set of pro-natalist policies. In the mid-1980s, Singapore's fertility rate dropped to 1.44 births per woman. Different educated groups have uneven replacement levels, and those in the higher socioeconomic brackets are not replacing themselves. Seeing the diminishing gene pool as a threat to the meritocratic-eugenic approach of the political order, the leadership worries that the quality nation's labor pool will dry up. Since 1987, the policies that applied the social services to penalize those with more children were reversed for the better educated. The units that once fielded the Disincentives against Higher Order Births have now come into line with eugenic pro-natalist policies. The Population Planning Unit is responsible for developing the new policies. This reversal aims to improve human capital amongst the populace and, some assert, to expand the Chinese section. Targeting the elite to bear more children, there is a wide range of benefits, including subsidies for child care, priority for public housing, and tax rebates for the better off. If the elite is encouraged to have more children, the poor are paid to have fewer. There is a sterilization cash incentive scheme for the purchase of an HDB flat. Differentiated hospital fees discourage high parity births (Singh, Fong, and Ratnam 1991).

The new policies place the burden on women to accede to their childbearing function. In fact, Singapore couples actually average two children, enough to replace themselves. However, many career women postpone marriage, and about one quarter of those women in their early thirties with a secondary education and over one third with a tertiary education remain single. For a while, the government became "matchmaker" by sponsoring social events and mixers. Going further, the state tries to reduce the proportion of women in advanced studies.[6]

The population transformation is a benchmark in Singapore's policies of structuring an industrial society. As in the past, the population profile reflects hard to legislate issues. Trends in the economy and society counter the legislation for more children. Having numerous children is not much help for parents' security.

For employed women, there is still a high level of work–family role conflicts (combining tasks of an employee, a spouse, a homemaker, mother) (Aryee 1992; Pyle 1997; Teo 1997; Yeoh and Huang 1995). Young educated parents put a lot of effort into raising their children which affects their daily life and future. Childbearing cannot be regulated directly by policy. The incentives have failed to bring a resurgence in births to educated women.

The "graying of the nation" dominates the political agenda of social services (Phillips and Bartlett 1995). It is estimated that in 2025, for every 100 Singaporeans of working age, 45 will be aged sixty or older. Over 85% of the elderly live with their children. Apart from normative obligations and emotional bonds, lack of independent government housing for seniors also plays a role (Harrison 1997; Mehta, Osman, and Lee 1995; Teo 1997; Teo and Kong 1997). To further the communitarian bent, HDB housing arrangements increasingly find ways to encourage adult children to live close to their parents. Limited numbers of nursing homes forces care of the elderly on adult children. Policies that reduce state responsibility for seniors include the Maintenance of Parents Act, Medisave, and raising the age of retirement.

Singapore has become a city-state of high-rises. A greater quantity of public-financed housing, with easier terms of purchase of HDB flats than before, has resulted in 87% of the population living in HDB apartments. The HDB's historical goal of facilitating home ownership was readily obtained through economic growth and public support. The success

[6] Women "flood" the medical and law faculties in such numbers that it is rumored that informal quotas limit their intake to one third.

was vital in the establishment of political legitimacy at the time of early development. Today, when around four-fifths of these flats are owned by their residents, the very success of the policy creates new tensions that need addressing, such as newly desired diversity in housing styles. HDB goals have changed from providing adequate quantity to improving the quality of life, but they cannot keep up with rising consumer expectations. Since different ethnic groups have unequal purchasing power, housing size reflects not only social class, but also ethnicity. An HDB flat is a quasi-market commodity, and providing housing for the people has political consequences. The opposition campaigns on the issue of equitable services, and areas that feel deprived of funds for better HDB housing did not turn out strong support for PAP candidates in recent elections. Finally, the earliest HDB policies of removing old ethnic settlements and widely resettling their habitants fracture ethnic communities, and new communities are not arising. The novel communitarian aim of developing community identity through housing remains a challenge (Chua 1995; Lim and Tay 1996; Teo and Ooi 1996).

Summary

Having traversed an economic and demographic path within decades that took Western nations a century to accomplish, Singapore now faces problems found in mature industrial nations. The city-state continuously needs to address issues of industry and society framed by its situation in the world economy.

The social services are part of the resolution of state–society conflicts. The public takes many services as a right. The issue of equalization of access, versus services as a reward to merit, is still forcefully felt, and political conflicts emerge over the distribution of social goods. There are popular pressures for state subsidies of health and other social safety nets. Access to social services has political significance. The leadership, however, does not entertain an alternative view of its social policies, and leads a frontal attack on the concept of a Singapore welfare state.

Its global position constrains the government's responses. Wary over the costs of paying for improved human capital, the state contrasts competitiveness to "over-spending." While social services are provided, they are not seen as "handouts," so to avoid the dependency that the government contends contributed to the economic and moral crises in the West. Competition is the most often used term for the majority, while meritocracy may be used to spur on the most disadvantaged sector, such as poor Malays (Yeo 1992).

In such contradictory ways, the government continues to use social policy to underpin its industrial plans, even as Singapore moves into a new industrial stage. The social services remain central to engineering the new social order. The delivery of these services is constructed as part of Singapore's positioning as a world city.

REFERENCES

Armunainathan, P. 1973. *Report on the Census of Population, 1970.* Singapore: Department of Statistics.

Arun, Mahizhnan and Yap, Mui Teng 2000. "Singapore: The Development of an Intelligent Island and Social Dividends of Information Technology," *Urban Studies*, 37 (10): 1749–1756.

Aryee, Samuel 1992. "Antecedents and Outcomes of Work–Family Conflict among Married Professional Women: Evidence from Singapore," *Human Relations*, 45 (8): 813–837.

Buchanan, Iain 1972. *Singapore in Southeast Asia.* London: G. Bell.

Chan, Angelique 1999. "The Role of Formal versus Informal Support of the Elderly in Singapore: Is there Substitution?," *Southeast Asian Journal of Social Science*, 27 (2): 87–110.

Chan, Heng-Chee 1976. *The Dynamics of One-Party Dominance: The PAP of the Grass Roots.* Singapore: Singapore University Press.

Chang, Chen-tung 1974. *Fertility Transition in Singapore.* Singapore: Singapore University Press.

Chiu, Stephen W. K., Ho, K. C., and Lui, Tai-lok 1997. *City-States in the Global Economy: Industrial Restructuring in Hong Kong and Singapore.* Westview, CO: Westview Press.

Chowdhury, A. 1993. "External Shocks and Structural Adjustments in East Asian Newly Industrializing Economies," *Journal of International Development*, 5 (1): 51–77.

Chua, Beng Huat 1995. *Communitarian Ideology and Democracy in Singapore.* London: Routledge.

1997a. "Between Economy and Race: The Asianization of Singapore," in Ayse Oncu and Petra Weyland (eds.), *Space, Culture and Power: New Identities in Globalizing Cities.* London: Zed Books, pp. 23–41.

1997b. "Still Awaiting New Initiatives: Democratisation in Singapore," *Asian Studies Review*, 21 (2–3): 120–133.

1999. "'Asian-Values' Discourse and the Resurrection of the Social," *Positions*, 7 (2): 573–592.

Chua, Wee Meng and Ho, Kun Ngiap 1975. "Financing Public Housing," in Stephen H. K. Yeh (ed.), *Public Housing in Singapore: A Multi-Disciplinary Study.* Singapore: Singapore University Press.

Clammer, John 1997. "Framing the Other: Criminality, Social Exclusion and Social Engineering in Developing Singapore," *Social Policy and Administration*, 31 (5): 136–153.

Doran, Christine and Jin, Jose 2002. "Globalization, the Patriachal State and Women's Resistance in Singapore," *Gender, Technology and Development*, 6 (2): 215–232.

Duff, John 1998. "Financing Foster Community Health Care: A Comparative Analysis." Paper presented at the XIV World Congress of the International Sociological Association (ISA), Montreal, 26 July–1 August.

Findlay, Allan M., Jones, Huw, and Davidson, Gillian M. 1998. "Migration Transition or Migration Transformation in the Asian Dragon Economies?," *International Journal of Urban and Regional Research*, 22 (4): 643–663.

Foucault, Michel 1973. *Discipline and Punish: The Birth of the Prison.* New York: Vintage.

FPPB and National Statistical Commission 1973. *Report of the First National Survey on Family Planning.* Singapore: FPPB and National Statistical Commission.

Goh, Chok Tong 1993. "Staying Competitive through Regionalisation," speech given at the Regionalisation Forum, Mandarin Hotel (Singapore) 221 May; reprinted in *Speeches: A Bimonthly Selection of Ministerial Speeches*. Singapore: Ministry of Information and the Arts (May–June), pp. 15–22.

Goh, Chor Boon 1998. "Creating a Research and Development Culture in Southeast Asia: Lessons from Singapore's Experience," *Southeast Asian Journal of Social Science*, 26 (1): 49–68.

Goh, Keng Swee and Education Study Team 1979. *Report on the Ministry of Education, 1978.* Singapore: Ministry of Education.

Gopinathan, S. A. F. 1999. "Preparing for the Next Rung: Economic Restructuring and Educational Reform in Singapore," *Journal of Education and Work*, 12 (3): 295–308.

Gunther, Albert C. and Peng, Hwa Ang 1996. "Public Perceptions of Television Influence and Opinions about Censorship in Singapore," *International Journal of Public Opinion Research*, 8 (3): 248–265.

Halliday, Jon 2000. "Productivist Welfare Capitalism: Social Policy in East Asia," *Political Studies*, 48 (4): 706–723.

Haque, Shamsul M. 1998. "New Directions in Bureaucratic Change in Southeast Asia: Selected Experiences," *Journal of Political and Military Sociology*, 26 (1): 97–119.

Harrison, James D. 1997. "Housing for the Ageing Population of Singapore," *Ageing International*, 23 (3–4): 32–48.

Hassan, Riaz 1977. *Families in Flats: A Study of Low-Income Families in Public Housing.* Singapore: Singapore University Press.

HDB 1980. *Annual Report. 1979/80.* Singapore: HDB.

Hill, Michael and Lian, Kwen Fee 1995. *The Politics of Nation Building and Citizenship in Singapore.* London: Routledge.

Ho, K. C. 1994. "Industrial Restructuring, the Singapore City-State, and the Regional Division of Labour," *Environment and Planning*, 26: 33–51.

1995. "Singapore: Maneuvering in the Middle League," in Gordon L. Clark and Won Bae Kim (eds.), *Asian NIEs and the Global Economy: Industrial Restructuring and Corporate Strategy in the 1990s.* Baltimore: Johns Hopkins University Press, pp. 113–142.

Jeon, Jei Guk 1995. "Exploring the Three Varieties of East Asia's State-Guided Development Model: Korea, Singapore, and Taiwan," *Studies in Comparative International Development*, 30 (3): 70–88.

Lee, Hsien Loon 1992. "Clans: Remaining Vibrant and Relevant," reprinted in *Speeches: A Bimonthly Selection of Ministerial Speeches*. Singapore: Ministry of Information and the Arts (September–October), pp. 120–123.

Lee, Soo Ann 1973. *Industrialization in Singapore*. Camberwell, Victoria: Longmans Australia.

Leung, Tang Kwong 1998. "East Asian Newly Industrializing Countries: Economic Growth and Quality of Life," *Social Indicators Research*, 43 (12): 69–96.

Lim, Cheng Tju 1997. "Singapore Political Cartooning," *Southeast Asian Journal of Social Science*, 25 (1): 125–150.

Lim, Chong Yah 1984. *Economic Restructuring in Singapore*. Singapore: Federal Publications.

Lim, Chong Yah and Tay, Boon Nga 1996. "Shelter for the Poor: Housing Policy in Singapore," *Population Review*, 40 (1–2): 84–101.

Lim, D. 1984. "Industrial Restructuring in Singapore," *Asian Employment Programme Working Paper*. Bangkok: ARTEP.

Low, Linda, 1998. "Health Care in the Context of Social Security in Singapore," *Journal of Social Issues in Southeast Asia*, 13 (1): 139–165.

Luke, Carmen 1998. "Cultural Politics and Women in Singapore Higher Education Management," *Gender and Education*, 10 (3): 245–263.

Mehta, Kalyani, Osman, Mohd Maliki, and Lee, Alexander E. Y. 1995. "Living Arrangements of the Elderly in Singapore: Cultural Norms in Transition," *Journal of Cross Cultural Gerontology*, 10 (1–2): 113–143.

Ministry of Health 1977. *Population and Trends*. Singapore: Ministry of Health.

Moore, R. Quinn 2000. "Multiracialism and Meritocracy: Singapore's Approach to Race and Inequality," *Review of Social Economy*, 58 (3): 339–360.

Mukhopadhaya, Pundarik 2000. "Education Policies as Means to Tackle Income Disparity: The Singapore Case," *International Journal of Sociology and Social Policy*, 20 (11–12): 59–73.

Phillips, David R. and Bartlett, Helen P. 1995. "Aging Trends Singapore," *Journal of Cross Cultural Gerontology*, 10 (4): 349–356.

Pyle, Jean Larson 1997. "Women, the Family, and Economic Restructuring: The Singapore Model," *Review of Social Economy*, 55 (2): 215–223.

Ramesh, M. 1995. "Social Security in South Korea and Singapore: Explaining the Differences," *Social Policy and Administration*, 29 (3): 228–240.

Rodan, Garry 1996. "Class Transformations and Political Tensions in Singapore's Development," in Richard Robison and David S. G. Goodman (eds.), *The New Rich in Asia: Mobile Phones, McDonalds, and Middle-Class Revolution*. London: Routledge, pp. 19–45.

Salaff, Janet W. 1988. *State and Family in Singapore: Structuring an Industrial Society*. Ithaca, NY: Cornell University Press.

Saw, Swee-Hock 1980, *Population Control for Zero Growth in Singapore*. Singapore: Oxford University Press.

Shadier, Bind 2001. "Shifting Paradigms of Globalization: The Twenty-First Century Transition towards Generics in Skilled Migration from India," *International Migration*, 39 (5): 45–71.

Shantakumar, G. 1996. "Preparing for the Greying Century: Lessons from an Industrializing Country and Future Developments," *Ageing International*, 23 (1): 52–65.

Singh, Kuldip, Fong, Yoke Fai, and Ratnam, S. S. 1991. "A Reversal of Fertility Trends in Singapore," *Journal of Biosocial Science*, 23: 73–78.

Teo, Peggy 1997. "Older Women and Leisure in Singapore," *Ageing and Society*, 17 (6): 649–672.

Teo, Peggy and Ooi, Geok Ling 1996. "Ethnic Differences and Public Policy in Singapore," in Denis Dwyer and David Drakakis-Smith (eds.), *Ethnicity and Development: Geographical Perspectives*. Toronto: John Wiley & Sons, pp. 249–270.

Teo, Siew Eng and Kong, Lily 1997. "Public Housing in Singapore: Interpreting 'Quality' in the 1990s," *Urban Studies*, 34 (3): 441–452.

Thompson, Mark R. 1996. "Late Industrialisers, Late Democratisers: Developmental States in the Asia Pacific," *Third World Quarterly*, 17 (4), special issue: 625–647.

Thomson, George G. and Smith, T. E. 1973. "Singapore: Family Planning in an Urban Environment," in T. E. Smith (ed.), *The Politics of Family Planning in the Third World*. London: George Allen and Unwin.

Thornton, William H. 1998. "Korea and East Asian Exceptionalism," *Theory, Culture and Society*, 15 (2): 137–154.

Tu, Wei-ming 2000. "Multiple Modernities: A Preliminary Inquiry into the Implications of East Asian Modernity," in Samuel P. Huntington and Lawrence E. Harrison (eds.), *Culture Matters: How Values Shape Human Progress*. New York: Basic Books, pp. 256–266.

Wong, Ting-Hong 2000. "State Formation and Chinese School Politics in Singapore and Hong Kong, 1945 to 1965," PhD thesis, University of Wisconsin, Madison.

Yeh, Stephen H. K. 1975. "Summary and Discussion," in Stephen H. K. Yeh (ed.), *Public Housing in Singapore: A Multi-Disciplinary Study*. Singapore: Singapore University Press.

Yeo, Cheow Tong 1992. "Social Problems among Malays," speech at the launch of AMP's Early Childhood and Family Education Programme, Singapore, Islamic Center, 18 July; reprinted in *Speeches: A Bimonthly Selection of Ministerial Speeches*, Singapore: Ministry of Information and the Arts (July–August), pp. 73–76.

Yeoh, Brenda S. A. and Huang, Shirlena 1995. "Childcare in Singapore: Negotiating Choices and Constraints in a Multicultural Society," *Women's Studies International Forum*, 18 (4): 445–461.

Yeung, Henry Wai-chung and Olds, Kris 1998. "Singapore's Global Reach: Situating the City-State in the Global Economy," *International Journal of Urban Sciences*, 2 (1): 24–47.

Yoshihara, Kunio 1976. *Foreign Investment and Domestic Response: A Study of Singapore's Industrialization*. Singapore: Eastern University Press.

Yun, A. H. 1997. "Industrial Restructuring and the Reconstitution of Class Relations in Singapore," *Capital and Class*, 62: 79–120.

9 Jakarta: globalization, economic crisis, and social change*

Dean Forbes

Jakarta is a mega-city which stands astride the economic, political, and (arguably) cultural landscape of Indonesia. As a center of finance and administration it is Indonesia's gateway to the global economy. However, its rapid and chaotic growth has created an urban fabric of complexity and contrast which has been impossible to service or manage in a comprehensive or effective way. Yet the city remains a key symbol in Indonesia, is regarded with genuine affection by many of its inhabitants, and is still a magnet for migrants from across the archipelago. It is sometimes represented as a city of villages that retain much of their rurality. Like a number of other cities, Jakarta embodies, in an exaggerated way, many of the core contradictions of modernity. Since 1997 Indonesia, and with it Jakarta, has experienced economic and political crisis and profound change. Few are able confidently to predict the outcome, but it has seriously slowed Jakarta's progression towards steadily acquiring a greater array of world city functions.

This chapter consists of three parts. In the first I make transparent the theoretical architecture which has guided construction of the chapter, then briefly outline Jakarta's history, establishing the foundations of its contemporary characteristics. The second part examines salient characteristics of Jakarta under the New Order (Order Baru) from 1965 until 1998, when the current infrastructure and modernist identity of the city was fashioned in its engagement with the global economy. In the third segment of the chapter I speculate about the impact the 1997 economic crisis and subsequent process of reform (reformasi) is having on Jakarta and its functioning within Indonesia and beyond.

* I am deeply thankful for Cecile Cutler's assistance in the preparation of this chapter. In addition, the ongoing discussions I have had with Indra Darmawan and Chairil Anwar in Adelaide, and with Triarko Nurlambang, Cholifah Bahudin, and Puguh Irawan (Jakarta), Tommy Firman (Bandung) and Yusrizal Yulius (Padang) have, over many years, informed and challenged my understandings of events in Jakarta and Indonesia more broadly.

A theoretical preamble

The twenty-first will, in all probability, be the century of the all-encompassing urban region, as the spread of the urban revolution embraces the great majority of the human population. The city, and indeed the fundamental restructuring of human organization of space, has been a subject of much theoretical conjecture over the last few decades. Perhaps the most powerful intellectual current of the last few years has centered on trying to understand the nature and consequences of global change, the intensification of which has been a feature of the last two centuries, and of much social research since the 1960s.

Two interrelated perspectives of globalization have proved particularly illuminating for urban research. On the one hand, writers have sought to understand how globalization, manifest through a continuous rejigging (or even reinvention) of global political economies, has permeated the cities and changed them and the lives of those who are affected by them. Thus post-Fordist industrial restructuring, the expansion of global communications and services, modernity, and the emergence of a network of world cities have all been discussed at length. On the other hand, researchers have explored the ways in which globalization has brought into focus a fractured multipolarity through the emergence of post-colonial identities, the identification of the significance of culture, the problematical nature of representation, post-modernity, the vernacular city, resistance, and the significance of civil society. I favor an approach that embraces both strands of the globalization literature, though in this chapter the emphasis is on political economy.[1]

A number of recent studies have reviewed the literature on Pacific Asian cities (Dick and Rimmer 1998; Forbes 1996; Forbes and Lindfield 1997; Forbes and Thrift 1987; Lin 1994; Schmidt 1998). Other accounts have looked at the broader processes reorganizing the social and economic spaces of Asia (Olds *et al.* 1999; Watters and McGee 1997, pp. 133–139). The predominant thrust of this work has been to situate Asian urban development within the discourse on the political economy of globalization (e.g., Olds 2001). A much smaller number of publications explore the social and cultural dimensions of globalization (e.g., Kim *et al.* 1997 on culture and the city). The common denominator has generally been the consistently fast economic growth rates which an increasingly large number of Pacific Asian countries have been able to achieve, though the arguments have been far from blind to the negative impacts on cities.

[1] In attempting to weave together two methodological strands my approach parallels, in some respects, that of authors such as Jacobs 1996 and Soja 1997. I have sketched my attempt to balance structure and agency in Forbes 1999, pp. 239–241.

Pacific Asian cities share problems with urban areas across the world such as urban traffic congestion, a loss of heritage architecture, and the challenges confronting the poor.

Yet emphasis has also been given to distinctive processes and patterns of Asian urban development. For example, few cities outside Asia have had to cope in recent years with consistently fast rates of industrial infrastructure investment, generally targeted on the underdeveloped peripheries of very large cities. Related to this, it is argued that the *desakota* or extended metropolitan region is specific to Asia, although other regions such as the northeastern seaboard of the USA have experienced a parallel kind of ribbon urban development. Further elaborations on this process include the hypotheses about the emergent mega-urban corridor regions that appear to be developing in a distinctive way in Pacific Asia. High levels of economic integration between countries (the so-called flying geese pattern) have been both a cause and a product of growing links between key cities. Thus there are several intersecting discourses, and equally interesting concepts, within which to situate an examination of Jakarta in its global context.

An historical introduction

Jakarta's history can be traced back to a twelfth-century trading port called Sunda Kelapa which serviced the Hindu-Javanese kingdom of Pajajaran. It was conquered by the Muslim sultanate of Banten in the 1520s and renamed Jayakarta. Dutch traders constructed warehouses on the opposite banks of the Ciliwung River in 1610, and gradually took control of the settlement, building a town which they called Batavia. The Dutch East Indies Company invested in infrastructure such as canals, modeled on towns in the Netherlands, and attracted residents from throughout Asia while excluding the local Javanese and Sundanese from the urban area. An influx of Chinese, Arabs, and Indians saw the emergence of a significant mestizo society. It was the Chinese, however, who prospered, prompting the Dutch to force them to reside outside the city walls in an area known as Glodok which remains a center of Chinese business activity. The high morbidity and mortality of the population in the swampy coastal settlement led to the city center being relocated further inland in the early nineteenth century to an area named Weltevreden (near present Senen).

As the Dutch colonial control increased during the nineteenth century, the role of Batavia changed, banks and offices were constructed, and a harbor at Tanjung Priok developed. The prosperous Dutch population congregated around Weltevreden, the Chinese residents of the city remained in the vicinity of Glodok, and the growing numbers of indigenous inhabitants moved into the deserted and rundown northern coastal parts of the city. Batavia's population reached 116,000 in 1900. By 1930 the city had increased to 533,000, some 37,000 of whom were Europeans, and 79,000 Chinese (see Abeyasekere 1987; Blusse 1985; Heuken 1989; Surjomihardjo 1977). Like many of its Pacific Asian contemporaries, Jakarta was once described as a "colonial" city.

The Japanese occupied the city in 1942 and renamed it Jakarta, but after their defeat in the Second World War they withdrew. Former Dutch residents, worried by the growing tide of nationalism and fighting between colonial troops and nationalists, began to depart in significant numbers after the republicans' unilateral declaration of independence in 1945. After the departure of the colonial regime in 1949, the Republican government moved back to Jakarta from Yogyakarta. A rapid influx of Indonesians into the void left by the departing Dutch raised the city's population from 823,000 in 1948 to 1,782,000 in 1952, and then to 2,973,000 in 1961. Their presence in such large and rapidly growing numbers overburdened the minimal infrastructure of the city. A plan for a new town – it later became a suburb – called Kebayoran was approved in 1950. Jakarta was granted the status of a province in 1961: instead of *kotapradja* it became Daerah Khusus Ibukota (DKI) Jakarta, or the Special Capital Region of Jakarta.

In 1959 President Sukarno sought to embellish the symbolic landscape of Jakarta by including it in his "lighthouse" (*mercusuar*) strategy through which he intended Indonesia to become the center of the world's "New Emerging Forces." He embarked on a massive building program that saw the construction of highways, luxury hotels, a department store, sports stadium, and the National Monument that sits in the center of Medan Merdeka. Huge socialist realist sculptures were erected at major intersections throughout the city. A process of "Indonesianization" of the city was taking place; it was said Jakarta would emerge as the "the birthplace of the New Indonesians" (Surjomihardjo 1977, p. 73). The lighthouse strategy skewed the development of the city, emphasizing the importance of prestigious streets and luxury buildings, and ignoring the needs of ordinary citizens (Surjomihardjo 1977, p. 77).[2]

The social composition of Jakarta in the 1950s and 1960s changed as a result of the influx of Indonesians into the city. A purposive sample survey

[2] Boddy 1983, p. 31, offers a scathing interpretation of the symbolism of Jakarta's monuments calling them "an almost perfect visual embodiment of the social forces at work in Indonesia in those times: a detached, elephantine, corrupt elite dropped onto a human grid of misery and neglect." See also the extensive treatment of architecture and urban symbolism in Indonesia in Kusno 2000.

of the Jakarta population undertaken in 1954 estimated that about 85% of Jakarta's annual increase in population was due to migration, most of which came from the surrounding province of West Java (Heeren 1955). Consequently, it was often remarked that Jakarta was a city of villages (or *kampong*) which retained much of their rural character. Locally born Jakarta residents (the *orang betawi*) were a relatively small proportion of the population.[3]

Jakarta and the "New Order"

Notwithstanding its colonial origins and the imprint of Sukarno in the 1950s and 1960s, contemporary Jakarta owes much of its profile to the "New Order" (1965–1998) established by Suharto following the overthrow of Sukarno.[4] In the wake of a ruthless purge of opponents that resulted in 500,000 to 1 million deaths throughout the archipelago, Suharto began to fashion an economic strategy designed to rescue Indonesia from the economic decline experienced in the late Sukarno years. It combined an emphasis on the market-oriented policies of econocrats (the "Berkeley mafia") with a contradictory emphasis on economic nationalism. This synthesis saw the emergence of some key Chinese-Indonesian entrepreneurs in partnership with an emergent indigenous business class, the most prominent of whom were members of the Suharto family and their close friends.[5] The rapid growth of Jakarta's population and economy during this period reflected the centralization of the Indonesian economy and polity that is a crucial legacy of Suharto.

Four aspects of the metropolis (as distinguished from the post-metropolis) form the substructure of this part of the chapter: population growth, migration, and the "livability" of the city (metropolarities); industrial development and the polarization of the Indonesian space economy (flexcity); the expansion of the services sector and its post-industrial character (cosmopolis); and the suburbanization of the city and the formation of Jabotabek and the extended metropolitan region (exopolis).[6]

[3] A later study by Castles (1967) compared Jakarta's population in the censuses of 1930 and 1961.

[4] I first visited Jakarta in 1975, and have made regular visits to the city ever since. The changes in that period have been extraordinary. During the 1970s Jakarta seemed somewhat preoccupied with its domestic role and separated from the rest of the world. During the 1990s its status as a component of the global economy was evident in everything from its department stores and supermarkets to the vehicles plying the streets and tollways.

[5] Transparency International ranked Indonesia the most corrupt country in Asia in 1998, and one of the six most corrupt (out of eighty-five) across the world (*Far Eastern Economic Review*, 8 October 1998, p. 108).

[6] The terminology is borrowed from Soja 1997, pp. 22–23.

Table 9.1 *Jakarta and Jabotabek, population, 1961–1995*

	1971	1980	1990	1995
Population ('000)				
DKI Jakarta	4,547	6,481	8,228	9,113
Bogor (Kabupaten)			3,736	4,415
Bogor (Kotamadya)			271	285
Bogor (Kabupaten and Kotamadya)		2,494		
Tangerang		1,529	2,765	3,589
Bekasi		1,144	2,104	2,757
Jabotabek	8,307	11,648	17,105	20,160
Rate of growth (% p.a.)	1961–1971	1971–1980	1980–1990	1990–1995
Jakarta	4.6	4.0	2.4	2.1
Jabotabek		4.1	3.8	3.3

Sources: Biro Pusat Statistik various years; Firman 1999, p. 51.

Each of these processes has been important in defining and elaborating the contemporary structure of Jakarta.

Metropolarities

Metropolarities is a discourse "on the restructured social mosaic and the emergence of new polarisations and inequalities" (Soja 1997, p. 22). Population growth has been one of the striking characteristics of modern Jakarta. In the 1970s former Governor Ali Sadikin attempted to halt migration to Jakarta by declaring it a closed city but failed. While local authorities try to maintain a register of residents in an attempt to dissuade migrants from staying in the city, any serious attempt to halt migration has long since been abandoned. DKI Jakarta, which is the administrative unit for governing the city proper, has grown from 2.9 million in 1961 to 9.1 million in 1995. Jakarta's population in the 2000 census was reported at 8.3 million, well below projections of 10 million, probably because of significant underenumeration in the census process (Biro Pusat Statistik 2001, p. 21). Growth rates, however, have been slowing. Jakarta grew at 4.6% p.a. in the 1960s, 4.0% in the 1970s, 2.4% in the 1980s, and 2.1% in the 1990s (Table 9.1). Nevertheless, the latter rate of growth still saw DKI Jakarta expanding in the second half of the 1990s by more than 190,000 people a year.

Slowing population growth within DKI Jakarta must be set against faster population growth in other parts of metropolitan Jakarta. Jakarta spills over its administrative boundaries into surrounding parts of West

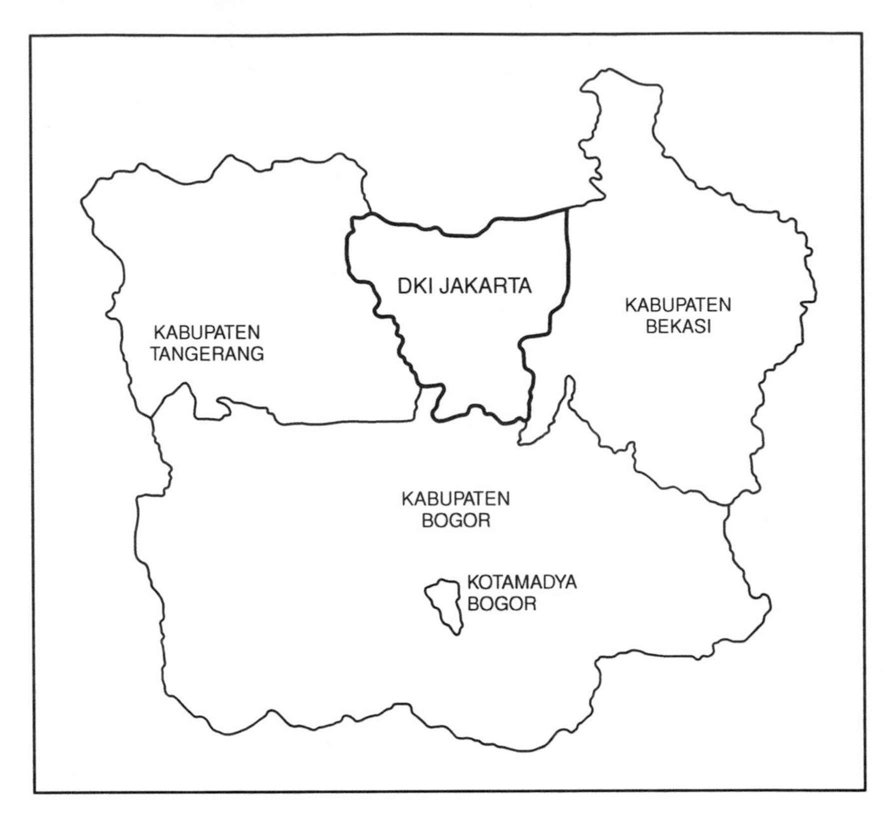

Map 9.1 Jabotabek

Java province. This has prompted the formation of the region known as Jabotabek, which combines DKI Jakarta with the *kabupaten* of Bogor, Tangerang, and Bekasi, along with *kotamadya* Bogor.[7] The Jabotabek region's population has increased from 11.6 million in 1980 to 17.1 million in 1990 and 20.2 million in 1995 (Table 9.1). Between 1971 and 1980 Jabotabek as a whole grew at 4.1% p.a., 3.8% p.a. from 1980 to 1990, and 3.1% p.a. from 1990 to 1995 (Table 9.1). Urban reclassification, natural increase, and migration each accounted for approximately one third of the population increase between 1980 and 1990 (Table 9.2). Rural to urban migration, which was responsible for 35.3% of the growth, has attracted the most scholarly attention (see Azuma 1995; Firman 1999; Gardiner 1997; Hugo 1996; Mamas *et al.* 2001).

[7] For an account of the structure of municipal government in Indonesia see Niessen 1999.

Table 9.2 *Decomposition of population growth rates in Jabotabek region, 1980–1990*

	%
Recorded growth rates p.a.	
Urban	5.8
Rural	−1.4
Total	3.5
Constant area growth rates p.a.	
1980 urban area	2.3
Expansion area	7.9
1990 urban area	3.6
Rural area	3.3
Dimensions of growth p.a.	
Reclassification	30.3
Natural increase	34.5
Net migration	35.3

Source: Gardiner 1997, p. 125.

The pattern of population growth, together with the distinctive kind of economic strategy adopted by the Suharto regime, has determined the city's social structure.[8] There is no doubt that Jakarta has become a city characterized by stark social and economic inequalities. On the one hand it is the home of Indonesia's rich, and increasingly of the wealthy middle class (who early during the New Order were more likely to be found in the resource-rich regions outside Java). On the other hand, there is no doubt that Jakarta has many pressing social problems associated with poverty. For example, the residents of inner-city settlements face pressure to relocate them (Jellinek 1991), child labor is a significant concern (Pardoen *et al.* 1996), the situation of women remains difficult (Murray 1991), and the lack of intergenerational socioeconomic mobility for those in the poorest parts of the city is a concern (Irawan 1999). Despite its attractiveness to migrants in search of paid work, and its undoubted attractions, especially to the middle class, conditions in much of Jakarta are poor (Jellinek 2000).

In 1999 *Asiaweek* magazine ranked forty Asian cities according to "livability." Jakarta was awarded thirty-fifth position, just above Phnom

[8] On housing and land in Jakarta, which can sometimes make more visible the social class structure of a society, see Dowall and Leaf 1991; Firman 1997; Jellinek 1997; Leaf 1993; Nurlambang 1993; and Setiono 1991.

Penh, but immediately below Karachi, Dhaka, and Delhi (Choong 1998). After an initial shock about the audacity of the exercise, few would have been surprised by Jakarta's ranking.

The *Asiaweek* survey measured city performance according to twenty-four indicators which formed a composite measure of economic opportunity, quality of education, environment and sanitation, health care, transportation, personal security, housing cost, and leisure (Choong 1998). In explaining the overall outcomes it was argued that good governance and the ability to deal with economic crisis were essential to a high ranking in the survey. Governance, in turn, depends on leadership, partnerships between government and civil society, and the absence of corruption. Jakarta's low rank reflects both its rapid growth and the failings of the administration to keep up with the changes required in order to make the city more "livable." Yet significant as these problems were, the onset of the 1997 economic crisis compounded the social problems confronting the Jakarta administration.

Flexcity

Flexcity is a term which draws attention to "the restructuring of the political economy of urbanisation and the formation of the more flexibly specialised post-Fordist industrial metropolis" (Soja 1997, p. 22). Jakarta's industrial capacity began to expand during the late colonial period, industries initially gravitating to the older parts of the city such as Kota and Pasar Ikan, and near the port at Tanjung Priok. Development was halting and suffered a setback in the 1960s when the Indonesian economy declined as a result of President Sukarno's neglect. Industry picked up again in the early 1970s with the development of the industrial estate at Pulo Gadung and the small-scale export-processing zone at Tanjung Priok (Castles 1989). Jakarta's industrial growth has continued to the present. Globalizing companies have been attracted to Indonesia, and Jakarta and West Java more specifically, by the low cost of labor and the generally favorable environment created by the government. Nike, which epitomizes the globalization of manufacturing, had about one third of its shoes produced in Java in 1996. Its factories, which are subcontractors, are staffed by a predominantly female labor force drawn from the local region.[9]

The economy of Indonesia has grown strongly since the early days of the New Order. Gross domestic product (GDP) increased by 7.2% p.a.

[9] Hancock's (1997, pp. 16–19) study is highly critical of the treatment of the female workforce in Nike's Banjaran, West Java factory.

Table 9.3 *Labor force growth, Jakarta, 1985–1995*

	1985	1995	Increase 1985–1995(%)
Manufacturing	393,408	571,693	45.3
Construction	158,198	173,169	9.5
Trade, restaurants, hotels	695,238	908,606	30.7
Transport, communications	208,119	235,788	13.3
Finance, insurance, property, and business services	51,534	238,952	363.7
Community, social and personal services	838,537	1,027,425	23.3
Total for Jakarta	2,395,437	3,222,288	34.5

Sources: Biro Pusat Statistik 1996, Table 20.3; 1986, Table 34.3.

during the 1970s, and 6.0% p.a. during the 1980s. In the first half of the 1990s GDP growth averaged 7.6% p.a. (Asian Development Bank 1996, p. 223). Industry has been important to that growth. Value added in industry increased by 6.1% p.a. in the 1980s and 10.5% p.a. between 1990 and 1995 (Asian Development Bank 1996, p. 226; Douglass 1997; Hugo 2000). Foreign investment, particularly from Pacific Asian countries, was an important factor in stimulating this growth. Indonesia was spoken of as an emerging, third generation, Asian tiger economy (or dragon, or flying goose, depending on the preferred metaphor).

Manufacturing employment in Jakarta grew by 45.3% between 1985 and 1995, compared to total growth in the labor force of 34.5% (Table 9.3). About 48.5% of the manufacturing workforce is in Jakarta, with the balance in the Botabek region. The distribution of manufacturing employment in the Jabotabek region can be determined by examining the 1995 Intercensal Population Survey (known as SUPAS) (summarized in Table 9.4). The manufacturing workforce in Jabotabek is distributed across an east–west axis, and along a north–south axis, paralleling the major transport arteries. The largest concentrations of manufacturing workers are in South Jakarta and Bogor, which together have a total of 350,046 workers, the majority of whom live in Bogor *kabupaten*. A second major concentration is in the east of the metropolitan area where East Jakarta and Bekasi account for 358,137 workers. The third major concentration is in West Jakarta and Tangerang which have 272,568 workers. Women constitute less than 30% of the manufacturing labor force.

Jakarta has been an important locus of economic growth within the Indonesian economy. In 1995 it accounted for about 16% of GDP (15% excluding oil and natural gas), regional GDP per capita was exceeded only by resource-rich East Kalimantan, and GDP growth rates were among

Table 9.4 *Manufacturing labor force, Jabotabek, 1995*

	Males		Females	
	Total	%	Total	%
South Jakarta	53,737	73.9	18,966	26.1
East Jakarta	114,559	72.8	42,728	27.2
Central Jakarta	35,190	74.7	11,934	25.3
West Jakarta	115,460	68.0	54,432	32.0
North Jakarta	81,859	65.7	42,728	34.3
Bogor	193,742	69.9	83,601	30.1
Bekasi	146,250	72.8	54,600	27.2
Tangerang	71,024	69.2	31,652	30.8
Bogor (Kotamadya)	15,276	76.1	4,788	23.9
Jabotabek total	827,197	70.5	345,429	29.5

Sources: Biro Pusat Statistik 1999a, 1999b, Tables 34.1, 34.2, 34.3.

the fastest in the country (Biro Pusat Statistik 1996, p. 570). A study by Soegijoko and Bulkin (1994, p. 31) argued that since the New Order government came to power almost half of all employment created by foreign and domestic investment in Indonesia has been located in Jabotabek. This combined with the higher wages and superior standards of living enjoyed by Jakarta residents has made the region a strong magnet for potential migrants.

Fifteen years ago Anne Booth (1989) predicted that, assuming Indonesia's industrial strategy was successful, and non-oil export targets were met, towards the end of the century Java would, for the first time since the 1920s, be producing around half of Indonesia's exports. As a result, Java would provide more employment opportunities in industry and ancillary service occupations than other parts of the country, and consequently household incomes and consumer expenditure would continue to grow faster than in the outer islands, exacerbating the in-migration of educated Indonesians to Java.

Java's position has indeed strengthened. Overall some 73% of Indonesia's jobs in manufacturing were on Java in 1985, and this had risen to 77% in 1995. Jakarta's share of manufacturing jobs, however, had shrunk from 6.8% in 1985 to 5.6% in 1995. This contrasted strongly with the province of West Java (which includes Botabek), where the share of manufacturing jobs had increased from 19.4% in 1985 to 25% in 1995 (based on the 1985 and 1995 SUPAS data).

It is sometimes said that export-oriented industry is more inclined to geographic dispersion than import-substitution-oriented industry, which is closely tied to local markets. This argument may be applicable to resource-based industries, but it is not relevant for the kinds of modern manufacturing concerns whose priorities include high-level financial and business services. Although Jakarta's share of these high-level services has fluctuated, its overall dominance of producer services provides a serious incentive for both domestic and foreign firms to locate within reasonable proximity to these services.

Cosmopolis

In Soja's (1997, p. 22) words cosmopolis refers to "the globalisation of urban capital, labour and culture and the formation of a new hierarchy of global cities." It draws attention to the key role of services in the urban economy, and the connectedness of the city with the global economy. Jakarta's significance as a center of both high- and low-order services complements its industrial role. Services range from transport and communications, to trade, public administration, and producer services. Together they accounted for 79% of Jakarta's labor force and 62% of GDP in 1997 (Badan Pusat Statistik 1999). Jakarta has dominated the provision of higher-order services in Indonesia for a long time. A study by Rutz (1987) developed a Central Place Facility Index (CPFI) for Indonesia in 1980. Jakarta achieved a weighted CPFI over six times larger than the second-ranked city (Medan), and larger than the next six biggest cities combined (including Medan). On a per capita basis, Jakarta's CPFI was the median figure for the five highest-ranked cities in Indonesia, i.e., the volume of central place services in Jakarta was approximately proportional to the population, Jakarta dominating the urban system in both. However, this is less important than its absolute ranking in the provision of central place services.

Wholesale and retail trade is the second most important sector of the Jakarta economy after manufacturing. It produced 22% of the city's GDP in 1997. Between 1985 and 1995 employment in trade, restaurants, and hotels grew by 30.7%; by 1995 it employed 908,606 people, or 28% of the city's workforce. For many years Jakarta has had a large informal sector of small-scale traders (microenterprises) able to provide cheap goods and services. The continuing rapid growth of Jakarta during much of the 1990s meant the informal sector has also continued to grow, especially in those parts of the city where migrants congregate. In 1991, the city boasted 156 markets and 68,202 registered market stalls, not including illegal and unregistered activities (Kantor Statistik, Propinsi DKI Jakarta 1992, Tables 8.3.1 and 8.3.3).

The city is the capital and home of the central government. Despite cutbacks in public sector spending due to reduced government oil revenues, the deregulation thrust of economic policy, and a desire to decentralize

Table 9.5 *Finance, insurance, property, and business services labor force, Jabotabek, 1995*

	Males		Females	
	Total	%	Total	%
South Jakarta	47,851	71.1	19,402	28.9
East Jakarta	47,742	71.9	18,639	28.1
Central Jakarta	21,624	67.5	10,404	32.5
West Jakarta	29,376	69.0	13,176	31.0
North Jakarta	22,563	73.4	8,175	26.6
Bogor	13,270	71.4	5,308	28.6
Bekasi	15,600	80.0	3,900	20.0
Tangerang	10,036	76.5	3,088	23.5
Bogor (Kotamadya)	1,596	97.3	114	6.7
Jabotabek Total	209,658	71.8	82,206	28.2

Sources: Biro Pusat Statistik 1999a, 1999b.

remaining bureaucratic power to the provinces and sub-provincial regions (such as municipalities), Jakarta has remained the center of national administration. Community, social, and personal services employed over 1 million people in 1995. However, new legislation announced in 1999 may have some impact on this in coming years.

Jakarta's producer services are closely connected to the internationalization of the city. The four main components of producer services are the banking subsector, insurance and other financial services, building rentals (not including house rentals), and business services. In just ten years, from 1985 to 1995, jobs in this sector grew nearly fivefold (Table 9.3). This massive expansion in employment reflects the rapid rise of the producer services in the late 1980s and through the 1990s, fueled by the growth of the Indonesian economy. Producer sector jobs, unlike manufacturing jobs, are concentrated in Jakarta, which accounts for 80.7% of jobs. The largest concentrations are in South and East Jakarta. The proportion of females in the sector is very similar to manufacturing (Table 9.5).

Over a decade ago Castles (1989) asked whether Jakarta was in transition from a pre-industrial to a post-industrial city, having skipped over the industrial phase. But he rejected the idea. Instead he argued that a post-industrial sector, centered on financial services, electronic communications, and air transport, had been grafted on a pre-industrial city, and supplemented by medium-technology manufacturing. Today, does Jakarta warrant being categorized as a post-industrial city? Castles (1989) had correctly predicted that declining oil revenues in the 1990s would encourage major industrial expansion, part of which would be export oriented, putting the Jakarta region in a conventional industrial stage. Manufacturing industry jobs in DKI Jakarta have increased by 45.3% between 1985 and 1995, but their share of the city's labor force has expanded from 16.4% to 17.7% (Table 9.3). New industry, however, has been attracted to Jabotabek where slightly more than half of the manufacturing labor force were found in 1995 (Table 9.4).

Despite this industrial growth, Jakarta has continued to develop a large and important services sector, and it dominates Indonesia in this respect. The sector as a whole has provided three-quarters of the jobs in Jakarta – this, of course, includes the informal sector. Still, an increasing proportion of the services jobs have been characterized by high levels of productivity and strong long-term growth. It is this growth that feeds speculation about the city's post-industrial character.

Whether we characterize Jakarta as a post-industrial city or not, segments of the services sector, producer services in particular, have matured over the last few years. As Jakarta's satellite urban centers develop in the Botabek region, attracting more industry along with the overspill of residential suburbs from the city, we may anticipate a greater degree of relocation of the producer services firms currently concentrated in East and South Jakarta. The post-industrial structures of the city are closely linked to its industrial future.

Exopolis

The term exopolis refers to "the restructuring of urban form and the growth of edge cities, outer cities and postsuburbia" (Soja 1997, p. 22). The spatial structure of Jakarta and the Jabotabek region more broadly is intimately connected to the pattern of transport development. Jakarta is the hub of the domestic and international transport networks, which in the Indonesian context means air, sea, rail, and road. Jakarta has the country's premier international airport, Sukarno-Hatta International Airport, opened in 1985. The value of exports shipped through the main port at Tanjung Priok in 1985, ranked behind only the resource-rich provinces of Riau, East Kalimantan, and Aceh. About one third of Indonesia's imports enter through Jakarta (Castles 1989), reflecting the industrial base of the city and the consumption levels of its inhabitants, as well as the dispersed geography of Indonesia.

Land transport systems also focus on Jakarta, including Java's railway network and its gradually expanding road network, which connects with ferries to Bali and Madura in the east, and Sumatra in the west (Dick and Forbes 1992). In 1995, some 40% of Indonesia's passenger vehicles and

45% of its buses were registered in Jakarta (Biro Pusat Statistik 1996, Table 8.2.2). Extensive investment in freeway development has occurred around Jakarta, joining it to the international airport, and upgrading the roads linking it to the main destinations in its hinterland, both in an east–west direction adjacent to the coast, and in a southerly direction. Equally, within Jakarta there has been massive investment in tollways criss-crossing the city, although rapid expansion in the number of private automobiles in the early 1980s has meant that traffic congestion in many parts of the city continues to get worse (Cervero and Susantono 1999; Pasaribu 1998). The city is the preeminent center of Indonesia's domestic and international communications. Jakarta in 1994 contained 35.9% of Indonesia's telephone sets, while, in 1988, 41.6% of international telegrams and 69.9% of out-going international telexes originated in the city (Biro Pusat Statistik 1989, 1996). Telecommunications within the city have improved vastly over the last decade, as have communications throughout Indonesia, due to the greater use of satellites.

The expansion of industrial employment and population around the outer edges of Jakarta has been remarkable (see also Henderson *et al.* 1996; Jones and Mamas 1996; Soegijoko 1999). However, while there has been significant dispersion of industrial enterprises into the Botabek region, the majority of producer services firms have remained close to the commercial centers of the city. The outward expansion of Jakarta has been examined by scholars who focus on the closely connected processes of suburbanization (Leaf 1994); urban fringe development (Browder *et al.* 1995), and the emergence of constellation (or satellite) cities (Ford 1993; Liu 1998).

The most significant of the city edge developments are the new, planned settlements. The Bumi Serpong Damai Project, on a 6,000 hectare site, was Greater Jakarta's first effectively integrated urban development. This project has been funded by a consortium of private developers and, unlike earlier attempts at "new town" development (such as Blok M), Bumi Serpong Damai will attempt to provide local work for 60–70% of its labor force. It is intended that this employment will be created with the development of a Hitech Park and associated Light Manufacturing Estate and in the normal range of retail and service occupations. The project is to be completed by the year 2005 and provide 139,000 dwellings (Dorleans 1994, p. 41; Pangestu and Dijkgraaf 1998; Rachmadi 1994, pp. i–viii). Another set of significant developments are Lippo Karawaci (Lippo Village) and Lippo Cikarang (Lippo City), two major, planned, privately developed residential areas each containing about 30,000 residents, and planned to expand to 1 million by 2020 (Hogan and Houston 2001).

There is little evidence of a hollowing-out of the city center of Jakarta, in the way that occurs in large Western cities. Instead, vacant land is rapidly being filled by offices, hotels, and expensive apartment blocks. The infill of the old Kemayoran airport, and the destruction of adjacent *kampung*, will create an area known as Bandar Kemayoran featuring the Indonesian International Trade Center (Jellinek 1997; Setiono 1991). Nor has the suburbanization occurred in quite the same way as in Western cities. Greenfields industrial development has drawn labor from semi-rural villages and satellite towns. New housing estates have proliferated on the outskirts of the city, but without a clear-cut focus on major service areas such as shopping centers. Satellite cities, such as Tangerang, Bekasi, Bogor, and Serpong, have provided nucleii for the suburbanization process. Housing estates are sometimes linked by freeway to Jakarta, but other transport connections are generally rudimentary.[10] The leapfrogging of industry to the semi-rural regions surrounding Jakarta contributes to the development of what McGee (1991a, 1991b) has termed *desakota*, now more commonly referred to as extended metropolitan regions (Firman 1992; Firman and Dharmapatni 1995; Jamieson 1991; Leaf 1996).

Economic crisis and 'reformasi'

Crisis and reform

Jakarta's world turned upside down in 1997. When the Thai economy suffered its financial crisis, Indonesia's soon followed. The causes of the crisis in Indonesia are too complex to deal with adequately here. In summary though, it was the coincidence of two separate (albeit interrelated) aspects of Indonesia in the 1990s which forced the country to the brink: an underlying weakness in the economy, particularly in the management of banking and finance; and widespread unease about the continuing stranglehold and abuse of power by President Suharto.

The overall economic impact of the crisis on Indonesia was both dramatic in its speed and profound in its consequences (Arndt and Hill 1999; Murphy and Dolven 1999, pp. 50–52). GDP growth dropped to 4.9% in 1997, and experienced negative growth (−13.4%) in 1998, and shrank again in 1999, before growing by about 4% in 2001 (*Far Eastern*

[10] Jabotabek is also a planning region, though less effective than it needs to be if it is to have a significant impact on the region (Clarke 1985; Forbes 1990; Giebels 1986; Soegijoko 1996).

Economic Review, 22 March 2001, p. 58). The economic consequences of the crisis remain severe. While the value of the Indonesian Rupiah stabilized at about Rp8,000 to $US1, nearly half of all Indonesian corporations are insolvent, and 60% of debt was owed to foreign creditors (World Bank 1999b, p. 5). A Jakarta initiative, established in an attempt to facilitate the voluntary out-of-court restructuring of corporations, registered 182 companies with foreign debts of about $20.8 billion and local debt of Rp11.6 trillion. The key sectors involved were basic industry, chemicals, and mining; property, trading services, and investment; and consumer goods, textiles, and garments.

The political consequences of the crisis have been equally powerful, leading ultimately to the resignation of President Suharto in May 1998. This event marked the end of the New Order. The incumbent vice president, B. J. Habibie, was installed as president in the wake of Suharto's resignation, though Suharto remained his mentor (as he had been since Habibie was a youth). Parliamentary elections were held in June 1999, and President Abdurrahman Wahid elected later in the year, but he resigned and was replaced by President Megawati Sukarnoputri in May 2001.

The social consequences

Given the magnitude of Indonesia's economic crisis, it is not surprising that the social consequences for the country have been significant.[11] Early in the economic crisis there were dire forecasts about the likely increase in poverty. The International Labor Organization predicted that the proportion of the Indonesian population in poverty would increase to about 48% in 1998. The Indonesian government itself anticipated about 39%. However, World Bank research suggested poverty increased from 11% of the population in 1997 to 18% in 1998, a much less significant increase than others anticipated.[12] It brought the number living under the poverty line to 36 million (*Inside Indonesia*, April–June 1999, p. 3; *Wall Street Journal*, 25 January 1999; Booth 1999, pp. 131–135; Cameron 1999, p. 24; World Bank 1999b, pp. 7–8).

[11] The World Bank (1999a) website on *The Social Crisis in East Asia*, referenced at the end of this chapter, has been an important source. On Indonesia see UNFPA (1998, pp. 43–71).

[12] Government policy in response to increased poverty has three priorities: maintaining food security; expanding employment and income-earning opportunities; and ensuring access to vital social services (World Bank 1999b, p. 7). Specific government initiatives which were allocated funding in mid-1998 included the Community Recovery Program (CRP) and the Social Protection Sector Development Scheme (UNFPA 1998, p. 46).

Unemployment did not worsen as much as anticipated. While some expected it to reach 22%, the proportion unemployed increased from 5.1% in February 1997 to 6.4% in February 1998 (Cameron 1999, p. 24). However, this is not surprising, in the absence of a welfare system that would allow people to be formally unemployed. For most, unemployment cannot be sustained: part-time or poorly paid jobs, such as in microenterprises, must, of necessity, offer a means to survive.

The impact of the crisis was specific to sectors and places. A Biro Pusat Statistik survey of household income in 100 *desa* (villages) conducted in May 1997, August 1998, and December 1998 suggested a differential regional impact, but it was not statistically representative. Agencies such as the World Bank (1999b, p. 7) believe that increases in poverty were most pronounced in the urban areas and on Java.[13] Undoubtedly the population of Jakarta has been hard hit. In contrast, the agricultural export-dependent provinces were rather less affected, and, on balance, may have benefited from the crisis.[14]

Construction workers in Jakarta and some other large cities on Java were seriously affected as large-scale building projects came to a halt. However, this did not have much of an impact on construction workers in other major cities, such as Makassar (formerly Ujung Pandang), with the result that the construction sector there has absorbed an influx of *mandur* (entrepreneurs) and construction workers from Java (Chairil Anwar, personal communication 1999). Among the consequences of the stagnation of the building sector in Jakarta were a reduction in the eviction of *kampung* residents and less harassment of petty traders, as authorities show leniency for the hardship experienced (Jellinek 1999a, pp. 4–6).

Urban residents were quick to reoccupy land set aside for new hotels and the like, growing fruit and vegetables and building shelters in which to stay. Similarly small enterprises such as blacksmithing, birdselling, and petty trade thrived throughout the cities and towns of Central Java (Jellinek 1999b, pp. 25–26). Such reports of expanding numbers of small-scale and microenterprises recall similar observations during Indonesia's previous serious economic crisis, in the mid-1960s, during the late Sukarno years. However, this does not mean all microenterprises were better off than before the crisis, as competition between entrepreneurs had also increased, while those dependent on the patronage of wage workers have sometimes suffered. Sex-workers reported declining incomes while there was thought to be an increased incidence of children being

[13] This observation was also made by Maxwell (1999), who worked in the Social Monitoring and Early Response Unit in Jakarta.

[14] As an illustration, one kilogram of exported black pepper would buy 9.8 kilograms of rice in May 1997, and 35.6 kilograms in May 1998 (Booth 1999, p. 134).

taken from the poorer parts of West Java to brothels in Jakarta (UNFPA 1998, pp. 50, 62–65).

In Jakarta's new outer suburbs, such as Depok, which straddles the border between Jakarta and West Java in the south of the city, the crisis has had dire consequences. Middle-class and lower-middle-class families had shifted to these suburbs, purchasing houses and commuting to the city to work, or finding employment in companies. Many lost their jobs, and found it impossible to create substitute jobs in microenterprises (UNFPA 1998, p. 48). Beyond these suburbs, in areas such as Cisauke, rice farmers sold their land in the 1980s and 1990s and took jobs in Jakarta, only to find the work has evaporated, leaving them dependent on subsistence farming on scraps of land (Jellinek 1999a, pp. 4–6).

As the capital and largest city, Jakarta has been the primary setting for the political and economic crises of the last few years (as it was the center of the dramatic events during the previous political transition in 1965–1966). Civil society is growing in strength in Jakarta, which has been a site of support for the existing regime, but also a key site of resistance. Student and worker demonstrations in Jakarta were an important catalyst in the events leading to the resignation of Suharto. Subsequently student groups maintained demonstrations of opposition to the new government of President Habibie, particularly in front of the houses of parliament (McBeth and Vatikiotis 1998, pp. 12–14). Students and other demonstrators provided an important source of support for the election of President Wahid and, to a lesser extent, his successor, President Megawati Sukarnoputri.

In the social unrest that flared in Indonesia during 1997 and 1998 (especially in May of 1998), attacks on Chinese-owned shops and enterprises were prominent (Murphy and Dolven 1999, pp. 50–52). In Jakarta, Chinese-dominated areas such as Kota and Glodok bore the brunt of rioting, looting, and burning of shops, factories, and shopping malls. Many Chinese Indonesians fled to Singapore, Perth, and other nearby cities, often transferring resources at the same time. Restoring the confidence and trust of Chinese Indonesians remains a challenge for the Indonesian government (World Bank 1999c, p. 19).

There are many more stories of the harsh consequences of the crisis. School enrollments in Jakarta declined as students were forced to drop-out in order to support parents or save the costs of attending school (Cohen 1998; World Bank 1999c, p. 10). The evidence suggests that while primary school enrollment remains almost universal, loss of income had a serious impact on higher levels of education, particularly for families in the poorest quintile (UNFPA 1998, p. 49). Increased government spending was intended to address the problem. The "Stay in School" Campaign was designed to provide scholarships to poor children in junior secondary school and facilitate greater community involvement in schools in poorer areas (World Bank 1999c, p. 11). Increasing crime levels have also been noted in Jakarta.

Jakarta and the regions

The economic and political crises have impacted on the relationship between Jakarta and its broader regional hinterland. Long-standing patterns of rural–urban migration have been altered. Anecdotal evidence suggests that migration to Jakarta slowed as a result of the crisis, and remittances from urban workers to rural villages have declined (World Bank 1999c, p. 16). At the same time, migration from Jakarta back to the rural areas increased. Such return migration has been observed previously when significant numbers of urban workers were displaced. Thus, when trishaws were banned in Jakarta in the early 1990s, trishaw drivers generally returned to rural areas including Indramayu in West Java and Tegal in Central Java (see Azuma 1995). It is evident that the companies worst affected by the crisis were concentrated in light and heavy manufacturing, construction, and property and investment services. Laid off manufacturing workers were often from the rural areas, so many returned to their villages – though not without exacerbating hardships, as much of rural Java has been drought-stricken in recent years.

Although the information available on the gender of displaced workers is limited, a case study in Tangerang in the western part of Jabotabek noted the high proportion of female workers retrenched from the shoe textile and garment industries. In addition, a report from the Ministry of Manpower in Jakarta in March 1998 indicated that 41% of laid-off workers were female (UNFPA 1998, pp. 50–52), which is considerably higher than the female share of the manufacturing workforce in Jakarta (Table 9.3).

On a more dramatic scale, an underlying concern in recent times has been that Indonesia risked disintegration in the aftermath of Suharto's resignation (Booth 1999). Regional tensions have existed in Indonesia ever since the nation was formed, the only logic for the territories included in the newly established republic being that they were all part of the Netherlands East Indies colonial entity. Highly visible resistance to Jakarta's rule in Aceh and, of course, East Timor, as well as less overt tensions in Irian Jaya and other regions of Indonesia, have demonstrated the precarious nature of Indonesia's territorial integrity.

The Suharto regime's commitment to regional development throughout Indonesia, manifest in several five-year plans, was intended to spread evenly the benefits of growth. In practice it left Java somewhat better off than might have been expected, and thus has exacerbated the concerns of people in other poor provinces. In April 1999, the Habibie government passed through parliament a Law on Intergovernmental Fiscal Relations, intended to represent a move towards greater regional autonomy by ceding to provinces greater control over revenue (Booth 1999; McBeth 1999). The aim was to give provinces much greater control over education, health, family planning, environmental protection, and economic planning. There remains much to do in order to operationalize the law, which was intended to be introduced during a two-year transitional phase, but it does seem to represent the discarding of Suharto's highly centralized model of governance. A decentralization law passed at the same time gives greater administrative power to the *kabupaten* (Indonesia has 306 such districts) and establishes that *kabupaten* heads are elected by local parliaments rather than appointed from Jakarta.

There are implications for the city of Jakarta. First, it is believed that many Jakarta bureaucrats[15] will eventually leave the city for posts in the provincial capitals where their functions have shifted along with budgets. Should this occur it will have implications for segments of the city's housing markets, various kinds of services, and other areas of urban economy. Second, the changes will represent a symbolic shift in the distribution of power within Indonesia, in turn reflecting on the way in which Jakarta is viewed by the remainder of the country. Yet Jakarta is sufficiently large and complex, and its role in Indonesia so powerful, that this will not fundamentally alter its overall key role in Indonesia, nor its international role.

Cosmopolis revisited: is Jakarta becoming a world city?

To what extent has Jakarta been able to take advantage of globalization and become a cosmopolis, acquiring "world city" characteristics? The question has been addressed in several publications (see Firman 1995, 1998; Forbes 1992; Schmidt 1998). Jakarta has a preeminent role in Indonesia and, in general, this has strengthened in recent years. In addition to this, Indonesia's economic planners and politicians have been fostering the international role of Jakarta. Transport, communications, hotels, financial reforms, and expansion of producer services all enhanced the city's ability to attract business people and investment from abroad. Improving the cost competitiveness of the city has also facilitated the development of non-oil exports.

[15] McBeth (1999, p. 28) says "tens of thousands" of government employees will shift to the provinces.

The social structure of the city reflects its cosmopolitan character. The growth of the middle class in Jakarta has created a demand for higher-quality, more expensive goods and services (Forbes 1996, pp. 54–58). The expanding urban middle class includes both foreigners and Indonesians. Housing estate developments such as the exclusive Pluit along a section of the Jakarta coast have become prominent features of the city. Citizens of foreign countries totalled 28,008 (3.9% of the population) in 1997, the majority of whom were concentrated in Central and West Jakarta, especially in Tambora, Taman Sari, and Sawah Besar, creating loosely defined foreign enclaves.

Travelling the major roadways and tollways of Jakarta invokes the dominant imagery of global cities. Extensive office block development remind the visitor of central business districts in many Asian countries, even if they display a distinctive Indonesianized outward appearance. Large, planned shopping malls have grown to provide services to the middle class. Five star international-standard hotels cluster in Central Jakarta. The cultural symbols of consumption are global in their resonance. The congested and generally poor *kampung* are hidden behind the modern façades.

While Jakarta is internationalizing, it is premature to call it a "world city" as its major role is as an economic intermediary, only rarely as a center for the control of investment outside the national boundaries. Indonesian entrepreneurs have used their Jakarta-based companies as a launching pad to invest overseas, particularly in Hong Kong, Bangkok, and other newly industrializing economies, and for securing investment from abroad, thus reinforcing the integration of the Indonesian and the global economy. However, Jakarta has yet to develop the global role of either Singapore or Hong Kong (alpha world cities in the classification mentioned earlier), or of Bangkok or Kuala Lumpur (both gamma world cities). Unlike them Jakarta is not a major transport hub, nor does it provide regional headquarters for a significant number of transnational corporations, nor is it a significant regional base for international organizations. Instead, its main function is to improve the economic links between Indonesia and the rest of the world, while building its central place services, enhancing its industrial base, and consolidating its position in the domestic economy.

Several authors have argued that an important dimension of the restructuring of Pacific Asia's space economy is the emergence of a network of large cities. These include the alpha world cities of Tokyo, Hong Kong, and Singapore, the beta world cities of Sydney and Seoul, together with Jakarta, Melbourne, Osaka, Taipei, Bangkok, Beijing, Kuala Lumpur, Manila, and Shanghai (all gamma world cities). These cities are in the process of creating a series of significant, regional mega-urban corridors.[16] The glue which binds these mega-urban corridors are the air, land, and sea transportation corridors, and the telecommunications networks which have emerged from the distinctive pattern of economic development in the Pacific Asian region. Jakarta is generally represented as the eastern node of a Southeast Asian urban corridor stretching from Bangkok through Kuala Lumpur and Singapore. Yet if there is any meaning to this corridor it is centered on Singapore, which is pivotal in terms of the services sector, not Jakarta.

Conclusion

Globalization and economic integration have had a determining influence on Jakarta's evolution, from its colonial history to its increasingly prominent regional – and emerging world city – role. The upside of this has been economic growth and its impact on Jakarta in terms of population growth and social structure, its industrial and services sector expansion, and the spread of the city into the extended metropolitan region. The downside of economic globalization is the particularly severe impact the economic crisis had on the city. The impact has been uneven. There appears to be a greater impact on the middle class than the poor; on the urban areas more than the rural; on large cities more than small cities; and on Java more than throughout the outer islands. Thus the population of Jakarta has been more affected than many other parts of Indonesia.

Beyond the present, Jakarta's likely future depends on the circumstances confronting Indonesia and the ability of governments to deal with them. President Wahid's term lasted just a short time before he was ousted, and President Megawati Sukarnoputri has only just begun to grapple with her new role. The situation in East Timor[17] has not engendered confidence in the military and regional problems persist. Yet a significant outcome of the increased democratization of national politics is that Indonesia has acquired a reputation for political instability. Despite some signs of economic recovery, Indonesia's attractiveness to foreign investors has declined significantly, thus reducing Jakarta's role in the global economy, and bringing to a halt its earlier growth in world

[16] A number of authors have contributed to these ideas; see the brief overview in Douglass 2000, pp. 2315–2335, and Forbes 1997, pp. 457–462.

[17] As a result of the crisis in East Timor, the international spotlight has recently focused on Jakarta. Van Klinken (1999) has speculated that Indonesia may, as a result, turn inward as Burma has, or remain globally oriented as Thailand has. Either pathway has significant implications for the kind of city Jakarta will be in the next decade.

city functions. Unless the incoming president can take a firm grip on domestic politics and the economy, it may herald a sustained downturn in Jakarta's prospects of expanding its role as a platform for increased engagement between the Indonesia and the global economy.

REFERENCES

Abeyasekere, S. 1987. *Jakarta: A History*. Singapore: Oxford University Press.

Arndt, H. W. and Hill, H. 1999. *Southeast Asia's Economic Crisis: Origins, Lessons, and the Way Forward.* St. Leonards, NSW: Allen and Unwin.

Asian Development Bank 1996. *Asian Development Outlook 1996 and 1997.* Hong Kong: Oxford University Press.

Azuma, Y. 1995. "Becak Drivers in Jakarta: A Study of Rural–Urban Circular Migration from Indramayu, West Java and Tegal, Central Java," Ph.D. dissertation, Flinders University, Adelaide.

Badan Pusat Statistik (Propinsi DKI Jakarta) 1999. *Jakarta Dalam Angka 1998.* Jakarta: BPS.

Biro Pusat Statistik 1986. *Statistik Indonesia, 1985.* Jakarta: BPS.

Statistik Indonesia, 1988. Jakarta: BPS.

1996. *Statistik Indonesia, 1995.* Jakarta: BPS.

1999a. *Penduduk DKI Jakarta: Hasil Survei Penduduk Antar Sensus 1995.* Jakarta: BPS, Seri S2.09.

1999b. *Penduduk Jawa Barat: Hasil Survei Penduduk Antar Sensus 1995.* Jakarta: BPS, Seri S2.09.

2001. *Penduduk Indonesia hasil Sensus Penduduk Tahun 2000.* Seri L.2.2. Jakarta: BPS.

Blusse, L. 1985. "An Insane Administration and Insanitary Town: The Dutch East India Company and Batavia (1619–1799)," in R. J. Ross and G. J. Telkamp (eds.), *Colonial Cities.* Dordrecht: Martinus Nijhoff Publishers, pp. 65–85.

Boddy, T. 1983. "The Political Uses of Urban Design: The Jakarta Example," in D. R. Webster (ed.), *The Southeast Asian Environment.* Ottawa: University of Ottawa Press, pp. 31–47.

Booth, A. 1989. "Repelita V and Indonesia's Medium Term Economic Strategy," *Bulletin of Indonesian Economic Studies*, 25 (2): 3–30.

1999. "The Impact of the Crisis on Poverty and Equity," in H. W. Arndt and H. Hill (eds.), *Southeast Asia's Economic Crisis.* Singapore: Institute of Southeast Asian Studies, pp. 128–141.

Browder, J., Bohland, J., and Scarpaci, J. 1995. "Patterns of Development on the Metropolitan Fringes: Urban Fringe Expansion in Bangkok, Jakarta and Santiago," *Journal of the American Planning Association*, 61 (3): 310–327.

Cameron, L. 1999. "Indonesia's Social Crisis," *Far Eastern Economic*, 8 July: 24.

Castles, L. 1967. "The Ethnic Profile of Djakarta," *Indonesia*, 1(3): 153–204.

1989. "Jakarta: The Growing Center," in H. Hill (ed.), *Unity in Diversity: Regional Economic Development in Indonesia since 1970.* Kuala Lumpur: Oxford University Press, pp. 232–253.

Cervero, R. and Susantono, B. 1999. "Rent Capitalization and Transportation Infrastructure Development in Jakarta," *Review of Urban and Regional Development Studies*, 11 (1): 11–23.

Choong Tet Siu 1998. "How to Make Cities Work," *Asiaweek*, 7 December 1998.

Clarke, G. T. R. 1985. "Jakarta, Indonesia: Planning to Solve Urban Conflicts," in J. P. Lea and J. M. Courtney (eds.), *Cities in Conflict: Studies in the Planning and Management of Asian Cities*. Washington, DC: World Bank, pp. 35–51.

Cohen, M. 1998. "Lessons in Hardship," *Far Eastern Economic Review*, 24 September: 42–44.

Dick, H. W. and Rimmer, P. J. 1998. "Beyond the Third World City: The New Urban Geography of South-East Asia," *Urban Studies*, 35 (12): 2303–2321.

Dorleans, B. 1994. "Perencanaan kota dan spekulasi tanah di Jabotabek," *Prisma*, 2: 41–61.

Douglass, M. 1997. "Structural Change and Urbanization in Indonesia: From the 'Old' to the 'New' International Division of Labour," in G. W. Jones and P. Visaria (eds.), *Urbanization in Large Countries: China, Indonesia, Brazil, and India*. Oxford: Clarendon Press, pp. 111–141.

2000. "Mega-Urban Regions and World City Formation: Globalization, the Economic Crisis and Urban Policy Issues in Pacific Asia," *Urban Studies*, 37 (2): 2315–2335.

Dowall, D. and Leaf, M. 1991. "The Price of Land for Housing in Jakarta," *Urban Studies*, 28 (5): 707–722.

Firman, T. 1992. "The Spatial Pattern of Urban Population Growth in Java, 1980–1990," 28 (2): 95–109.

1995. "Urban Restructuring in Jakarta Metropolitan Region: An Integration into a System of 'Global Cities'." *Cities and the New Global Economy*, Conference Proceedings Volume 1. Melbourne: OECD/Australian Government, pp. 200–216.

1997. "Land Conversion and Urban Development in the Northern Region of West Java, Indonesia," *Urban Studies*, 34 (7): 1027–1046.

1998. "The Restructuring of Jakarta Metropolitan Area: A 'Global City' in Asia," *Cities*, 15 (4): 229–243.

1999. "Metropolitan Expansion and the Growth of Female Migration to Jakarta," *Asia Pacific Viewpoint*, 40 (1): 45–58.

Firman, T. and Dharmapatni, I. A. I. 1995. "The Emergence of Extended Metropolitan Regions in Indonesia: Jabotabek and Bandung Metropolitan Area," *Review of Urban and Regional Development Studies*, 7: 167–188.

Forbes, D. K. 1990. "Jakarta towards 2005: Planning Mechanisms and Issues," *Bulletin of Indonesian Economic Studies*, 28 (2): 95–109.

1992. "The Internationalisation of Jakarta and the Growth of the Services Sector," in E. J. Blakely and R. J. Stimson (eds.), *New Cities of the Pacific Rim*. University of California at Berkeley, Monograph 43, pp. 16.1–16.22.

1996. *Asian Metropolis: Urbanisation and the Southeast Asian City*. Melbourne: Oxford University Press.

1999. "Globalisation, Postcolonialism and New Representations of the Pacific Asian Metropolis," in K. Olds, P. Dicken, P. F. Kelly, L. Kong and H. W.

Yeung (eds.), 1999. *Globalisation and the Asia-Pacific: Contested Territories*. London: Routledge, pp. 238–254.

Forbes, D. K. and Lindfield, M. 1997. *Urbanisation in Asia: Lessons Learned and Innovative Responses*. International Development Issues No. 51, AusAID, Canberra.

Forbes, D. K. and Thrift, N. J. 1987. "International Impacts on the Urbanization Process in the Asian Region," in R. Fuchs, G. Jones, and E. Pernia (eds.), *Urbanization and Urban Policies in Pacific Asia*. Boulder: Westview Press, pp. 67–87.

Ford, L. 1993. "A Model of Indonesian City Structure," *Geographical Review*, 83 (4): 374–397.

Gardiner, P. 1997. "Migration and Urbanisation: A Discussion," in G. Jones and T. Hull (eds.), *Indonesia Assessment: Population and Human Resources*. Canberra: Institute of Southeast Asian Studies, Singapore and Australian National University, pp. 118–133.

Giebels, L. J. 1986. "JABOTABEK: An Indonesian-Dutch Concept on Metropolitan Planning of the Jakarta Region," in P. J. M. Nas (ed.), *The Indonesian City: Studies in Urban Development and Planning*. Dordrecht: Foris Publications, pp. 101–115.

Hancock, P. 1997. "The Walking Ghosts of West Java," *Inside Indonesia*, 51: 16–19.

Heeren, H. J. (ed.) 1955. "The Urbanisation of Djakarta," *Ekonomi dan Keuangan Indonesia*, 8 (11): 5–43.

Henderson, J. V., Kuncoro, A. and Nasuution, D. 1996. "The Dynamics of Jabotabek Development," *Bulletin of Indonesian Economic Studies*, 32 (1): 71–95.

Heuken, A. 1989. *Historical Sights of Jakarta*. 3rd edition. Singapore: Times Book International.

Hogan, T. and Houston, C. 2001. "Corporate Cities – Urban Gateways or Gated Communities against the City? The Case of Lippo, Jakarta," *Globalization and World Cities Study Group and Network Research Bulletin 47*. Web URL www.lboro.ac.uk/gawc/rb/.

Hugo, G. J. 1996. "Urbanization in Indonesia: City and Countryside Linked," in J. Gugler (ed.), *The Urban Transformation of the Developing World*. New York: Oxford University Press, pp. 132–183.

2000. "Indonesia," in T. R. Leinbach and R. Ulack (eds.), *Southeast Asia: Diversity and Development*. New Jersey: Prentice Hall, pp. 304–340.

Irawan, P. 1999. "Intergenerational Transmission of Poverty in the Enclaves of Jakarta," Ph.D. dissertation, Flinders University, Adelaide.

Jacobs, J. 1996. *Edge of Empire*. London: Routledge.

Jamieson, N. 1991. "The Dispersed Metropolis in Asia: Attitudes and Trends in Java," in N. Ginsburg, B. Koppel and T. G. McGee (eds.), *The Extended Metropolis: Settlement Transition in Asia*. Honolulu: University of Hawaii Press, pp. 275–297.

Jellinek, L. 1991. *The Wheel of Fortune: The History of a Poor Community in Jakarta*. Honolulu: University of Hawaii Press.

1997. "Big Projects, Little People," *Inside Indonesia*, 50: 18–19.

1999a. "The New Poor," *Inside Indonesia*, 57: 4–6.
1999b. "Blacksmith Boom," *Inside Indonesia*, 59: 25–26.
2000. "Jakarta, Indonesia: Kampung Culture or Consumer Culture?," in N. Low, B. Gleeson, I. Elander, and R. Lidskog (eds.), *Consuming Cities: The Urban Environment in the Global Economy after the Rio Declaration*. London and New York: Routledge, pp. 265–280.
Jones, G. W. and Mamas, S. G. M. 1996. "The changing Employment Structure of the Extended Jakarta Metropolitan Region," *Bulletin of Indonesian Economic Studies*, 32 (1): 51–71.
Kantor Statistik, Propinsi DKI Jakarta 1992. *Jakarta Dalan Angka 1991*. Jakarta.
Kum, W. B., Douglass, M., Chae, S. C. and Ho, K. C. (eds.) 1997. *Culture and the City in East Asia*. Oxford: Clarendon Press.
Kusno, A. 2000. *Behind the Postcolonial: Architecture, Urban Space and Political Cultures in Indonesia*. London and New York: Routledge.
Leaf, M. 1993. "Land Rights for Residential Development in Jakarta, Indonesia: The Colonial Roots of Contemporary Urban Dualism," *International Journal of Urban and Rural Research*, 17: 477–491.
1994. "The Suburbanisation of Jakarta: A Concurrence of Economics and Ideology," *Third World Planning Review*, 16 (4): 341–356.
1996. "Building the Road for the BMW: Culture, Vision and the Extended Metropolitan Region of Jakarta," *Environment and Planning A*, 28: 1617–1635.
Lin, G. C.-S. 1994. "Changing Theoretical Perspectives on Urbanization in Asian developing Countries," *Third World Planning Review*, 16 (1): 1–24.
Liu, Thai-Ker 1998. "From Megacity to Constellation City: Towards Sustainable Asian Cities," in Toh Thian Ser (ed.), *Megacities, Labour Communications*. Singapore: Institute of Southeast Studies, pp. 3–26.
McBeth, J. 1999. "Too Little, Too Late," *Far Eastern Economic Review*, 13 May: 28–30.
McBeth, J. and M. Vatikiotis 1998. "Dazed and Confused," *Far Eastern Economic Review*, 26 November: 12–14.
McGee, T. G. 1991a. "Southeast Asian Urbanization: Three Decades of Change," *Prisma*, 51: 3–16.
1991b "The Emergence of *Desakota* Regions in Asia: Extending a Hypothesis," in N. Ginsburg, B. Koppel, and T. G. McGee (eds.), *The Extended Metropolis: Settlements Transition in Asia*. Honolulu: University of Hawaii Press, pp. 3–25.
Mamas, S. G. M., Jones, G., and Sastrasuanda, T. 2001. "Demographic Change in Indonesia's Megacities," *Third World Planning Review*, 23 (2): 155–174.
Maxwell, J. 1999. "The Social Impact of the Economic Crisis in Indonesia," in *Indonesia – A Neighbour in Transition*. Seminar organized by the Center for Development Studies and the Department of Asian Studies and Languages, Flinders University, Adelaide, 17 September.
Murphy, D. and Dolven, B. 1999. "Now, Back to Work," *Far Eastern Economic Review*, 24 June: 50–52.
Murray, A. 1991. *No Money, No Honey: A Study of Street Traders and Prostitutes in Jakarta*. Singapore: Oxford University Press.

Niessen, N. 1999. *Municipal Government in Indonesia: Policy, Law, and Practice of Decentralization and Urban Spatial Planning*. Leiden: CNWS Publications No. 77.

Nurlambang, Triarko 1993. "Middle and High Class Housing Development and its Impact on Regional Development in Jakarta," Ph.D. dissertation, Flinders University, Adelaide.

Olds, K. 2001. *Globalization and Urban Change: Capital, Culture, and Pacific Rim Mega-Projects*. Oxford: Oxford University Press.

Olds, K., Dicken, P., Kelly, P. F., Kong, L., and Yeung, H. W. (eds.) 1999. *Globalisation and the Asia-Pacific: Contested Territories*. London: Routledge.

Pangestu, P. E. and Dijkgraaf, C. 1998. "Mobilizing Financial Resources for Urban Infrastructure – a Case Study: The New Town of Bumi Serpong Damai," *Urban Infrastructure Development*, UNCRD Proceedings Series 26, Tokyo: 55–82.

Pardoen, S. R., Adi, R. and Prasadja, H. 1996. *Children in Hazardous Work in the Informal Sector in Indonesia*. International Programme on the Elimination of Child Labour (IPEC) in cooperation with Atma Jaya Research Center, Jakarta.

Pasaribu, M. 1998. "The Role of Toll Roads in Promoting Regional Development: Private Sector Participation: A Case Study of Jabotabek," *Urban Infrastructure Development*, UNCRD Proceedings Series 26, Tokyo: 143–164.

Rachmadi, A. B. 1994. "Bumi Serpong Damai: kota madiri berawasan lingkungan dan teknologi," *Prisma*, 2 Supplement I–VIII.

Rutz, W. 1987. *Cities and Towns in Indonesia: Their Development, Current Positions and Functions with Regard to Administration and Regional Economy*. Berlin: Gebruder Borntraeger.

Schmidt, J. D. 1998. "Globalisation and Inequality in Urban South-East Asia," *Third World Planning Review*, 20 (2): 127–145.

Setiono, Djoko 1991. "Bandar Kemayoran: New Town in Town: An Evaluation of the Effect of the Development of Bandar Kemayoran on the Urban Problems of Jakarta," M.A. dissertation, Flinders University, Adelaide.

Soegijoko, B. T. S. 1996. "Jabotabek and globalization," in F-c. Lo and Y-m. Yeung (eds.), *Emerging World Cities in Pacific Asia*. Tokyo: United Nations University Press, pp. 377–416.

1999. "National Urban Development Strategy in Indonesia – Case Study: Jabotabek," in J. Brotchie, P. Newton, P. Hall, and J. Dickey (eds.), *East West Perspectives on 21st Century Urban Development: Sustainable Eastern and Western Cities in the New Millennium*. Aldershot: Ashgate, pp. 125–144.

Soegijoko, B. T. S. and Bulkin, I. 1994. "Arahan kebijaksanaan tata ruang nasional: studi kasus JABOTABEK," *Prisma*, 23 (2): 21–39.

Soja, E. W. 1997. "Six Discourses on the Postmetropolis," in S. Westwood and J. Williams (eds.), *Imagining Cities: Scripts, Signs, Memory*. London: Routledge, pp. 19–30.

Surjomihardjo, Abdurrachman 1977. *Pemekaran Jakarta*. Jakarta: Penerbit Djambatan.

United Nations Population Fund (UNFPA) 1998. *Southeast Asian Populations in Crisis: Challenges to the Implementation of the ICPD Programme of Action*. New York: UNFPA and the Australian National University.

Van Klinken, G. 1999. "Burma or Thailand? Two Asian Roads for Indonesia Today," in *Indonesia – A Neighbour in Transition*. Seminar organized by the Center for Development Studies and the Department of Asian Studies and Languages, Flinders University, Adelaide, 17 September.

Watters, R. F. and McGee, T. G. (eds.) 1997. *Asia Pacific: New Geographies of the Pacific Rim*. London: Hurst & Co.

World Bank 1999a. *The Social Crisis in Asia*. Website URL http://www.worldbank.org/poverty/eacrisis.

1999b. *Indonesia*. Website URL http://www.worldbank.org/poverty/eacrisis.

1999c. *Social Issues Arising from the East Asia Economic Crisis*. Work-in-Progress, URL http://www.worldbank.org/poverty/eacrisis.

Part 3

The impact of popular movements

10 São Paulo: the political and socioeconomic transformations wrought by the New Labor Movement in the city and beyond

Maria Helena Moreira Alves

São Paulo was founded by Jesuits in 1554, on a plateau 2,493 feet (760 meters) above sea level, as a mission center for early settlers and the Indians who lived in the area. São Paulo was the first highland settlement established in Brazil, occupying the lower terraces of the Rio Tiete, in the midst of tall grasses and scattered scrub trees. The community grew very slowly and had only 300 inhabitants by the end of the sixteenth century. Seventeenth-century São Paulo was a base for expeditions (bandeiras) into the hinterland by armed explorers (bandeirantes) in search of Indian slaves, gold, silver, and diamonds. In 1560 São Paulo became a township and had a town council that could enact and enforce local laws. For a long time São Paulo remained a small town, but its location was ideal for commerce and trade, capitalizing on waterways and easy access to the sea. The sea port of Santos, even at that early time one of the most important trading routes of the country, was located only 45 miles (72 kilometers) from the new city. In 1711 São Paulo attained the status of a city, yet it remained an agrarian town.

Around 1850 São Paulo began to grow and become richer because of the highly productive coffee plantations of the state of São Paulo. The coffee planters were the center of production, living in large coffee plantations in the interior of the state, but with important middlemen activities, packing, distribution, and export being organized in the city of São Paulo for coffee to be transported to the port of Santos and shipped to world markets. The social and political history of São Paulo is marked by its development as a trade center for the "coffee barons." The plantations demanded a large number of slaves as laborers and several thousand Africans were to arrive, via the port of Santos, to work the plantations in the state. The planters also needed qualified labor, however, and financed the immigration of Europeans to work as indentured servants in the farms. In order to maintain dominance over the laborers, the planters organized the enactment of legislation which gave them complete authority, enforcing absolute obedience, not only over their

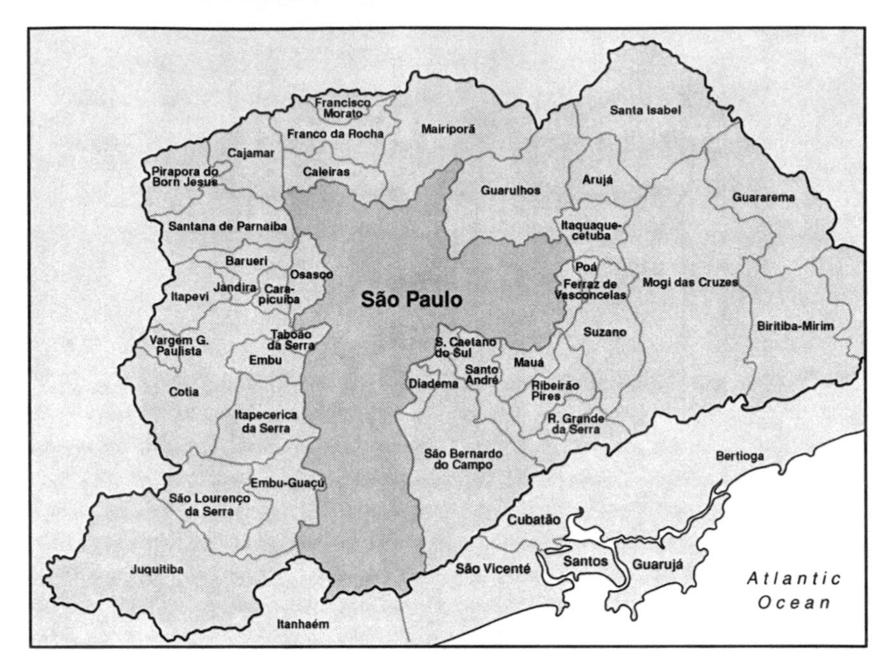

Map 10.1 São Paulo

slaves but also over the indentured laborers who had come from Europe. However, once the Europeans worked off the debts incurred by transference from Europe to Brazil, they were free to leave the plantations. Most came to live in the city of São Paulo, building a growing economic base of small artisans, commerce, trade, and forming the initial industrial laboring class for incipient industrialization (Morse 1958). The importance of the coffee plantations in the economy of the city as well as the state built a sociopolitical environment of authoritarianism. The authority of the planters was extended to urban areas to form a strong rural–urban bourgeoisie that imposed its ideology through complete control of political power and strong patriarchal social organization both in the plantations and in the city.

Before 1874 there was little capital available for industrial expansion, but two important events changed the economic scenario and created an incentive to divert private capital and immigrant labor to industry: the growing coffee crisis due to oversupply, which dramatically decreased the profits of the planters, and the building of the Santos–Jundiaí Railway by British capital. Capital investment in industry became more attractive to the newly formed rural–urban bourgeoisie. As the world coffee price crisis deepened, the planters definitively moved to the city to engage in industrial, bureaucratic, and commercial activities. They formed a new capitalist class which merged their patriarchal rural origin, continuing their investments in coffee, with a growing involvement in industry. This capitalist class was further complemented by entrepreneurial immigrants from Europe who concentrated their activities in the importing sector. Warren Dean (1969, p. 125), in his study of the industrialization of São Paulo, points out that "the importers who complemented the planter-entrepreneurs in the development of the *Paulista* industry were almost always immigrants."

The needs of the growing industry encouraged the organization of immigration, financed both by the planter-industrialists themselves, and by European governments bent on providing escape valves for their own socioeconomic problems at home. The population of São Paulo grew rapidly (Morse 1958, p. 225). Waves of immigrants from Europe arrived in the port of Santos. Most came to São Paulo to work in technical and commercial occupations. The more entrepreneurial joined the rural–urban "planter bourgeoisie," engaging in a variety of activities and becoming a new capitalist class in São Paulo, of foreign descent. These immigrants provided the needed commercial and technical support for the very early stages of industrialization. Such names as Raffin, Nardelli, Kleeberb, Christofani, Fowles, Weltmann, Sydow, Matarazzo, Maggi, Falchi, Stupakoff, Zimmerman, Scorzato, and Witte became common brand names (Morse 1958, p. 225). A French observer, traveling in São Paulo at the time, noted that there was a division of the capitalist class, by nationality, according to specialization in industrial areas. For example, Germans, French, and Italians shared the dry goods sector with Brazilians. Foodstuffs was generally the province of either Portuguese or Brazilians, except for bakery and pastry which was the domain of the French and Germans. Shoes and tinware were mostly controlled by Italians. However, the larger metallurgical plants were in the hands of the English and the Americans (Van Putte 1890, p. 34). Most immigrants from Europe, however, came to work as industrial laborers, in more qualified jobs that were not available to free slaves. According to Morse (1958, p. 226), 75% to 85% of the proletariat were foreign. By 1897 Italians outnumbered Brazilians two to one in São Paulo.

A second wave of immigration, in the twentieth century, increased the diversity of the population of São Paulo, assuring its unique status as a cosmopolitan city within Brazil and in Latin America. During the quarter century after 1908, a million foreigners entered via Santos and more than half a million settled around São Paulo (Morse 1958, p. 228). This new period of immigration included people from Lebanon, Turkey, and Middle East countries. Brazilians commonly join them all under the generic name of *turcos*. After the First World War the Japanese government organized a program for Japanese to migrate to Brazil, and the numbers of Japanese immigrants increased rapidly. More than 1 million Japanese entered through the port of Santos to settle in São Paulo between 1930 and 1934. The nationality of the labor force was thus changed, with the Japanese making up 28% of workers, and the once dominant Italians only 3%. Although a majority of the Japanese immigrants settled in rural areas of São Paulo, and became a leading force for a new form of agri-industrial business, a significant number also took jobs in the industrial sectors of São Paulo. Today, there are more Japanese in the metropolitan area of the city of São Paulo than in any other community outside Japan, and Japanese farmers who settled in areas adjoining the city are the suppliers of most of the fruit and vegetables sold in the markets.

The worldwide depression of the 1930s deeply affected Brazil and brought the expansion of the city of São Paulo to a grinding halt. In 1934, in response to growing pressures for jobs, the government of Getúlio Vargas imposed restrictive immigration quotas, cutting the influx of foreigners to a minimum. Internal migration from other states of Brazil was encouraged and supported by the federal government. Thus, between 1935 and 1939, 96% of the state's immigrants were Brazilian nationals, coming especially from the impoverished northeast of Brazil to escape widespread drought.

São Paulo's history of industrial development is marked by the social origins of both an immigrant bourgeoisie and an immigrant proletariat from Europe, the Middle East, and Japan. With the Great Depression this pattern changed abruptly with internal migration from other states of Brazil, particularly from the northeast, becoming the single most important factor in the formation of the urban working class. This history gives the city its unique cosmopolitan blend with all classes merging nationalities and origins. Internal and external migration processes entailed a significant historical difference in the experiences of different population sectors of the city. Internal migrants from Brazil, many the descendants of Indians or African slaves, were totally abandoned to their own endeavors in the city, with no governmental subsidies, no programs of immigration support, no job training, and no housing programs to help the process of adaptation. In short, the Brazilian migrants found themselves pushed into a *social apartheid* in the slums of the city, their jobs limited to those that whites would not touch, such as garbage removal, hard construction work, and menial jobs in industry. In contrast, many European and Japanese immigrants came under the auspices of programs organized by their governments which assisted them with the cost of their transportation and of housing, helped them find employment, trained them, and provided a number of other benefits.

Politically and socially the city of São Paulo is marked by its past as a patriarchal society, dominated by a highly coherent bourgeoisie that united European immigrant entrepreneurs and rural–urban plantation "coffee barons." The industrial and plantation ruling-class families intermarried and formed giant firms. These still exist today, and are economically organized as *grupos* that often have oligopolistic control over entire industrial sectors (Dean 1969, pp. 116–122). These families have not only achieved material control of the forces of production but have also shaped the city's political life, giving the polity its distinct brand of patriarchal authoritarianism which supports a degree of segregation in terms of class and race. On the other hand, the cosmopolitan nature of the city, with the mixture of nationalities, races, and social origins of the proletariat, brought with it ideals of struggles and organizational experiences from anarchists and syndicalists who pushed the working class towards independent political and economic action. Hence São Paulo is at the same time a strongly exclusionary society with distinct class and race differences and a city that experiences constantly flowing social movements, struggles for reform, for revolution, for creative change, and for political and democratic organization.

The importance of São Paulo in contemporary Brazil cannot be overestimated. Metropolitan São Paulo has been described as the powerful engine that leads the nation. The state of São Paulo produces 36% of the gross national product, and almost 20% comes from the metropolitan region (PNAD 1998). Although the economy of São Paulo, and in particular its industry, suffered severely from the recession that began in 1997, the level of production remains one of the most impressive in Latin America. Besides being the economic motor of the nation, São Paulo is also the most important provider of health treatments and other services for Brazilians who come to the city from all regions of the country. And the city continues to be the primary destination of internal migrants who move in search of work. By 2000, 12 million people lived in the municipality of São Paulo, 18 million in the metropolitan area, making it the third largest city in the world.

The industrialization of São Paulo

Industrialization patterns and governmental economic policies

The early capitalists of São Paulo operated in a complete laissez-faire system. Neither the federal nor the state government concerned itself with practical matters of economic control, and, aside from import and export duties, nor did they regulate or otherwise become involved with the activities of private capital. Monopoly control of industrial sectors became common as rural–urban "coffee baron" elites merged with newer immigrant capitalists to form large industrial concerns which often controlled production at all levels. As early as the 1920s, São Paulo industrialists began a process of pooling capital to control lines of production (Dean 1969). To understand São Paulo as a city, one has to appreciate the strength of these early arrangements and the control these alliances of rural–urban plantation owners and immigrants still hold over a large part of São Paulo's industry, trade, and finances. Their economic power is directly transferred to political control of all governmental structures, thus impeding socially oriented reforms and public policies that might affect their inherited privileges.

Working conditions in industry were extremely exploitative. The laissez-faire approach embraced by both federal and state governments did not regulate or otherwise legislate to protect the interests of workers. Not until widespread working-class riots broke out in 1917 did the government begin to think about legislation to ameliorate the plight of the workers. The dismal working conditions led to the rapid organization of trade unions and other forms of working-class associations, inspired both by anarcho-syndicalist ideals brought by European immigrants, and, later, by the impact of the Russian revolution. The Communist Party of Brazil was established in 1922, one of the first to be founded in Latin America, and it had considerable influence among workers in São Paulo. One could say that the roots of the modern "New Labor Movement" in São Paulo were in fact laid during the early period of industrialization. The dual influence of syndico-anarchism and of communism shaped the struggles of elements of the working class throughout the political and social history of São Paulo since the early 1920s. Organization became widespread in large industrial and commercial concerns and led to new governmental policies to control labor after 1930.

In order to bring labor under the control of the state, the Getúlio Vargas government institutionalized forms of domination in the *Estado Novo* (New State). Taking fascist Italy as a model, corporative state structures were built both to control labor and to implement social programs that provided workers with certain legal rights. The trade unions were organized corporatively in top-down structures that gave the government complete power over their operations. Elections were regulated, and the government could intervene, at any time, to depose union officials who were undesirable or deemed to cause too much unrest among workers. The top-down structure of organization was insured by a system of confederation, federation, and local, territorially based trade unions that had representative rights over an entire industrial sector. This organizational format ensured complete control of representative rights by only one trade union group of organizers and impeded more independent efforts to organize workers' struggles. The top-down structure was reinforced by considerable financial endowments, which were entirely controlled by the federal government: trade unions were financed by a system of taxes collected on all workers' paychecks, independently of their personal involvement in trade unions. One day's salary was deducted from paychecks directly by employers, under the law, and deposited in a special fund controlled by the Ministry of Labor. This money was then divided up between confederations, federations, and local unions, in all trade, commercial, industrial, and financial sectors. The state determined the amount to be received by each. Finally, working-class organizations were obligated by law to fulfill certain welfare roles such as providing educational training and health programs for their affiliates, thus freeing the state from having to institutionalize social programs. After the period of the *Estado Novo*, the corporative structure of the organization of labor in Brazil enabled the state effectively to control the working class, eliminating unwanted anarcho-syndicalist and communist influences and fostering a pro-business elite of working-class leaders who became known in Brazilian working-class politics as *pelegos*. This term denotes the sheepskin used by gauchos in the south of Brazil to put upon the saddle and thus soften the impact of the horse's gait. *Pelego* thus characterizes the role of the leaders within the corporative union structure as intermediaries who control and soften the impact of working-class unrest upon capital. This corporative structure of labor control was in place from the 1930s until very recently. In fact, even the more democratic governments that came after military rule modified it only partly in the Constitution of 1988.

The automobile industry in São Paulo: forming a globalized working class

The worldwide depression which followed the crash of 1929 significantly affected the industrial development of São Paulo. Growth slowed to a crawl in the years between 1930 and 1955. In response, successive governments implemented policies of import substitution: erecting trade barriers to limit imports and providing incentives for local companies, so as to protect Brazilian industry and encourage investment. The strongest effort to encourage development through the use of import-substitution policies was carried out by President Juscelino Kubitschek (1956–1961) with his program *50 Anos em 5* (Fifty Years in Five). This was a coherent economic and political program that combined trade barriers, tax incentives, and regulation of industry. It was meant not only to protect local capital but also to attract multinational corporations with a system of incentives that would make it profitable for them to transfer full production to Brazil. The centerpiece of Kubitschek's import-substitution program was the automobile industry. Brazil had, at that time, a significant local industrial park, especially in São Paulo, which produced auto parts and assembled kits from foreign auto manufacturers. There was, however, little full production of automobiles in Brazil since the big auto companies preferred simply to assemble their kits rather than build from scratch, which would have required significant investments and technology transfers (Shapiro 1994).

Once aggressive European auto manufacturers came in, especially Volkswagen and Mercedes-Benz, the US Big Three were quick to follow. GM, Ford, and Chrysler began a major program of direct investment, building modern manufacturing plants in São Paulo. The state of São Paulo immediately offered other incentives for corporations to build there: exemption from local value-added taxes, exemption from property taxes, and significant commitments of state investment to build the necessary infrastructural improvements to provide the basis for the installation of a large industrial park. These offers guaranteed the state of São Paulo priority for the new automotive investments. Another important factor was the proximity to autoparts manufacturers and producers of important raw materials (steel, electrical equipment, glass, leather) needed by the automotive industry. Multinational corporations concentrated plants in a relatively small area for optimal use of infrastructure and proximity to the most promising markets of São Paulo and the south of Brazil.

Eventually the majority of the automotive multinationals installed manufacturing assembly plants within a radius of 60 kilometers, encompassing four municipal districts of the metropolitan area. The installation of so many large automobile factories in one area brought with it hundreds of other connected industries for components and autoparts. The region became known as the ABCD metropolitan area of São Paulo for its four districts, Santo André, São Bernardo do Campo, São Caetano do Sul, and Diadema. It has helped to make São Paulo the most important industrial park of Latin America. The physical placing of the automobile giants, one next to the other in a very tight geographic area, has been very important both for the ease of production, with shared raw materials and access to inputs, and for the format of labor organization which arose in São Paulo. Ford, GM, Chrysler, Volkswagen, Saab-Scania, and Mercedes-Benz all installed immense manufacturing factories side by side, providing for the direct employment of approximately 300,000 people and the indirect employment of over 1 million in autoparts and other connected input industries. The corporations took advantage of this situation to keep wages under control by instituting a system of "labor rotation" whereby workers would be massively dismissed by, say, Ford and almost immediately rehired by Volkswagen, GM, or another automotive giant. This rotation could be accomplished with little effort and expense in training costs, since the worker would be usually hired to do the same job he performed in the previous company, but for lower, entry-level pay (Alves 1984a, pp. 256–257).

During the "miracle years" of the 1970s, when annual growth rates of the economy reached 12% to 17%, the economic policy of the military governments was directed at encouraging the multinational automobile corporations to produce not only for the internal market but also for export. Incentives were provided for exported cars, with a reduction or elimination of value-added taxes. Import duties for needed parts and materials were also eliminated. However, the military maintained the requirement that at least 70% of every car had to be made in Brazil. Peter Evans (1979) describes how the military built an economic model based on a tripartite division of the economy, known as the Tripé Economico. For the automobile industry this meant a clear distinction of areas of investment: the manufacturing of cars was freely opened to multinational investment; autopart manufacturing and the provision of raw materials were by law reserved exclusively for wholly owned or majority-owned Brazilian capital; infrastructural investment was the exclusive realm of the Brazilian state.[1] This period fostered a very protected industry based on international, private Brazilian, and state capital. Today, the automobile industry continues to be one of the most important sectors of the economy. It has continued to produce well over 1 million vehicles a year.

In the last few years São Paulo has lost its privileged position as the only state with automobile production. There has been an increasing tendency for new automobile production to move to other states, in particular in the south and the northeast, as states have engaged in a veritable fiscal war, outbidding each other to attract multinational automobile manufacturers. States in the northeast have also attempted to convince multinationals to move from São Paulo with the argument that the lower levels of labor organization result in significant wage differentials: workers in

[1] The most comprehensive study of the tripartite nature of the economic development model of the military in Brazil is Evans's (1979) outstanding work on the Brazilian economy during the military period. At the time of the so-called "Brazilian Miracle" of accelerated economic growth there was a prolific debate about the impact of the economic model on the poor. See in particular Bacha 1978; Bresser Pereira 1977; Furtado 1975; and Singer 1972, 1977.

the northeast of Brazil earn half the wages paid to workers in São Paulo. This trend has had a negative impact upon the industrial sectors in the metropolitan region of São Paulo and has often been used as a weapon to pry concessions from the strong *paulista* trade unions (Rodríguez-Pose and Tomaney 1999, pp. 479–498).

The New Labor Movement

Organizing in resistance to authoritarianism

The populist period of democratic governments that followed the *Estado Novo* changed the composition of the working class, increasing its number and power, but did not affect its inability to influence politics and become an independent political actor. Populist political parties of that period used the working class to form their own political base. They were, however, usually also controlled by the same elites, albeit in a more liberal-minded manner. Workers did not hold leadership positions in these parties and were not political candidates themselves or hold political office in government. The left political parties, the Brazilian Communist Party (PCB) and other parties that split from the PCB, were closer to workers, and they did include them in their leadership and roster of candidates, but the party leadership controlled working-class movements directly in a top-down, centralized manner.

The years of military rule in Brazil, from 1964 to 1984, were particularly difficult for the working class. Harsh military action repressed any attempt at organizing. Strikes were broken by troops armed with machine guns. Workers were violently repressed and discipline inside the factories was sometimes enforced with armed guards. In addition to the repression, the corporative structure of trade unions impeded any independent organization as the military frequently utilized the available legal mechanisms of trade union intervention, intimidation, and direct control of unions by government-appointed trade union officials. Particularly after 1968, when the military hardened its control over the country, workers in São Paulo labored in silence, unable to meet to discuss their grievances: a meeting of more than five people was defined under the National Security Law as a "crime against the state," punishable with prison. The majority of trade unions were under direct government intervention, run by state-appointed officials (Alves 1983b, pp. 149–160).

Churches were among the few places where workers could meet safely. The Catholic Church was going through a deep transformation under the impact of the social doctrines of the Vatican II Council, the advent of the Liberation Theology and, particularly, of the educational theories of the Catholic educator Paulo Freire. His many works were prohibited by the military, and he himself was banned from the country and deprived of his citizenship rights. His works, however, were copied and distributed widely in thousands of Christian Base Communities, small Catholic community groups which discussed the Testaments in the light of the Liberation Theology and practiced the theories of Paulo Freire's Education for Liberation. Between 1970 and 1978, a new generation of working-class leaders, social Catholic organizers, and progressive intellectuals established forms of organization deeply rooted in community work, collective sharing, and democratic leadership in São Paulo (Alves 1984b).

The growing importance of urban social movements in São Paulo characterized the period from 1976 to 1978. Most organization developed around specific issues of concern to the urban poor: land tenure, housing, and infrastructural improvements such as sewage and potable water (Assies 1993, pp. 39–58). Broader issues also elicited strong population support, as was the case, for example, with the *Movimento Contra o Custo de Vida* which, in 1978, mobilized over 100,000 people for demonstrations against the high cost of living (*Isto É*, 22 March 1978). The experience of organizing in urban social movements was a very important step towards the democratization of popular organization, establishing strong links between community groups, the Catholic Church, trade unions, and political parties. New political actors would influence public policy not only in the city of São Paulo itself, but increasingly in many other cities and states of Brazil (Moisés 1978; Singer and Caldeira Brant 1981).

The metallurgical workers of the automobile industry felt this influence and began to discuss, in small groups meeting in the churches of São Bernardo do Campo, ways to form a more independent, factory-floor-based trade union movement that could break the corporative structure of the official trade unions and draw support so as to challenge the military state itself (Alves 1984a, pp. 240–278). New leadership developed and began to win electoral posts in local unions until they were able to elect an entirely new board of directors that was combative. Luis Ignácio da Silva, known by the workers simply as Lula, was elected President of the Metalworkers and Automotive Workers Union of São Bernardo do Campo. Organization began rapidly to grow on the factory floor of most of the automobile factories of the ABCD region. The organizational format followed closely the base-related and democratic structures learned in the years of repression and community work. Intellectuals were called forth by union leaders to aid in the process of organization and a popular education process began in the São Bernardo do Campo trade union.

Professionals were asked to study the automotive industry and work out with factory workers and the leadership the best way to organize.[2] Careful study indicated the advantage of striking in two multinational companies whose sales contracts with foreign distributors had heavy penalties for failure to meet deadlines for delivery. The analysis made by lawyers and leaders indicated that time could be gained by taking advantage of a legal loophole in the anti-strike legislation of the military governments. A strike was punishable with prison, but it was defined as "not going to work." Hence was born the strategy to prepare quietly in the factories. The element of surprise was crucial. On the 12th of May 1978, 1,600 workers of Saab-Scania, in São Bernardo do Campo, went to work, punched their cards, turned on their machines, and then stood next to them, arms crossed and immobile. The strike movement rapidly picked up, and in the late morning all workers at the nearby Ford plant also crossed their arms and stood by their machines. The movement rapidly spread to other factories and other towns close to São Bernardo do Campo, until, within a few days, over 120,000 workers were on strike. This was a turning point. The movement known as *Bracos Cruzados Máquinas Paradas* (Arms Crossed and Machines Stopped) had succeeded: negotiations with the multinational corporations began at the request of managements, which were concerned about incurring contract penalties or altogether losing contracts if they did not meet their export obligations on time; the military did not interfere (Alves 1989b).

The lessons learned in that first strike have marked the New Labor Movement to this day. To work at the base level, including as many workers as possible in discussion, organization, and leadership; to inspire solidarity among workers in other plants and industries; to organize support from community organizations, church groups, university students, political representatives; to use the knowledge of professional people such as economists, sociologists, and lawyers, better to understand the system of production, the legal system, the social and political repressive mechanisms; and to work collectively to develop the most effective counter-strategies. The most important lesson is the need to maintain the contact between leadership and workers, developing a democratic organizational format that includes sharing of responsibility and rotation of

[2] At that time I participated in a study of Ford. We analyzed documents and contracts, investment plans, and balance sheets. Our reports were discussed with workers on the factory floor who sometimes had inside information that was crucial to the understanding of the company and its production plans. Eventually, all the different reports would be discussed with the leadership. In this manner the strike could be planned so as take maximum advantage of the constraints the company faced in terms of sales contracts with foreign distributors. The plan was to strike at a time when the company was most pressed for fast production, betting on management's will to negotiate more rapidly.

leadership. The fear was broken. The movement spread rapidly throughout the region of São Paulo. The strikes which began in São Paulo were repeated all over the country over the next two years, until over 3 million workers in eighteen different states and from sectors as different as the automotive, commerce, construction, banking, education, and health had taken their destiny into their own hands and faced not only their employers but, above all, the military state. Middle- and upper-class sectors of the opposition to the military regime joined in and supported the strikers until the military could no longer hold on to power and began negotiations for the transition to democratic government after 1978 (Alves 1984a, pp. 225–314).

The New Labor Movement was the seed of a larger political and social movement which changed the political scene of São Paulo and of Brazil (Alves 1988, 1989a). The very vastness of the modern multinational industrial park had established a new type of labor force characterized by highly qualified workers in a global industry and with connections with working-class organizations across the globe. International solidarity brought workers into close touch with European, North American, and Latin American trade unions which supported the struggles of the factory workers and encouraged their efforts to organize independently. A new, globalized labor force had been formed in São Paulo, and it would have a profound impact upon the city and the nation (Sader 1988).

The political organization of the New Labor Movement and the establishment of the Workers' Party

The years from 1980 to 1988 were marked by the growing organization of the working class in São Paulo in a manner unprecedented in the city's history. Inspired by the experiences gained during the strikes of 1978, 1979, and 1980, workers who participated in the New Labor Movement deepened their community ties and worked closely with church activists, members of political parties, university students, and intellectuals to lay the groundwork that would enable the working class to break the tight political hold of the elites. The experiences gained in the local, base-level organizations, the factory committees, the neighborhood associations, and the Christian Base Communities of the Catholic Church enabled workers, for the first time, to engage directly in politics, to become primary political actors in the city of São Paulo.

On 28 August 1983, in São Bernardo do Campo, 5,059 delegates, who represented 912 organizations from different trades, met to found the *Central Única dos Trabalhadores* (CUT), the Central Confederation of Workers. The CUT followed the format of organizations built during the years of collaborative work at the base level. Organized from the factory floors, workplaces, schools, universities, construction yards, and rural areas, the CUT would serve as the trampolin from which the working class would be catapulted to the political scene of São Paulo and of Brazil. By 1988 the CUT had become a strong, nationwide organization with over 8 million members representing different trades, urban and rural, from all states of Brazil. From the automobile workers of São Paulo to the rubber tappers of the Amazon, the CUT joined the strength of working people collectively to force their entry into local and national politics. The CUT broke with past relationships with the state by continuing the dual strategy of organization that had first brought Lula to the presidency of the São Bernardo Metalworkers Union in 1978: to organize the rank-and-file at the workplace, forming factory committees (workplace committees in other trades) that were elected by plant sectors or by departments, spreading leadership across as many people as possible, winning elections within existing state-controlled trade unions, and fighting the federal state directly on the streets, in the trade unions, and even in the courts when the government "intervened" to remove elected officials from office. The new leadership learned to negotiate directly with employers to draft collective contracts that would be binding as private agreements between employers and workers. In this manner they bypassed the legal union if it was under government intervention. The CUT formed a parallel form of trade union organization which, although illegal until 1988, was the *de facto* representative organization with which employers negotiated collective bargaining contracts. This process gave workers experience in negotiation, and in dealing with complex economic, social, and political issues, while at the same time increasing the self-confidence and political awareness of the working class in general. It "democratized" the economic and political scene of São Paulo and of the nation, forcing recalcitrant elites to share power and decision making with once-excluded sectors of the population. By 1991 the CUT reported 1,679 member unions in all industries and professional categories, representing a total of 15,097,183 workers. Their ranks had increased to 2,703 affiliated trade unions, representing 19,331,301 workers throughout the country, by 1999. Its strongest base remains in metropolitan São Paulo where it represents over 1 million workers.[3]

All this activity was organized with the help of many intellectuals, particularly sociologists, economists, lawyers, doctors, architects, engineers, urban planners, and educators. It also drew on the aid of international

[3] On the CUT, see Gacek 1999.

organizations and trade unions in Europe, the US, Canada, and Latin America. International solidarity played a crucial role not only in the defense of the nascent movement against state and employer repression but also in the sharing of information and techniques of negotiation and management. In these years much learning took place in widespread popular education courses, organized by the CUT, the Catholic Church, universities, and in international programs. Research and development projects, financed by foreign non-governmental organizations (NGO's), trade unions, and foundations, helped workers understand the complexities of organization and economics and the functioning of multinational corporations.[4] Courses taught business administration, multinational finance, corporate structure, investment planning, administration of trade unions and other NGOs, experiences of workers' control in other nations, health and safety in the workplace.

In 1983, the *Instituto Cajamar* was founded, with Paulo Freire as its leading figure. The labor movement transformed a semi-abandoned motel on the outskirts of São Paulo into the "University of Workers," offering courses in business, economics, sociology, history, politics, and administration to thousands of groups from trade unions, neighborhood organizations, shanty towns, farms, construction trades, rural workers, and rubber tappers from the Amazon. There people who had no access to formal education, and sometimes a low self-image, were able to meet, study, learn, and grow in self-esteem – to become full-fledged educated citizens capable of wresting a share of power from elite groups that had enjoyed exclusive control of politics as well as education.

In all these educational experiences, one theme came to the surface of the debate time and again: workers can organize at the base level, win power in class-based organizations, and even influence their contractual situation with employers, but this is not sufficient to change their lives.

[4] The Social Science Research Council funded a large post-doctoral research project, "Labor Unions and Working Conditions: A Comparative Analysis of the Automobile Industry in Brazil, United States/Canada and Sweden," from 1984 to 1986. I was the principal investigator, but this was really a participatory research project that involved workers of the Ford and Saab-Scania plants in São Bernardo do Campo as well as leadership of the United Auto Workers (UAW) in the United States, Canada, and Sweden. We were particularly interested in understanding Quality Control Circles and Employee Involvement Programs in the Ford plants of the United States and Canada. We also compared health and safety programs and automatic safeguards in Sweden and in the US/Canada plants. This research was used to provide collective bargaining leverage in order to achieve the same rights – especially as to safety – for workers in the Brazilian subsidiaries of the two multinational corporations. The UAW, the Canadian Labor Congress, and the Swedish Metalworkers Union were especially helpful and built strong solidarity ties with the automobile workers in Brazil. Participatory research that can advance the causes of workers has become an integral part of political life in Brazil.

They must have access to government so they can affect public policy, influence governmental decisions, and change the political environment of the city and the nation. Most issues that concern workers are not decided at the negotiating table with employers, but are decided behind closed doors in secretive meetings between elite groups and their political representatives. It was necessary, therefore, to build the mechanisms through which workers could participate in decisions that affected their lives and make themselves heard in the political arena. To "open political space for the rank-and-file," workers of the New Labor Movement began to organize a new kind of political party, in their own image, and built upon the basis of their own past organizational experience. A "party of the workers," they would say, by workers, and for the interests of workers. Hence was born in 1980 the *Partido dos Trabalhadores* (PT), the Workers' Party.

The PT grew between 1980 and 1999, looking very much like the labor and social movements themselves that gave it energy: a militant movement of working-class people, at first strongly based in the automobile plants, then broadening to include people from all trades, eventually spreading to rural areas, and as far as the rubber tappers in the Amazon region. The PT emerged in close association with activists committed to Catholic Liberation Theology who had participated in the resistance to the military governments for many years. Finally, born from the direct experience of base-level organization, the PT also included many middle-class people from professional groups: teachers, university professors, health workers, engineers, sociologists, political scientists, economists, architects, medical doctors. The ties which were forged between middle-class and working-class groups, from urban and from rural areas, would give the PT its distinct profile that defies ideological definition. In the ideological discussions even its name, Workers' Party, was made more inclusive to mean "all those who do not live by the exploitation of the labor of others, and who struggle for the interests of all who are socially and economically excluded – those who do not have a voice." In this definition one notes the influence of the Liberation Theology of a Catholic Church that has redefined its political and social role in Brazil as "the voice of those who do not have a voice" (Alves 1985, 1990).

The PT was built true to the ideals that inspired it: democratic, class-based, a party of the masses, both urban and rural. "Democratic" in the conception of the PT means a party which is dedicated to opening up the political space, bringing the working class to the political scene as a primary actor and not merely as masses to be used, as in populism, or exploited, as with the economic policies of the right. In this process the PT has helped to create a debate on democracy itself, interpreting the term to mean not only political (electoral) democracy but also social and popular democracy, referred to as "Participatory Democracy." The question of democracy within the party itself has been a constant, and sometimes turbulent, effort to build institutional mechanisms within the party itself that enable the participation of different ideological groups, women, racial and sexual minorities, to impact policies, programs, alliances, and to give them proportional representation in the elections of party leaders and political candidates (Alves 1991; Keck, 1992). Thus quotas were established for women in party offices and as political candidates at the PT National Congress in 1996, and the number of women elected increased considerably, even if much remains to be done.[5]

The impact of the first administrations of the Partido dos Trabalhadores *in Diadema and São Paulo*

The collective effort of workers to open the political space paid off with increasing victories of the PT in many municipal elections in Brazil. The PT grew to be one of the most important political forces in the country. It participated in four presidential elections (1989, 1994, 1998, 2002), with Lula as its candidate. Three times Lula was one of the two leading candidates and went to the second round of balloting. Then in 2002 he became President Luis Ignácio da Silva.

The PT has been concerned to institutionalize mechanisms of participation in government that allow as many people as possible to be actively involved in policy making, budget decisions, the allocation of public funds, and the programatic solution of urban social problems.

[5] The PT has several ideological roots, which can be recognized as "tendencies" that may develop their own programatic alternatives and compete for representation on the local, state, regional, and national boards of the Party. The largest "tendency" within the PT is known as *Articulacao* and is composed of trade unionists, rural workers, members of the Landless Peasants Movement (*Movimento dos Sem Terra*) – one of Brazil's largest social movements, Catholic members who espouse the Liberation Theology, and other social movements. The last national congress of the PT, the *II Congresso Nacional do Partido dos Trabalhadores* in November 1999, brought together 914 delegates who had been elected by 15,000 delegates in state-level congresses. They represented over 800,000 PT members from all states of Brazil. In this national congress the tendency *Articulacao* received ample support for its platform and elected almost 60% of the national board of directors as well as the President of the party, José Dirceu, a Congressman from São Paulo, now a minister in Lula's government. In political terms, one of the most important decisions focused on the internal democratization of the PT itself, including direct elections of board members at the municipal, state, and national levels in 2001. The *Congresso Nacional* also decided to broaden the politics of alliance with other sectors and other progressive political parties in future elections. On the history of the PT, see Alves 1990, 1991; and Keck 1992. Because of this policy of alliances, the PT was able to get Luis Ignácio Lula da Silva elected as Brazil's President in the Presidential elections of 2002.

Institutionalized forms of popular participation, developed in the different PT governments, have led to new approaches to policies, problem-solving activities, and alternative local government. In general one can say that the mark of the PT in the city of São Paulo, as in the other cities where it has been in government, has been to develop an inclusionary politics so that marginalized sectors of the population can be actively involved in the discussion and development of public policy.

The first PT government in the São Paulo metropolitan area was in Diadema. The PT administration implemented programs that were based on popular participation. The PT developed an innovative format of organization by encouraging citizens to participate in *Conselhos Populares* (Popular Councils), composed by people elected by their neighbors in the different districts of the city. Public policy, in all areas of government, is discussed, drafted, and implemented with the direct participation of the elected members of the *Conselho Popular* concerned with the issues and object of the policy or program. Thus the health program was developed through health councils that met with government health officials, medical doctors, and health workers to study the city's budget for health and develop a program that would establish investment priorities. The building of local-level clinics for preventive and primary care, closer to people who did not have access to health facilities, was the first priority.

The housing program was faced with the challenge that one third of the population lived in *favelas* (shanty towns), distributed in approximately 120 different settlements. In the *favelas* in Brazil, the poor usually build their shacks one against the other so as to save materials by sharing as many walls as possible. The proximity and fragility of the shacks makes it impossible to build urban sewage and water systems since there are no roads and only very small passing areas. Electricity is, for the most part, "hung," i.e., taken illegally from neighboring urban areas where *favela* residents attach electricity wires to connect to their own shacks. Most previous administrations had either ignored the shanty towns or pursued repressive policies, dismantling the shanties and expelling families by force. The PT administration set out to encourage the organization of the *favelados* themselves in an effort to work together with government technicians to develop a coherent approach. The administration hired engineers, topographers, architects, and urban planners. They had the specific mission to work with the residents and find alternatives for the development of the *favelas*. This meant, first of all, the dismantling of all the shacks, in order to build roads and squares that would enable the installation of sewage pipes, potable water systems, garbage collection, and electricity lines. The residents elected representatives, forming a committee of approximately 200 people to work directly with the government technicians. They drafted possible solutions, and these were taken back to meetings with the community. Eventually, the accepted proposals were put together as a development plan and approved by the *favela* residents by majority vote in open-air public assemblies. Then the dismantling process began. The people themselves tore down their shacks, saving every bit of material that could be saved. The government organized collective purchasing agreements of cheap materials. It also encouraged scientists at the University of São Paulo to develop an alternative technology for cement and tile construction that could be employed by the residents themselves. Known as *solo cimento* (cement soil), this new technology enabled poor people to produce their own bricks by using the earth dug for the foundation of the house, mixing it with cement and other components, pressing it in a simple press, and drying it in the sun. This technology was so successful that all the 120 *favelas* in Diadema were rebuilt in the four years of the first PT administration. The technology was also used to build, with collective labor, municipal buildings such as schools, day-care centers, the new 180-bed hospital, and three health clinics. Scientists from the University of São Paulo eventually designed a complete factory that mass-produces the *solo cimento* bricks now sold to governments, NGOs, and individuals all over the country (Alves 1983a). The redevelopment program of Diadema has been a model for other cities, including Porto Alegre, where the PT is in its third administration, Belo Horizonte, Santos, and the city of São Paulo itself.

In 1988 the PT won the government of the municipality of São Paulo and elected Luiza Erundina the first woman mayor in the city's history. The São Paulo PT government (1988 to 1992) would become a model for popular participation in public policy throughout Brazil. Concerned with the spatial distribution of housing, the PT administration established a Municipal Low Income Housing Policy to take advantage of progressive elements of the new Constitution of Brazil, enacted in 1988, which gave municipalities legal power to use property taxes progressively and to determine the uses of urban land. These allowed the government to put to use idle land, including land acquired for speculative purposes by individuals and corporations. Such land was allocated to housing developments for poor people. The municipality worked with Citizen Councils and experts, especially urban planners, to develop a series of laws pertaining to urban planning strategy. By 1992, the city approved a New Building Code which simplified construction norms, ensured safety regulations for construction, limited illegal construction, and discouraged corruption (Cotter 1994).

In this governmental experience the impact of participatory democracy policies resulted in a body of legislation that greatly aided the development of popular housing programs that answered the needs of the poor (Kowarick and Singer 1993; *Paoli* 1992, 1995; Rolnik 1989, 1992, 1995). Other mechanisms to encourage citizen participation in public policy were the *Conselhos Municipais de Saúde* (Municipal Health Councils) which worked together with government to establish priorities of investment and health policy. The previous experience with the Municipal Health Councils in Diadema enabled the PT government in São Paulo to institutionalize a mechanism of popular participation in health-related issues (Araújo 1999; Bittar 1992; Wampler 1997). The PT also introduced innovative social and educational programs for abandoned children who live in the streets of the city. The administration's "Team Work to Mothers Head of Families" program has been included in the United Nations "Best Projects" list. It encouraged and financed collective housing built by women heads of families. The food cooperatives and the "Large Food Basket" program for low-cost vegetables, fruit, eggs, chicken, fish, and other products to be sold directly at municipally supported fairs, without the cost of intermediaries, is now widely used in other cities of Brazil as part of municipal programs to alleviate malnutrition and combat inflationary food prices.

Policy experiences which began with the first municipal government of São Paulo were later developed into full-fledged state and national level programs. This is the case, for example, of the Minimum Family Income Program (*Programa de Renda Mínima*). This program was first developed by Senator Eduardo Matarazzo Suplicy (of the PT of São Paulo) as a national law proposal to Congress which would guarantee each citizen of Brazil a minimum income. It was later implemented in seventy-six major cities. In addition, the educational program *Bolsa Escola*, implemented by the PT administration of Cristóvam Buarque in the Federal District of Brasília, guaranteed a minimum income to families for each child that continued in school and maintained a good performance level so as to persuade poor families to keep their children in school, rather than taking them out to work or spend their days in the streets to sell candy and other small goods so as to supplement family income (Buarque 1998). The *Bolsa Escola* program was recommended by UNESCO, as a "UNESCO Favorite Program," to serve as a model for poor countries because of its impact in decreasing poverty and guarranteeing equal access to education.

Perhaps the most important contribution of the first PT government in the city of São Paulo to the process of increasing citizen participation in public policy came with the tenure of Paulo Freire as Secretary of Education. He introduced new public education policies based on "The Pedagogy of Hope" (Freire 1992). The educational program, "Change the Face of the Schools," not only built many new schools, but also transformed the learning experience of the children of the city of São Paulo. Education for Liberation meant transforming schools into centers of creativity where teaching and learning could be joyous and democratic, respecting the poor children's life-experience and specific language as well as teaching them mainstream language and skills so they could become active and participatory citizens capable of developing their own potential and of transforming society. The government convened meetings with university professors and curricular specialists across various disciplines to discuss potential reforms. After these initial meetings, the government held meetings with other educators, students, parents, and grassroots groups to determine what they needed and wanted from schools. They formed *Plenárias Pedagógicas* (Pedagogical Plenaries), educational councils that discussed, designed, and analyzed government budgets for education and established the priorities for change both in the curriculum and in investment. Freire concluded that it was the curricular reform, along with the ongoing teacher education program organized by the government and the Pedagogical Plenaries, that led to the dramatic reduction of student failure and drop-out rates in São Paulo (Freire 1992, 1998).

São Paulo at the crossroads: clientelism or participatory democracy?

The major problems of São Paulo are directly related to the uneven nature of Brazil's developmental model, specifically to the highly skewed distribution of income that reflects the severe poverty of a large proportion of the population. While the per capita income of metropolitan São Paulo was US$8,245 in 1998, this did not reflect reality for most of the population. The prevalent poverty can best be evaluated by other indicators such as the high infant mortality rate of 25 per 1,000 live births that same year, and an illiteracy rate of over 7%, with functional illiteracy at about 24% (PNAD 1998). Income inequality and discrimination for jobs in almost all economic activities remains profound, in particular for women and the black population.

Between 1994 and 2002, the government of President Fernando Henrique Cardoso strictly followed the adjustment program imposed by the International Monetary Fund (IMF). This program has increased inequality at the national level and has also deeply affected São Paulo and its metropolitan region. While the wealth of those in the upper classes increased, the income of middle- and working-class groups was dramatically reduced. The concentration of income has encouraged the acquisition of land for investment in the metropolitan region – diminishing the supply of land for middle-class and popular housing. And the reduction in the income of the majority of the population has decreased access to education, health care, and affordable transportation (Jacobi 1994, pp. 6–16). Because of the highly skewed wealth and income distribution, the city of São Paulo has experienced increased violence and growing conflicts over housing and other infrastructural needs (Silva 1994). The access to health has also been a major problem for excluded sectors of the population of the city such as the black population (Minayo 1995).

Social inequality and poverty can become the basis for political clientelism and populism. This happened in the municipality of São Paulo which split between the perspective of citizen participation in public policy, represented by the PT, and a populist-clientelistic form of government based on personal favors and individual aid. Clientelism as a form of government has been the historic basis of power of elite groups seeking to maintain their privileges, while providing minimal aid to poor families on an individual basis in exchange for their loyalty in elections. Paulo Maluf, a charismatic populist leader, became the most effective "political boss" in São Paulo (both in the municipality and the metropolitan region), basing his political influence on a classic clientelistic organization. Carefully cultivating a political and popular clientele network, Paulo Maluf defeated the candidate of the PT in the 1992 municipal election to become mayor of the municipality. During his administration (1992–1996) Maluf reversed the citizen participatory policies of the previous PT government and used public funds to finance a growing network of political support in the City Council. Clientele relations with local-level leadership were extended by introducing a system of personal and individual attention rather than collective and participatory citizen actions. The municipality of São Paulo was divided into "districts" commanded by members of the City Council loyal to Paulo Maluf. Public funds were distributed by these local bosses to the population according to their loyalty to Maluf's network. Jobs, scholarships, housing, access to public health, food and transportation vouchers, were all distributed to the poor in return for their commitment at the elections. The extreme poverty of key sectors of the population of São Paulo provided fertile ground for a system of political clientelism similar to that of Mexico. In the 1996 municipal election, Celso Pitta, who worked closely with Paulo Maluf, was chosen to succeed him. Celso Pitta was the first black candidate for mayor in the history of São Paulo and received significant support from the black population. Celso Pitta also drew on the political and financial support of Paulo Maluf and of the influential and well-organized Middle Eastern community. Once again the coalition was able to defeat the PT candidate. Celso Pitta's administration reversed whatever had remained of the social, educational, health, and transportation programs implemented by the PT during the administration of Luiza Erundina. Instead, the administration of Celso Pitta concentrated public funds almost exclusively in expensive public works and highway projects meant to "modernize" the city. Social programs were reduced to a minimum. As a result, the established pattern of segregation and inequality was magnified to the point that the city has been described as a "segmented metropolis," where the central question remains one of the distribution of wealth and unequal access to collective infrastructure.

The elections for mayor of São Paulo in 2000 had candidates from many different political parties and coalitions. But the second round of the elections presented the clear choices available to citizens of São Paulo: the clientelistic form of government represented by Paulo Maluf and the option of participatory democracy offered by Marta Teresa Suplicy, the candidate of the PT. Marta Suplicy may be seen as a synthesis of the recent social and political history of the metropolis. She comes from one of the most aristocratic families of Brazil. At the time of the campaign for mayor of São Paulo she was married to Eduardo Matarazzo Suplicy who in 1998 had been elected senator for São Paulo. He in turn is related to one of the city's most important immigrant industrial families, the Conde Matarazzo. Apart from their incursion into politics, they are both very well-known professionals. Eduardo Matarazzo Suplicy is a leading economist and professor at the prestigious University *Fundacao Getúlio Vargas*. And Marta Suplicy is a widely known psychologist who specializes in sexology. She was one of the leading founders of the Brazilian feminist movement and became best known for her program *TV Mulher* which was shown on *TV Globo*, Brazil's largest television network. In 1996 Marta Suplicy was elected to the National Congress, representing the state of São Paulo. As a legislator she actively promoted laws pertaining to the rights of women and minorities, sexual rights, and health issues. In 1998, Marta Suplicy was the candidate of the PT for governor of the state of São Paulo and lost narrowly. In spite of their class background, both Marta and Eduardo Suplicy were founders of the *Partido dos Trabalhadores*.

Beginning a process of recovery: "São Paulo Dá a Volta Por Cima"

The campaign slogan of the PT during the elections of 2000, "Sao Paulo Dá a Volta por Cima," can perhaps best be translated as "Sao Paulo Rises from the Ashes." The slogan is a popular expression in Brazil, deeply ingrained in the culture, meaning that when things go very wrong one should not give up, but rather reconsider, pick up the pieces, and go on to begin afresh with renewed strength – like the Phoenix rising from the ashes. The most important message of the campaign was that the population of São Paulo should reconsider all the possibilities and decide between a clientelistic government or the responsibility implicit in direct participation in the drafting of public policy. São Paulo could only recover if all sectors of the population contributed, including the middle and upper classes, who had to accept redistribution of income in exchange for social peace. Marta Suplicy, as a member of the upper class but representing the working class, was able to convince a large majority of the population of the need for an interclass alliance to save the city from utter chaos and violence. She was elected mayor of São Paulo, easily defeating Paulo Maluf.

There is much discussion as to the "governability" of São Paulo and the difficulty of solving the severe social and economic problems that have accumulated historically (Ramos Schiffer 1998). The city is a quagmire of contradictions. Important sectors of modern globalized development stand side by side with decaying housing, lack of urban infrastructure, lack of sanitation, pavement, little access to public health or education. Some of the best education available in Brazil, comparable to that of developed countries, contrasts with public schools which do not even have desks for students to work on, schools that lack both infrastructure and teachers. In the midst of the wealth produced in metropolitan São Paulo, which boasts the highest per capita income in Brazil, the majority of the population continues to live in poverty. The city stagnates in inequality, particularly for women and for the black population.

Marta Suplicy inherited a most difficult situation, the challenge of turning around patterns of inequality, poverty, and violence strongly established in history and made more severe by the policies of the eight years of the administrations of Paulo Maluf and Celso Pitta as well as by the overall economic crisis of Brazil. Since Marta Suplicy took office in March 2001, the citizens of São Paulo have been mobilized to participate in drafting many policies. The government of São Paulo has also actively engaged members of the middle and the upper class to contribute to the process of discussion that led to drafting the budget priorities for 2002. The government is seeking the cooperation of businesses as partners in social, health, and educational programs targeted at the most vulnerable groups. Citizens are encouraged to participate in local forums, by district, to define investment priorities for the budget. Citizen Councils are also active in drafting policies for health, education, to combat poverty, to provide greater opportunities for marginalized youth, and combat discrimination.

Conclusion

The ideas which sprung from the São Paulo working class more than twenty years ago are now clearly defined in the challenges of government that lie ahead. These include the need to construct a new understanding of fiscal responsibility that does not exclude social priorities; of government based on public participation in policy making and transparency as well as the development of innovative programs that will reduce the lack of low-income public housing, of providing access to health, education, and public transportation for the poorest sectors of the population. The experiences of the PT represent an important contribution to democratic forms of government that include all sectors of the population and encourage practical solutions through government–business–community projects.

São Paulo has become an "exporter of ideas," especially so for its contribution to debates on democratization, popular participation, citizen participation in public policy, alternative technology, social programs, urban development programs, urban social architecture, health, and educational policies in Latin America. The movement which began in the early eighties, almost exclusively among workers in multinational corporations, was the seed of important historical events that changed the political, historical, and economic scenario of São Paulo. The ideas proposed and implemented in a variety of governmental experiences over the last twenty years are spreading to other nations. NGOs from Latin America, the United States, Canada, and Europe have paid attention to the innovative programs carried out by the PT in cities where it has been in power for more than ten years. The *Orcamento Participativo* (Participatory Budget) experience of Porto Alegre has, perhaps, become the most studied as a successful example of citizen participation not only in the discussion and drafting of public policy but also in deciding budget priorities and overseeing their implementation. It was chosen by the United Nations to be included in the "Best Projects List" for its importance in encouraging base-level democratic government and containing corruption in the disbursement of public funds.

Many newly formed international organizations that now regularly meet to discuss and promote alternative policies for sustainable development, fiscal responsibility, and participatory democracy began in São Paulo. The *Fórum de São Paulo*, an organization which now includes over 200 social organizations, trade unions, and political parties representing most Latin American nations, first met in 1990 in São Paulo. The *Fórum Social Mundial* (World Social Forum) began its organization in the city, though the latest international assemblies have been held in Porto

Alegre. This organization works to draft economic, social, and ecological projects as alternatives to the neoliberal economic policies advocated by the IMF. It coordinates the work of 700 NGOs from Europe, the US, Canada, and Latin America. It has received worldwide attention because of the public protests it organized during Group 8 meetings in Ottawa and in Genoa where approximately 50,000 people demonstrated against the IMF's policies in the Third World. The *Fórum Social Mundial*, however, is not merely concerned with international protests. Rather it supports working projects that effectively combat poverty and discrimination and develop sustainable ecological and development alternatives.

The São Paulo "new union movement" has been an important influence in establishing the international organization of Factory Committees, base-level organizations inside the factories that connect internationally through regularly held meetings as well as through the internet and video conferences. The Factory Committees discuss concerns of workers that may be negotiated internationally with the managements of parent and subsidiary companies. These include job safety programs, unemployment insurance, regulations to diminish job discrimination, general collective salary agreements, layoff plans, and alternative programs to avoid layoffs. One of these negotiated agreements is the *Programa Banco de Horas* (Bank of Hours Program), where workers reduce their working hours in exchange for keeping their jobs in times of crisis. Pay is not reduced while the hours not worked are put in a "Hour Bank" as a credit to the company. When production resumes workers repay the hours accumulated in their "Hour Bank" by working extra hours or reducing their paid vacation time. This has been a rather controversial program, and not all trade unions agree with it.

The Brazilian trade unions also played a crucial role in what has been perhaps the most effective initiative of internationalized labor, the push for protections for labor in the negotiations to develop *Mercado del Como Sur* (MERCOSUR), the Common Market of Southern Cone Nations. The *Coordenadora de Centrais Sindicais do Cone Sul* (CCSCS) coordinates the work of the *Centrais Sindicais* (Central Unions) of the Southern Cone nations that are involved in the commercial agreements of MERCOSUR. It was founded in a meeting in Buenos Aires in 1986 with the main objective of working for human rights and democracy at a time when many nations were still governed by authoritarian regimes. Subsequently the CCSCS became an active participant in the development of MERCOSUR and obtained formal recognition to participate in the *Grupo Mercado Comum*, the board of directors of MERCOSUR.

Metropolitan São Paulo is not only the industrial, financial, and commercial center of Latin America; the format of the organization of its working class has shaped events far beyond the city. Innovative ideas and programs have been implemented elsewhere in Brazil and "exported" as models that can be adapted to effect historic transformations in governments and economic policies in Latin America and the Third World. It all began in 1978 when workers downed their tools in São Paulo.

REFERENCES

Alves, Maria Helena Moreira 1983a. "Diadema, an Experience of Popular Government within an Authoritarian Context." Paper presented at the XI International Congress of the Latin American Studies Association (LASA) Mexico City, Mexico.

1983b. "Mechanisms of Social Control of the Military Governments in Brazil (1964–1980)," in David H. Pollock and A. R. M. Ritter, (eds.), *Latin American Prospects for the 1980s: Equity Democratization and Development.* New York: Praeger Press, pp. 240–303.

1984a. *O estado e a oposição no Brasil (1964–1984*). Rio de Janeiro: Editora Vozes. English trans. *State and Opposition in Military Brazil.* Austin: Texas University Press, 1985.

1984b. "Grassroots Organizations, Trade Unions and the Church: A Challenge to the Controlled Abertura in Brazil," *Latin American Perspectives*, 11 (1): 73–102.

1985. "The Indirect Elections and the PT," *Sociology Review*, September.

1988. "Dilemmas of the Consolidation of Democracy from the Top in Brazil: A Political Analysis," *Latin American Perspectives*, 15 (3).

1989a. "Interclass Alliances in the Opposition to the Military in Brazil: Consequences for the Transition Period," in Susan Eckstein (ed.), *Power and Popular Protest: Latin American Social Movements.* Berkeley: University of California Press.

1989b. "Trade Unions Brazil: A Search for Autonomy and Organization," in Edward C. Epstein (ed.), *Labor Autonomy and the State in Latin America.* Boston: Unwin Hyman.

1990. "Building Democratic Socialism: The Partido dos Trabalhadores in Brazil," in *Monthly Review*, 42 (4): 1–16.

1991. "New Trends of Democratic Socialism in Latin America: The Experience of the Partido dos Trabalhadores in Brazil," in Barry Carr and Steve Ellner (eds.), *Latin American Leftist Parties since Allende.* Westview Press: Boulder.

Araújo, Maria José de Oliveira 1999. "The Role of Local Authorities in Implementing Health Care with the Gender Perspective: The Case of the Women's total Health Care Program in Sao Paulo, Brazil," in UNESCO papers. Available at www.unesco.org.

Assies, Willem 1993. "Urban Social Movements and Local Democracy in Brazil," *European Review of Latin American and Caribbean Studies*, 55: 39–58.

Bacha, Edmar 1978. *Política e distribuição de renda.* Rio de Janeiro: Editora Paz e Terra.

Bittar, Jorge 1992. *O modo petista de governar*. Caderno especial de *teoria & debate*, Publicação do Partido dos Trabalhadores, Diretório Regional de São Paulo.

Bresser Pereira, Luis Carlos 1977. *Desenvolvimento e crise no Brasil*. São Paulo: Editora Brasiliense.

Buarque, Cristóvam 1998. *Lugar de crianca é na escola: como estamos fazendo em Brasília*. Governo do Distrito Federal, Secretaria de Comunicação Social, Secretaria de Educação e Fundação Educacional, Brasília.

Cotter, Lisa 1994. "Municipal Low Income Housing Policy in the New Republic: Sao Paulo 1989–1991," in Program Research Papers, Lyndon B. Johnson School of Public Affairs, University of Texas at Austin.

Dean, Warren 1969. *The Industrialization of Sao Paulo 1980–1945*. Institute of Latin American Studies. Austin: University of Texas Press.

Evans, Peter 1979. *Dependent Development: The Alliance of Multinational, State, and Local Capital in Brazil*. Princeton: Princeton University Press.

Freire, Paulo 1992. *Pedagogia da esperanca: um reencontro com a pedagogia do oprimido*. Rio de Janeiro: Editora Paz e Terra. English trans. *The Pedagogy of a City*. New York: Continuum Publishing Company.

1998. *Teachers as Cultural Workers: Letters to Those Who Dare Teach*, trans. Donaldo Macedo, Dale Koike, and Alexandre Oliveira. Boulder: Westview Press.

Furtado, Celso 1975. *Diagnosis of the Brazilian Crisis*. Berkeley: University of California Press.

Gacek, Stanley 1999. "Labor Union Power in Brazil." Document of the International and Foreign Affairs Department of United Food and Commercial Workers International Union, Washington, DC.

Isto É 1978. 22 March.

Jacobi, Pedro Roberto 1994. "Políticas sociales y pobreza en el Brasil de la década perdida: desigualdades y alternativas ciudadanas en São Paulo," *Cadernos CEDEC*, 36.

Keck, Margaret 1992. *The Workers Party and Democratization in Brazil*. New Haven: Yale University Press.

Kowarick, Lucio and Singer, André 1993. "A experiencia do PT na prefeitura de São Paulo," *Novos Estudos*, 35: 195–216.

Minayo, Maria Cecília de Souza (ed.) 1995. *Os muitos brasis: saúde e população na década de 80: São Paulo*. São Paulo: HUCITEC/ABRASCO.

Moisés, José Álvaro 1978. "Experiencia de mobilização popular em São Paulo," in *Contraponto*, Ano III, N. 3, Sept., Rio de Janeiro, Centro de Estudos Noel Nuttels, pp. 84–93.

Morse, Richard M. 1958. *From Community to Metropolis: A Biography of Sao Paulo*. Gainesville: University of Florida Press.

Paoli, Celia 1992. "Citizenship and Inequalities: The Making of a Public Space in the Brazilian Experience," *Social and Legal Studies*, 1: 134–159.

1995. "Movimentos sociais no Brasil: em busca de um estatuto político," in M. Hellman (ed.), *Movimentos sociais e democracia no Brasil*. São Paulo: Editora Marco Zero, pp. 24–55.

PNAD (Pesquisa Nacional por Amostra de Domicílios) 1998. Instituto Brasileiro de Geografia e Estatística (IBGE).

Ramos Schiffer, Sueli 1998. "Sao Paulo: The challenge of Globalization in an Exclusionary Urban Structure." United Nations University /Institute of Advanced Studies "Project on Global Cities – The Impact of Transnationalism and Telematics."

Rodríguez-Pose, Andrés and Tomaney, John 1999. "Industrial Crisis in the Centre of the Periphery: Stabilisation, Economic Restructuring and Policy Responses in the Sao Paulo Metropolitan Region," *Urban Studies*, 36 (3): 479–498.

Rolnik, Raquel 1989. "El Brasil urbano de los años 80: un retrato," in Mario Lombardi (ed.), *Las ciudades en conflicto: una perspectiva latinoamericana*. Montevideo: Centro de Informaciones y Estudios del Uruguay, pp. 175–194.

1992. "Citizenship and Inequalities: The Making of a Public Space in Brazilian Experience," *Social and Legal Studies*, 1: 134–159.

1995. "Movimentos sociais no Brasil: em busca de um estatuto político," in M. Hellman (ed.), *Movimentos sociais e democracia no Brasil*. São Paulo: Editora Marco Zero, pp. 24–55.

Sader, Emir 1988. *Quando novos personagens entraram em cena – experiencias e lutas dos trabalhadores na Grande São Paulo*. Rio de Janeiro: Editora Paz e Terra.

Shapiro, Helen 1994. *Engines of Growth: The State and Transnational Auto Companies*. Cambridge: Cambridge University Press.

Silva, Ana Amélia 1994. "Sao Paulo and the Challenges for Social Sustainability: The Case of an Urban Housing Policy," in Program Research Papers, Lyndon B. Johnson School of Public Affairs, University of Texas at Austin.

Singer, Paul 1972. "O milagre brasileiro: causas e consequencias," *Cadernos CEBRAP*, 6, São Paulo.

1977. *A crise do milagre: a interpretação Crítica da economia brasileira*. Rio de Janeiro: Editora Paz e Terra.

Singer, Paul, and Caldeira Brant, Vinicios 1981. *São Paulo: o povo em movimento*. Rio de Janeiro: Editora Vozes.

Van Putte, Hubert 1890. *La Provence de São Paulo du Bresil*. Bruxelles: Vanderauvera Presse.

Wampler, Brian 1997. "Popular Participation and Reform: Municipal Health Councils in Sao Paulo," in *Policymaking in a Redemocratized Brazil*, Policy Research Report 119, Policy Research Project on Public Policies in Brazil, University of Texas at Austin.

11 Bombay/Mumbai: globalization, inequalities, and politics

Sujata Patel

In both popular and academic literature Bombay is typically characterized as India's most modern city. In view of its range of manufacturing, finance, and service activities Bombay has been described as the first Indian town to experience economic, technological, and social changes associated with the growth of capitalism in India. Though colonial capitalism fostered dependent economic development and unevenness in urban growth, Bombay represented for many commentators what is possible despite these odds. It symbolized the paradigm associated with achievements of colonial and post-colonial India both in its economic sphere and its cultural sphere.

Bombay[1] enters the twenty-first century with a continuing population explosion. It is still working out the consequences of the heritage of its beginnings on a small island; its political structures are still coping with the groups and interests of its cosmopolitan mix of people; its housing and its public facilities are still struggling with its growth as the logic of its transition from an industrial base to service industries is being realized. It is the blends of all these things in the context posed by the post-colonial state that is India and by the overarching cultures of that state which makes Mumbai different from other world cities. Just what these differences are will emerge in the pages that follow.

Located on the eastern shores of the Arabian Sea, Bombay is the capital of the state of Maharashtra whose population speaks the Marathi language. But by the early twentieth century Bombay had established an identity as a city of many tongues and many cultural expressions. Bombay's economic expansion in the late nineteenth century and early twentieth century attracted a range of ethnic groups from the north, east, and southern parts of India. It soon developed a reputation of being the cosmopolitan city of India. It is thus no surprise to note that it has

[1] Bombay was renamed Mumbai when the Shiv Sena party took over the Maharashtra government in March 1995. In this chapter I use the name Bombay interchangeably with Mumbai.

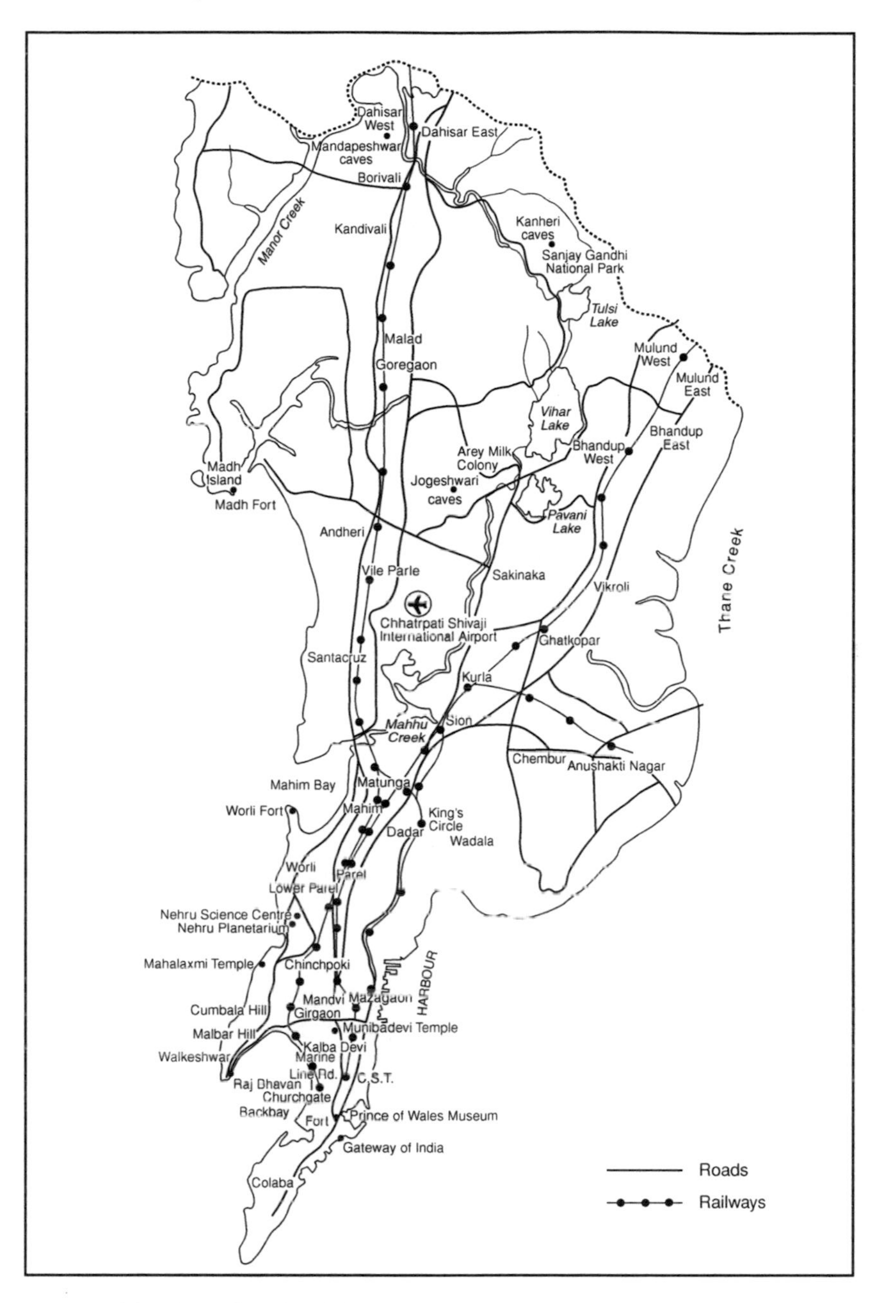

Map 11.1 Bombay/Mumbai

been the home of the country's premier cultural industry, the Hindi film industry, popularly known as Bollywood.[2] It has also nurtured schools of modern Indian painting and progressive modern theatre in English and native languages. Indian English literature has found an expression in this city, which has also nurtured *Dalit* literature, radical literature in Marathi of the oppressed (in this case the scheduled castes).[3]

Today, Bombay's reputation as a city of many tongues and many cultural expressions is under threat. This threat is directly related to the growth of a chauvinist and vigilante movement since the 1960s, called the Shiv Sena,[4] which sought to change the city's character and image from that of cosmopolitanism to a city of the Marathi-speaking underclass. The growth of such a chauvinist movement in Bombay should be seen in context with trends in the country at large as well as in terms of the changing nature of the city's economy. From the 1960s onwards various communal[5] and regional movements emerged as the result of the crisis in the legitimacy of the state. While class-based movements grew in the countryside and urban areas, these were soon superseded by an ethnic and religious upsurge. By the 1980s populist religious mobilization had replaced class-based movements, especially in urban India. This has its reflection in legislative politics with non-secular and Hindu-oriented parties coming to power both at the center and in the state. The growth of chauvinist politics in Bombay has certainly reiterated the trend in the country. In this chapter I analyze the specific features of a city's economy that is strongly associated with this trend in politics and has indeed reinforced it. I relate the growth of the Shiv Sena to changes in Bombay's economy as it liberalized in the context of policies of globalization enunciated by the Indian state. I concentrate on contemporary developments but adopt a historical perspective.

Before I explore the context of Bombay in the contemporary world of globalization, I clarify in the next section the way this chapter interfaces with the contemporary perspectives on globalization and more specifically theories that explore the relationship between globalization and cities.

[2] The term Bollywood is a corruption of Hollywood, with the B of Bombay substituting for H in Hollywood. It is difficult to trace the exact date when it became popular in colloquial language. Film magazines and chat-shows started using it in the early nineties.

[3] See Dalmia 1995; Gangar 1995; and Gokhale 1995 for details on painting, films, and theatre.

[4] Shiv Sena literally means the army of Shivaji who established power during the sixteenth century in this region.

[5] In India the term communal violence denotes religious violence.

Mumbai and the globalizing world

More than two decades ago Friedman and Wolff (1982) suggested that the urban system plays a critical role in the global economy dominated by new technologies such as telematics. They argued that cities are organized in terms of hierarchies and form basic nodes in the emerging world economy and that the city's local character and internal economic and social structure reflect its particular position and function in the world system. As a result contemporary research perceived cities as command and control centers while classifying them in a global urban hierarchy. Three primary cities were identified: London, New York, and Tokyo with a second layer such as Paris and Los Angeles and so on. In the earlier stages of research scholars examined the economic fabric and social relations of the city – the way the globalization of economic activity has raised the scale and complexity of economic transactions feeding into the expansion of scope of firms and services and thereby increasing the service intensity of organization of the economy (Sassen 1991), and related these to the latter's external economic linkages. Presently, the scope of research is widened to incorporate social and cultural dimensions of globalization, such as lifestyles, more evident in concepts such as *macdonaldization* of society. However, globalization and the city have been primarily understood in economic terms – the city as a production site with research emphasizing the following features: the nature of spatial agglomeration of the city and the relationship between space and power; the secular decline of manufacturing and the growth of services; and new forms of polarization and marginalization.

In this chapter I explore the above features, such as the decline of manufacturing and the growth of service industries, locational issues, and reorganization of space, and relate it new forms of marginalization and inequalities. However, I would argue that these features have to be understood in the way the local, regional, and national processes have interfaced with the global processes to restructure the economy of Mumbai. More particularly it is not the external economy that has oriented the city to globalization but the national policy of the government. Of particular importance in the case of India has been the contradictory impact of the structural adjustment and liberalization policies initiated by the government of India after it negotiated a new loan from the International Monetary Fund. This policy changed the earlier program of development – state-induced social change – at an ideational level from that of balanced growth and social justice, social responsibilities and accountability, equity and self-reliance to an emphasis on private enterprise and the withdrawal of the state from social welfare schemes. The specific programs initiated by the state of fiscal austerity, monetary and credit contraction, and liberalization packages such as the deregulation of trade and finance and the labor market led to a recessionary trend in the economy as public expenditure and public investment on long-term development programs were curtailed.

Commentators have suggested that the program of structural adjustment and liberalization in the case of India has led to contradictory trends. While on one hand partial convertibility and entrance of foreign firms have increased equity participation, expanded the nature of the stock market, and changed the nature of manufacturing, making it more service-oriented and related to global markets, in the absence of a political will to increase direct taxes on higher income group or cut down wasteful expenditure, there was a heavy cut in welfare expenditures such as water supply and health and a cut in subsidies on basic needs and amenities such as food and electricity. Additionally, as a result of the policy of privatization, there has been reorganization of public sector corporations – most of them located in big cities. Thus unemployment has increased and so have inequalities while there has been an extension of the scope of the non-organized economy; the latter having got further impetus due to the service orientation of the new economies. These features are spread over the entire country, but they are unevenly distributed; this unevenness being related to the specific history of different regions and the way urbanization has developed historically in these regions.

In this context Bombay because of its history and the way it represents the contradictory strands of the global economy presents an interesting case to examine the specific form the globalizing process takes in India. Bombay's growth as a colonial city with its manufacturing oriented to an export market, financial and corporate headquarters, and after independence, a national market for its products, together with a developed media and film industry, and a multiethnic entrepreneurial group, made it more apt to accept the new global economies. And yet the synergy developed by the globalizing process did not engulf the city's entire economy. Most of Bombay's population remains employed in production and service processes employing archaic and pre-global technology. This unevenness in the internal structure of the economy manifests itself in the way inequalities in the city are structured. These inequalities relate to the lack of integration and organic connection between old and new economies and are not representative of the features of the fully developed global economy. Within the city this has meant an unusual interest by the business groups in short-term profits, especially in activities such as real estate, leading to highly skewed distribution of land use. This has further aggravated the inequalities already increasing as a result of the structural adjustment policies. Additionally, the lack of integration of the city with the global economies makes it open and vulnerable to regional political demands as seen from the case of the growth and spread of the Shiv Sena examined below. These specific features, indigenous to the city, I argue, determine the issues facing globalizing Bombay.

To summarize my arguments, inequalities in Mumbai have been exacerbated by an internal reorganization of the economy as well as external influences relating to the uneven spread of capitalism due to the colonial experience and as well as to globalization. The changing character of the economy has affected the nature and structure of the poor and laboring class. The issue of housing and access to space has supplanted earlier conflicts over wages. This change in the structure of the urban economy and the issues determining popular conflicts and inequities has been detrimental to political movements that mobilized the working class and has limited their range of political influence among the underclass and in the city's politics. This political vacuum has been filled by the growth of Shiv Sena, the movement and the party of chauvinist ethnic and religious ideologies on one hand and the promoter of vigilante politics on the other. Lastly, with this party taking control of local political institutions, and in 1995 the state of Maharashtra, cultural traditions of democracy, multiculturalism, and civility have declined in the city.

The economy

Like other metropolitan cities in India such as Calcutta and Chennai,[6] Mumbai is a colonial city and has a short history as a major urban settlement that set it apart from the subcontinent's old cities, such as Delhi, Agra, Lahore, Varanasi, Hyderabad, or Ahmedabad. Ceded by the Portuguese to the British in 1661 as part of the dowry of Princess Katherine, the seven islands that constitute what is known as Greater Bombay remained undeveloped for a long time.[7] Even in the late eighteenth century, Bombay was primarily a marine supply point, which, unlike Calcutta and Madras, had few linkages with its hinterland.

Bombay's early growth was dependent on imperialist interests. Till early in the nineteenth century Britain used Calcutta as its main port. Eventually, several specific economic factors spurred the growth of

[6] Chennai is the new name for Madras.

[7] Bombay proper can trace its genesis to a modest Quinta (Manor House) built by the Portuguese physician and botanist who leased the Bombaim Island from the then Portuguese regime in the mid-sixteenth century.

Bombay: the development of foreign shipping services which wanted to take advantage of a port closer to Europe than Calcutta; the extension of the railway line to the cotton-growing areas in the hinterland of Bombay; the rise of world cotton prices due to the shortages caused by the American Civil War; and the opening of the Suez Canal in 1869. The initial boom led to an increase of wealth. This in turn led to the establishment of the textile industry in Bombay by Europeans with Indians as their junior partners. Ethnic divisions were institutionalized in this process. The business communities of Gujarat dominated both manufacturing and trade, while the workers manning the ports and manufacturing industry came from the Marathi-speaking region.

The establishment of the cotton industry in the mid-nineteenth century encouraged further population growth, with skilled and educated migrants coming from the south. However, manufacturing never superseded completely the service orientation of the city.[8] Bombay continued to be first and foremost a port city with extensive networks into the hinterland, exporting raw resources such as cotton-spun yarn, and eventually cloth, as part of multilateral trade agreements fashioned by the colonial authorities. Thus when the city became the headquarters of financial and corporate houses, as well as the stock market, the orientation of these institutions remained linked to imperialist interests.

Colonial ties loosened to a significant extent in the interwar period and the textile industry developed a domestic market. This labor-intensive industry saw its workforce peak during this period. This was also the period of the growth of a radical working-class movement and of the nationalist movement in Bombay.

The profits accruing through the boom of the textile industry were reinvested in capital-intensive industries such as engineering, petrochemicals, food processing, pharmaceuticals, and fertilizers. The development of these industries attracted educated migrants to the city. The majority of the unskilled migrants became dependent on employment in services as ever fewer of them were absorbed by the textile industry, which declined and was restructured.

The Bombay textile industry has been undergoing a major restructuring since the 1960s. Consequent to modernization, there has developed a differentiation between the units in the city. Part of the industry

[8] On the basis of a survey done in 1955–1956, Lakdawala *et al.* (1963) suggest that if the number of workers in manufacturing and processing continued to increase, the number in the service sector other than in commerce remained steady at about one third of the total working force. If employment in commerce is taken into account, the number employed in service industries shoots up to 56% of the city's employed. Once the textile industry collapsed, the numbers employed in services increased again, as we will see below.

became automated. This led to a sharp retrenchment of labor: formal employment decreased by half. Even though workload and productivity increased, wages did not rise, while those in capital-intensive industries have remained relatively high (Sherlock 1996).

The pace of decline and the subsequent restructuring of the textile industry was hastened by a strike in 1982–1983 which continued for more than eighteen months before petering out.[9] The textile industry, already in the process of restructuring, took full advantage of the collapse of the strike to shut down definitively a considerable number of mills. In 1976, 27% of the city's organized force had found employment in the textile industry. By 1991 the figure had dropped to 12.5%. In absolute terms, the employment in textile industry had fallen from 600,000 in 1981 to 400,000 in 1991 (Bakshi 1986). Over the same period there was a growth of unregistered units with downgraded technology and substantial part of manufacturing was contracted out to informal processes. One estimate suggests that such establishments increased from 39% in 1951 to 60% in 1991 (Deshpande and Deshpande 1999, p. 8).

These statistics are confirmed by other figures, for the retrenched textile workers had little possibility of finding other factory jobs and were forced to survive by moving into informal processes. The total decline in the manufacturing sector has led to an increase in unemployment. Between 1981 and 1996 the total number of unemployed more than doubled.[10] Using data from the Establishment Census, Sudha and Lalit Deshpande (1997) estimated that the proportion of employed in the informal sector increased from 27% in 1970 to 33% in 1980. According to a second estimate, calculated from the Employment Market Information Program, the proportion employed in the informal processes increased from 49% in 1971 to 55% in 1981. Current figures confirm this trend. For 1991, the estimate computed from Employment Market Information is 65.6%. Another estimate suggests an increase from 27.4% in 1970 to 46.3% in 1991 of units employing workers less than ten workers.[11]

While organized sector jobs in manufacturing have decreased, there has been an increase in jobs associated with producer services related to globalization. Today Bombay accounts for 61% Indian jobs in the oil sector and 41% in domestic air traffic. Its airport handles 75% of the

[9] The failure of this longest textile strike in world history, which displaced more than 100,000 workers, has generated a heated debate about its causes and its conduct. Starting on a bonus issue, the movement rapidly turned into a massive expression of a whole series of long-standing grievances, the most critical of which was the rejection of the legitimacy of the trade union recognized by government as the sole accredited representative for textile labor in industrial negotiations in Mumbai.

[10] Fact Book on Mumbai 2000, Table 29, p. 22.

[11] Fact Book on Mumbai 2000, Table 27, p. 20.

country's air cargo imports and 64% of exports. Employment in financial and business services has increased by 43% between the 1970s and the 1980s. Bombay collects 25% of income tax revenues and 60% of custom revenues of the country. Its banks control 12% of national deposits and a quarter of the country's outstanding credits. The number of new issues listed on the Bombay stock exchange grew from 203 in 1991–1992 to 694 in 1993–1994, and the amount of fresh capital in old and new companies increased from Rs. 54 billion to 213 billion between these years (Deshpande 1996; Harris 1995, p. 54).

The growth of the financial sector and the entrance of international financial groups in Bombay's stock exchange led to ancillary developments such as an increase in investments in the communications industry[12] and an expansion of related service industries, specifically the film and music industry. This trend accelerated in the mid-nineties after Bombay became the hub of the telecommunications industry. In July 1994, the runaway success of the film *Hum Aapke Hain Kaun* (Who Am I of Yours?) established the importance of the overseas market for Indian movies: a quarter of the revenues of this film came from the overseas market.[13] Given the synergistic relationship between the film and audio industry,[14] globalization of the film industry led to a boom in the audio cassette industry. In response audio companies are now increasingly producing films.[15] With an average of 140 Bollywood releases and exports per year, the economics of the film and audio industry have radically changed, and they have affected the growth of other service industries such as the travel, tourism, and hotel trade as well as television.

The expansion of these economic activities has led to the growth of a new class, which is linked to the world of international finance and producer services. At the same time the interests of much of Mumbai's workforce are no longer defended by militant trade unions. The bulk of the city's workforce has fallen far behind.

Sudha and Lalit Deshpande (2003) have suggested that there has been a modest increase in income in the city and a slight reduction of poverty. An expenditure survey conducted in 1958–1959 and in 1981–1982 estimated that average family income increased by 0.88% per annum. They

[12] Telecommunications has increasingly become a high-profile industry over the past decade. Bombay is the principal hub for this industry. In 1994 Bombay was connected to the rest of the world through an analog cable. Fibre-optic cables were laid from 1994 onwards.

[13] In 2000 the film *Taal* (Rhythm) changed the economics altogether when its overseas market grossed Rs. 2 million of revenues, 50% more than the Indian market.

[14] The overseas market in this area has also expanded in conjunction to that of films as most films in India have at least five or six songs.

[15] Personal communication from Taran Adarsh, editor, *Trade Guide*.

also report that the real wages of the factory worker increased marginally by 2.68% between 1975–1977 and 1985–1987. They argue that there has also been an increase in the wages of casual workers. They conclude that the share of poor declined from 15% in 1987–1988 to 5% in 1993–1994.

Even when income and earnings have risen, basic conditions of work and living environment have not changed for many of Mumbai's citizens. Swaminathan (2003), in a longitudinal study of some settlements, has shown that the issues of deprivation and poverty have to be examined not only in context to income and earnings but also in terms of access to land and housing, health and education, environment and population density, and occupation of citizens.[16] In Bombay today, whether in manufacturing or in services, most employment is unregulated in respect of wages, working conditions, security of tenure, rights to health care, and retirement benefits. Most of the workers in this mode of activity not only use their own labor but also their residence and infrastructure, e.g., electricity and water for the manufacture of goods and services. Critical to gaining employment is a need for the laborer to have access to housing. Access to these services, subsidised earlier through urban development programs, has become more difficult. An electricity meter, which was available in Mumbai for Rs. 306 in 1990, cost Rs. 2006 by the end of 1995, while electricity bills increased by 100%.

Population

In the rather short history of Mumbai, three demographic trends stand out. One is the continuous increase in the population of the city; particularly during the period between 1941 and 1971. Another is the male-biased sex ratio of the city. Finally, there was a shift of the population towards the northeast and northwest suburbs, and that of industries northwards, with the subsequent reorganization of the boundaries defining the city.

The population of Bombay was estimated to be around 10,000 in 1861, and at the first census in 1872 the count was 644,400. Initially push factors such as famines and epidemics led to increases in migration to Bombay. Later, once industries were established, pull factors dominated. The growth of the population of Bombay during the nineteenth century was therefore erratic. The period 1901–1921 saw relatively fast growth, and by 1921 the population had reached 1.4 million. The nationalist

[16] For instance, in the Dharavi slum of central Bombay air and water pollution created by 400 leather-processing units determines the conditions of living quite apart from income.

Table 11.1 *Population of Greater Mumbai, 1901–1991*

Year	Population	Decadal change	Percentage change	Males	Females	Sex ratio F/M × 1,000
1901	927,994	561,825		366,169	652	
1911	1,148,757	220,763	23.8	731,634	417,123	570
1921	1,380,448	231,691	20.2	884,301	496,147	561
1931	1,397,812	17,364	1.3	878,102	519,710	592
1941	1,801,357	403,544	28.9	1,114,983	686,373	616
1951	2,994,444	1,193,088	66.2	1,868,335	1,126,109	603
1961	4,152,056	1,157,612	38.7	2,496,176	1,655,880	663
1971	5,970,575	1,818,519	43.7	3,478,378	2,492,197	716
1981	8,505,380	2,534,805	42.5	4,808,137	3,697,243	769
1991	9,925,891	1,420,511	16.7	5,460,145	4,465,746	818

Sources: For 1901 to 1981, Karkal 1982; for 1991, Census of India 1991.

non-cooperation movement resulted in under-reporting in the 1931 census. By 1951 Bombay's population had swelled by an influx of refugees following the partition of the country in 1947 in addition to migrants from the rest of Maharashtra whereas the 1991 census showed a sharp decline in population growth.

In the early days deaths exceeded births in Bombay, and the city's growth came entirely from the surrounding region and then from farther afield. Young male adults used to dominate amongst migrants, and Mumbai's sex ratio was highly imbalanced. Once housing developed, family migration became more common. In recent years increasing numbers of young females appear to have migrated to Mumbai for education and employment. Finally in the 1980s the increased share of natural increase in the population growth also contributed to a more balanced sex ratio. Bombay Municipality used to be conterminous with the island city, covering 67.67 square kilometers. In 1950 the limits of the city were extended to include eastern and western suburbs, adding 187.46 square kilometers, and giving rise to Greater Bombay. The process of suburbanization was accelerated in 1957 as the administrative limits of Bombay were extended further with the addition of another 174.76 square kilometers, bringing the total area of Greater Mumbai to 429.89 square kilometers. For planning purposes an even larger metropolitan region administered by the Mumbai Metropolitan Regional Development Authority (MMRDA) was established in 1965.

The partition of the country brought in large numbers of refugees and saw many of them settling in the suburbs. Other migrants came from the Maharashtra interior. They too settled in the northern suburbs. While the population outside the island city expanded rapidly from

Table 11.2 *Percentage of Greater Bombay's population by areas, 1901–1991*

Year	Island city	Suburbs	Extended suburbs	Total
1901	83.62	7.70	8.68	100
1911	85.26	7.14	7.60	100
1921	85.18	8.57	6.25	100
1931	83.09	10.10	7.81	100
1941	82.71	11.40	5.89	100
1951	77.78	17.04	5.18	100
1961	66.76	24.97	8.27	100
1971	51.43	39.61	8.96	100
1981	39.85	42.58	17.57	100
1991	31.99	41.99	26.02	100

Sources: For 1901 to 1981, Karkal 1982; for 1991, Census of India 1991.

thereon, the population on the island grew more slowly and eventually declined in the 1980s. By 1991 two-thirds of Greater Bombay lived outside the island city.

This process of suburbanization was characterized by a spatial order of succession. The northward creep along the rail-cum-road corridors, crystallizing into dormitories around the railheads, was the first phase. The westside developed first. The building of the Express Highways brought subsequent eastside development. Areas extending outwards from the railheads were developed in the next phase. With railheads as focal points of commuter traffic, roads leading to these railheads became shopping fronts. In the southern part of the city, land was reclaimed to build housing for middle- and upper-class society, with hutments developed in niches thereby sheltering shanties.

The suburbs have become a mix of people of varied linguistic, religious, and caste groups living together in housing stratified by income. Due to the concentration of business activities there is a movement southwards in the mornings. However, an opposite movement of employment opportunities is now gaining strength, with the growth of industrial and service jobs in the suburbs. Also, new industries have been established on the eastern corridor of the city, increasing the east–west flows within the suburbs and beyond.

Poverty, space, and deprivation

The city remains a study of extreme contrasts. More than half of the city's population does not have legal tenure of the land they occupy. In 1971, the slum population was estimated at 1.25 million. Data collected in 1985 suggested that slum dwellers constituted more than half of the city's 9 million people, but that they occupied only 2,000 of the 43,000 hectares of its land area. At that time there were 10,000 hectares of vacant land, most of it owned by governmental organizations, in particular the Bombay Port Trust. About ninety landlords owned more than half of the vacant land in the possession of private builders. More than half of Bombay's population live on 6% of its land area (Patel 1985).

Concentration of ownership reinforces inequities in land and housing. It also made for fictitious scarcity, speculation, and capital accumulation through rent. Efforts have been made by the state through legislation, in particular the Urban Land Ceiling and Regulation Act, to redistribute land, but results have run counter to expressed aims (Narayanan 2003). While the area on which lower- and middle-class housing could be built increased, most of the poor live in slums or are altogether homeless. Many are crowded together in tight clusters of one-room huts. Others have to struggle to find and then to retain unoccupied spaces under bridges, along railway tracks, even on pavements or rooftops. Many do not have access to clean water or to waste disposal systems.

Living quarters in the slums are cramped, overcrowded, and without proper ventilation. In most slums the area available per person is of the order of 50 square feet. Because of the scarcity of land, a range of income groups is found even within slums. For the poorer, housing is typically a small space enclosed on two sides by gunny bags, long lengths of cloth, sometimes saris, old sheets of plastics, tarpaulin, and a couple of wooden rods.[17]

Many Bombay residents do not have access to clean water. A majority of slums do not have systems of sanitation for the disposal of excreta, sewage, and silage. This is one of the biggest health hazards to the city. In a census of 619 notified slums in Bombay, 174 reported no toilets. Where there were toilets, an average rate of 94 persons per toilet was recorded (Swaminathan 2003).

Most Mumbai workers live on the margins both figuratively and metaphorically. Their work in informalized modes of manufacturing and services is unsteady, unprotected, and unregulated. Instability and deprivation rule their lives. They have broken the bonds of community in the village, but they have not become part of an urban-industrial culture. Their life remains restricted to overcrowded dense areas where there is constant struggle to live and reproduce themselves, physically and culturally. In these circumstances, a reaffirmation of community gets translated

[17] Eighty-eight slums reported ceilings of highly toxic asbestos (Swaminathan 2003, p. 9).

into small slum communities of regional, ethnic, and religious groups. Identification with the local dominates consciousness. This is the class that identifies with the Sena. Kin and caste networks, as well as ethnic and religious affiliation, shape settlement patterns and divide space within the slums.

The Shiv Sena

The Shiv Sena's development can be traced to the growth and expansion of a regional movement for separate statehood for Maharashtrians, and the demand that Bombay be made its capital, in order to give employment opportunities to the Marathi-speaking population in the area.[18] Contemporary commentators (Gupta 1982; Katzenstein 1979) suggest that these demands were linked to another one, that Bombay invest its wealth in the state of Maharashtra.

The Shiv Sena was established in 1966, six years after Maharashtra state had been created and Mumbai made its capital. The late sixties were a period of political and economic crisis in India, a period of protests against rising prices, against exploitation by landlords, against one-party rule, and against the government for not giving jobs to the migrants flooding the urban areas. The Shiv Sena was a child of these times, a movement that emerged from the crisis of legitimation faced by the Congress party. It projected itself as an anti-Congress party, channeling and articulating the protest of the city's populace against the policies that the Congress Party was pursuing at the behest and in consort with the ruling groups.

Bombay had been facing critical problems. Its population had increased dramatically and the city's economy was being restructured. Shiv Sena initially mobilized the middle class facing inflation, a decline in real wages, and soaring land and housing prices. The Sena was able to exploit their discontent and direct it at the in-migration of south Indians. It thus earned the title of being nativist. Its strategy was to use confrontational politics and violence to project itself as the only true movement for and on behalf of Maharashtrians. In the process, it was able to exploit long-standing perceptions of disadvantage among desperate class and caste groups of Maharashtrians in the city and mobilize them against the establishment.

[18] Bombay Presidency, and later Bombay State, consisted of present-day Gujarat and Maharashtra. Regional movements in both areas led ultimately to the formation of two separate states.

During this phase attempt was made by the Sena leaders to elaborate a theory of discrimination faced by the Marathi-speaking population in the city. They articulated the "sons of soil" ideology encapsulated in its slogan, Mumbai for Maharashtrians. Disdain towards institutionalized democracy – which it debunked as non-Maharashtrian and elitist made possible an interrogation of established power systems in the city based on class and community. If one ideological element signed the Sena's narrative in this phase, it was anti-communism. It entered trade union politics and attempted to take control of it. It also sought to enter other formal structures of power, specially the Municipality, in order to legitimize its goals. Within two years of its creation, Sena gained about 47% of the seats it contested and 30% of the total seats in the municipal elections. It thus emerged as a key player in local politics and could distribute resources and employment opportunities to some if not all of its supporters.

The Shiv Sena is structured as a two-tiered system: the elite are entrenched members of the large family networks of the Thackeray family. Their followers are connected to various branches of this organization. They are often characterized by a distinctive style: aggressive, chauvinist, and macho. For most, affiliation with the Sena is not long term. For some it is subsidiary to other political affiliations, for others in lieu of any other political affiliation.

Soon vigilantism, a political strategy of using violence to ensure its influence, engulfed Shiv Sena politics. It introduced a new political culture in a city which had earlier developed a culture of mass democratic protests as a result of the growth and spread of both the nationalist and organized trade union movements over four decades prior to the Sena's formation. Through vigilantism the Sena soon became associated with extortion and protection rackets. One commentator characterized this development as the growth of predatory capitalism (Lele 1995). After the communal riots of 1984, the Sena cultivated an image of a religiously oriented movement and party, and of protecting the rights of the Hindus, while its latent intention was to promote the economic regime that was emerging in the city through globalization.

The Shiv Sena endorses two agendas: religious chauvinism and globalization. To realize the latter, it is involved in sponsoring lifestyles and providing systems of consumption that are associated with and thus represent the global economy in the city. These are in three spheres: food, leisure, and housing.

The Sena's involvement in these economies started in the late 1960s but became more significant from the 1970s onwards. With no decline in in-migration, the employment opportunities for the migrants and those who were displaced by restructuring only increased the 'informal' economy. Slums became the main centers for the expansion of these activities. The Sena's solution was to encourage employment in the 'informal sector' through the provision of fast food stalls selling *vada-pav* (a vegetarian hamburger) to the newly arrived migrants. Petty businesses were encouraged, such as selling vegetables and fruits in the market, setting up food stalls around railway stations, or retailing to provide consumption goods to the burgeoning population of the city. These small businesses needed little finance. Sometimes Sena leaders would finance such activities.

Most of these activities needed licensing, and the Sena started encouraging its members to establish networks with municipal officials through kin and linguistic linkages. Drawing on these connections, the Sena procured licenses for others and collected commission. The origin of the protection and extortion rackets associated with the Sena grew out of these economic activities that were started to give employment to the unemployed.

The Shiv Sena's entrance into the slums occurred in the early 1970s when the issue of obtaining land to build became critical. At that time there was a boom in housing construction for the middle and upper classes. The Sena was able to organize *dadas*[19] to encroach land both for constructing slum settlements and for selling it to builders. Violence or the threat of violence was essential. As the extortion and protection business expanded, it needed the help of gangs. By the late 1970s, there were clear indications that Mafia gangs were primarily involved in smuggling activities moved in on the land, building, and housing businesses. With escalating land prices their involvement in this business increased, and uneasy alliances with various sections of the Sena were forged. Within the slums a culture around the figure of the *dada*, a culture of brotherhood, emerged.

For young male underemployed slum dwellers, the Shiv Sena represents the family, its local chief the father or elder brother, *dada*. It gives them a sense of identity, organizing them in various cultural activities as they hang around in corner *paan*[20] shops. It taps their restlessness and articulates their anger at being part of an unrecognized group in the city. The *mitra mandals* (youth clubs) have provided a space for youth to meet, to play games, and to read magazines and books. Women's circles discuss and organize activities involving households.

[19] In Marathi *dada* means an elder brother. In Bombay colloquial language it means a Mafia don or his representative, who is the "protector."
[20] Corner stalls which sell beetle leaf and cigarettes.

The Sena has been able to bolster its legitimacy as the movement of the people through its success in organizing festivals on a grand scale. To a considerable degree mass sports, cinema, and television have substituted games, *bhajan* (prayer) singing, and play-acting. People who formerly created their own entertainment have been metamorphosed into spectators. The Sena thrives by creating spectacles. Initially its activities were oriented to organizing the *Ganesh* (elephant-headed god) festival with each slum having its own representation. Then it started organizing all other Hindu festivals, including the *Durga puja* (prayers to Goddess *Durga*) and the *garbaas* (dances) during *Navraatri* (nine-day festival in honor of the Goddess *Amba*, another name for *Durga*). Recently it began to organize Michael Jackson shows. These festivals have served two functions. They have mobilized the local slum community, giving them an identity as part of a pan-Hindu community and lessening their feelings of deprivation. At the same time these activities have helped the Sena legitimize its power and extend its influence in organizing other commercial activities such as extortion and protection rackets.

The Sena adopts, interprets, mediates, transforms, and negotiates the symbols that arouse responses in a city largely populated by rural immigrants, packed densely in degraded areas and slums, and subject to feelings of cultural *angst*. It recognizes the need to promote the dreams, fantasies, and aspirations of youth. Their restlessness and their instability are thereby captured and manipulated to burst out in vigilantism.

The way in which these economies of consumption are organized in various localities determines the Sena's effectivity and influence among the local population. Some *shakhas* (branches) are well organized. Their chiefs control almost all aspects of life through the provision of systems that organize the consumption of various goods including leisure. The Sena is also involved in social activities: it arranges marriages, assists with medical problems of slum dwellers, and organizes arbitration of family and economic disputes through a people's court. In other areas of the city, the *shakhas* do not have this kind of control. They rely on violence or threat of violence to obtain control over the economy.

The Sena's appeal does not seem to lie in a coherent ideology and program of political action. We have seen how its agenda has been shifting over the years. Earlier it portrayed itself as a movement fighting for the rights of the sons-of-the-soil, now it is projecting itself as a Hindu party. When it fought the Municipal elections, it confronted the party in power over the program of slum demolition. Yet when it came to power, it called for modernizing the city, erasing the slums and developing new green areas, thereby participating in the scam of de-reserving existing green areas. Though its agenda tends to change, it seems to be clear about its enemies: the communists and the secularists.

The Sena's success has to be seen in the context, on one hand, of the absence of political strength and a clear ideological agenda of the trade union movement and of the organized political parties which had earlier mobilized the working class and created democratic traditions in the city. On the other hand, it is also related to the political mobilization of the people of region on identity issues such as language and region in the late fifties and sixties and religion in the eighties and nineties. Today, the Sena draws its legitimacy from the crystallization of a new deprived class, a new form of mobilization, and through an involvement in the economies of consumption and culture.

Conclusion

The growth and legitimation of the Shiv Sena is related to the way in which Bombay's cosmopolitanism was constructed within dependent colonialism. The uneven growth of labor-intensive industry and its decline, the shift to capital-intensive industry and then the growth of economic activities related to globalization, each in turn furthered extreme inequities. They encouraged the growth of narratives regarding a culture of deprivation that identity movements such as the Shiv Sena have been able to mobilize.

The unequal institutionalization of the new economies has had altogether negative implications for the poor and the deprived in the city. It has not only increased social and spatial inequities, but it has also tied and identified a significant proportion of the underclass to a chauvinist and vigilante movement. What are the prospects for the future? The Sena leadership sits uneasily between its mass followers and the rich as it mediates between these two in its quest to continue its hold on power in the city and the state.[21] During its five-year term in office as a coalition partner – from 1995 to 2000 – it was associated with the growth and expansion of "small capital" in the consumption sector. Its attempts to provide housing to the poor through the slum redevelopment program did not take off. Its effort to provide cheap food through the *zunkha bakhar* (a bread made of millet with lentil soup) flopped within months of its inception. It retains control of the leisure industry and continues to play a role in its

[21] A crisis may emerge if the linkages between the two arms of the organization, the elite and their mass following, disintegrate. Death of the patriarch, Thackeray, may precipitate such a process.

expansion. Despite these contradictory trends, the Shiv Sena though out of power presently retains its influence as a party because it is also a civil society organization that can organize the poor in the city. The crisis of the city is the crisis of politics, that of the absence of a political alternative to the Sena.

REFERENCES

Bakshi, Rajni 1986. "The Long Haul: The Historic Bombay Textile Strike." Bombay: Build Documentation Center (mimeo).

Dalmia, Yashodhara 1995. "From Jamshetjee Jeejeebhoy to the Progressive Painters," in Sujata Patel and Alice Thorner (eds.), *Bombay: Mosaic of Modern Culture*. Bombay and Delhi: Oxford University Press, pp. 182–193.

Deshpande, Lalit 1996. "Impact of Globalization on Mumbai." Paper presented for UNU-Unesco Workshop on Globalization and Mega City Development in Pacific Asia, Tokyo (mimeo).

Deshpande, Sudha and Deshpande, Lalit 1997. "Problems of Urbanization and Growth of Large Cities in Developing Countries: A Case Study of Bombay." Population and Labour Studies Program Working Paper No. 17, World Development Program Research (mimeo).

2003. "Work, Wages and Well Being in Bombay of 1950s to Mumbai of 1990s," in Sujata Patel and Jim Masselos (eds.), *Bombay and Mumbai: The City in Transition*. Delhi: Oxford University Press, pp. 53–80.

Fact Book on Mumbai 2000. Bombay: Bombay First.

Friedmann, J. and Wolff, G. 1982. "World City Formation: An Agenda for Research and Action," *International Journal of Urban and Regional Research*, 6: 309–344.

Gangar, Amrit 1995. "Films from the City of Dreams," in Patel and Alice Thorner (eds.), *Bombay: Mosaic of Modern Culture*. Bombay and Delhi: Oxford University Press, pp. 210–224.

Gokhale Shanta 1995, Poor Theater. Rich Theater, in Sujata Patel and Alice Thorner (eds.), *Bombay: Mosaic of Modern Culture*. Bombay and Delhi: Oxford University Press, pp. 194–209.

Gupta, Dipankar 1982. *Nativism in a Metropolis, Shiv Sena in Bombay*. Delhi: Manohar.

Harris Nigel 1995. "Bombay in the Global Economy," in Sujata Patel and Alice Thorner (eds.) *Bombay: Metaphor for Modern India*. Bombay and Delhi: Oxford University Press, pp. 47–63.

Karkal, Malini 1982. "Population Growth in Greater Bombay: Some Emerging Trends," *Economic and Political Weekly*.

Katzenstein, Mary F. 1979. *Ethnicity and Equality: The Shiv Sena Party and Preferential Politics in Bombay*. Ithaca: Cornell University Press.

Lakdawala, D. T. Sandesara, J. C., Kothari, V. N. and Nair, P. A. 1963. *Work, Wages and Well-Being in an Indian Metropolis: Economic Survey of Bombay City*. University of Bombay Series in Economics No. 11. Bombay: University of Bombay.

Lele, Jayant 1995. "Saffronization of the Shiv Sena: The Political Economy of City, State and Nation," in Sujata Patel and Alice Thorner (eds.), *Bombay: Metaphor for Modern India*. Bombay and Delhi: Oxford University Press, pp. 185–212.

Narayanan, H. 2003. "Politics of Urban Ceiling Act," in Sujata Patel and Jim Masselos (eds.), *Bombay and Mumbai: The City in Transition*. Delhi: Oxford University Press, pp. 183–206.

Patel, S. 1995. "Bombay's Urban Predicament," in Sujata Patel and Alice Thorner (eds.), *Bombay: Metaphor for Modern India*. Bombay and Delhi: Oxford University Press, pp. xi–xxxiii.

Sassen, S. 1991. *The Global City: New York, London, Tokyo*. Princeton: Princeton University Press.

Sherlock, Stephen 1996. "Class Re-formation in Mumbai: Has Organised Labour Risen to the Challenge?," *Economic and Political Weekly*, 31 (28): L34–L38.

Swaminathan, Madhura 2003. "Aspects of Poverty and Living Standards," in S. Patel and J. Masselos (eds.) 2003. *Bombay and Mumbai: The City in Transition*. Delhi: Oxford University Press, pp. 81–110.

12 Johannesburg: race, inequality, and urbanization*

Owen Crankshaw and Susan Parnell

The city of Johannesburg lies at the heart of a sprawling metropolis. This metropolis, which we shall call the Johannesburg region, roughly corresponds with the boundaries of Gauteng Province.[1] It stretches from Soshanguve in the north to Vanderbijl Park in the south and from Carletonville in the west to Springs in the east (Map 12.1). While Johannesburg is an obvious example of a large city in a poor country that is riddled by social and economic inequality, there is a certain irony in its portrayal as a world city. After all, only five years ago Johannesburg was the hub of a pariah nation that was the object of one of the most successful international sanctions campaigns (see Gelb 1991). Notwithstanding the impact of the boycott against apartheid, Johannesburg has long served as the major urban center of southern Africa. It is an unusually cosmopolitan city, with extensive demographic, political, and economic connections with Africa, Asia, Europe, and North America that date back to colonial times (Goty and Simone 2002; Parnell and Pirie 1991). Increasingly strong links are now also being forged with Australasia through immigration and sport.

Johannesburg is the economic hub of both South Africa and of the southern African region. As an urban giant located in a middle-income

* Financial assistance from the National Research Foundation and the University of Cape Town for this research is hereby acknowledged. Opinions expressed in this chapter and conclusions arrived at are those of the authors and are not necessarily to be attributed to the National Research Foundation.

[1] A note on terminology: this metropolis used to be called the "PWV," an acronym for the "Pretoria-Witwatersrand-Vereeniging Complex." The functional importance of this region has since been given the status of a province and is now known as "Gauteng" (the place of gold). However, the names "PWV" and "Gauteng" are not known in international circles so, for the purposes of this chapter, we have chosen to name this metropolitan area the "Johannesburg region" or simply "Johannesburg." When we refer to the city of Johannesburg, we will refer to its formal administrative designation of the "Greater Johannesburg Metropolitan Area" or simply as the "city of Johannesburg." The Greater Johannesburg Metropolitan Council was an interim municipal authority that incorporated, amongst others, the erstwhile local authorities of Johannesburg, Randburg, Roodepoort, Sandton, and Soweto (see Map 12.1).

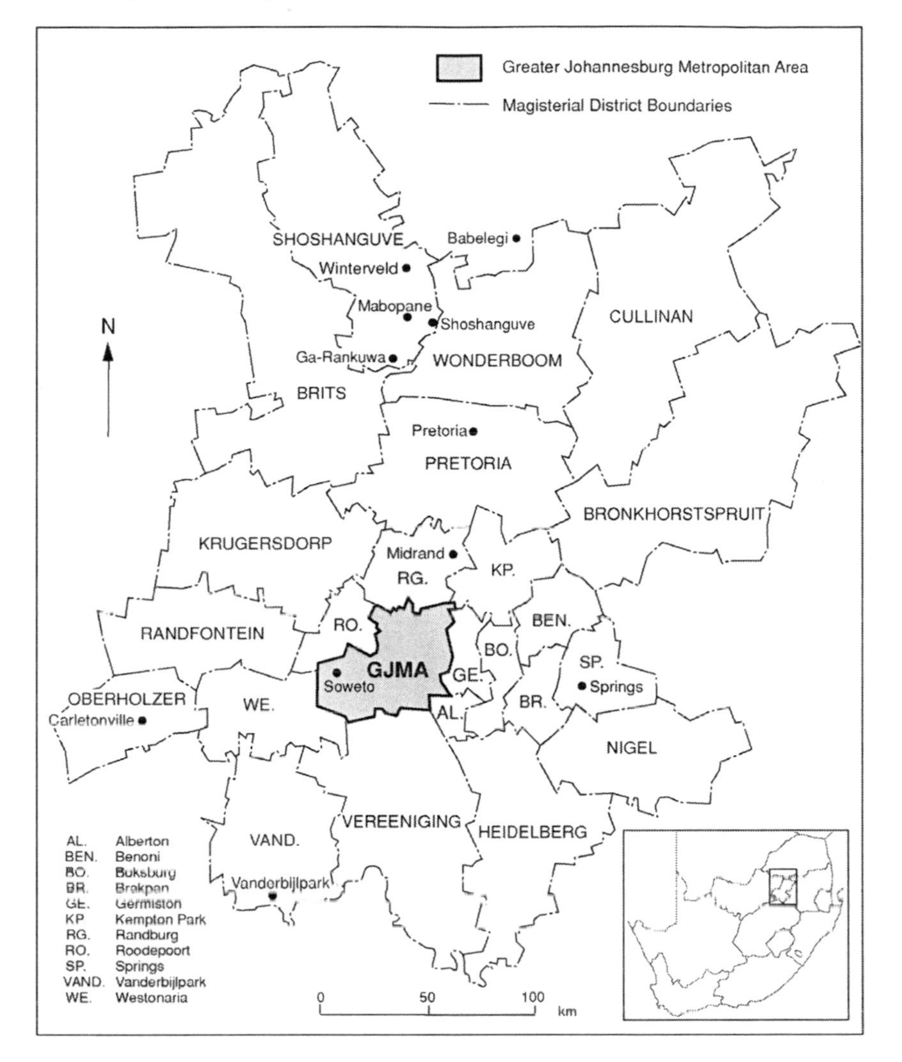

Map 12.1 The Johannesburg region

country amidst extremely poor nations like Mozambique, Lesotho, Zimbabwe, Botswana, Namibia, and Swaziland, Johannesburg dominates the southern African region.[2] Within South Africa, the dominance of the Johannesburg region is unquestioned. The coastal centers of Cape Town

[2] The sum of the 1997 gross national products (GNP) of these countries is less than one sixth of South Africa's GNP, United Nations Development Programme 1999, pp. 180–3.

and Durban, although they are large and important cities, do not compete with the political and economic power of the Johannesburg region. Johannesburg is therefore set to remain the economic heart of both South and southern Africa (Rogerson 1995).

A number of authors have made the case for Johannesburg to be seen as a regional, if not a world, city (Friedman 1995; Simon 1995). This claim has some substance. Even by global standards the numbers of international flights from Johannesburg airport are significant. The Johannesburg stock exchange is the twelfth most powerful in the world, reflecting the place of South Africa at the leading edge of emerging nations (Beavon 1997). Other indicators of global connectivity abound, from telephone links to Internet usage (South Africa ranks twentieth in connections) (*National Geographic* 1999); the 5.9 million square meters of high-quality office space (to which thousands of meters of new A-grade office space is added each year) (Beavon 1997); the concentration of office head quarters (Rogerson 1984); and the growing percentage of the working population who were born outside of the country (Morris 1999; South African Migration Project).

Our concern in this chapter is not to follow the train of analysis that lists the indicators of Johannesburg's world city status, or that which seeks to debate the opportunities or the constraints of globalization for southern Africa's primary city. Instead, we have chosen to reflect on the world city literature to extract analytical tools for reinterpreting urban change in Johannesburg in the post-Second World War period. Our specific attention falls on the utility of linking global economic and demographic shifts to the changing patterns of employment inequality within the city. This chapter is thus a study of the changing relationships between urbanization, racial inequality, and the structure of the labor market in the Johannesburg region.

Race, inequality, and urbanization in the Johannesburg region

Since Johannesburg was first settled in the late nineteenth century, it has been a city of immigrants. Migration from places as diverse as Greece, Britain, Germany, Zambia, Angola, India, and Malaysia meant that it was also an ethnically and racially mixed city (Parnell 1991). As a quasi-colonial city, it was structured in ways that reinforced racial inequality. However, this pattern of racial inequality has changed dramatically over the last half century. Whereas racial inequality was once the touchstone of social inequality in South Africa, inter-racial inequality is increasingly being overshadowed by intra-racial inequality. The most recent analysis of national trends in household income show that, although inter-racial inequality has decreased over the past two decades or so, this trend has not been accompanied by any decrease in inequality among the population as a whole (Whiteford and McGrath 1994). Instead, figures for 1975 and 1991 show that household income inequality remained very high and unchanged, hovering at a Gini coefficient of 0.68.[3]

Whiteford and McGrath argue that the erosion of inter-racial inequality has not been accompanied by a general decline of inequality because intra-racial household income inequality has grown. In other words, although there has been a general redistribution of income from whites, on the one hand, to Africans, coloreds and Indians, on the other, this has not affected the general pattern of household income inequality because most of the increased income which accrued to the black population has gone to the richest black households. Their evidence from the Population Censuses shows that between 1975 and 1991 the richest 20% of black households became richer in absolute terms. By contrast, the poorest 80% of black households became poorer. This shift in the racial distribution of household income has increased intra-racial inequality to the extent that the Gini coefficient for African households was as high as 0.62 in 1991, almost as high as the Gini coefficient for all households (Whiteford and McGrath 1994, p. 51). This means that intra-racial household income inequality contributed as much as 75% to overall inequality, with inter-racial inequality contributing only 25% (Whiteford and McGrath 1994, p. 57). Rising income inequality was not restricted to black households. Although the incomes of the richest 20% of white households remained unchanged, the incomes of the poorest 40% of white households fell in absolute terms (Whiteford and McGrath 1994, pp. 42–5).

These findings upset the conventional interpretations of South African society that have tended to emphasize the extent and character of inter-racial inequality rather than intra-racial inequality (see Lemon 1991). The reasons why South African scholarship has tended to emphasize inter-racial inequality is obvious: since the earliest colonial times, the South African state has pursued racially discriminatory policies. In more recent decades, the apartheid state was responsible for racially discriminatory policies and laws which regulated the urbanization, education, employment, residence, and political rights of black South Africans. Scholars who opposed the racist policies of the apartheid government were therefore keen to identify the relationship between racially discriminatory state policy, on the one hand, and racial inequality, on the other. Although this

[3] South Africa has one of the highest Gini coefficients in the world, comparable with that of Brazil: Whiteford *et al.* 1995, p. 21.

approach to urban studies correctly identified the extent and character of inter-racial inequality and its relationship to government policy, it has generally failed to identify, let alone explain, the rise in intra-racial inequality over the past few decades.

There is another obvious reason why we can no longer rely on racially discriminatory government policies to explain inequality in South Africa. This is because the new democratically elected South African government has abolished all racially discriminatory legislation, including job reservation. Of course, the historical effects of racial discrimination during the apartheid period will continue to cause inter-racial inequality for many years to come. Nonetheless, the evidence suggests that there are other causes of inequality that are at work in South Africa and that these causes are driven by intra-racial divisions. Moreover, these intra-racial dynamics of inequality are increasingly the main cause of inequality within South African society generally, and urban society more directly. Whereas the most startling feature of the South African city was once its division along racial lines, new and less obvious cleavages are now more significant, especially within the African urban population.

Recent research has examined in detail trends in intra-racial inequality in South Africa as a whole (Bhorat *et al.* 2001; Nattrass and Seekings 2001; Seekings and Nattrass forthcoming). But there has been little work focusing specifically on intra-racial inequality in urban areas. In this chapter we draw upon ideas developed to explain inequality in other world city contexts, to examine certain social dynamics which may be contributing towards rising inequality amongst the African population.[4]

In our search for fresh ideas about the relationship between urbanization and racial inequality, we were drawn to the international literature on social polarization, the underclass, and the emergence of global cities (Fainstein *et al.* 1992; Mollenkopf and Castells 1991; O'Loughlin and Friedrichs 1996; Sassen 1994; Waldinger and Bozorgmehr 1996; Wilson 1987). Although contributions to this literature may disagree on the character of the changes and their implications for racial and ethnic inequality, their arguments share the following conceptual structure. Inequality is explained, at least in part, in terms of the changing relationships between the urban demand for different kinds of labor, on the one hand, and the level of skill that is offered by newcomers to the city, on the other. For example, the most common argument is that newcomers, be they urbanizing rural migrants or foreign immigrants, are poorly educated

[4] This analysis of inequality from the perspective of the relationship between the changing labor force and urban population growth builds on earlier work on Johannesburg that sought to contextualize the growth in urban poverty (Beall *et al.* 2002).

and therefore eligible for relatively unskilled manual jobs. However, during the second half of this century there have been important changes in the demand for such unskilled manual work in the cities which has changed patterns of urban inequality.

Up until the 1960s, newcomers to the city could be assured of unskilled employment in the unionized manufacturing sector. This form of employment offered relatively high and stable wages as well as the opportunity for upward mobility. Since then, however, many cities in the advanced capitalist countries have seen the decline of the manufacturing sector and the rise of the service sector. Unlike the manufacturing economy of old, the new service economy lacks jobs in the middle-income range. Instead, it features a polarized job market, requiring high levels of skill at the professional end and low skills at the other, with little opportunity for upward occupational mobility. Furthermore, the proportion of low-skilled jobs in the new service economy is relatively low. This economic restructuring has meant that unskilled newcomers to the city are less likely to secure employment. And even if they do find employment, it is more likely to be in dead-end and low-paying service sector jobs. In the United States, this argument has been used to explain, at least in part, the poor performance of racial and ethnic minorities in the urban labor market (Ortiz 1996, pp. 274–5; Wilson 1987, pp. 39–46). With this general hypothesis in mind, we now turn to the analysis of population and employment trends in the Johannesburg region.

These population and employment trends are based on data from the Population Censuses of 1946, 1951, 1960, 1970, 1980, 1991, and 1996. Population and employment estimates are published for each magisterial district. The boundaries of these magisterial districts usually coincide with the boundaries of local authorities. Where boundaries of these administrative bodies do not coincide, the Census reports provide tables which allowed us to correct the population and employment estimates for each local authority. Obviously, the boundaries of the magisterial districts have changed considerably over the years. However, the pattern was for magisterial districts to be subdivided as their populations grew in size. This made it possible for us simply to add new magisterial districts to our list as the number of magisterial districts within the boundary of the present-day Johannesburg region grew. The population and employment estimates for the Johannesburg region are therefore the sum of the figures for the magisterial districts of Alberton, Benoni, Boksburg, Brakpan, Brits, Bronhorstspruit, Cullinan, Germiston, Heidelberg, Johannesburg, Kempton Park, Krugersdorp, Nigel, Oberholzer, Pretoria, Randburg, Randfontein, Roodepoort, Soshanguve, Springs, Vanderbijl Park, Vereeniging, Westonaria, and Wonderboom.

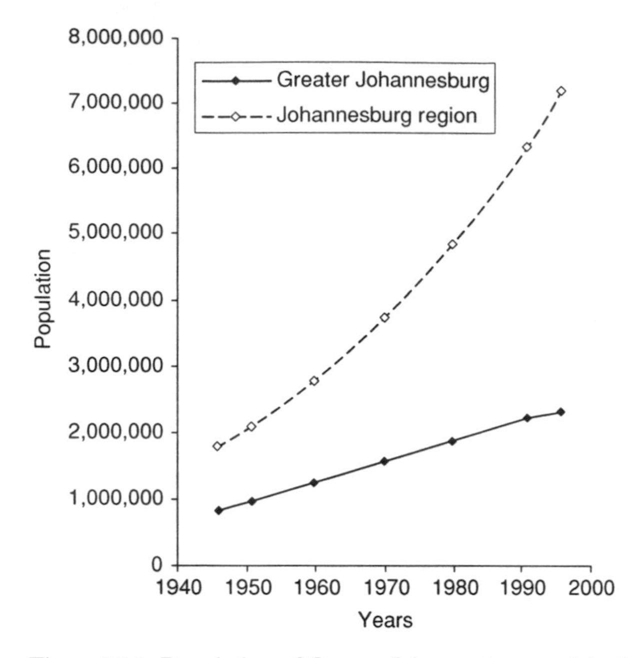

Figure 12.1 Population of Greater Johannesburg and the Johannesburg region, 1946–1996

The estimates for the Greater Johannesburg Metropolitan Council are the sum of the estimates for the magisterial districts of Johannesburg, Randburg, and Roodepoort.

Population trends

In 1996, the urban population of the Johannesburg region was about 7.3 million, which is one third of the national urban population of 21.8 million. The annual growth rate of the population of the Greater Johannesburg Metropolitan Council has declined from 3.2% between 1946 and 1951 to 0.7% between 1991 and 1996. By comparison, the population of the Johannesburg region as a whole has shown a higher and more enduring rate of growth. The annual population growth rate of the Johannesburg region grew from 4.0% between 1946 and 1951 to 6.0% between 1960 and 1970. Thereafter, the population growth rate declined, falling to a rate of 2.8% per annum between 1991 and 1996 (Figure 12.1). The main reason for these divergent trends is that the boundaries of the Greater Johannesburg Metropolitan Council are hemmed in by other urban settlements, except in the southwest. Consequently, whereas

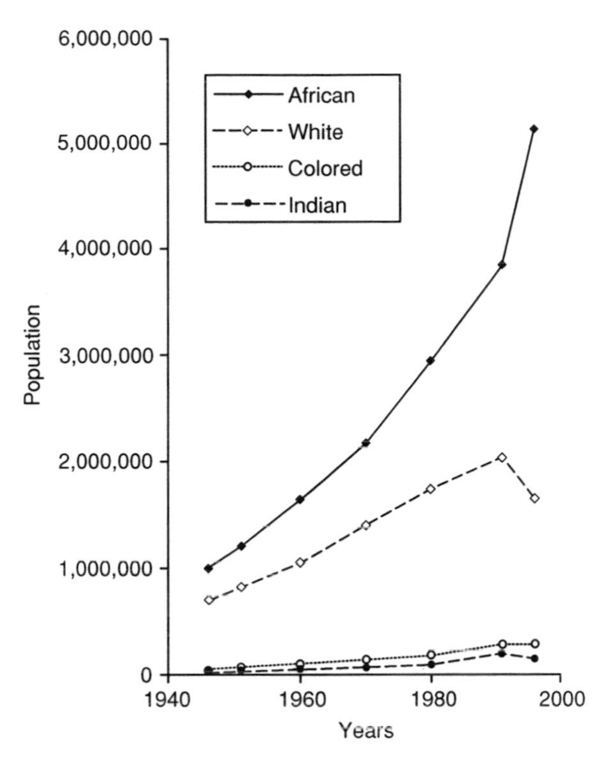

Figure 12.2 Urban population of the Johannesburg region by race, 1946–1996

Johannesburg has almost reached the geographical limits of its expansion, the surrounding regions of the East and West Rand, Pretoria, and the Vaal Triangle have continued to expand outwards.

The racial composition of the Johannesburg region has undergone a radical transformation over the past four decades. When the National Party ushered in the apartheid period in 1948, about 40% of the population of the Johannesburg region were white and most of the remainder was African. Coloreds and Indians together made up less than 4% of the population. Since then, in spite of apartheid policies to achieve quite the opposite, the African population has grown steadily in both relative and absolute terms. By 1996 the proportion of white residents had dropped to one fifth of the population (Fig.12.2). Correspondingly, the African population grew steadily so that by 1996, African residents made up 71% of the population. The population of coloreds and Indians increased, but still remained relatively insignificant in 1996, contributing only 4% and 2%, respectively, to the total population of the Johannesburg region. The primate metropolis of South Africa has therefore undergone a demographic transition that has mirrored the political transition to black majority rule.

The population data represented in Figure 12.2 exaggerate the rate of increase of the African population since 1991. This is because the official Population Censuses for 1980 and 1991 excluded settlements such as Mabopane, Ga-Rankuwa, Winterveld, and Babalegi that lie to the north and northwest of Pretoria. These areas fell within the boundaries of the Bophuthatswana "homeland" and, in keeping with the policy that granted this territory "independence" from South Africa, the apartheid government excluded these areas from its Population Censuses for those years (Smith 1982). However, since townships such as Mabopane and Ga-Rankuwa were officially established in the early 1970s, their populations grew steadily as a result of both forced relocation from Pretoria and from urbanization that was displaced by influx control to the Bophuthatswana homeland (Hattingh and Horn 1991). The inclusion of the populations of these settlements in the latest census more accurately reflects the *de facto* integration of these populations as long-range commuters in the Johannesburg regional economy (Pirie 1992).

These trends in the racial composition of the population show that Africans comprise the vast majority of Johannesburg's residents. Moreover, according to these trends, the proportion of Africans in the population will increase even further. For the purposes of this study, this means that it is the social characteristics of the African population that will drive the social characteristics of Johannesburg's population in the future. Specifically, as non-Africans become a smaller and smaller proportion of Johannesburg's population, so the contribution of inter-racial inequality to overall inequality will decline. Conversely, as Africans increasingly predominate in the population, so intra-racial inequality among Africans will increasingly contribute to overall inequality. The following section of this chapter therefore turns to an analysis of employment trends in the Johannesburg region with a view to understanding how these trends have shaped inequality amongst the African population.

Trends in employment by economic sector

Although the community, social, and personal services sector remained the single largest employer for most of the apartheid period, there have been substantial employment shifts in other sectors. Before the 1960s, the mining sector was the single largest employer of labor. However, as the gold ore in the Witwatersrand mines was steadily worked out, mining

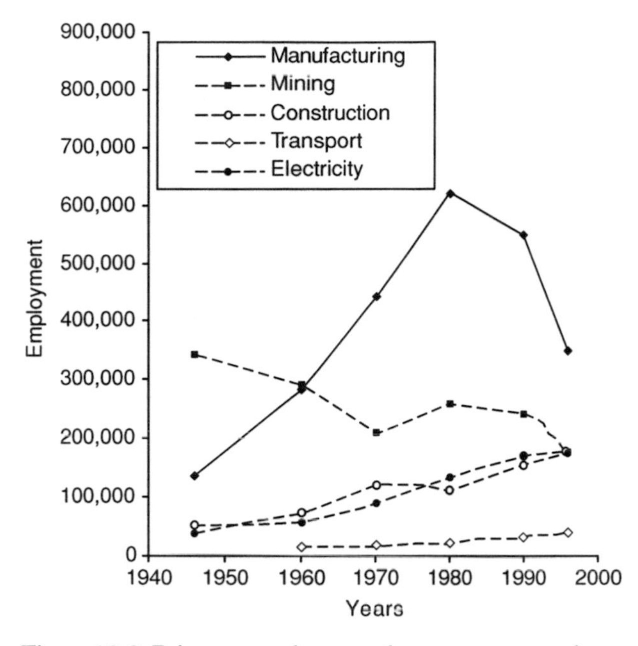

Figure 12.3 Primary and secondary sector employment in the Johannesburg region, 1946–1996

employment moved out of the Johannesburg region to the new gold fields being opened up in the Orange Free State. The sudden increase in mining employment between 1970 and 1980 was due to the development of new mines on the West Rand (Figure 12.3). The manufacturing sector, which started out as a service industry to the gold mines, grew steadily so that by the 1960s it had become the largest sector after the community, social, and personal services sector. Manufacturing employment grew steeply during the boom years of the 1960s and early 1970s. However, with the onset of a long-term phase of lower output growth, manufacturing employment went into sharp decline thereafter. Although employment in the smaller industrial sectors of (i) construction, (ii) electricity, gas, and water, and (iii) transport and communication grew at a much slower rate during the 1960s and 1970s, it did not follow the decline of manufacturing employment after 1970. Instead, employment in these sectors, apart from a temporary drop in employment in the construction sector, continued to grow, albeit at a relatively slow rate.

In contrast to employment trends in the manufacturing and mining sectors, employment in the tertiary sector continued to grow between 1980 and 1991 (Figure 12.4). Only after 1991 was there a sharp downward

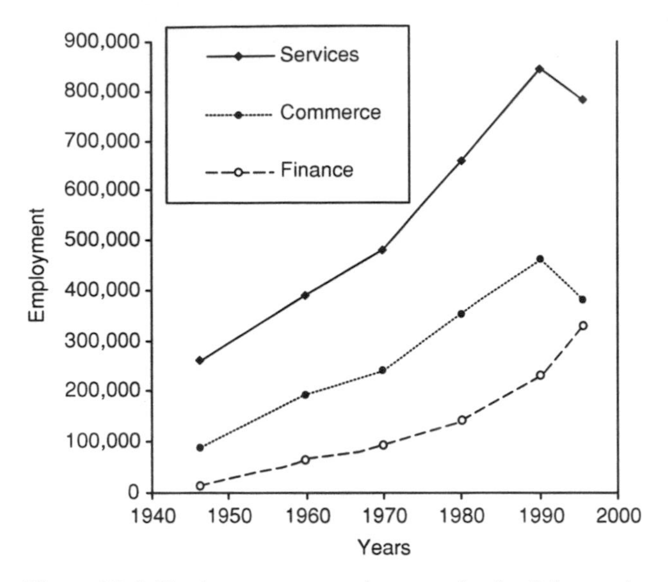

Figure 12.4 Tertiary sector employment in the Johannesburg region, 1946–1996

employment trend in the community, personal, and social services sector and the commercial sector. However, the financial sector continued to grow, employment increasing even more rapidly between 1991 and 1996.

What are the likely causes of this precipitous decline of the manufacturing sector? There is some agreement among scholars that South Africa's manufacturing sector did not achieve its potential growth. In other words, output has been less than what would have been expected, given the available resources for economic growth (Joffe *et al.* 1995, p. 12; Moll 1991, p. 289). This weak economic performance has, at least in part, been attributed to poor macro-economic management, on the one hand, and inappropriate domestic policies on the other. Specifically, the expansion of the manufacturing sector under the policy of import substitution during the 1960s and 1970s was constrained by the lack of foreign exchange. This problem was not remedied by the switch to an export-led policy of industrialization in late 1970s because of high interest rates that made loans prohibitively expensive. As far as domestic policies were concerned, there were at least two important policies that restricted manufacturing growth in Johannesburg. These were the industrial decentralization policy and education policy, both of which aimed to curb African urbanization. The former policy forced manufacturers either to cut back on African labor or to relocate to remote decentralization districts. Education policy was to limit African urbanization by restricting the provision of secondary education in Johannesburg. This obviously had the effect of exacerbating an already chronic shortage of skills.[5]

These sectoral employment trends for the Johannesburg region suggest that the urban labor market has undergone a major structural shift. The only common feature of the early and late apartheid periods was the consistently high level of employment in the community, social, and personal services sector. In all other respects, there have been dramatic changes in the sectoral composition of employment. The early apartheid period was characterized by relatively high levels of demand for unskilled and semi-skilled labor in the mining and manufacturing sectors. The late apartheid period, by contrast, was characterized by the increased demand for skilled white-collar and professional employment in the commercial and financial sectors. Specifically, in 1970, manufacturing employment accounted for 25% of all employment, whereas the commercial and financial sectors accounted for 13% and 5%, respectively. By 1996, employment levels in the manufacturing, commercial, and finance sectors had almost converged. Whereas the percentage of the workforce employed in the manufacturing sector had dropped to only 14%, the percentages for the commercial and financial sectors had increased to 15% and 13%, respectively.

The 1996 Population Census provides us with useful data for testing our hypothesis because it recorded the economic sector of each employed resident. The theory that social polarization of cities is due to economic change associated with the shift from manufacturing employment to employment in the tertiary sector hinges upon the argument that income and skill distributions are more polarized in the service sector than in the manufacturing sector (Sassen 1994). We have tested this theory by comparing the occupational profiles of employers in the mining, manufacturing, and service sector. We have broken down service sector employment into three categories. The first category is what is often classified as "commerce." This sector includes (i) all wholesale and retail trade, (ii) the repair of motor vehicles, motor cycles, and personal and household goods, and (iii) the hotel and restaurant trade (*Standard Industrial Classification* 1993). The second category is "Community, social, and personal services." The most important areas of employment within this category are (i) government administration, (ii) the defence force, (iii) public and private educational services, (iv) public and private health services, and (v) personal services (particularly domestic service). The third category is "Financial intermediation, insurance, real estate, and Business Services."

[5] For a more detailed review of this question, see Beall *et al.* 2002.

Table 12.1 *Distribution of employment in major occupational groups by sector in the Johannesburg region, 1996*

	Mining and quarrying	Manufacturing	Commerce (wholesale and retail trade)	Financial, insurance, real estate, and business services	Community, social, and personal services
Legislators, senior officials, and managers	2%	6%	11%†	8%	2%
Professionals	5%	5%	2%	17%†	21%†
Technicians and associated professionals	3%	7%	7%	17%†	7%
Clerks	3%	8%	14%†	26%†	7%
Service workers, shop, and market sales workers	3%	4%	28%†	18%†	11%†
Craft and related trades workers	49%*	36%*	17%†	4%	2%
Plant and machine operators and assemblers	22%*	20%*	5%	3%	2%
Elementary occupations	13%*	12%*	16%	6%	44%
Total	100%	100%	100%	100%	100%

* Important shrinking occupations
† Important expanding occupations
Source: Calculated from the community-profile database of the 1996 Population Census provided by Statistics South Africa, Pretoria.

Occupational profiles prepared from the 1996 Population Census suggest that these service sectors are associated with greater skill polarization. Table 12.1 shows that the tertiary sectors employ somewhat higher proportions of managers, professionals, and technicians/semi-professionals than the manufacturing and mining sectors. Similarly, the tertiary sectors employ a relatively higher proportion of "elementary" or unskilled workers than the manufacturing and mining sectors. Specifically, the managerial, professional, and technical occupations account for 20% of all employment in the commerce sector, 42% in the finance sector, and 30% in the community, social, and personal service sector. These percentages are substantially higher than the 10% and 18% for the mining and manufacturing sectors, respectively (Table 12.1). The same can be said for the category of "elementary" or unskilled occupations. Unskilled employment accounts for 44% of jobs in the community, social, and personal service sector and 16% of jobs in the commerce sector. This is somewhat higher than the 13% and 12% for the mining and manufacturing sectors, respectively. The only tertiary subsector that does not follow the pattern is finance, which has a very low percentage (6%) of unskilled employment (Table 12.1).

This structural shift in the demand for employment has been an important cause of rising inequality among the urban African population. We argue that the urban labor market of the pre- and early apartheid period needed a relatively high proportion of unskilled manual labor. This period therefore offered employment opportunities for poorly educated rural migrants, many of whom used this opportunity to urbanize permanently. However, the late apartheid period saw the decline in the demand for unskilled labor and even semi-skilled manual work and the relative rise in demand for white-collar employment. This meant that during the 1980s and 1990s, educated Africans who had urbanized during the early apartheid period were relatively well placed to secure employment in these more skilled jobs. By contrast, poorly educated rural migrants, who were qualified for only unskilled work, were much more likely to face unemployment. In other words, much greater levels of social polarization are evident in the later period. This argument is elaborated in the following sections.

African differentiation in the urban labor market[6]

Throughout its history, the gold mining industry on the Witwatersrand has relied primarily upon the cheap labor of rural migrants. The relatively

[6] This section draws upon Crankshaw 1997.

small number of skilled jobs were occupied by whites who, through their trade unions and with government support, jealously guarded their wages and jobs against undercutting by unskilled African labor. Employment opportunities for African workers were therefore numerous, but restricted to unskilled and semi-skilled manual jobs. Consequently, Africans who worked in the mining industry were poorly educated rural migrants who had few other opportunities for urban employment. The manufacturing industry was not much different. White workers, usually from urban backgrounds and with higher levels of education, were in a better position than Africans to secure the top-end of semi-skilled factory jobs. The skilled trades were also dominated by white workers who excluded Africans from apprenticeships and employment in the skilled trades. When the jobs of white workers were threatened by undercutting from cheaper African labor, they were usually successful in lobbying the government to reserve certain occupations for white employment only. So, in a similar fashion to the mining industry, African employment in the manufacturing sector was restricted to unskilled and lower-paid levels of semi-skilled work which was attractive to poorly educated rural migrants.

We know very little about the urbanization careers of these African workers subsequent to their arrival in Johannesburg. However, we do know that the African population of Johannesburg grew steadily as a result of the demand for their labor in the mines and factories. By the 1940s, this led to a housing crisis and squatter movements sprang up all over the Witwatersrand (Bonner 1990). The response of the government was to provide low-cost public housing for Africans on an unprecedented scale during the 1950s and early 1960s. Although the provision of this housing went hand in hand with forced removals, tight controls over the urbanization of Africans and the racial segregation of Johannesburg's residential areas, it nonetheless granted permanent urban status to a large number of African families. In the subsequent decades of the 1960s and 1970s, government policies and laws continued to draw a deep division between Africans with urban rights and those without them (Hindson 1987). Africans who were not born within the urban boundaries of the Johannesburg region could not qualify for permanent urban residence. These rural-born migrants who were employed in the Johannesburg region were granted only temporary urban rights and were forced to live in hostels while their families continued to live at their rural home. By contrast, Africans with urban rights were free to live and work in the Johannesburg region, although only in prescribed areas and jobs. The overall impact of these policies was to reinforce and perpetuate the division between urbanized and migrant Africans.

During the 1960s and 1970s, the Johannesburg region experienced sustained and rapid growth in employment. This led to a chronic shortage of white labor, first in the skilled manual trades and then later in white-collar occupations. Employers responded to this shortage by calling for the fragmentation of the skilled trades and for the employment of African labor in these fragmented semi-skilled tasks, which were the preserve of skilled white artisans. This entailed confronting white trade unions and lobbying the government to reform both its employment and educational policy towards urban Africans. During the late 1960s and early 1970s, a set of compromises between business, white unions, and the government were struck. The essence of these agreements, across a variety of sectors, was that Africans could be advanced into semi-skilled, supervisory, and white-collar jobs on the condition that it did not adversely affect the employment conditions of white workers. This period of accelerated growth in output therefore saw the expansion of semi-skilled machine operative employment, which entailed precisely those jobs which had been opened up for African employment. However, not all Africans benefited equally from this growth in semi-skilled employment. Since employers were increasingly obliged to train African workers for these more skilled jobs, they began to switch from a low-wage, low-skill employment strategy to a high-wage, high-skill strategy. By increasing wages, employers aimed both to attract and to retain better-educated labor. Since migrant workers were both less educated and had a higher turnover, employers began to prefer urbanized African workers (Crankshaw 1997, pp. 110–12). So, whereas up until the 1950s, manufacturers usually preferred to employ migrant workers because they were cheaper, by the end of the 1960s, these same employers were turning to urbanized African workers instead (Posel 1991, p. 169).

Somewhat later, shortages of white labor began to manifest themselves in the tertiary sector. These sectors were poorly unionized and white workers showed little inclination to resist the employment of Africans in routine clerical and sales work. Under pressure from business, state educational policy was reformed to increase the supply of educated African labor in urban areas. Consequently, businesses began to employ Africans in white-collar and semi-professional occupations from the late 1960s. The beneficiaries of these reforms were mostly urban Africans who were educated in the new urban high schools that were established from the early 1970s.

However, if opportunities for upward occupational mobility were improving for educated Africans, the reverse was true for those whose education had not prepared them for anything but unskilled manual work.

The growing preference of employers for more capital-intensive methods of production and the employment of semi-skilled African machine operatives resulted in the steady decline in the demand for unskilled manual labor. The falling demand for unskilled workers coincided with growing unemployment levels. The relatively low rate of employment growth from the mid-1970s did not keep up with the population growth rate and the discrepancy in these growth rates has been the major cause of rising unemployment in South Africa since the end of the 1960s (Bell and Padayachee 1984).

So, the late apartheid period was characterized by the occupational differentiation of the urban African population. On the one hand, reforms to apartheid policy opened up more skilled and professional work for educated and urbanized Africans in the secondary and tertiary sectors. On the other hand, employment opportunities for unskilled African workers, who were usually rural migrants, declined.

There is some quantitative evidence to support our argument concerning the causes of increasing differentiation within the African population of Johannesburg. This evidence is based on the results of a household survey of Soweto, the largest African township in the Johannesburg region.[7] These results are based on interviews with a senior adult in the household, who was usually the major breadwinner. The interviewers recorded the respondents' place of birth and when they were born. If the respondent was not born in Greater Johannesburg, the interviewer recorded the year in which s/he first moved there. The interviewers also recorded the respondents' employment status and occupation. We then categorized the respondents into four groups according to where they were born and when they entered the urban labor market. We chose 1980 as the cut-off point because this was the Census year that marked the beginning of employment decline in the manufacturing industry. So, respondents who were born outside the Johannesburg region were divided into two groups: those who arrived in the region before 1980 and those who arrived in 1980 or later. For respondents who were born in the Johannesburg region, we assumed that they entered the labor market at the age of twenty and

[7] The questionnaire and sample were designed by Owen Crankshaw in consultation with other members of the Soweto in Transition Committee, Sociology Department, University of the Witwatersrand. The logistical aspects of the fieldwork were managed by Progressus cc. and the quality of the interviews and the sample was monitored in the field by Owen Crankshaw. The authors are grateful to the members of the Soweto in Transition Committee (Sociology Department, University of the Witwatersrand) for their permission to use the results of the Soweto Household Survey. We also acknowledge the financial contributions made to the Soweto Household Survey by the Johannesburg Metropolitan Council, the Anglo American Chairman's Fund and the Human Sciences Research Council.

divided them into those who were born before 1960 and those who were born in 1960 and later. Controlling for place of birth, our aim was to compare the employment status and occupation of respondents who entered the labor market before 1980 with those who had entered the labor market during and after 1980.

The results of this analysis show that there is a distinct difference in the employment status of residents who were either born in the region or who urbanized before 1980, on the one hand, and those who urbanized after 1980. Whereas the former have an unemployment rate of about 25%, the latter have an unemployment rate of 30% (Table 12.2). In other words, respondents who were born in the Johannesburg region had the same unemployment rate, regardless of when they entered the labor market. By contrast, there was quite a distinct difference among rural-born respondents in the proportion of unemployed respondents who entered the labor market before and since 1980. Whereas 22% of the rural-born respondents who urbanized before 1980 were unemployed, the percentage of rural-born respondents who urbanized since 1980 was significantly higher at 30% (Table 12.2).[8]

Similarly, there is some evidence to show that Sowetan adults who were born in the Johannesburg region or who urbanized there before 1980 were more likely to establish themselves in clerical and sales jobs or semi-professional, professional, and managerial careers than their fellow residents who urbanized from 1980 onwards. The percentage of respondents employed in these white-collar occupations who were either born in the Johannesburg region or arrived there before 1980 was almost twice that of those who urbanized from 1980 onwards (Table 12.3). Specifically, the percentage of respondents employed in these white-collar jobs who were born in the Johannesburg region was 33% (born before 1960) and 36% (born after 1960). Those respondents who urbanized before 1980 were somewhat less successful in securing white-collar employment, with a percentage of 26%. Respondents who urbanized after 1980 were even less successful, with only 18% of them employed in such white-collar jobs. So, these findings suggest that more recent newcomers to the Johannesburg region have been less successful at securing white-collar employment than established urbanites and those who arrived before 1980.

On the face of it, these results do not support our hypothesis as strongly as we expected them to. One reason for this may be that Soweto is atypical of African townships in the Johannesburg region. It is generally understood to have a population that is relatively better off than most other

[8] The sample sizes for these estimates are large enough to ensure confidence intervals of not more than 5% at a probability level of 95%.

Table 12.2 *Distribution of employment status of Sowetans by year of birth or arrival in the Johannesburg region, 1997*

	Born in the Johannesburg region		Born outside the Johannesburg region	
	Born before 1960	Born in 1960 or later	Arrived before 1980	Arrived in 1980 or later
Employed full time	63%	60%	65%	56%
Employed part time	5%	6%	4%	9%
Self-employed	6%	10%	10%	5%
Unemployed	25%	24%	21%	30%
Total	100%	100%	100%	100%
Sample size	955	380	652	451
Correlation coefficient (Cramer's V)		0.34		0.49

Sources: The results presented in this table are based on a household survey of the African townships of Greater Soweto which was conducted during February 1997. Altogether, 2,947 interviews were conducted, using a stratified cluster sample. The respondent in each household was a senior adult, usually a major breadwinner. For a detailed discussion of the sampling method, refer to Morris *et al.* 1999.

Table 12.3 *Distribution of the occupations of employed Sowetans by year of birth or arrival in the Johannesburg region, 1997*

	Born in the Johannesburg region		Born outside the Johannesburg region	
	Born before 1960	Born in 1960 or later	Arrived before 1980	Arrived in 1980 or later
Never employed	4%	5%	3%	5%
Unskilled manual workers	30%	14%	36%	25%
Semi-skilled manual workers	30%	42%	30%	39%
Routine security workers	2%	2%	4%	11%
Clerical or sales workers	17%	25%	14%	13%
Professionals, semi-professionals and managers	16%	11%	12%	5%
Other	1%	2%	1%	2%
Total	100%	100%	100%	100%
Sample size	955	380	652	451

Source: See Table 12.2.

townships, including the formal townships of the East Rand (Seekings n.d.). If survey results of Alexandra (a poorer township to the north of Johannesburg), Orange farm (a new informal settlement), or Winterveld (a sprawling homeland settlement near Pretoria) were considered, the differences in unemployment rates between urbanites and recent migrants are likely to be greater. Unfortunately, there are no appropriate survey data for these areas.

Conclusion

In this chapter, we have made an attempt to identify and measure the relationship between urbanization and inequality in the Johannesburg region. Our starting point is the finding that inequality in South Africa is increasingly being driven by causes that are intra-racial in character rather than inter-racial. We have explored the hypothesis that there is an important division between urbanized Africans on the one hand, and rural migrants or recently urbanized, rural-born Africans, on the other. Our inspiration for this hypothesis comes from the literature on social polarization, which identifies a relationship between deindustrialization and rising inequality among new arrivals in major urban centers.

We have tested this hypothesis by examining changing urbanization policy and employment trends during the apartheid period. Our findings show that the Johannesburg region has experienced a dramatic decline in manufacturing employment since the late 1970s. Over the same period, there has been an increase in service sector employment. In conjunction with the probable effects of apartheid policies on African urbanization, education, and employment, these overall employment trends have, at least in part, contributed towards growing inequality between established urban Africans, on the one hand, and rural-born migrants, on the other. This finding therefore suggests that income inequality in Johannesburg is being shaped to some extent by deindustrialization and its associated pattern of social polarization.

REFERENCES

Beall, J., Crankshaw, O., and Parnell, S. 2002. *Uniting a Divided City: Governance and Social Exclusion in Johannesburg*. London: Earthscan.

2000. "The Genesis of Urban Poverty in Post-Apartheid Johannesburg," *Tijdscrift voor Economishe en Sociale Geografie*, 91 (4): 379–396.

Beavon, K. 1997. "Johannesburg," in C. Rakodi (ed.), *The Urban Challenge in Africa: Growth and Management of its Large Cities*. Tokyo: United Nations Press, pp. 150–191.

Bell, T. and Padayachee, V. 1984. "Unemployment in South Africa: Trends, Causes and Cures," *Development Southern Africa*, 1 (3 and 4): 426–438.

Bhorat, H., Leibbrandt, M., Maziya, M., van der Berg, S., and Woolard, I. 2001. *Fighting Poverty: Labour Markets and Inequality in South Africa*. Cape Town: University of Cape Town Press.

Bonner, P. 1990. "The Politics of Black Squatter Movements on the Rand, 1944–1952," *Radical History Review*, 46/47: 889–916.

Crankshaw, O. 1997. *Race, Class and the Changing Division of Labour under Apartheid*. London: Routledge.

Fainstein, S., Gordon, I., and Harloe, M. (eds.) 1992. *Divided Cities: New York and London in the Contemporary World*. Oxford: Blackwell.

Friedman, J. 1995. "The World City Hypothesis," in P. Knox and P. Taylor (eds.), *World Cities in a World System*. Cambridge: Cambridge University Press, pp. 317–331.

Gelb, S. 1991. *South Africa's Economic Crisis*. Cape Town: David Philip.

Goty, G. and Simone, A. 2002. "On Becoming and Belonging in African Cities," in R. Tomlinson, B. Beauregard, L. Bremner, and X. Mangcu (eds.), *Emerging Johannesburg: Perspectives on the Post-Apartheid City*. London: Routledge, pp. 123–147.

Hattingh, P. and Horn, A. 1991. "Pretoria," in A. Lemon (ed.), *Homes Apart: South Africa's Segregated Cities*. London: Paul Chapman, pp. 146–161.

Hindson, D. 1987. *Pass Controls and the Urban African Proletariat*. Johannesburg: Ravan Press.

Joffe, A., Kaplan, D., Kaplinsky, R., and Lewis, D. 1995. *Improving Manufacturing Performance in South Africa: Report of the Industrial Strategy Project*. Cape Town: University of Cape Town Press.

Lemon, A. (ed.) 1991. *Homes Apart: South Africa's Segregated Cities*. London: Paul Chapman.

Moll, T. 1991. "Did the Apartheid Economy Fail?," *Journal of Southern African Studies*, 17 (2): 271–291.

Mollenkopf, J. and Castells, M. (eds.) 1991. *Dual City: Restructuring New York*. New York: Russell Sage Foundation.

Morris, A. 1999. *Bleakness and Light*. Johannesburg: Witwatersrand University Press.

Morris, A., Bozzoli, B., Cock, J., Crankshaw, O., Gilbert, L., Lehutso-Phooko, L., Posel, D., Tshandu, Z., and van Huysteen, E. (eds.) 1999. "Change and Continuity: A Survey of Soweto in the Late 1990s," Department of Sociology, University of the Witwatersrand.

National Geographic 1999. June (Culture Pullout Chart).

Nattrass, N. and Seekings, J. 2001. "'Two Nations': Race and Economic Inequality in South Africa Today," *Daedalus*, 130 (1): 45–70.

O'Loughlin, J. and Friedrichs, J. (eds.) 1996. *Social Polarization in Post-Industrial Metropolises*. New York: Walter de Gruyter.

Ortiz, V. 1996. "The Mexican-Origin Population: Permanent Working Class or Emerging Middle Class?," in R. Waldinger and M. Bozorgmehr (eds.), *Ethnic Los Angeles*. New York: Russell Sage Foundation, pp. 274–277.

Parnell, S. 1991. "Sanitation, Segregation and the Natives (Urban Areas) Act: African Exclusion from Johannesburg's Malay Location," *Journal of Historical Geography*, 17: 171–188.

Parnell, S. and Pirie, G. 1991. "Johannesburg," in A. Lemon (ed.), *Homes Apart: South Africa's Segregated Cities*. London: Paul Chapman, pp. 129–145.

Pirie, G. 1992. "Travelling under Apartheid," in D. Smith (ed.), *The Apartheid City and Beyond: Urbanisation and Social Change in South Africa*. London: Routledge, pp. 172–181.

Posel, D. 1991. *The Making of Apartheid, 1948–1961: Conflict and Compromise*. Oxford: Clarendon Press.

Rogerson, C. 1984. "The Spatial Concentration of Corporate Control in South Africa," *South African Geographical Journal*, 66: 97–100.

1995. "South Africa's Economic Heartland: Crisis, Decline or Economic Restructuring?," *Africa Insight*, 25: 241–247.

Sassen, S. 1994. *Cities in the World Economy*. Thousand Oaks: Pine Forge Press.

Seekings, J. (n.d.). "Why Was Soweto Different? Urban Development, Township Politics, and the Political Economy of Soweto, 1978–1984," unpublished paper.

Seekings, J. and Nattrass, N. forthcoming. *From Race to Class: Inequality, Unemployment and the Social Structure in South Africa*. New Haven: Yale University Press.

Simon, D. 1995. "World City Hypothesis: Reflections from the Periphery," in P. Knox, and P. Taylor (eds.), *World Cities in a World System*. Cambridge: Cambridge University Press, pp. 132–155.

Smith, D. 1982. "Urbanization and Social Change under Apartheid: Some Recent Developments," in D. Smith (ed.), *Living under Apartheid: Aspects of Urbanization and Social Change in South Africa*. London: George Allen and Unwin, pp. 38–44.

South African Migration Project. *Migration Policy Series*. Cape Town: Idasa.

Standard Industrial Classification 1993. *Standard Industrial Classification of all Economic Activities (5th Ed.), Report 09-90-02*. Pretoria: Central Statistical Service.

United Nations Development Programme 1999. *Human Development Report 1999*. Oxford: Oxford University Press.

Waldinger, R. and Bozorgmehr, M. (eds.) 1996. *Ethnic Los Angeles*. New York: Russell Sage Foundation.

Whiteford, A. and McGrath, M. 1994. *Distribution of Income in South Africa*. Pretoria: Human Sciences Research Council.

Whiteford, A., Posel, D., and Kelatwang, T. 1995. *A Profile of Poverty, Inequality and Human Development in South Africa*. Pretoria: Human Sciences Research Council.

Wilson, W. 1987. *The Truly Disadvantaged: The Inner City, the Underclass and Public Policy*. Chicago: University of Chicago Press.

Afterword

Saskia Sassen

Cities around the world are the terrain where multiple global processes assume concrete and localized forms. These localized forms are, in good part, what globalization is about. Incorporating cities in analyses of globalization means recovering this multiplicity of presences and dynamics in the urban landscape. But herein also lies one of the theoretical and methodological challenges for the new field of research on cities and globalization. It is intrinsic to major cities to have enormous visual, organizational, and historic specificity. The global will inevitably be a partial condition in such cities, unlike for instance, what it might be in an export-processing zone, and it will be inflected by the specificities of each city. Methodologically we confront the problem of detecting the global under conditions of enormous variability across cities and specificity inside cities. Theoretically, we confront the challenge of interpreting an attribute that is systemic at a global scale yet assumes specific forms and meanings in each city.

This volume adds to this large and challenging enterprise by introducing a perspective on major cities in the global south, and their specificities. This is an enormously important step in a field dominated by studies of cities in the global north. Through its distinctive focus this volume contributes to de-center the production of knowledge about globalization and cities. It shows us the enormous variability among these cities, but also that there are certain shared patterns beneath these sharp differences. Most notable perhaps are the massive but highly selective investments for redevelopment and the growing numbers of high-income professional workers and low-income service workers. This in turn has contributed to new types, or to sharpen old types, of socio-spatial inequality evident in all these cities, even when this inequality has been constituted through a great diversity of mechanisms and processes.

But at the heart of each chapter in this volume is a concern with the particulars of one city, and, further, with one distinct issue, which allows for an in-depth inquiry into each city. The concern in these chapters is not with drawing comparisons or generalizing across cities. This task fell to

Josef Gugler who has done this admirably in his introduction. I have been asked to add to the analytics of the effort, to situate the contributions of these scholars in a broader empirical and theoretical landscape. A brief afterword can contribute only a few elements to this effort.

Understanding the analytic effort represented by this collection of chapters requires navigating among three framing conditions. One of these is the rich and important empirical information contained in each of these chapters; the second is the particular conceptual orientation of each of these chapters; and the third is a broader analytic architecture that must inevitably sacrifice much of the detail even as it situates the specific contribution of each chapter in this broader analytic frame. It entails examining also processes that precede or condition some of the issues discussed in these chapters, as well as their outcomes or significance beyond a single-city perspective. This is a task that would ideally be a whole book in itself. In this afterword I will have to confine myself to only a few of the many issues addressed in these chapters.

In what follows, then, I discuss some of the key contributions these chapters make to various analytic and methodological efforts in the broader field of research on cities and globalization. My concern is not to describe the key findings as much as to advance the analytic project, a task I am better prepared for than an in-depth discussion of these cities which I am not sufficiently familiar with and whose long histories and complexity are daunting to an outsider. I will select three particular angles from which to do this. The first concerns the question of whether these are world cities. The second one focuses on the meaning of the vast investments in urban redevelopment and the consequent inequalities evident in all these cities. The third one examines the meaning of politico-cultural processes and actors in global cities.

Distinguishing world and global cities

A first question one might ask is whether these are indeed world cities, a question warranted by the fact that many of the chapters do not quite focus on the articulations of these cities with world processes in the past or today.

Several of these cities have histories that cover many centuries and have been at the center of major historical processes, most notably Cairo and its multimillennial history, but also Shanghai, Bombay, and Moscow. In this regard we can immediately recognize that they are world cities in the general sense of that term. But others are more difficult to think of as world cities, notably São Paulo, Mexico, Jakarta, and Johannesburg, and perhaps even Hong Kong given a somewhat narrowly defined and highly functional type of role in past world processes. Yet we also know that today each one of the cities covered in this volume is articulated with major global economic circuits. Might these be global cities without being in all cases world cities?

There are today several closely linked terms used to capture a particular intersection between global processes and cities. (For overviews see Paddison 2001: ch.1; Savitch 1996; and Stren 1996.) The most common is world cities, a term attributed to Goethe and then relaunched in the work of Peter Hall (1966) and more recently respecified by John Friedmann (Friedmann and Wolff 1982). Other, related terms are "superville" (Braudel 1984) and informational city (Castells 1989). If we historicize the world economy and specify what is distinct today, we need to differentiate an older literature focused on past world cities (Braudel 1984), as well as more recent work on urban hierarchies in the world system (Chase Dunn 1985).

Choosing how to name a configuration has its own substantive rationality. The decision to formulate the term "global city" (Sassen 1984) stemmed out of a recognition of the specificity of the current period. The term world city has precisely the opposite attribute: it refers to a type of city which we have seen over the centuries (Braudel 1984; Hall 1966; King 1990), and most probably also in much earlier periods in Asia than in the West (Abu-Lughod 1989; Patel and Thorner 1995). In this regard it could be said that most of today's major global cities are also world cities, but that there may well be some global cities that are not world cities in the full, rich sense of that term. This is partly an empirical question; further, as the global economy expands and incorporates additional cities into various cross-border networks, it is quite possible that the answer to that particular question will vary over time. Thus the fact that Miami has developed global city functions beginning in the late 1980s does not make it a world city in that older sense of the term (Nijman 1996). (See generally Sachar 1990; Scott 2001; Short and Kim 1999.)

In the current literature on global cities the determining factor is a cross-border, global network of cities that function as strategic sites for the management and specialized servicing of global economic operations. There is no such entity as a single global city, as there was with the capital of earlier empires. By definition, the global city is part of a network of cities. There is enormous hierarchy in the worldwide network of global cities, but there is also an increasingly complex interdependence, perhaps most clearly evident at this time in economic processes, particularly global finance. This network also facilitates the emergence of other forms of interdependence and other types of circulation in a very broad range of domains, such as cross-border policy regimes, illegal trafficking in people, and international art festivals.

Notwithstanding their sharp differences, each of the cities covered in this volume is articulated with multiple global economic, political, cultural, and civic circuits. When it comes to economic circuits, each of these cities has the density of resources and the levels of specialization necessary to operate in such circuits. Hong Kong, Singapore, Seoul, Bangkok, Mexico, Bombay, São Paulo, and Johannesburg are by now well-established financial centers, deeply articulated with global capital markets. Moscow, Shanghai, and Jakarta are each, in their particular way, becoming established, with Shanghai recognized by late 2001 as having one of the fastest-growing stock market valuations in the world. Finally, Cairo is moving slowly towards becoming integrated into what is emerging as a potentially very dynamic Middle Eastern/Persian Gulf region in the global economy.[1] While much of the effort in this book is centered on emphasizing the distinctiveness of each city, I would argue – taking the liberty of an analytic optic – that each chapter captures particular outcomes of that city's articulation with global circuits. This is so even when the authors do not focus on these circuits or even recognize them as such.

Socio-spatial conditionings and consequences

Each of these cities can be seen as reaching a threshold of complexity we could describe as representing global city functions, achieved through a mix of national and foreign investors and corporate services firms, markets, infrastructure, and a supply of highly educated national and foreign professionals. To house these functions each of these cities has launched massive investments in construction and infrastructure, including investments to meet the needs of the new, rapidly growing professional classes that are part of these global city functions. (For a variety of perspectives, see Gugler 1997; Marcuse and van Kempen 2000; Peraldi and Perrin 1996; Santos *et al.* 1994.)

At this point we can reenter these chapters' narratives about the rebuilding, renovation, and expansion of central urban areas, and the presence

[1] This is predicated on a mix of conditions, notably, the reentry of Beirut as a significant regional center, the successful transformation of Dubai from an exclusively oil-exporting country to a powerful regional commercial, financial and tourism center, and, given growing government deficits, the need of the region for its own oil-export profits and hence the need for regional financial capabilities to recirculate these profits (for a more detailed dicussion see Huybrechts 2002; Parsa and Keivani 2002).

in most of these cities of a growing high-income workforce. As patterns they come through in many of these chapters, no matter what the particular focus and regardless of the often very different mechanisms involved. Shanghai (Wu and Yusuf, this volume) is perhaps the most dramatic case with its government-led massive, multiyear construction program. Investments in the center of Moscow (Bater, this volume; see also Bater 1996), in Hong Kong (So, this volume; see also So and Chiu 1997) and in Jakarta (Forbes, this volume; see also Forbes 1996), aimed at strengthening the space for global city functions, have been enormous over the last few years compared with investments in other parts of these cities. Webster's (this volume) examination of investments in Bangkok signals a similar effort. While the chapters on Mexico (Ward, this volume), São Paulo (Alves, this volume), and Bombay (Patel, this volume; see also Patel and Thornton 1995) do not focus on this issue, we know from other evidence that these three cities have similarly made major investments in construction and high-priced rebuilding of central areas over the last few years (see, e.g., Schiffer Ramos 2002; Ward 1998).

The patterns of investment in upgrading and developing central urban areas in the rest of the cities covered in this volume are somewhat different. Singapore (Salaff, this volume) and Seoul (Kim, this volume) stand out for having used very distinct strategies, with the first determined to provide housing and services to all (Salaff 1988), and the second using Olympic Games as an anchoring strategy for urban development. One cannot help but notice, however, that part of the effort in these cities also produced or enhanced the conditions for housing global city functions. Cairo and Johannesburg are perhaps the two cities that have undergone the least, or a more gradual transformation in this regard. Cairo (Abu-Lughod, this volume) began its opening to foreign capital in the 1970s and initiated its renovation and upgrading of key urban areas at the time. Abu-Lughod shows us how these policies resulted in a sharpening of spatial and social inequalities between those segments of the economy and workforce linked to early forms of emergent global city functions and the rest of the city. Given its history of racial domination and apartheid, Johannesburg has long been marked by sharp uneven investment in its built environment and, after apartheid, the development of whole new "central" areas on the outskirts of Johannesburg. While the chapter does not focus explicitly on urban investments privileging the housing of global city functions, Crankshaw and Parnell (this volume) show us that the question of developing global city functions maps on to both the black–white division and, perhaps more significantly for central Johannesburg today, the growing intra-black inequality (see also Crankshaw 1997; Parnell and Mabin 1995).

One might ask, why this particular pattern of urban investments aimed at the housing of global city functions is happening today when there is a global economy dominated by electronic markets and dematerialized finance? This brings up a major issue essential for thinking about cities and globalization. The understandings and the categories that dominate mainstream discussions about the future of the advanced urban economy suggest that the city has become obsolete for leading economic sectors. We need to subject these notions to critical examination and allow for the possibility that there are instances of the global economy that have not been recognized as such. At the same time, it is clear that these new technologies have altered the locational options of firms and households. The next two sections develop these two issues.

Recovering place and work process in the global economy

Many of the resources necessary for global economic activities are not hypermobile and are, indeed, deeply embedded in places, notably places such as global cities, global city regions, and export-processing zones. This entails a whole infrastructure of activities, firms, and jobs, necessary to run the advanced corporate economy.[2] These industries are typically conceptualized in terms of the hypermobility of their outputs and the high levels of expertise of their professionals rather than in terms of the production or work process involved and the requisite infrastructure of facilities and non-expert jobs that are also part of these industries. When we incorporate these material and place-bound dimensions of the global information economy we can also explain the new or accentuated forms of socio-spatial polarization evident in most of the cities described in this volume. There is a disproportionate concentration of very high and very low-income jobs in these cities compared with what is the case at a larger scale such as the region or the country, where many of the effects and components of the global economy might either be absent, more diluted, or exclusive and in that regard monochromatic, as in export-processing zones or export-oriented plantations.

A focus on the actual practices and structures necessary to run, organize, service, and finance the global economy draws the categories of place

[2] To some extent, it is global cities in the highly developed world which most clearly display the processes I discuss, or best lend themselves to the heuristics I deploy. But increasingly these processes are emerging in cities in the global south as well: here they are often submerged under the megacity syndrome. Sheer population size and urban sprawl create their own orders of magnitude; and while they may not much alter the power equation I describe, they do change the weight and the importance of some of these dynamics.

and work process into the analysis of economic globalization. These are two categories easily overlooked in accounts centered on the hypermobility of capital and the power of transnationals. Developing categories such as place and work process does not negate the centrality of hypermobility and power. Rather, emphasizing place, infrastructure, and non-expert jobs matters precisely because so much of the focus has been on the neutralization of geography and place made possible by the new technologies and on the need for high-level professionals. In brief, place is central to the multiple circuits through which economic globalization is constituted. One strategic type of place for these developments is the city.

Cities in this regard are key sites where we can study a broad range of mixes of these various components and maximize our chances of including into the analysis components, notably low-wage service jobs and low-income urban neighborhoods, usually excluded from analyses of the global information economy (e.g., Allen *et al.* 1999; Low 1999; Pozos Ponce 1996; Scott 2001). The global city literature has made a significant contribution to the unpacking of what it is we are actually naming when we use the term global information economy.[3] This volume adds to this literature by focusing on major cities in the global south.

The spatialities of the center

The concept of the city is complex, not very precise, and charged with specific historical meanings. I prefer a more abstract category: centrality. One of the properties that cities have historically provided/produced is centrality. The question is, then, what are the conditions for the continuity of centrality in advanced economic systems in the face of major new technologies that maximize the possibility for geographic dispersal at the regional, national, and, indeed, global scale.[4] Historically, centrality has largely been embedded in cities. One of the changes brought about by

[3] Including cities in the analysis of economic globalization is not without conceptual consequences. Economic globalization has mostly been conceptualized in terms of the duality national–global where the latter gains at the expense of the former. And it has largely been conceptualized in terms of the internationalization of capital and then only the upper circuits of capital. Introducing cities in an analysis of economic globalization allows us to reconceptualize processes of economic globalization as concrete economic complexes situated in specific places. One effect is that it decomposes the nation-state into a variety of subnational components, making clear that some are profoundly articulated with the global economy but others not. It also signals the declining significance of the national economy as a unitary category insofar as it contributes to fragment the "territoriality" of the nation-state (Sassen 2000a).

[4] My concern here is not with matters such as the boundaries of cities or what cities actually are. These are partly empirical questions: each city is going to have a different configuration of boundaries and contents.

the new information technologies is the reconfiguring of centrality: cities are today but one form of centrality. Important emerging spaces for the constitution of centrality range from the new transnational networks of cities to electronic space. (See also for the question of the diversity of urban scales Clark 1996; Peraldi and Perrin 1996; Rutherford 2004; Simmonds and Hack 2000; see papers at GaWC.)

The combination of the new capabilities for mobility along with patterns of concentration and operational features of the cutting-edge sectors of advanced economies suggest that spatial concentration remains as a key feature of these sectors. But it is not simply a continuation of older patterns of spatial concentration. Today there is no longer a simple straightforward relation between centrality and such geographic entities as the downtown, or the central business district (CBD).

The new technologies and organizational forms have altered the spatial correlates of centrality. Thus the center can be the CBD, as it still is largely for some of the leading sectors, notably finance, or an alternative form of CBD, such as Silicon Valley. Yet even as the CBD in major international business centers remains a strategic site for the leading industries, it is one profoundly reconfigured by technological and economic changes. This is the case for several of the cities covered in this volume, notably São Paulo, Bombay, Moscow, Shanghai, Jakarta, and Singapore. Second, the center can extend into a metropolitan area in the form of a grid of nodes of intense business activity. This is the case today for Johannesburg, where finance remains anchored downtown, even as whites have mostly left the center and are developing alternative centers in the outskirts.[5] This is a partly deterritorialized space of centrality.[6]

Third, we are seeing the formation of a transterritorial "center" constituted via intense economic transactions in the network of global cities (see, e.g., Lo and Yeung 1996; Sassen 2000a; Simmonds and Hack 2000).

[5] One might ask whether a spatial organization characterized by dense strategic nodes spread over a broader region does in fact constitute a new form of organizing the territory of the "center," rather than, as in the more conventional view, an instance of suburbanization or geographic dispersal. Insofar as these various nodes are articulated through digital networks, they represent a new geographic correlate of the most advanced type of "center."

[6] This regional grid of nodes represents, in my analysis, a reconstitution of the concept of region. Further, it should not be confused with the suburbanization of economic activity. I conceive of it as a space of centrality partly located in older socioeconomic geographies, such as that of the suburb or the larger metropolitan region, yet distinct precisely because it is a space of centrality. Far from neutralizing geography, the regional grid is likely to be embedded in conventional forms of communication infrastructure, notably rapid rail and highways connecting to airports. Ironically perhaps, conventional infrastructure is likely to maximize the economic benefits derived from telematics. I think this is an important issue that has been lost somewhat in discussions about the neutralization of geography through telematics.

These transactions take place partly in digital space and partly through conventional transport and travel. The result is a multiplication of often highly specialized circuits connecting sets of cities. These networks of major international business centers constitute new geographies of centrality. The most powerful of these new geographies of centrality at the global level binds the major international financial and business centers: New York, London, Tokyo, Paris, Frankfurt, Zurich, Amsterdam, Los Angeles, Sydney, Hong Kong, among others. But this geography now also includes the cities covered in this volume. In the case of a complex landscape such as Asia's we see in fact several geographies of centrality, one global, and others regional (Lo and Yeung 1996; Mayer 2002; So and Chiu 1997; Yeung 2000).[7]

The city as a nexus for new politico-cultural alignments

One of the contributions of this volume to the larger scholarship on global cities is its focus on political and cultural variables. This is particularly evident in the chapters on São Paulo (Alves, this volume; see also Alves 1991) and Bombay (Patel, this volume) which focus explicitly on popular movements, respectively the role of the Workers Party in dislodging the military dictatorship in Brazil, and the ascendance of Shiv Sena as a major force organizing political passions in Bombay, including anti-globalization struggles. Less explicitly, all of these chapters signal the fact that urban space has become subject to new or sharpened contestation. This is more evident in Mexico (Ward, this volume; see also Ward 1998), Johannesburg (Crankshaw and Parnell, this volume), Cairo (Abu-Lughod, this volume) and Moscow (Bater, this volume), than in the rest of these cities, but it is present in all of them.

Theoretically, we can posit that the urban investment patterns described in many of these chapters, and the sharpening socio-spatial polarization they entail, reconfigure the legitimacy of the different types of claims on the city and its resources. These investment patterns legitimate the claims connected to global city functions. An explicit or sometimes mere side-effect is to delegitimate the claims by the poor, the shanty dwellers, and even the older types of middle-income strata. Investments in selective urban upgrading on the scales on which they are occurring in most of these cities contain the seeds for conflict over urban space when

[7] Methodologically, I find it useful to unpack these intercity transactions into the specific, often highly specialized circuits that connect particular sets of cities. For instance, when examining futures markets, the set of cities includes São Paulo and Kuala Lumpur. These two cities fall out of the picture when examining the gold market; this market, on the other hand, includes Johannesburg and Sydney (Harvey forthcoming).

redevelopment aimed at elites encroaches on the spaces of the disadvantaged.

One can capture these systemic trends also in those cases where this is not an explicit condition. Bater (this volume; see also Ward 1998) examines the uneven geography of investment in housing construction and physical upgrading of different neighborhoods in Moscow and focuses especially on the expansion of a high-income segment in the most central area in that city linked to some of the new economic dynamics (see also Bater 1996). Further, such systemic trends can also be seen in conditions where the "self-evident" conflict runs along other lines. Crankshaw and Parnell (this volume) examine how different educational levels and employment opportunities in an expanding service economy with growing numbers of both high-level and low-level jobs contributes to a sharpening inequality within Johannesburg's black population, a fact that is charged with the potential for conflict among blacks who now are the main occupants of the city, most whites having left for the suburbs and the new edge city of Sandton (now incorporated in Metropolitan Johannesburg). However, apartheid state housing policy forced black residents out of inner-city areas into an exclusively black "township on the suburban periphery during the late 1950s and early 1960s" (Soweto houses about 1 million blacks in the suburban southwest of the city). So although there is racial segregation, it does not follow a simple division between a black inner city and white suburbs. In fact, it makes more sense to see Johannesburg in terms of a spatial division between the white northern suburbs and black inner-city and southern suburbs (Beall *et al.* 2002; see also Crankshaw 1997).

The large city has probably always been a strategic site for a whole range of new types of operations – political, economic, "cultural," subjective. This is certainly also the case today, as is so forcefully described in the chapters on São Paulo (Alves, this volume) and Bombay (Patel, this volume).

Spatialized power projects

Cities have long been key sites for the spatialization of power projects – whether political, religious, or economic. There are certain properties of power that make cities strategic. Power is a very abstract concept. It needs to be historicized. Power is actively produced and reproduced. Does power have spatial correlates, does it have a spatial moment?

There are multiple instances that capture this spatialization of power in cities and metropolitan regions (see, e.g., Abu-Lughod 1999; Kostinsky 1997; Levy 1997; Souza 1994; Tardanico and Lungo 1995). We can find it in the structures and infrastructures for control and management functions of past colonial empires and of current global firms and markets. We can also find it in the segregation of population groups that can consequently be more easily produced as either cheap labor or surplus people. It is present in the choice of particular built forms used for representing and symbolic cleansing of economic power, as in the preference for "greek temples" to house stock markets. It is present also in what we refer today as high-income residential and commercial gentrification to accommodate the expanding elite professional classes, with the inevitable displacement of lower-income households and firms. And we can see it in the large-scale destruction of natural environments to implant particular forms of urbanization marked by spread rather than density and linked to specific real estate development interests, such as the uncontrolled strip-development and suburbanization we see in many major US cities, notably the Los Angeles region.

Cities are also key sites for the spatializing of a different type of power project, perhaps better thought of as contestatory (Drainville 2004; Hamilton and Chinchilla 2001; Levy 1997; Sassen 2002a). The space of the city is a far more concrete space for politics than that of the national polity (e.g., Isin 2000). A city can accommodate a broad range of political activities – squatting, demonstrations against police brutality, fighting for the rights of immigrants and the homeless, the politics of culture and identity, gay and lesbian and queer politics.

Much of this becomes visible on the street. Street level politics makes possible the formation of new types of political subjects that do not have to go through the formal political system. In this sense, the city becomes a place where non-formal political actors can be part of actual political processes in a way that is much more difficult at the national level. Nationally, politics needs to run through existing formal systems: whether the electoral political system or the judiciary (taking state agencies to court). Non-formal political actors are rendered invisible in the space of national politics. Much of urban politics is concrete, enacted by people rather than dependent on massive media technologies.

Forging new political subjects

This concreteness of politics in the city and the possibility for non-formal political actors to participate can make a difference for those who lack power. Those who are disadvantaged, outsiders, discriminated minorities, can gain *presence* in global cities, presence vis-à-vis power and presence vis–à-vis each other (Sassen 2002a). This signals, for me, the possibility of a new type of politics centered in new types of political actors. It is not simply a matter of having or not having power (see, e.g., Bartlett forthcoming; Drainville 2004; Evans 2002; Lustiger-Thaler 2004; Sandercock 2003; Sassen 2002a). There are new hybrid bases from which to act. This a counter-spatialization of power in the city. The struggles by inner-city residents in Mexico (Ward, this volume) and the success of the Shiv Sena among the disadvantaged in Bombay (Patel, this volume) in some ways illustrate these new politics. In contrast, the political mobilization of the Workers Party in São Paulo, while benefiting from the concreteness of city political activity, is not an instance of the new politics (but see Buchler 2002).

The emphasis on the transnational and hypermobile character of capital has contributed to a sense of powerlessness among local actors, a sense of the futility of resistance. But an analysis that emphasizes place suggests that the global city is a terrain for politics and engagement. The loss of power at the national level produces the possibility for new forms of power and politics at the subnational level. Further, insofar as the national as container of social process and power is cracked (Abu-Lughod 2000; Brenner 1998; Taylor 2000) it opens up possibilities for a geography of politics that links subnational spaces across borders. Cities are foremost in this new geography. The incorporation of cities into a new cross-border geography of centrality also signals the emergence of a parallel political geography. One question this engenders is how and whether we are seeing the formation of a new type of transnational politics that localizes in these cities.[8]

Migration, for instance, is one major process through which a new transnational political economy and translocal household strategies are being constituted (Ehrenreich and Hochschild 2003; Samers 2002). All the cities covered in this volume, except for Shanghai at the time of closed communist rule, have multiple cross-border networks through migrations. Migration is, in many regards, one of the constitutive processes of globalization today, even though not recognized or represented as such in mainstream accounts of the global economy.

Researching and theorizing these issues will require approaches that diverge from the more traditional studies of political elites, local party

[8] See, e.g., digital technology, and notably the Internet, is contributing to this transnationalizing of contestatory politics (Sassen 2002b). Political activists can use digital networks for global or non-local transactions *and* they can use them for strengthening local communications and transactions inside a city (or rural community). Recovering how the new digital technology can serve to support local initiatives and alliances across a city's neighborhoods is extremely important in an age where the notion of the local is often seen as losing ground to global dynamics and actors and the digital networks are typically thought of as global.

politics, neighborhood associations, immigrant communities, and so on through which the political landscape of cities and metropolitan regions has been conceptualized in urban studies. One way of thinking about the political implications of this strategic transnational space anchored in global cities is in terms of the formation of new claims on that space. The city has indeed emerged as a site for new claims: by global capital which uses the city as an "organizational commodity," but also by disadvantaged sectors of the urban population, frequently as internationalized a presence in large cities as capital.

This is a space that is both place-centered in that it is embedded in particular locations; and it is transterritorial because it connects sites that are not geographically proximate yet are intensely connected to each other. If we consider that large cities concentrate both the leading sectors of global capital and a growing share of disadvantaged populations – migrants, many of the most disadvantaged women, masses of shanty dwellers – then we can see that cities have become a strategic terrain for a whole series of conflicts and contradictions. In this regard cities are a site for new types of political operations and for a whole range of new "cultural" and subjective operations (Allen *et al* 1999; Sassen 2000b). The centrality of place in a context of global processes makes possible the formation of new claims, notably rights to place. At the limit, this could be an opening for new forms of "citizenship" (Isin 2000; Holston 1996).

REFERENCES

Abu-Lughod, Janet L. 1989. *Before Hegemony: The World System A.D. 1250–1350.* New York: Oxford University Press.

1999. *New York, Chicago, Los Angeles: America's Global Cities.* Minneapolis: University of Minnesota Press.

Abu-Lughod, Janet L. (ed.). 2000. *Sociology for the 21st Century.* Chicago: Chicago University Press.

Allen, John, Massey, Doreen and Pryke, Michael (eds.) 1999. *Unsettling Cities.* London: Routledge.

Alves, Maria Helena Moreira 1991. "The Workers Party of Brazil: Building Struggle from the Grassroots," in William Tabb (ed.) *The Future of Socialism.* New York: Monthly Review Press.

Bartlett, Anne forthcoming. "Political Subjectivity in the Global City." Ph.D. dissertation, University of Chicago.

Bater, James H. 1996. *Russia and the Post-Soviet States: A Geographical Perspective.* London: Edward Arnold.

Beall, J., Crankshaw, O. and Parnell, S. 2002. *Uniting a Divided City: Governance and Social Exclusion in Johannesburg.* London: Earthscan.

Braudel, Fernand 1984. *The Perspective of The World*, vol. III. London: Collins.
Brenner, Neil 1998."Global Cities, Glocal States: Global City Formation and State Territorial Restructuring in Contemporary Europe," *Review of International Political Economy*, 5 (2): 1–37.
Buchler, Simone 2002. "Women in the Informal Economy of Sao Paulo." Paper prepared for the National Academy of Sciences, forthcoming in *Background Papers: Panel on Cities*. Washington DC: National Academy of Sciences.
Castells, M. 1989. *The Informational City*. London: Blackwell.
Chase-Dunn, C. 1985. "The System of World Cities A.D. 800–1975," in M. Timberlake (ed.), *Urbanization in the World Economy*. New York: Academic Press.
Clark, David 1996. *Urban World/ Global City*. London: Routledge.
Crankshaw, O. 1997. *Race, Class and the Changing Division of Labor under Apartheid*. London: Routledge.
Drainville, Andre 2004. *Contesting Globalization: Space and Place in the World Economy*. London: Routledge.
Ehrenreich, Barbara and Hochschild, Arlie (eds.) 2003. *Global Woman*. New York: Metropolitan Books.
Evans, Peter (ed). 2002. *Livable Cities? Urban Struggles for Livelihood and Sustainability*. Berkeley: University of California Press.
Forbes, D. K. 1996. *Asian Metropolis: Urbanisation and the Southeast Asian City*. Melbourne: Oxford University Press.
Friedmann, John and Goetz Wolff 1982. "World City Formation: An Agenda for Research and Action," *International Journal of Urban and Regional Research*, 6: 309–344.
GaWc. http://www.lboro.ac.uk/GaWC.
Gugler, Josef (ed.) 1997. *Cities in the Developing World: Issues, Theory, and Policy*. London: Oxford University Press.
Hall, Peter 1966. *The World Cities*. New York: McGraw Hill.
Hamilton, Nora and Chinchilla, Norma Stoltz 2001. *Seeking Community in a Global City: Guatemalans and Salvadorans in Los Angeles*. Philadelphia: Temple University Press.
Harvey, Rachel forthcoming. "Global Cities of Gold." Ph.D. dissertation, University of Chicago.
Holston, James (ed.) 1999. *Cities and Citizenship*. Durham, NC: Duke University Press.
Huybrechts, Eric. 2002. "Beirut: Building Regional Circuits," in Saskia Sassen (ed.), *Global Networks, Linked Cities*. New York and London: Routledge, pp. 237–247.
Isin, Engin F. (ed.) 2000. *Democracy, Citizenship and the Global City*. London and New York: Routledge.
King, A. D. 1990. *Global Cities: Post-Imperialism and the Internationalization of London*. London: Routledge.
Kostinsky, Grigory 1997. "Globalisation de l'economie et notions urbanistiques," in P. Claval and A.-L. Sanguin (eds.), *Metropolisation et politique*. Paris: L'Harmattan, pp. 17–25.
Levy, Evelyn 1997. *Democracia nas cidades globais: um estudio sobre Londres e Sao Paulo*. São Paulo: Studio Nobel.

Lo, Fu-chen and Yue-man Yeung (eds.) 1996. *Emerging World Cities in Pacific Asia*. Tokyo: United Nations University.
Low, Setha M. 1999. "Theorizing the City," in Setha M. Low (ed.) *Theorizing the City*. New Brunswick, NJ: Rutgers University Press, pp. 1–33.
Lustiger-Thaler, Henri (ed.) 2004. "Social Movements in a Global World," *Current Sociology*, 52 (4): 657–674.
Marcuse, Peter and van Kempen, Ronald 2000. *Globalizing Cities: A New Spatial Order*. Oxford: Blackwell.
Mayer, David R. 2002. "Hong Kong: Global Capital Exchange," in Saskia Sassen (ed.), *Global Networks, Linked Cities*. New York and London: Routledge, pp. 249–271.
Nijman, Jan 1996. "Breaking the Rules: Miami in the Urban Hierarchy," *Urban Geography*, 17 (1): 5–22.
Paddison, Ronan (ed.) 2001. "Introduction," *Handbook of Urban Studies*. London: Sage.
Parnell, S. and Mabin, A. 1995. "Rethinking Urban South Africa," *Journal of Southern African Studies*, 21: 39–61.
Parsa, Ali and Keivani, Ramin 2002. "The Hormuz Corridor: Building a Cross-Border Region between Iran and the UAE," in Saskia Sassen (ed.), *Global Networks, Linked Cities*. New York and London: Routledge, pp. 183–207.
Patel, Sujata and Thorner, Alice (eds.) 1995. *Metaphor for Modern India: Bombay*. New Delhi: Oxford University Press.
Peraldi, Michel and Perrin, Evelyne (eds.) 1996. *Reseaux Productifs et Territoires Urbains*. Toulouse: Presses Universitaires du Mirail.
Pozos Ponce, Fernando 1996. *Metropolis en reestructuracion: Guadalajara y Monterrey 1980–1989*. Guadalajara, Mex.: Universidad de Guadalajara.
Riemens, Patrice and Lovink, Geert 2002. "Digital City Amsterdam: Local Uses of Global Networks," in Saskia Sassen (ed.), *Global Networks, Linked Cities*. New York and London: Routledge, pp. 327–345.
Rutherford, Jonathan 2004. *A Tale of Two Global Cities: Comparing the Territoriality of Telecommunications Developments in Paris and London*. Aldershot: Ashgate.
Sachar, A. 1990. "The Global Economy and World Cities," in A. Sachar and S. Oberg (eds.), *The World Economy and the Spatial Organization of Power*. Aldershot: Avebury, pp. 149–160.
Salaff, Janet W. 1988. *State and Family in Singapore: Structuring an Industrial Society*. Ithaca, NY: Cornell University Press.
Samers, Michael 2002. "Immigration and the Global City Hypothesis: Towards an Alternative Research Agenda," *International Journal of Urban and Regional Research*, 26 (2): 389–402.
Sandercock, Leonie 2003. *Cosmopolis II: Mongrel Cities in the 21st Century*. New York and London: Continuum.
Santos, Milton, Souze, Maria Adelia A. De and Silveira, Maria Laura (eds.) 1994. *Territorio Globalizacao e Fragmentacao*. Sao Paulo: Editorial Hucitec.
Sassen, Saskia 1984. "The New Labor Demand in Global Cities," in M. P. Smith (ed.) *Cities in Transformation*. Beverly Hills, CA: Sage, pp. 139–171.
2000a. "Territory and Territoriality in the Global Economy," *International Sociology*, 15 (2): 372–393.

2000b. "New Frontiers Facing Urban Sociology," *British Journal of Sociology*, 51 (1), Special Millennial Issue: 143–159.

2002a. "The Repositioning of Citizenship: Emergent Subjects and Spaces for Politics," *Berkeley Journal of Sociology: A Critical Review*, 46: 4–26.

2002b. "Towards a Sociology of Information Technology," *Current Sociology*, Special Issue: *Sociology and Technology*, 50 (3): 365–388.

Savitch, H. V. 1996. "Cities in a Global Era: A New Paradigm for the Next Millennium," in Michael A. Cohen, Blair A. Ruble, Joseph S. Tulchin, and Allison M. Garland (eds.), *Preparing for the Urban Future. Global Pressures and Local Forces*. Washington DC: Woodrow Wilson Center Press, pp. 39–65. (Distributed by the Johns Hopkins University Press.)

Schiffer Ramos, Sueli 2002. "São Paulo: Articulating a Cross-Border Regional Economy," in Saskia Sassen (ed.), *Global Networks, Linked Cities*. New York and London: Routledge, pp. 209–236.

Scott, A. J. 2001. *Global City-Regions*. Oxford: Oxford University Press.

Short, John R. and Kim, Y. 1999. *Globalization and the City*. Harlow: Longman.

Simmonds, Roger and Hack, Gary 2000. *Global City Regions: Their Emerging Forms*. London and New York: E&FN Spon/Taylor & Francis.

So, Alvin Y. and Stephen Chiu 1997. "Current Perspectives on East Asian Development: A Critical Review," in Kam-Yee Law (ed.) *Behind the Miracle: Modernization in Asia*. Hong Kong: Oxford University Press, pp. 1–24.

Souza, Maria Adelia Aparecida de 1994. *A identidade de metropole: a verticalizacao em São Paulo*. São Paulo: Hucitec.

Stren, Richard 1996. "The Studies of Cities: Popular Perceptions, Academic Disciplines, and Emerging Agendas," in Michael A. Cohen, Blair A. Ruble, Joseph S. Tulchin, and Allison M. Garland (eds.), *Preparing for the Urban Future: Global Pressures and Local Forces*. Washington DC: Woodrow Wilson Center Press, pp. 392–420. (Distributed by the Johns Hopkins University Press.)

Tardanico, Richard and Mario Lungo 1995. "Local Dimensions of Global Restructuring in Urban Costa Rica," *International Journal of Urban and Regional Research*, 19 (2): 223–249.

Taylor, Peter J. 2000. "World Cities and Territorial States under Conditions of Contemporary Globalization," *Political Geography*, 19 (5): 5–32.

Ward, Peter M. 1998. *Mexico City*, 2nd edn. Chichester and New York: John Wiley and Sons.

Yeung, Yue-man 2000. *Globalization and Networked Societies*, Honolulu: University of Hawai'i Press.

Index

Page references followed by "tab" indicate tables. Endnotes are designated by "n"

Printed in the United States
126250LV00003B/52-57/P